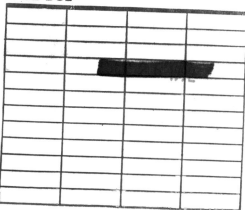

78

BALZAC AND THE FRENCH REVOLUTION

La Révolution continue, elle est implantée dans la loi, elle est ecrite sur le sol, elle est toujours dans les esprits (Duc de Chaulieu, *Mémoires de deux jeunes mariées*)

BALZAC and the FRENCH REVOLUTION

RONNIE BUTLER

CROOM HELM
London & Canberra

BARNES & NOBLE BOOKS
Totowa, New Jersey

© 1983 R. Butler
Croom Helm Ltd, Provident House, Burrell Row,
Beckenham, Kent BR3 1AT

British Library Cataloguing in Publication Data
Butler, R.
  Balzac and the French Revolution.
  1. Balzac, Honoré de —— Criticism and interpretation
  I. title
  843'.7   PQ2178
  ISBN 0-7099-3208-1

First published in the USA 1983 by
Barnes and Noble Books,
81 Adams Drive,
Totowa, New Jersey, 07512

ISBN 0-389-20406-4

Printed and bound in Great Britain by
Biddles Ltd, Guildford and King's Lynn

CONTENTS

Pour les voix chères qui se sont tues

ACKNOWLEDGEMENTS

This book would not have been possible without the help of certain people. In particular, I should like to thank Mr F.W. Saunders for putting his constructive and judicious criticism at my constant disposal, and Dr A.I. Forrest, whose valuable suggestions ensured that the material benefited from a salutary historical discipline.

I am also greatly indebted to Professor Colin Smethurst for advice generously given, and to Dr A.W. Raitt, whose patient encouragement was the ultimate deciding factor in the publication of this study.

Finally, may I express my gratitude to Mrs Veronica Green for the excellent job of work which she performed in completing the typescript.

FOREWORD

Priorities and Dimensions

'*La Comédie humaine*, ou Des conséquences de la Révolution française.'[1] André Wurmser's definition identifies the starting-point of this study. While concentrating on the socioeconomic evidence of the *Comédie humaine*, I have also tried, in conclusion, to suggest how Balzac's political beliefs arose out of his response to what he saw as the irreversible effects of the Revolution.

In undertaking such a task, I have to admit to several misgivings. The need for a serious project of historical verification in relation to the *Comédie humaine* has long been recognised. Bernard Guyon, for example, has made an urgent plea in this direction. Regretting the lack of attention given to Balzac by historians, by what he calls 'vérificateurs de Balzac', Guyon remarks: 'Je les trouve trop rares, un peu paresseux, et même méprisants *a priori*, pleins de méfiance à l'égard de ce fabricateur de fictions. Un champ immense reste à labourer. Seule pourra le faire une équipe où participeront activement des historiens patentés. Qui nous diront par exemple: "Voilà ce qu'était le vignoble sancerrois à l'époque de *La Muse du département*, voilà comment on pouvait en effet faire fortune dans les Assurances au temps de Gaudissart, ou dans les achats de biens nationaux au temps de Grandet".'[2]

In this instance, I have not been able, alas, to collate the findings of a team of specialist historians. The fact that I am not myself a professional historian is, I recognise, also a problem. Inevitably, therefore, this undertaking will fall short of the ambitious aims suggested by its title. Nor will it even cover some of the areas mentioned by Guyon. There will necessarily be omissions, although it is hoped that none of them will be of the first magnitude; I can only request indulgence for any errors which have escaped the vigilance of revision; finally, some of the interpretations and emphases will no doubt appear tendentious or questionable.

I have not allowed myself, however, to be deterred by an awareness of the problematic nature of the subject from pursuing it to a conclusion. My commitment to it has been sustained by the hope that, when completed, the investigation might provide a useful addition to Balzac studies in precisely that area of historical illumination indicated by

Bernard Guyon. If this study helps to vindicate Balzac as a superb historian of post-revolutionary society, it will have achieved more than its author dare expect. Otherwise, if it enables those who may be interested in reading it to know more about Balzac and about the society which emerged from the Revolution, then it will have done something from which the author himself is grateful to have benefited. Finally, I have relied throughout on the new Pléiade edition of the *Comédie humaine*, details of which can be found in the bibliography. The references in footnotes are all based on this edition. In the case of the *Oeuvres Diverses*, the Conard edition has been used.

Whatever one's ultimate view of Balzac's merits and value as a historian may be, several facts are beyond dispute. First, Balzac took himself very seriously as a historian, insisting on numerous occasions that he was more of a historian than a novelist. Secondly, it is clear where Balzac chose to place the emphasis in his historical investigation. From *Les Chouans* onwards, Balzac consistently rejected the kind of history which deals exclusively with the arid recording of isolated facts. At the same time, Balzac affirmed his intention to write 'l'histoire des moeurs', or, as he stated in the introduction to *Les Chouans*, 'l'esprit d'une époque'.[3] It was in July 1840, in the 'Lettres sur la littérature', as Mme Ambrière-Fargeaud reminds us, that Balzac insisted on the need for the novelist-historian to enter 'dans le milieu social au lieu de se placer dans la haute région des faits politiques' if he is to capture 'l'esprit et les moeurs' of contemporary society.[4]

There are other aspects, however, of Balzac's contribution as a historian which are less well appreciated and which have important implications for an understanding of his entire work and outlook. It is for this reason that the research which is embodied in the critical prefaces of the new Pléiade edition of the *Comédie humaine* is of great significance.

In her introduction to *Les Petits Bourgeois*, Mme Meininger concludes that 'Balzac s'occupe moins de grands accidents que de vie quotidienne . . . Balzac n'est pas historien des faits, il est historien des moeurs'.[5] This raises the question of what one understands when one refers to Balzac as the 'historien des moeurs'. Applied to Balzac, the notion means more than a picture of manners in the tradition of Jane Austen. To illustrate her point, Mme Meininger claims that, in *Les Petits Bourgeois*, Balzac takes no account of the working-class unrest which occurred in Paris in July 1840. Mme Meininger also argues that the political 'conjoncture' is subordinated to the speculation in 'rentes' which it provoked. Mme Meininger's argument is perfectly valid in emphasising the 'historien des moeurs' in Balzac as distinct from the 'historien des faits', but it also points to the fact that, when Balzac speaks of writing 'l'histoire des moeurs', he assumes that the discussion of socioeconomic realities is part of it.

At the same time, one has to be careful not to take Balzac too superficially at his own word and to write him off as 'l'historien des faits'. One can only do so in the sense referred to earlier of Balzac's disdain for the historian who is content to remain the desiccated chronicler of unrelated facts. On the other hand, it would be a gross error not to recognise that Balzac is supremely concerned with facts where they constitute an integral part of his analysis of the broader developments which they express. It is with this in mind that Louis Chevalier praises Balzac as the historian 'non des idées mais des faits'.[6] Although, in fact, it challenges her conclusion that Balzac is not interested in facts, the force of this tribute is recognised by Mme Meininger when she makes the point that 'la littérature et les critiques, même balzaciens, sont souvent en retard sur l'histoire et les historiens. Les faits sont ignorés ou méconnus'.[7]

Louis Chevalier's tribute to Balzac is quoted by Mme Meininger in support of her contention that Balzac's aesthetic priorities make it a waste of time to attempt to relate Balzac's views to various currents of ideology, either contemporary or subsequent. Mme Meininger refers to the pronouncement of Léon de Lora in *Les Comédiens sans le savoir* – 'L'opinion d'un artiste doit être la foi dans ses oeuvres' – and asserts: 'Voilà le vrai credo de Balzac, autrement inexplicable ou si souvent mal expliqué, en particulier par les gens "à opinions", au prix d'étonnantes virtuosités dialectiques'.[8] One knows well enough the kind of Marxist acrobatics which are Mme Meininger's legitimate target, but no great dialectical virtuosity is needed, as it is hoped that this study will show, to reveal the reactionary nature of Balzac's political ideology.

Above all what the contributors to the new Pléiade edition have emphatically confirmed is Balzac's permanent preoccupation with the long-term effects of the Revolution. Suzanne Bérard is a lone voice in suggesting that, after the writing of *Un Episode sous la Terreur*, Balzac's interest in the Revolution receded and was revived only after a long interval. 'Puis son attention se détourna de la Révolution et de ses thèmes', she concludes. 'Il ne devait y revenir que beaucoup plus tard.'[9] This is true only in the sense that the events of the Revolution were never of great interest to Balzac. The themes associated with the Revolution, however, conceived in terms of its lasting consequences, continued to engage Balzac's attention, to permeate his work and to influence his thinking.

From *Les Chouans* to *Le Député d'Arcis*, as members of the Pléiade team convincingly show, the historical unity of the *Comédie humaine* is constructed around Balzac's assessment of the changes in French society produced by the Revolution. Lucienne Frappier-Mazur's view of *Les Chouans* is that in the novel 'le sens s'organise autour du mythe de 1789', so that 'l'intrusion de la Révolution dans la vie de chacun' dominates the action.[10] For René Guise, *La Rabouilleuse* represents 'l'histoire d'une fortune sur trois générations'. The Descoings have made their fortune out of selling wool and buying 'biens nationaux'. 'Supprimez cette fortune initiale', Guise emphasises, 'il n'y a plus de roman. Tout part de là.'[11] In her introduction to *Ursule Mirouët*, Madeleine Ambrière-Fargeaud retraces its historical theme, which she defines as 'le magistral tableau d'un siècle d'histoire, ... de l'Ancien Régime et du siècle des Lumières à la monarchie de Juillet et au règne d'argent'.[12] Finally, Colin Smethurst identifies the historical interest of *Le Député d'Arcis* in the account of 'tous les débris des antagonismes surgis, puis mal éteints, transformés enfin à travers les trois générations qu'a connues la France depuis la Révolution'.[13]

It is this authoritative reaffirmation of the historical implications of Balzac's work, with its focal point in the Revolution, which encourages me to believe that, whatever its results, the aims of the following study are fully justified.

Notes

1. André Wurmser, *La Comédie Inhumaine*, 2nd edn (Paris, 1965), p. 570.

2. Bernard Guyon, 'La Province dans le roman'. *Stendhal et Balzac II, Actes du VIIIe Congrès International Stendhalien*, Nantes, 27-29 May 1971 (Nantes, 1978), p. 127.

3. Balzac had expressed the same conviction a year earlier in the 'Avertissement' to *Le Gars*, the original title of *Les Chouans*. Roland Chollet traces it to the fragment called *Histoire de ma vie* which Balzac wrote in 1822. See the article by Roland Chollet, ' "Une Heure de ma vie" ou Lord R'hoone à la découverte de Balzac', *L'Année Balzacienne* (1968), pp. 121-34.

4. Madeleine Ambrière-Fargeaud, introduction to *Ursule Mirouët*, 2nd Pléiade edn, III, 739. The passage referred to in the 'Lettres sur la littérature' can be found in the Conard edition, *Oeuvres Diverses*, III, on p. 286 of vol. 40 of *Oeuvres Complètes de Honoré de Balzac* (eds M. Bouteron and H. Longnon, 40 vols. (Conard, Paris, 1926-63), p. 286.

5. Anne-Marie Meinger, introduction to *Les Petits Bourgeois*, Pléiade, VIII, 10.

6. Preface to the Folio edition of *Les Paysans* (Paris, 1975), p. 12.

7. Anne-Marie Meininger, introduction to *Les Comédiens sans le savoir*, Pléiade, VII, 1150.

8. Ibid., p. 1149.

9. Suzanne J. Bérard, introduction to *Un Episode sous la Terreur*, Pléiade, VIII, 431.

10. Lucienne Frappier-Mazur, introduction to *Les Chouans*, Pléiade, VIII, 885.

11. René Guise, introduction to *La Rabouilleuse*, Pléiade, IV, 266.

12. Madeleine Ambrière-Fargeaud, introduction to *Ursule Mirouët*, Pléiade, III, 737.

13. Colin Smethurst, introduction to *Le Député d'Arcis*, Pléiade, VIII, 702.

PART ONE:

REPUBLIC AND EMPIRE.
REVOLUTION AND COUNTER-REVOLUTION

INTRODUCTION

In keeping with Balzac's declared intention of giving priority to analysing the effects of the Revolution, the references to the events of the Revolution and to the measures which it introduced are rigorously subordinated to the discussion of the long-term consequences to which they contributed. In turn, Balzac's method is to treat the issues raised by the Revolution in terms of a series of opposing categories representing the forces of revolution and counter-revolution. Thus the Civil Constitution of the Clergy is less a factor in itself than the opposition of 'prêtres assermentés' and 'prêtres non-assermentés'. The 'réquisition', to take another example, is seen in the light of its impact on the various 'réquisitionnaires' who are featured in the *Comédie humaine*, together with the rebellious population on whom they were visited.

It is through the representatives of various revolutionary and counter-revolutionary groups, and in his account of both beneficiaries and victims of the Revolution, that Balzac develops his view of the Revolution in the *Comédie humaine*. L'abbé Janvier, for instance, who acts in *Le Médecin de campagne* as the co-spokesman of Balzac's legitimism, turns out to have been an unlikely 'assermenté'. Balzac's method can be seen in the way in which he deals with a particular creation of the Revolution, the 'maximum'.[1] The 'maximum' affects Balzac's characters in different ways. M. Guillaume and Pillerault, though hit by the 'maximum', survive its worst effects. The Poiret brothers, on the other hand, who helped in administering the 'maximum', suffer in the end when, because of their revolutionary associations, their promotion as 'petits fonctionnaires' is blocked under the Restoration. For Cardot, the 'maximum' works to his advantage. In acquiring the business of his employer who had been ruined by the 'maximum', Cardot takes the first important step in a career of uninterrupted success.

In Balzac's analysis of the social and economic effects of the Revolution, the proliferation of bourgeois categories contrasts with the narrow range of groups adversely affected by and opposed to the Revolution. This balance both makes historical sense and corresponds to a hostile vision of the Revolution which induces Balzac to see it in terms of a variety of bourgeois predators feeding off the corpse of the *ancien régime*. The bourgeois categories in the *Comédie humaine* are numerous. Apart from the 'accapareurs', who are given short shrift by the

Revolutionary tribunals, Balzac's bourgeois who emerge from the Revolution are, with few exceptions, remarkably successful. This is notably true of the 'fournisseurs' and of those who acquire a business in the Revolution. The 'fournisseurs' include some of the most striking examples of bourgeois ascension in the *Comédie humaine*, such as du Bousquier and Gaubertin. In addition to Cardot, Goriot, Grandet and Séchard all owe their promotion from worker or artisan to bourgeois to a Revolution which, in its various effects, had made available to them the business of their ruined employer.

Despite the interest which this revelation of other social groups has, and despite the richness of its documentation, they are dominated in the *Comédie humaine* by Balzac's concentration on what he saw as the essential expression of the opposition of bourgeoisie and aristocracy in the continuing struggle of Revolution and counter-revolution, the confrontation of 'acquéreurs' and émigrés.

Note

1. The first law imposing a ceiling on the price of 'les grains et les fourrages' was introduced on 4 May 1793, followed by 'la loi du maximum général' affecting both prices and wages on 29 September. Widely resisted and evaded, the 'maximum' was abolished on 24 December 1794.

1 'LES ACQUÉREURS DE BIENS NATIONAUX'

The sale of 'biens nationaux', a question of continuing curiosity to historians, also attracted the attention of nineteenth-century novelists. Its profound effect on the development of French society is attested, for example, by the *Rougon-Macquart*. Zola, when he discusses the history of certain properties under the Second Empire, mentions how they changed hands during the Revolution and came to belong to the family of their present bourgeois owners. In *Germinal*, it is revealed that the father of Leon Grégoire acquired the family house, la Piolaine, 'comme bien national, pour une somme dérisoire'.[1] Similarly, in *La Terre*, la Borderie, the farm owned by Hourdequin, had been bought as a 'bien national' in 1793 by Hourdequin's father, in the face of peasant competition, from the father of Fouan.[2]

It is above all, however, in Balzac's work that the issue of 'biens nationaux' appears as a major theme, since it is treated in a large number of the novels of the *Comédie humaine*. It was a subject, moreover, which was directly linked to the experience of Balzac's own family, Balzac's father having himself been an 'acquéreur'.[3] Recent research has emphasised the historical dimension of Balzac, and it is for this reason that a study of the place of the sale of 'biens nationaux' in the *Comédie humaine* is of especial interest.[4]

Balzac's attack on post-revolutionary society is focused on the socioeconomic changes arising from the Revolution. The sale of 'biens nationaux' is at the centre of Balzac's analysis and fundamental to his conception of the Revolution. It was during the critical period of the Revolution, Balzac observes, that 'la vente des biens nationaux était l'arche sainte de la politique'.[5] Two questions are immediately prompted. First, is Balzac's picture complete? Secondly, is his account historically accurate? In the final analysis, such questions can only be answered by comparing Balzac's version of events with the conclusions of historians who have made a special study of the sale of 'biens nationaux'.

Of the problems identified by Marion, Balzac leaves aside those which are of a statistical nature, such as the amount of property sold and the number of 'acquéreurs' involved.[6] On other occasions, when he is not completely silent, Balzac is often imprecise about other important aspects of the sale of 'biens nationaux'. In some cases, it is not certain whether a particular character is an 'acquéreur' or not, even when the evidence may point strongly in that direction. Balzac, for instance, describes d'Aldrigger as being, in 1800, 'à l'apogée d'une fortune faite pendant la Révolution'.[7] The description of Minoret-Levrault, though less equivocal, stops short of identifying him explicitly as an 'acquéreur'. 'En trente-six ans', Balzac simply states, 'il avait, la Révolution aidant, gagné trente mille livres de rente, en prairies, terres labourables et bois'.[8]

At other times, it is not clear whether it is Church or émigré property which is involved, especially in relation to 1793.[9] Nor is Balzac concerned with the relative proportions of the two categories of 'biens nationaux'. Although the Comédie humaine shows more émigré property sold than Church property and thus accords with the historical facts, it is a reality which emerges independently of Balzac's intentions, fortuitously rather than by methodical analysis.[10]

Balzac is less preoccupied with the quantitative details than with the long-term effects of the transfer of 'biens nationaux'. What essentially concerns him is the process set in motion by the sale of 'biens nationaux' which resulted in the domination of landed property passing from the aristocracy to the bourgeoisie and thereby profoundly shaping the character of post-revolutionary society. The Comédie humaine contains important evidence of the sale of 'biens nationaux' which is remarkable in its scope and perceptiveness and for the individuality of its viewpoint. Not to take account of it would be to omit a vital element in Balzac's historical outlook. In order to understand Balzac's reaction to the Revolution and to the changes which it brought about in French society, it is necessary to appreciate the role which the sale of 'biens nationaux' plays in Balzac's work.

Balzac's account of the sale of 'biens nationaux' is particularly interesting in that it touches on questions which have continued to preoccupy historians. One important question concerns the size of the gains made by the 'acquéreurs' and the means which they used to achieve them; another consists in determining whether the acquisition of 'biens nationaux' signified the creation of a new propertied class or whether, on the other hand, the confiscated property was acquired by existing property owners, either urban bourgeois or landowning peasants. Finally, through his discussion of the sale of 'biens nationaux', Balzac pursues his fundamental purpose of analysing and judging the society created by the Revolution and shaped to a significant degree by the impact of their transfer.

When he gives details of the benefits gained from the purchase of 'biens nationaux', Balzac again shows little concern for historical precision. Instead of indicating which of the two categories of 'biens nationaux' might have been the more profitable, Balzac is content to note their general profitability by giving numerous examples taken from each group.[11] In some instances, Balzac does not specify which type of 'biens nationaux' is involved. When he refers, for example, to the parents of Mlle Descoings, Balzac gives only a general indication. 'Sortis des laines', he states, 'ils employaient leurs fonds à l'achat des biens nationaux: autre toison d'or!'[12] It is only the incidental reference to the date, 1792, which enables one to conclude that the 'biens nationaux' which the Descoings acquire are in fact Church property, since, as Marion points out, the first sales of émigré property did not take place until the autumn of 1793.[13]

In describing the 'biens nationaux' which were acquired by the father of Angélique Bontems, Balzac suggests that the 'force biens nationaux achetés à vils prix' may have included both types. 'D'abord il n'a eu que des prés de moines qui ne reviendront jamais', Balzac reveals. Despite the greater precision and the added hint, the identification remains finally inconclusive. What is certain is the value of the financial gains made by the bourgeois 'acquéreurs'. The 'biens nationaux' acquired by M. Bontems give him 50,000 'livres de rente'. The 'toison d'or', which Balzac speaks about in reference to Descoings, is worth 30,000 'livres de rente' to Descoings' son-in-law, Rouget, on his wife's death in 1799.

The most celebrated purchaser of Church property is Grandet. When the property of the clergy was put up for sale in Saumur, Grandet acquired the best vineyards and pasture-land in the area. On his death Eugénie inherits a fortune of 17 million francs, the origins of which can be identified in Grandet's acquisition of a choice sample of 'biens d'église'. Professor Castex sees in Grandet 'le type même du bourgeois conquérant' produced by the Revolution and who owed his social ascension essentially to his acquisition of 'biens nationaux'.[14] The experience of Grandet and Bontems supports, moreover, the findings of Marion, who claims that 'il y a à peu près unanimité parmi les historiens pour enseigner que c'est surtout à la bourgeoisie qu'ont passé les biens de première origine'.[15]

Among the 'acquéreurs' of émigré property, Malin and du Bousquier are particularly prominent. Malin's gains are made in three successive stages. His career as 'acquéreur' begins with his purchase of the best Church land in the Aube department. Then he acquires the Gondreville estate formerly belonging to the Simeuse family and confiscated as émigré property. Finally, Malin uses his influence under the Directory to make further acquisitions of 'biens nationaux'. The examples which Balzac gives have no bearing on Marion's conclusion that Church property, though smaller in amount, was more profitable to the 'acquéreurs' than émigré property.[16] However, the testimony of these examples is important in other respects.

The co-operation of Marion and Grévin, for example, in Malin's transactions illustrates what Balzac denounced as the disastrous power conferred by the Revolution on the legal professions. To appreciate the important message which emerges from the example of Balzac's 'acquéreurs', one has, however, to consider their subsequent careers. Between them, they represent the three types of acquisition. An 'acquéreur' of Church property such as Grandet, while he has neither social nor political ambitions, becomes enormously wealthy in consequence of his purchase of 'biens nationaux'. Du Bousquier, whose profits are made entirely from émigré property, becomes a powerful financier and a 'grand propriétaire' before the end of the Restoration. Having acquired both types of 'biens nationaux', Malin appears as a leading 'notable' under the Empire, the Restoration and the July Monarchy. Grandet reigns over Saumur as du Bousquier dominates Alençon. In *La Paix du ménage*, Malin, now comte de Gondreville, awaits Napoleon in his drawing room. Du Bousquier's triumph is equally emphatic in the presence of his vassals who come to pay him homage in the house of his wife, the former Mlle Cormon.[17] With few exceptions and interruptions, the history of Balzac's 'acquéreurs' is one of outstanding success in every sphere of 'la société révolutionnée'.

The lucrative purchase of 'biens nationaux' is not simply expressed in the *Comédie humaine* in financial terms or by examples of social promotion. Balzac also refers to the acquisition of separate lots or individual items which serve the purpose of personal adornment or consumption. In *Le Cabinet des Antiques*, Chesnel's role as 'acquéreur national' is not confined to his repurchasing on behalf of the marquis d'Esgrignon property lost during the Revolution. The marquis d'Esgrignon's salon is furnished with objects bought by Chesnel in sales of 'biens nationaux'. The same is true of the Thuillier family in *Les Petits Bourgeois*, whose silverware and table-linen are 'le fruit d'achats faits pendant la Révolution par le père Thuillier'.[18] Even Rigou's liqueurs betray their revolutionary origin, Balzac observing that 'l'usurier en avait acquis une provision pour le reste de ses jours, au dépeçage d'un château de Bourgogne'.[19]

Balzac thus agrees with historians in showing the significant number of large individual fortunes made through the acquisition of 'biens nationaux'. His account is also orthodox in two other respects. The first concerns the various means adopted by the 'acquéreurs' to consolidate their gains from 'biens nationaux'. The second concerns whether the transfer of 'biens nationaux' created an important category of new landowners.

On the question of the resale of 'biens nationaux' Marion is categorical. On the basis of his analysis of the Gironde and the Cher, Marion estimates 'à environ au 1/6e la proportion des achats suivis de revente volontaire par les acquéreurs primitifs'.[20] Marion's finding is reflected in the *Comédie humaine*, which contains very few examples of resale. Apart from du Bousquier, the only 'acquéreurs' who resell are Rigou and Sauviat. Referring to Sauviat, Balzac reveals that 'en 1973, il put acquérir un château vendu nationalement, et le dépeça; le gain qu'il fit, il le répéta sans doute sur plusieurs points de la sphère où il opérait'.[21] The profits made by Sauviat from reselling his 'biens nationaux' give him the necessary capital to embark on a scheme of large-scale investment. The case of du Bousquier is particularly interesting. Closely linked with Ouvrard, 'un des matadors de la finance', du Bousquier first achieved a meteoric rise under the Directory.[22] In describing the initial stages of du Bousquier's career, Balzac displays a remarkable historical accuracy. It is du Bousquier 'qui faisait confisquer des biens d'émigrés pour les acheter et les revendre'.[23] Du Bousquier represents the trend identified by Lefebvre, whereby 'sous le Directoire, la prédominance des acheteurs bourgeois, incontestable déjà dans l'ensemble, devint vraiment écrasante'.[24] The manner in which du Bousquier makes his fortune was made possible by laws passed under the Directory. It was the laws of 28 ventôse and 6 floréal, Year IV, which explained, Marion indicates, why 'les spéculateurs, achetant pour revendre, furent très nombreux'.[25]

Sauviat and du Bousquier represent a minority tendency among Balzac's 'acquéreurs', who, in general, prefer to retain the property they acquire rather than resell it. The type of behaviour associated with Grandet is more common than that which is embodied by du Bousquier. In this sense, Balzac's indications are once again in line with the conclusions of historians. As Marion notes, 'acquéreurs' who bought 'biens nationaux' with a view to holding on to them were more numerous (in a ratio of 6 to 1, as noted above)[26] than those whose aim was to resell.[27] Whether they speculate in 'biens nationaux' or exploit them directly, whether they acquire Church property or émigré property, Balzac's 'acquéreurs' considerably increase their wealth through their acquisitions. In many cases, they go on to achieve political power as a result and, more often than not, their increased wealth and authority is accompanied by an enhancement of their social status.

Du Bousquier's achievements suggest that the exploitation of the advantages derived from the acquisition of 'biens nationaux' began to bear political fruit towards the end of the Restoration. In his study of the Gironde and the Cher, Marion found that the 'acquéreurs' formed an overwhelming majority of the registered electors at this period.[28] Here again, Balzac and historians are in full agreement. Du Bousquier is not the only example in the *Comédie humaine* of an 'acquéreur' emerging as a 'notable' at the end of the Restoration. The liberal faction in Provins is largely made up of 'acquéreurs', while the shareholders in a new liberal newspaper are mainly recruited 'parmi les électeurs propriétaires de biens nationaux à qui les journaux libéraux faisaient concevoir des craintes'.[29] Balzac's historical accuracy and insight, on this occasion, are beyond dispute.

At the same time that he confirms the judgement of historians that the resale of 'biens nationaux' was a less frequent phenomenon than their retention, Balzac lends support to another interpretation concerning the acquisition of 'biens nationaux' to which historians have attached great importance. They are unanimous in concluding that the 'biens nationaux', far from creating by their transfer an important new class of property owners, were essentially acquired by existing proprietors. Marion's view is that 'les biens nationaux ont été achetés surtout par ceux qui en possédaient déjà d'autres'.[30] Soboul reaches a similar conclusion, namely that 'la vente des biens nationaux renforça la prépondérance des possédants'.[31]

The 'acquéreurs' in the *Comédie humaine* bear out this view. Almost without exception, they already own property or have a fortune which is consistent with its possession when they acquire their 'biens nationaux'. Descoings has a wool business, Bontems a property near Bayeux. Where the nature of their property is not specified, bourgeois 'acquéreurs' have the necessary amount of ready capital which would enable them to defeat peasant bids, while their profession or function in society is such as to denote the ownership of property. Everything in the *Comédie humaine* therefore points to the view of historians that the sale of 'biens nationaux' chiefly benefited those who already owned property. Balzac, moreover, suggests the important implication of this: the accession of the urban bourgeoisie to a significant share of landed property at the expense both of the clergy and the aristocracy, via the acquisition of 'biens nationaux'. That Balzac himself was aware of this reality is made clear in *Les Chouans*, when he lets it be understood that the enthusiasm of the Republican forces combating the Chouans was partly explained by their concern to retain their 'biens nationaux'. 'Néanmoins', Balzac hints, 'les bienfaits de la Révolution mieux appréciés dans les villes entraient aussi pour beaucoup dans cette ardeur.'[32]

The range of Balzac's 'acquéreurs' is considerable. A former opera singer, Mlle Laguerre, exists alongside the Bonapartist fanatic Bartholoméo di Piombo and the Protestant, Moïse Piédefer.[33] In *Les Paysans*, there is the case of a 'bien national' purchased by the local commune. Of all the buildings in Soulanges, Balzac remarks, 'la plus magnifique est l'ancien bailliage. Vendue nationalement, elle fut achetée par la commune, qui en fit la mairie et y mit le tribunal de paix.'[34] Despite this individual variety, the important fact remains that the bulk of the 'acquéreurs' in the *Comédie humaine* is composed of bourgeois property owners.

There is, however, a striking omission in Balzac's account of the sale of 'biens nationaux'. One of the questions which has particularly engaged the attention of historians of the Revolution has been to determine to what extent and in what sense the peasantry benefited from the process. It is generally accepted that the effect of peasant acquisitions was to reinforce an existing category of proprietors rather than to create a new landowning class. While acknowledging that a certain number of peasants became landowners for the first time through the purchase of 'biens nationaux', Marion nevertheless concludes that 'ceux qui possédaient déjà furent parmi eux l'immense majorité'.[35] Lefebvre reaches the same conclusion when he stresses that 'même au moment le plus favorable pour les ruraux, la vente aux enchères avantagea de beaucoup les laboureurs aisés et les grands fermiers, en sorte que s'affermit l'ascendant de ce qu'on peut appeler la bourgeoisie paysanne'.[36]

It is surprising to find that, except in a general way in *Les Paysans*, peasant 'acquéreurs' scarcely exist in the *Comédie humaine*. Otherwise, the category is represented only by Violette in *Une Ténébreuse Affaire*. Employed by Marion to inform him of the activities of his 'régisseur' Michu, Violette is paid for his services in 'biens nationaux' and thus, from being a landless peasant, becomes a 'petit propriétaire'. A study of *Les Paysans* encourages a hypothesis which might explain what appears to be a surprising absence in the *Comédie humaine*. It is not Balzac's purpose in *Les Paysans* to undertake a thorough and detailed analysis of peasant conditions under the Restoration. As far as Balzac is concerned, the important fact is already established, the unlimited and universal division of land resulting from the sale of 'biens nationaux'.

Every peasant is therefore considered as an 'acquéreur' and, as such, as a new proprietor whose increased appetite for land makes him envy the estates of the bourgeois who have replaced many of his old noble masters. This is a position far removed from that represented in de Tocqueville's statement: 'C'est donc suivre une erreur commune que de croire que la division de la propriété foncière date en France de la Révolution; le fait est bien plus vieux qu'elle'.[37] If one is to believe Balzac, the peasant 'acquéreur', 'cet infatigable sapeur, ce rongeur qui morcèle et divise le sol, le partage, et coupe un arpent de terre en cent morceaux'[38] signifies the emergence of a new monolithic and dangerous class in society.

This conviction that the acquisition of 'biens nationaux' brought into existence a powerful body of new peasant proprietors is reiterated by the duc de Chaulieu in the *Mémoires de deux jeunes mariées*. The consequences of this, he claims, are the disastrous breaking-up of landed estates and the increased danger of social upheaval.[39] The same argument is restated by Clousier and Grossetête in *Le Curé de village*, who add to it an important new element. The peasants were only able to acquire their 'biens nationaux', they maintain, through the intervention of bourgeois who often resold to peasant buyers the land which they had acquired. Clousier undoubtedly exaggerates the significance of bourgeois resales, of which Balzac, as we have seen, provides few examples, just as Balzac magnifies the extent of 'morcellement'. On the other hand, when he describes the exploitation of the peasant by the bourgeoisie under the Restoration, Balzac is on perfectly safe ground. The 'acquéreur' is often a moneylender as well. This is the dual role of d'Orgemont during the Republic.[40] The practice was still in force under the Restoration. In *Les Paysans*, it is the 'acquéreur' Rigou who lends Courtecuisse money at an excessive rate of interest to enable him to become a 'propriétaire'.[41]

Whereas Marion notes 'un léger surcroît de morcellement', Balzac persists in the erroneous view of the peasantry as comprising an infinite number of 'acquéreurs' who have only become landowners in the Revolution through their acquisition of 'biens nationaux'.[42] According to Balzac, the peasant, determined to maintain and extend his gains, was to look towards Napoleon as 'l'homme qui lui assurait la possession des biens nationaux'.[43] It is not difficult to see in these views the impact of Balzac's political thinking. His fundamental hostility to the Revolution, in the first place, leads Balzac greatly to exaggerate the extent of the division of land resulting from the sale of 'biens nationaux', a view which has been totally invalidated by historical research.

It is also appropriate to Balzac's legitimism that he should present the behaviour of Republicans involved in the sale of 'biens nationaux' in an unfavourable light. In Balzac's defence, it has to be emphasised that the picture he gives is a reasonably balanced one, from which acts of Republican generosity are not excluded. There are instances of Republicans who, out of selfless motives and at considerable risk to themselves, protect émigrés threatened with the loss of their property.[44]

In contrast, the closer one approaches the centre of operations of the sale of 'biens nationaux', the more damning the picture becomes. The Republican officials who profit from the traffic in 'biens nationaux' are numerous in the *Comédie humaine*. In some cases, like that of the 'chef de district', Bontems, the motive is the personal gain of 'biens nationaux'. On other occasions, it is an influentially placed Republican who ensures that 'biens nationaux' pass into certain hands. It is in complicity with 'le Syndic de la Commune' that du Bousquier is able to buy and to resell émigré property. Grandet owes the basis of his fortune 'au farouche républicain qui surveillait la vente des domaines nationaux', and who, in exchange for 'deux cents doubles lois' offered by Grandet's father-in-law, obtains for Grandet 'pour un morceau de pain, légalement, sinon légitimement, les plus beaux vignobles de l'arrondissement, une vieille abbaye et quelques métairies'.[45]

This is the starting-point of Grandet's remarkable career under the Republic. By exploiting his revolutionary contacts, Grandet, as wine-supplier to the Republican armies, 'se fit payer en superbes prairies dépendant d'une communauté de femmes que l'on avait réservée pour un dernier lot'. Already an 'acquéreur' of Church property, Grandet acts as a double agent, playing a counter-revolutionary role in the Republican administration of Saumur, of which he finally becomes mayor. 'Politiquement', Balzac adds, 'il protégea les ci-devant et empêcha de tout son pouvoir la vente des biens des émigrés.[46] The same far-sighted determination to get the best of both worlds out of the Revolution is shown by Goulard. Having, like Grandet, acquired Church land, Goulard is unusually well-disposed towards the nobility. 'Semblable à beaucoup de parvenus', Goulard, Balzac comments, 'une fois sa fortune faite, recroyait aux vieilles familles et voulait s'y rattacher.'[47]

However, a Republican does not have to show generosity towards the nobility to earn Balzac's approval. Balzac also pays tribute to those Republicans whose integrity resists the opportunity of acquiring 'biens nationaux'. The outstanding example is that of Niseron. An incorruptible idealist, in whom revolutionary fervour is reconciled with religious faith, 'il refusa d'acheter des biens nationaux, il déniait à la république le droit de confiscation'. While applauding the individual example of Niseron, Balzac is careful to maintain his ideological distance. Niseron remains for Balzac 'ce sublime républicain, qui rendrait la république acceptable s'il pouvait faire école'.[48] Sceptical admiration easily turns to contempt, if not for the values represented by Niseron, for, in Blondet's words, 'le vertueux Robert Lindet, qui n'a su tirer parti ni des assignats, ni des Biens Nationaux'.[49]

Balzac's parting shot is nevertheless aimed at Niseron. The final judgement on the logic of Niseron's behaviour is unpitying. 'En réponse aux demandes du Comité du (sic) Salut Public, il voulait que la vertu des citoyens fît pour la sainte patrie les miracles que les tripoteurs de pouvoir voulaient opérer à prix d'or.'[50] Balzac had few illusions about the realities of the sale of 'biens nationaux'. They merely strengthened his conviction that the Revolution represented the triumph of corruption and the death of an impotent idealism.

Balzac's error is not simply to exaggerate the extent of the division of land arising out of the sale of 'biens nationaux'. All the conclusions which he draws from this assertion turn out to be incorrect, like so many deductions based on a false axiom. The hypothesis of an excessive redistribution of landed property leads Balzac to take for granted the creation of a new class of landowners recruited from the peasant masses. In terms of the economic effects of the acquisition of 'biens nationaux', Balzac's account is equally in conflict with the historical facts. In *Les Paysans*, he attacks the policy of 'morcellement', claiming that the breaking-up of land, accentuated by the sale of 'biens nationaux', by favouring small-scale farming, had had disastrous consequences for French agriculture. Marion's conclusion is the very opposite. After first pointing out that small-scale farming had co-existed with large estates before the Revolution, he then goes on to emphasise that, far from showing a fall, agricultural production had increased following the sale of 'biens nationaux'.

It is therefore perfectly logical that, on the question of the long-term effect of the sale of 'biens nationaux', Balzac should have taken up a position contrary to that held by historians, for whom their transfer did not represent a fundamental change in the character of landed property. Making allowance for the losses suffered by the Church and the aristocracy, historians have underlined the conservative nature of the revolutionary land settlement. This point of view is well expressed by Soboul, who echoes Marion and Lefebvre in concluding: 'La révolution agraire n'en demeure pas moins, en dépit des apparences, modérée dans ses effets et, selon Georges Lefebvre, "conservatrice". Désormais, une puissante minorité de paysans propriétaires, attachée à l'ordre nouveau, rallia la bourgeoisie dans ses options conservatrices.'[51]

Balzac, on the other hand, misled by his systematic aversion for the Revolution, exaggerates the consequences which the sale of 'biens nationaux' had for the structure of landed property. Its effect, Balzac insisted, had been to give free rein to bourgeois materialism, the precedent of which the masses would not be slow to emulate. Whereas, for historians, that section of the peasantry which acquired 'biens nationaux' represented a powerful conservative force, Balzac saw it as a subversive threat which those in authority must repress at all costs.[52]

The account of the sale of 'biens nationaux' in the *Comédie humaine* reveals as much about the political convictions of Balzac as it does of the nature of post-revolutionary society. The points on which Balzac agrees with historians are less numerous and less important than the differences that divide them. Such affinities that exist are the result of diffuse observations rather than of systematic analysis. On the other hand, Balzac's historical misjudgements are often redeemed by the imaginative power of the novelist whose inventions enliven the sober reality of events. Balzac is wrong less on the facts of revolutionary history than in respect of the conclusions which he draws from them. He is vulnerable as a political polemicist rather than as the 'secrétaire' of contemporary society. Balzac's discussion of the sale of 'biens nationaux', as well as containing one major error, betrays an unresolved ambivalence. On the one hand, he incorrectly insists on the revolutionary potential of the peasantry. At the same time, Balzac's cult of the dynamic forces in society, which the acquisition of 'biens nationaux' by the bourgeoisie expressed, is in conflict with his nostalgic evocation of an aristocracy which had lost the first important battle in the struggle for the control of landed property.

Notes

1. Zola, *Les Rougon-Macquart*, Pléiade, vol. III (Paris, 1964), p. 1198.
2. Zola, *Les Rougon-Macquart*, Pléiade, vol. IV, pp. 392, 440.
3. The role of Balzac's father as an 'acquéreur' is the subject of an article by Jean Dutacq, 'La Maison de famille', *Le Courrier Balzacien*, nos. 3, 4, 5.
4. For an interesting historical appraisal of Balzac see J.-H. Donnard, *Les Réalités économiques et sociales dans l'oeuvre de Balzac* (Paris, 1971). From a Marxist point of view, the most characteristic of the numerous publications of Pierre Barbéris are *Balzac et le mal du siècle*, 2 vols. (Paris, 1970a) and *Le Monde de Balzac* (Paris, 1973).
5. *Le Député d'Arcis*, VIII, 725.

6. Marcel Marion, *La Vente des biens nationaux pendant la Révolution* (Paris, 1908), Introduction, pp. v-vi.

7. *La Maison Nucingen*, VI, 359.

8. *Ursule Mirouët*, III, 772.

9. Marion reveals, for example, that 'les premières ventes de biens d'émigrés n'ont pas eu lieu avant octobre 1793: elles n'ont eu de véritable activité que dans le courant de l'an II et de l'an III'. Marion, *Les Ventes des biens nationaux*, p. 160.

10. On this question see Marion, ibid., Introduction, p. vi.

11. For an explanation of the greater profitability of Church property see Marion, ibid., pp. 157-60.

12. *La Rabouilleuse*, IV, 273.

13. See note 9.

14. P.-G. Castex, *Eugénie Grandet* (Classiques Garnier, Paris, 1965a), 'Note préliminaire', pp. xiii-xiv. See also section IV of the Introduction to this edition, in which Grandet is seen as representing the new landowning bourgeoisie.

15. Marion, *La Vente des biens nationaux*, Introduction, p. vii.

16. See note 11.

17. For the genesis of the character of du Bousquier see P.-G. Castex, *La Vieille Fille* (Classiques Garnier, Paris, 1957), pp. xvi-xxi. Professor Castex provides some interesting information about the elements which went into the creation of du Bousquier, especially concerning his similarities with Ouvrard.

18. *Les Petits Bourgeois*, VIII, 104.

19. *Les Paysans*, IX, 244.

20. Marion, *La Vente des biens nationaux*, p. 364.

21. *Le Curé de village*, IX, 643.

22. *La Vieille Fille*, IV, 827.

23. Ibid.

24. Georges Lefebvre, *La Révolution Française*, 1st edn (Paris, 1957), p. 586.

25. Marion, *La Vente des biens nationaux*, p. 273.

26. Ibid., p. 364.

27. 'Nombreux aussi, plus nombreux même', Marion states, 'furent les acheteurs qui achetèrent pour conserver.' Ibid., p. 354.

28. Ibid., pp. 390-3.

29. *Pierrette*, IV, 90.

30. Marion, *La Vente des biens nationaux*, p. 412.

31. Albert Soboul, *Précis d'histoire de la Révolution Francaise* (Paris, 1962), p. 170.

32. *Les Chouans*, VIII, 1156.

33. The marriage of Dinah Piédefer and Polydore de la Baudraye is of particular significance in that it brings together the daughter of an 'acquéreur' and the son of a dispossessed émigré.

34. *Les Paysans*, IX, 255.

35. Marion, *La Vente des biens nationaux*, p. 414.

36. Lefebvre, *La Révolution Française*, p. 586. The law of 12 prairial year III (31 May 1795) replaced sale by auction by direct sale. Confiscated property was henceforth sold 'au premier venu' instead of 'au plus offrant'. The result was to provoke a flood of successful bids from the urban bourgeoisie to the detriment of the peasantry, and to encourage a wave of speculation.

37. A. de Tocqueville, *L'Ancien Régime et la Révolution* (Paris, 1887), livre II, chapître I.

38. *Les Paysans*, IX, 49.

39. *Mémoires de deux jeunes mariées*, I, 242-4.

40. As an 'acquéreur', d'Orgemont has his predecessors in the 'romans de

jeunesse'. D'Orgemont's appearance in *Les Chouans* establishes him as the first of a long line of 'acquéreurs' in the *Comédie humaine*.

41. This observation has been made by J.-H. Donnard in his analysis of Balzac's attitude to the peasantry. *Les Paysans* (Classiques Garnier, Paris, 1964), pp. xxvi-xxxiv.

42. Marion, *La Vente des biens nationaux*, p. 362.

43. *Les Paysans*, IX, 127.

44. This theme is discussed in detail on pp. 37, 39 and 41-2.

45. *Eugénie Grandet*, III, 1030-1.

46. Ibid., 1031. *La Cousine Bette* confirms that the dying request made by Montauran in *Les Chouans* that Marshal Hulot should look after the interests of his younger brother has been fully respected. Hulot, it is revealed, 'avait si bien accepté le testament verbal du noble, qu'il réussit à sauver les biens de ce jeune homme alors émigré'. *La Cousine Bette*, VII, 353.

47. *Une Ténébreuse Affaire*, VIII, 551.

48. *Les Paysans*, IX, 222.

49. *La Maison Nucingen*, VI, 379.

50. *Les Paysans*, IX, 222.

51. Soboul, *Précis d'histoire de la Revolution Française*, p. 477.

52. Balzac's view of the peasantry is compared with that of Zola by J.-H. Donnard in his article ' "Les Paysans" et "La Terre" ', *L'Année Balzacienne* (1975), pp. 125-42. Pages 137-42 of Donnard's article are especially interesting for their discussion of the historical factors which enabled Zola, in contrast to Balzac, to make a correct assessment of the conservative tendencies of the peasantry.

2 THE EMIGRÉS

I Dimensions and Priorities

The emigration emerges as a subject of high-ranking importance in the *Comédie humaine*, being treated, with varying degrees of emphasis, in the majority of Balzac's works. The significance which it assumes extends beyond the phenomenon itself. Through his reactions to the emigration which are revealed in his writing, Balzac provided a powerful indication of his view of the Revolution and of the nature of post-revolutionary society.

Balzac's interest in the emigration no doubt had its origin in his personal experience and relationships. It is very likely that Balzac gained his early knowledge of the emigration during his spell of legal work between 1816 and 1819, first for the lawyer Guillonnet-Merville and then for the solicitor Me Passez. Among the law-suits which he must have come across at this time there are bound to have been numerous cases involving émigrés. This initiation was subsequently reinforced by two other factors: first, by Balzac's reading of the various Memoirs of the Revolution which appeared during the Restoration; and secondly, by the contacts which he made in the salon of the duchesse d'Abrantès from 1826 and, after 1830, his relationship with the duc de Fitz-James, himself a former émigré, and the marquise de Castries, the wife of an émigré.[1]

Judged by strictly historical standards, Balzac's approach to the emigration is far from systematic, for it is lacking in both rigour and completeness. There is nothing in the *Comédie humaine* which approximates to the detailed analysis of the emigration which has been undertaken by Greer,[2] Gain,[3] Marion[4] and, most recently, by Vidalenc.[5] Nor does one find in Balzac a study of ideological differences among the émigrés which one associates with the work of Baldensperger.[6] Balzac's account of the emigration is fragmentary and subjective. It does not always faithfully reproduce the facts of history. Where such inaccuracies occur, attention has been drawn to them. Nevertheless, in its scope and diversity, the independent perspective which Balzac offers of the emigration is one which may usefully be measured against the findings of historians.

If Balzac's treatment lacks depth, his terms of reference are impressive.

Whereas Greer limits himself to the period from July 1789 to December 1799, from the flight of the comte d'Artois to Bonaparte's closing of the émigré lists, Balzac's discussion of the emigration continues up to the final years of the Restoration. Moreover, although Balzac is mainly concerned with the effects of the sale of émigré property, it is not his only preoccupation. Unlike Marion and Gain, Balzac presents a picture of émigré *mores* and values as well as evaluating the historical role of the émigrés.

There are a number of important aspects of the emigration which are sufficiently dealt with by Balzac for the question of historical authenticity to be seriously considered. The first concerns the social incidence of the emigration. Secondly, Balzac, by the number and variety of the examples he gives, raises the question of the extent to which the émigrés were successful in avoiding expropriation. Essentially, however, Balzac's analysis concentrates on the effort made by the émigrés to regain the preponderant position in French society from which they had been ousted by the confiscation and sale of their property. Above all, Balzac is concerned to examine the émigré recovery prior to the indemnity of 1825 and the impact of the indemnity itself, which is dealt with in chapter 5.

II The Social Incidence

Greer found that the majority of émigrés (51 per cent) were from the Third Estate, compared with only 25 per cent from the clergy and 17 per cent from the nobility, the remaining seven per cent being classed as unidentifiable.[7] Although, by discounting the six departments of heaviest emigration, where civil war and invasion greatly swelled the proportion of émigrés from the Third Estate, Greer acknowledges that 'the emigration from the greater part of France was essentially clerical and aristocratic',[8] he effectively demolishes, in his appraisal of 'the Legend of the White and the Black', the myth of a wholly aristocratic and clerical emigration.[9]

The *Comédie humaine* conveys a totally different impression in terms of the social pattern of the emigration. Balzac's émigrés are almost exclusively aristocratic; clerical émigrés are virtually absent. As for the Third Estate, it is simply ignored by Balzac as a factor in the emigration. There are neither industrial labourers nor artisans among Balzac's émigrés; the bourgeoisie is no more represented than the peasantry.

In describing his aristocratic émigrés, Balzac gives a similarly distorted picture. Only in respect of the military emigration can he be said to be accurate in this area. The considerable number of military émigrés, all of them army officers and therefore perforce noble,[10] in the *Comédie humaine*, accurately reflects Greer's estimate that they made up ten per cent of the total number of émigrés and represented the largest category (35 per cent) among the émigré nobility.[11] On the other hand, just as he excludes the Third Estate from a share in the emigration, so Balzac omits the 'noblesse de robe' in favour of the 'noblesse de cour' and the 'noblesse de province'. Greer, however, reveals that, while the court and provincial nobility formed the majority of the aristocratic émigrés, the 'noblesse de robe' nevertheless constituted an important element in the emigration, including, for example, 872 out of 2,000 members of the sovereign courts. One should not expect to find therefore in the *Comédie humaine* a reliable indication either of the composition of the aristocratic emigration or, more importantly, of the social distribution of the emigration as a whole.

III The Return of the Emigrés

In leaving France for the most part before the end of 1792, Balzac's exclusively noble émigrés support Greer's conclusion that the aristocratic emigration was essentially completed before 1793.[12] More than their departure, the question of the date of the return of his émigrés is of great importance for Balzac, linked as it is in his analysis with their attempt to regain their former preponderance.

The fact that non-aristocratic émigrés scarcely exist in the *Comédie humaine* leaves irrelevant Greer's view that 'probably a heavy proportion of all the Third Estate exiles had come home by the end of 1795 in virtue of or in defiance of the laws'.[13] It is, however, worth examining how the evidence of the *Comédie humaine* fits Greer's general conclusion that 'very likely the great majority of the émigrés were in France by the autumn of 1800'.[14]

Greer's assertion is based on his study of the 72 departments for which reliable information is available. It takes account of two important factors. The first concerns the great number of émigrés, both lay and clerical, who returned although still officially proscribed. Thus the figure of 145,000 uncancelled émigrés given in the 'Liste générale' in October 1800, on the eve of Bonaparte's first amnesty, becomes meaningless. The second factor has to do with the effect of Bonaparte's measures on the volume of the return flow of émigrés. After the lists had been closed with effect from the end of 1799, the partial amnesty of October 1800 affected a further 52,000 émigrés. After the second amnesty of April 1802, only 1,000 émigrés, those considered implacably hostile to the Revolution, were still banned from returning.[15]

The account of the return of Balzac's émigrés is altogether different from the timetable proposed by Greer. First, there is not a single instance in the *Comédie humaine* of an émigré returning before 1800, which means that no account is taken of the post-Thermidor influx.[16] Where the amnesty of 1800 is concerned, Balzac stresses the ease with which émigrés were able to return in 1800. 'En 1800', he states, 'quelques émigrés rentrèrent en France, les radiations des noms inscrits sur les fatales listes s'obtenaient assez facilement.'[17] From this three points emerge. First, Balzac does not directly relate the trend he describes to Bonaparte's first amnesty. Secondly, Balzac's reference is in keeping with what historians have said about the way in which the émigrés responded to Brumaire. Greer asserts that Brumaire encouraged émigrés to return, although the ban was officially still in force.[18] Gain lends support to this view when he states that 'Dès l'an VIII la rentrée des émigrés se poursuit rapidement'.[19] Finally, Balzac's use of the term 'quelques émigrés' suggests that the number of émigrés who returned in 1800 was significantly lower than the proportion indicated by Greer.

When one looks at specific examples, one finds that Balzac's dating of the return of his émigrés is often imprecise. In *Le Colonel Chabert*, comte Ferraud is simply referred to as having returned under the Consulate. All we are told of the father of Polydore de la Baudraye is that 'il revint à Sancerre en 1800'.[20] Whether this occurred as a result of the amnesty or not is not made clear. In *L'Envers de l'histoire contemporaine*, the references are even vaguer. The uncle of Mme de la Chanterie, M. de Boisfrelon, may have returned at any time up to the moment when the action begins in 1803, by virtue of either amnesty or in circumstances independent of both. Balzac merely mentions that M. de Boisfrelon had been removed from the émigré lists and had returned from exile to Paris.

The account of the return of M. de Mortsauf is particularly confusing. 'Après douze ans de misère', Balzac records, 'il tourna les yeux vers la France où le décret de Napoléon lui permit de rentrer.'[21] By which amnesty one is not told. The uncertainty is made worse by the fact that, before referring to M. de Mortsauf's 'douze ans de misère', Balzac announces that he is prematurely aged by 'les dix années d'émigration'.[22] In general, the information which Balzac gives concerning the date of the return of his émigrés is slender, vague and unhelpful.

In contrast, Balzac is firm to the point of being dogmatic in identifying the period when the return from emigration reached its general peak. 'Pendant les années 1804 et 1805', he maintains, 'les deux tiers des familles émigrées revinrent en France, et presque toutes celles de la province où demeurait le marquis d'Esgrignon se replantèrent dans le sol paternel.'[23] Balzac is consistent with his own statement in the sense that relatively few of his émigrés are reported as having returned before 1804. Nevertheless, Balzac's claim that two-thirds of the émigrés came back in 1804-5 cannot be taken seriously. Even if one accepts that Balzac is thinking solely of aristocratic émigrés, his assertion is quite unacceptable. Greer's figures speak for themselves, while historians have concluded that Bonaparte's amnesties were successful in inducing many of the remaining émigrés to return under the Consulate.

One might therefore reasonably presuppose that, in so far as dates are given at all, the majority of Balzac's émigrés would be described as having returned in 1804-5. This is far from being the case, however. The only clear-cut instance of émigrés returning at that period is that of the duc and duchesse de Grandlieu, 'rentrés en 1804'.[24] To this one might reply that the absence of an explicit date is not important since, if it does not support Balzac's contention that the bulk of the émigrés returned in 1804-5, it in no way invalidates it either. There the matter might rest, were it not for a significant fact. There are an important number of Balzac's émigrés who return, not in 1804-5 but in 1814-15. The father of the duc d'Hérouville is referred to as having 'revenu avec le roi en 1814'.[25] There are the examples of the vicomte de Troisville, 'revenu d'émigration en 1815',[26] and of Mme de Grandlieu, 'rentrée en France avec la famille royale'.[27]

Balzac thus gives a misleading impression. The diehard émigrés numbered only a few thousand and, as Gain observes, their ranks were even thinner by 1806, when they had to opt between fighting against the advancing French armies or serving in them.[28] In concentrating his attention on the type of intransigent émigré who was either excluded from Bonaparte's second amnesty or chose to ignore it, preferring to return only with the Bourbons, Balzac encourages the false assumption that the number of émigrés who did not return until 1814-15 was greater than was in fact the case.

IV The Emigré Recovery

(a) The Decade of Revolution (1789-99)

(i) The Avoidance of Expropriation. The date of the return of Balzac's émigrés only acquires full significance when it is seen as part of Balzac's analysis of the émigrés' attempt to recover the ground which they had lost in the Revolution. In some cases, the process of recovery was facilitated, in advance of the émigrés' return, by various factors which combined to take some of the sting out of the revolutionary legislation directed at the émigrés. This important first stage in the revival of émigré fortunes, which occurred while the émigrés were still in exile, is finely demonstrated in the *Comédie humaine*.

As Marion has pointed out, there were many exceptions in the sale of 'biens nationaux'.[29] The point is confirmed by Balzac, who gives numerous examples of the ways in which, short of directly repurchasing it themselves, émigrés were able to avoid the sale and, in some cases, even the confiscation of their property. In showing how some émigrés, in this respect, fared better than others, Balzac does not always explain the reason for their good fortune. The comte de Granville, for example, is spared for no reason, while the Lenoncourts' 'château' unaccountably escapes the fate of the rest of their property. In *Les Chouans*, la Billardière simply tells Montauran, 'vos biens n'ont pas été vendus'.[30]

The manner in which Balzac deals with the experience of the Sérisy family is at once revealing and baffling. On the positive side, Balzac illustrates, in the case of the comte de Sérisy's father, how the true total of émigrés was inflated by what Marion calls the 'pseudo-émigrés'.[31] If, like the marquis d'Esgrignon and the comte de Fontaine, a noble were a rebel allied to interventionist foreign powers, he was almost certain to be classed and treated as an émigré. Yet it was enough, on some occasions, for a noble to be arrested by virtue of his mere status and to have his property confiscated as an émigré.[32] The Sérisy family clearly comes into this category. Having established this, however, Balzac does not make it clear precisely what happened to the Sérisy property during the Revolution. Referring to the intervention of Moreau, the father of the present manager of the Sérisy estates, who had been 'procureur-syndic' at Versailles at the time, Balzac leaves one guessing when he states that 'Moreau père avait presque sauvé les biens et la vie de messieurs de Sérisy père et fils'.[33]

Such instances are exceptional, however. Normally, Balzac is scrupulously concerned to reveal the circumstances which enable émigrés to avoid expropriation, whether it is a question of escaping the sale of their property or of being spared confiscation altogether. In those cases where émigré property remains unconfiscated, chance may play a decisive part. As the heiress of émigré property, Mlle Félicité des Touches keeps it within the family through being orphaned at the age of two in 1793. 'Ses biens', Balzac explains, 'échappèrent ainsi aux confiscations qu'auraient sans doute encourues son père et son frère.'[34]

Emigré relatives are frequently mentioned in the *Comédie humaine* in connection with the legislation affecting émigré property. In some cases, they suffer themselves as a result. Malin ensures, for example, that because of her brothers' activities, Laurence de Cinq-Cygne should have only 'sa légitime', 'la Nation étant au lieu et place de l'émigré, surtout quand il portait les armes contre la République'.[35] Otherwise, in the examples which he provides, Balzac emphasises the important role of relatives in helping émigrés avoid confiscation. This particular service on the part of émigré relatives is performed by, among others, the sister of the baron du Guénic. 'Avant de partir', Balzac reveals, 'il avait vendu tous ses biens à sa soeur aînée, mademoiselle du Guénic', which, according to Balzac, constituted 'un trait de prudence unique dans les annales révolutionnaires'.[36] As the self-appointed secretary of contemporary French history, Balzac took occasional liberties with the minutes. The act of caution which Balzac refers to was no doubt unique in the *Comédie humaine* rather than in the history of the Revolution. What is important, however, is that the baron du Guénic is able to save his property from confiscation. Moreover, his sister, who receives the income from it, arranges for it to be transferred to him by fishing boat in his Irish exile from 1802 to 1813.

Similarly, the marquis d'Esgrignon, a rebel falsely included in the émigré lists, owes the retention of part of his property to his sister. Finally, there is the behaviour of Mme de Dey in *Le Réquisitionnaire*. Already a widow, she had left the court at the beginning of the emigration to take refuge on her estates in Basse-Normandie. When her only son, who is a cavalry officer, decides to emigrate, Mme de Dey stays on at the risk of her life in order to preserve the family heritage on behalf of her son while émigré property in the surrounding area is being confiscated.

When one tries to establish whether Balzac's references to émigré relatives are consistent with the historical facts, two observations may be made in Balzac's favour. First, there is the negative point that none of his dating conflicts with the realities of the legal situation. The law confiscating the property of émigré relatives which was passed on 17 frimaire, year II (7 December 1793) remained in force until 20 floréal, year IV (May 1796). There is no example in the *Comédie humaine* of the seizure of relatives' property at any period, nor are the actions of the relatives of Balzac's émigrés situated during the period when they would have been preoccupied with protecting their own property as well as that of émigrés which might be in their safekeeping.[37]

If Balzac ignores the legal aspect of the question, he none the less provides a remarkable illustration of the various ways in which émigré relatives might play a decisive part in helping émigrés to avoid confiscation. As male relatives were more likely to have joined the head of family in emigrating, the role is shown by Balzac to have been essentially assumed by female relatives.

Thus, Mlle des Touches escapes as a young orphan. The sister of the marquis d'Esgrignon successfully claims the right of pre-succession to part of her brother's estates because she is a minor. But the most masterly demonstration which Balzac gives of the success of an émigré relative in preserving property from confiscation occurs in the case of Mme de Dey. In November 1793, which is the date of the action in *Le Réquisitionnaire*, the legislation aimed at émigré relatives was still a month away. In addition, there are two factors which enable Mme de Dey to avoid extra-legal victimisation and to ensure that the period of legal liability can be negotiated without serious danger. The first is Mme de Dey's correct calculation that the effects of the Revolution will be less severe in Carentan than elsewhere. 'La Révolution', Balzac confirms, 'exerça peu de ravages en Basse-Normandie.'[38]

The second reason for Mme de Dey's success lies in her effective cultivation of the local bourgeoisie. Not for the first time, Balzac highlights the complicity of Republican officials in saving émigré property from confiscation and sale. Finally, Balzac adds a coquettish ingredient to the familiar theme of Republican connivance at émigré evasion. Mme de Dey's aristocratic charms are widely felt among the bourgeois who frequent her salon, to embrace even 'les juges du tribunal révolutionnaire'. Her most important conquest, however, is the 'accusateur public'. Formerly in charge of her affairs, he alone knows the true amount of her fortune and subsequently, for two-and-a-half years from December 1793 to May 1796, the full extent of her liabilities as the mother and next-of-kin of an émigré.

When he discusses cases of émigré property which, though confiscated, had still escaped sale, Balzac observes some important historical distinctions. The category of exemptions will be examined later. One must first, however, consider what evidence the *Comédie humaine* contains of émigré property which was not exempt from sale, yet nevertheless remained in émigré hands. Balzac distinguishes three distinct factors which explain why this happened: the element of chance; the nature of the property itself; and the actions of individuals intervening on behalf of émigrés.

It frequently happened that confiscated émigré property failed to find a buyer simply because it was economically unattractive. The church and presbytery of Cinq-Cygne remain unsold because they are not sufficiently profitable. Infertility and problems of cultivation might also explain why émigré land escaped sale. This happens in the case of the duc de Navarreins, 'dont les terres avaient échappé à la vente ordonnée par la Convention, autant par leur infertilité que par l'impossibilité reconnue de les exploiter'.[39] Here Balzac is on firm ground. Poor fertility was aggravated by attendant factors. Marion makes the point that the neglected and devastated condition of émigré property was one of the main reasons for its inferior profitability compared with Church land.[40] When the émigré owners had left, their property was often pillaged by vindictive marauding bands and even by their successors. Hence the difficulties encountered by the revolutionary authorities in trying to sell it.

Just as the relatives of émigrés help in protecting property from confiscation, so outside agents are instrumental in preventing its sale. A combination of chance and the initiative of a well-disposed tenant-farmer is responsible for the happy experience of M. de Mortsauf. 'A demi mourant', Balzac relates, 'il atteignit le Maine, où, par un hasard dû peut-être à la guerre civile, le gouvernement révolutionnaire avait oublié de faire vendre une ferme considérable en étendue, et que son fermier lui conservait en laissant croire qu'il en était propriétaire.'[41]

The decisive service is often performed by lawyers. One far-sighted form of emigration is that adopted by Paul de Manerville's father, who departs for Martinique in 1790 ostensibly to look after his wife's property on the island, leaving the direction of his estates to the solicitor's clerk, Mathias. The gamble succeeds since, as Balzac notes, 'à son retour, le comte de Manerville trouva ses propriétés intactes et profitablement gérées'.[42]

Another important phenomenon, which contributed to this phase in the recovery achieved by the émigrés in anticipation of their actual return, was repurchase. The part played by émigré relatives in repurchase, which has been underlined by historians, is in fact never mentioned by Balzac.[43] The one example in the *Comédie humaine* of repurchase carried out on behalf of émigrés is not the work of relatives but that of the solicitor Chesnel, who is responsible for looking after the affairs

of a 'pseudo-émigré', the marquis d'Esgrignon. Benefiting from Bonaparte's first amnesty, the marquis d'Esgrignon emerges from hiding on
his estates in October 1800, to find that Chesnel has excelled himself.
The property which Chesnel has bought back in his own name is
largely intact and efficiently managed. Along with the rest of his
property, the old house known as the 'hôtel d'Esgrignon' is now restored
by Chesnel to the marquis. 'Moyennant cinq cents louis', Balzac concludes, 'l'acquéreur national rétrocéda ce vieil édifice au légitime
propriétaire.'[44]

In describing how some of his émigrés are indebted for their recovery
largely to the services performed on their behalf in their absence by
non-relatives, Balzac identifies an important reality which has been
singled out by historians. 'Telle famille', Marion emphasises, 'ayant eu
l'heureuse chance d'avoir trouvé quelque homme dévoué pour veiller
à ses intérêts pendant la tourmente, sortit sans trop de pertes de la crise
révolutionnaire.'[45]

If Chesnel's action is the only one of its type to be found in the
Comédie humaine, it had already featured in Balzac's earlier work.
Donnard has drawn attention to the prominence given in Balzac's
'romans de jeunesse' to the discussion of the basic issues arising out of
the Revolution, above all of the related questions of the emigration and
the acquisition of 'biens nationaux'. Donnard demonstrates that the
themes which repeatedly recur in the *Comédie humaine*, the return of
the émigrés, the efforts which they make to recover their property and
the means which they devote to that purpose, have a place in Balzac's
first novels. Thus, in *Jean Louis*, Antoine, the valet of the duc de
Parthenay, repurchases his master's property and hands it back when
the duc de Parthenay returns from emigration. In *Wann-Chlore*,
Guérard does the same for the benefit of Horace Landon, and so, with
Antoine, sets the precedent for the action taken by Chesnel in *Le
Cabinet des Antiques*.[46]

A further factor in the émigré recovery which Balzac consistently
highlights is the way in which émigrés were helped by the gestures
of individual Republicans. We have already noted the inconclusive
example of Moreau père in the case of the Sérisy family. There are
other instances which are less ambiguous. In *Les Paysans*, Mouchon, a
former 'conventionnel', protects the lives and property of the Ronquerolles. Gaubertin père is described in *Les Paysans* as 'l'accusateur
public qui sauva les Soulanges'.[47] Mathias, the solicitor of the Manervilles,
'qui donnait alors dans les idées nouvelles', exploits his revolutionary
credibility to safeguard the interests of his émigré clients.[48] Balzac's

émigrés indeed frequently find help from the most unlikely quarters. Emigrés, as we have already seen, variously benefit from the calculated behaviour of Grandet and the magnanimity of Marshal Hulot.[49]

Finally, a remarkable example of the ingenious play of Balzac's historical imagination can be seen in the experience of the father of Charles Mignon. His response to the threat posed to his class by the Revolution is to become the Republic's executioner. 'Le comte de la Bastie', Balzac relates, 'devenu le citoyen Mignon, trouva plus sain de couper les têtes que de se laisser couper la sienne.' The device succeeds until the events of Thermidor make his new identity hazardous. As a result, 'ce faux terroriste disparut au Neuf Thermidor et fut alors inscrit sur la liste des émigrés'. This, in turn, means that 'le comté de la Bastie fut vendu', and the Mignon family is massacred, leaving Charles as the sole survivor.[50]

For all its picturesqueness, the 'vignette' involving Mignon père is atypical of the experience of Balzac's émigrés in ensuring their own survival and in preserving their property from sale or even confiscation. The success with which they avoid expropriation accurately reflects the fact that the émigrés suffered less than the clergy from the seizure by the Revolution of the property of its enemies. This aspect of their recovery which emerges so clearly in the *Comédie humaine* helps demonstrate why, in Lefebvre's phrase, 'la classe des ci-devant n'était pas dépouillée au même degré des sources matérielles de son influence'.[51] The factors which contributed to that achievement are referred to by another historian, Soboul, when he observes that 'les divorces fictifs, les rachats par des prête-nom permirent à des émigrés de sauvegarder des terres ou de les récupérer'.[52] It is a measure of Balzac's creative sense of history that the means which are employed in this process in the *Comédie humaine* are more numerous and more resourceful than those which have been traditionally recognised.

(b) Consulate and Empire (1799-1814)

(i) Exemption and Restitution. The Position of Forest-land. Thus far, in assessing the factors at work in the recovery of Balzac's émigrés prior to their return from exile, apart from the question of émigré relatives, no account has been taken of official legislation. When examining the fortunes of the émigrés after their return, the intervention of legal factors assumes greater importance.

The outstanding area of legislation affecting the sale of émigré property was that which related to forest-land. On frequent occasions Balzac refers specifically to the fate of forests owned by émigrés. It is interesting therefore to consider the historical implications of the way in which Balzac handles this particular question, especially in respect of the legal issues surrounding it.

The revolutionary legislation governing forest-land had a complex history. In the case of Church property, it had been exempted from sale as early as August 1790, less than a year after 'les biens d'église' had been declared national property in November 1789, and only three months following the laws of May 1790, which laid down the conditions of sale. The important difference as far as the legislation was concerned which affected the forest-land of émigrés was that the gap between the law authorising its sale along with the rest of émigré property and that which made it illegal was considerably greater than in the case of Church property. Confiscation was decreed in February 1792, and the sale of émigré property established in principle in July of the same year. The detailed provisions for sale were not finalised, however, until a year later, in July 1793. It was only in December 1795, in one of the first laws passed by the Directory, that 'par la loi du 2 nivôse an IV', émigré forest-land was made ineligible for sale.[53]

If one takes into account the fact that the first sales of émigré property did not take place until near the end of 1793, one therefore finds that there was a period of just over two years, from October 1793 to December 1795, when the sale of émigré forest-land was legally authorised.[54] As this was the period in which the sale of émigré property reached its peak, it is safe to assume that forest-land had a significant share in it. It is for this reason that Balzac's references to the sale or otherwise of émigré forest-land take on fresh significance.

When he describes how the rebel marquis d'Esgrignon was unjustly treated as an émigré, Balzac mentions that 'les bois furent nationalement vendus'.[55] The princesse de Cadigan tells a different story, however. 'J'avais une belle fortune', she confesses to d'Arthez, 'soixante mille livres de rente en forêts, que la Révolution avait oublié de vendre en Nivernais ou n'avait pu vendre.' The uncertainty betrayed by the afterthought of the princesse de Cadignan is highly revealing. The fact that her forest-land escaped sale is more likely to be explained, as she herself vaguely hints, by the law of December 1795, forbidding its sale than by any fortuitous oversight on the part of the revolutionary authorities.[56] Conversely, the marquis d'Esgrignon's forest-land may have been sold legally at any time from October 1793 to December 1795. Although Balzac gives no precise dates and takes no account of the legal factors which determined what happened to émigré forest-land, his contrasting references in fact betray no historical inconsistency. One cannot, of course, rule out the possibility that Balzac's treatment of the question is entirely random. Despite this, the fact remains that, in showing some of his émigrés to have avoided the sale of their forest-land, Balzac faithfully reproduces the fluctuating history of a particular category of 'biens nationaux' in which revolutionary legislation was a key factor.

Marion makes the point that among the émigrés who were especially favoured in minimising the losses inflicted on them by the Revolution was 'telle famille ayant eu l'heureuse chance d'avoir en bois quelque notable partie de sa fortune'.[57] Marion's point is, as we have indicated, confirmed by Balzac. The interesting question which remains to be investigated by the study of further examples in the *Comédie humaine* is how Balzac's evidence compares with the historical facts concerning the manner in which the émigrés were able to recover the forest-land which, apart from the two-year period between 1793 and 1795, had been precluded from sale by government legislation.

Balzac returns to the question of forest-land in discussing the émigré revival under the Consulate and Empire. The 1802 amnesty, for example, at the same time that it allowed the great majority of the remaining émigrés to return to France, entitled them to reclaim any of their confiscated property that had not been sold. None of Balzac's émigrés is, in fact, shown as benefiting in this way from the 1802 amnesty. This omission is not serious, however, and may even be regarded as appropriate since the provisions of the amnesty were, for the most part, not applied. As Gain recalls, the stipulations of the amnesty which provided for the restitution of émigré property contained too many exemptions.[58] Moreover, many émigrés had either not had their property confiscated at all or else it had all been seized and sold.

Most significant of all, the forest-land which had remained unsold by virtue of the law of December 1795, was exempted from restitution in the 1802 amnesty. Officially at least, Bonaparte did not overturn the belief of his Republican predecessors that forest-land was of top national priority and that only the state could keep it properly maintained. The retention of the legal ban on its sale, together with the deterrent problems of cultivation, explain why so much forest-land was available for restitution at the first Restoration. The forest-estates of the duc de Navarreins, for example, 'l'immense forêt dite de Montégnac', would be affected by both factors.[59]

By this time, forest-land was virtually the one important type of 'biens nationaux' which had not been sold and one which, it must be remembered, was not eligible for restitution.[60] How is one therefore to regard Balzac's statement that those émigrés who rallied to the imperial cause invariably recovered their wealth, including their forest-land, with the result that, as Balzac puts it, 'tous ceux qui entrèrent dans le mouvement impérial reconstituèrent leurs fortunes et retrouvèrent leurs bois par la munificence de l'Empereur'?[61]

The historical explanation of this apparent contradiction is simple. It lies in Napoleon's circumventing of the ban which had made illegal first the sale of émigré forest-land and then its return to its former owners. The imperial decrees which Napoleon employed for this purpose, Gain points out, 'rendaient . . . des forêts officiellement déclarées inaliénables'.[62] While he is therefore correct in emphasising the importance of the gains made by the émigrés from imperial restitutions, particularly in the form of forest-land, Balzac nevertheless does not give a single example of an émigré who recovers forest-land in this way.

There is, however, an indirect piece of evidence which can be reconstructed from the experience of comte Ferraud. By his uncompromising opposition to Napoleon, comte Ferraud rejects any possibility of recovering his unsold property under the Empire. 'Il appartenait . . .', Balzac says of him, 'à cette partie du faubourg Saint-Germain qui résista noblement aux séductions de Napoléon', including the promise of 'la restitution . . . de ses biens non vendus.'[63] The fact that comte Ferraud regains 'deux forêts' at the first Restoration is an indication of Napoleon's readiness to restore to émigrés their unsold forest-land.

Balzac undoubtedly exaggerates when he claims that all those émigrés who responded to Napoleon's overtures were successful in recovering their wealth and, in particular, their forest-land. Some no doubt suffered from the change of policy which Napoleon adopted in 1809. The undesirable effect of his restitutions, Napoleon decided, could only be 'de rendre aux émigrés la totalité de leurs biens'. Therefore, he announced, 'j'ai retiré pour 30 à 40 millions de forêts', concluding ruefully, 'mais il en reste beaucoup trop à grand nombre d'entre eux'.[64] This decision of Napoleon, combined with what was left over after imperial restitutions, explains why so much forest-land was available for return to its original émigré owners on the return of the Bourbons.

The law of December 1814, authorising émigrés to reclaim that part of their property which was still unsold, put an end to the ban of the restitution of forest-land. Indeed, the law was introduced essentially to deal with the problem of the return of forest-land, since it comprised

95.7 per cent of the total amount of unsold émigré property which thus reverted to its former owners. The evidence of the *Comédie humaine* fully accords with Gain's conclusion that, 'importante dans l'histoire des biens des émigrés, la loi de 1814 l'est . . . surtout dans celle du domaine forestier'.[65]

Of the estimated value of nine million francs which it represented in annual revenue, just under half went to the prince de Condé and the duc d'Orléans between them. What Balzac confirms, however, is that, although only a small number of émigré families benefited from the law of December 1814, the important minority of forest-owners whom it concerned did well out of it.[66] Comte Ferraud regains 'deux forêts et une terre dont la valeur avait considérablement augmenté pendant le séquestre'.[67] The duc de Lenoncourt also recovers two forests, while his wife, 'rentra dans ses biens non vendus qui avaient fait partie de la couronne impériale'.[68]

Balzac tends to suggest that the émigrés gained more from the law of December 1814 than has been generally recognised by historians. Comte Ferraud, as we have seen, benefits considerably, both in a territorial and a financial sense, from the measure. It is because her parents, the Lenoncourts, recover so much of their property in 1814 that Mme de Mortsauf becomes 'l'une des plus riches héritières du Maine'.[69] The picture which Balzac presents is therefore somewhat at variance with Gain's view that 'un nombre très restreint de dépossédés ont profité de la loi du 5 décembre, 1814, et parmi ces favorisés, le sort fait à chacun d'eux a été extrêmement inégal'.[70]

(ii) The Imperial Balance-sheet. When one tries to assess how reliable Balzac's testimony is of the fortunes of the émigrés under the Empire, one's task is not made easier by the fact that the period has received relatively little attention from the historians who have studied the emigration. The Empire falls outside Greer's terms of reference, and it is only briefly discussed by Marion and Vidalenc. Gain, however, deals with the question of the experience of the émigrés under the Empire at much greater length and thus provides a valuable point of reference by which to evaluate Balzac's treatment of a particularly vital phase of the emigration.

One point on which historians are in agreement is that the recovery achieved by the émigrés was completed before the indemnity of 1825. Their unanimous conclusion is expressed by Gain when he affirms that 'en plus d'une région c'est bien avant l'indemnité que les anciens propriétaires ont recouvré leurs biens'.[71] It is therefore appropriate, at this point, to ask what indication Balzac gives of the ground regained by the émigrés under the Empire and then, in a later chapter, to raise the same question in respect of the reign of Louis XVIII.

The two factors which were chiefly responsible for the economic gains made by the émigrés under the Empire were repurchase and restitution. One is surprised to discover that Balzac offers virtually no evidence of either. In the area of repurchase, there is no imperial example to match the initiative taken by the father of Polydore de la Baudraye under the Consulate, who, Balzac indicates, 'revint à Sancerre en 1800, et racheta la Baudraye'.[72] Gain, however, shows that, although émigrés had bought back significant amounts of property before Bonaparte's first amnesty, repurchase continued to be an important method of recovery under the Empire.[73] As for imperial restitutions, the only instance which Balzac provides concerns the duc and duchesse de Grandlieu, who recover 'tout ce qui se trouvait à la maison de Grandlieu dans le Domaine, environ quarante mille livres de rentes'.[74]

In the absence of specific examples with which to illustrate the process of émigré recovery under the Empire, Balzac relies almost exclusively on general statements in order to make his points. One has already seen how this applies in the case of forest-land. Balzac resorts to the same kind of generalisation when he outlines the principal ways in which émigrés reintegrated themselves into the fabric of imperial society. 'Quelques gentilshommes prirent du service', Balzac declares, 'soit dans les armées de Napoléon, soit à sa cour; d'autres firent des alliances avec certains parvenus.'[75]

This uncharacteristic reliance by Balzac, in describing the resurgence of the émigrés under the Empire, on generalised judgements unsubstantiated by individual illustration, is puzzling. In order to account for it I can offer only a tentative explanation. The reason can hardly be that, in tracing the progress of his émigrés under the Empire, Balzac was dealing with a period which ended before he had acquired first-hand, adult knowledge of society, and for which he could therefore supply no case-histories drawn directly from either his own experience or from his contacts with contemporary witnesses. After all, the analysis of the ways in which émigrés might escape the sale or confiscation of their property during their absence is richly illustrated by reference to particular examples. I can only suggest an explanation in which both aesthetic and political considerations have a part. Despite Balzac's criticism of ultra intransigence, the nostalgia inspired by the splendid remains of a ruined aristocracy never diminished. His susceptibility to the impotent grandeur of an aristocratic gesture remained as strong as ever. In this sense, it is interesting to note that, in his discussion of émigré fortunes under the Empire, Balzac refers to the majority of 'ralliés' in terms of broad generalities, whereas the detailed study of individual examples is reserved for the handful of nobles who steadfastly oppose Napoleon and whose colourful eccentricities distinguish them from the amorphous mass of their more pragmatic fellow-émigrés.

Comte Ferraud and the comte de Fontaine are equally proof against Napoleon's blandishments. Like the comte de Fontaine, the marquis d'Esgrignon is a rebel who is treated as an émigré and loses much of his property as a result. The 'hôtel d'Esgrignon' becomes a meeting-ground for returned émigrés resolutely opposed to any form of compromise with Napoleon.

Balzac makes it clear, however, that these are exceptions. 'Il y eut huit ou neuf familles nobles', he emphasises, 'qui demeurèrent fidèles à la noblesse proscrite et à leurs idées sur la monarchie écroulée.'[76] The situation described in *Le Cabinet des Antiques* is true of the *Comédie humaine* as a whole. Moreover, it accurately depicts the historical balance in presenting a rallying to the Empire as the norm among the émigrés. It is this response which enables the majority of Balzac's émigrés to recover part of their wealth and property and to acquire a new role and status in society.

The whole climate of the Empire, in fact, is shown by Balzac to have been favourable to an émigré revival. The careers of the young émigrés in *Une Ténébreuse Affaire* confirm that even those who had been involved in attempts to abort the Empire were not beyond the reach of imperial reconciliation. As their former defence-counsel, the comte de Granville is afraid lest, as he confesses, 'mon dévouement à ces malheureux émigrés me nuisait'.[77] He need have no such fears in 1805, as the 'Grand-juge' Régnier reassures him that a pro-émigré past is not necessarily a handicap to a successful imperial career.

The explanation of Napoleon's favourable treatment of the émigrés, Balzac suggests, lies in his incorrigible prejudice in favour of the aristocracy. In *Une Ténébreuse Affaire*, Corentin tells l'abbé Goujet that he and his aristocratic friends can count on Bonaparte's protection since 'le premier Consul aime les ci-devant et ne peut souffrir les républicains'.[78] Similarly, when the comte de Soulanges objects that his prospects of becoming a marshal are nil because of Napoleon's disdain for the artillery, Montcornet insists that he, Napoleon, 'adore la noblesse et vous êtes un ci-devant!'[79] Balzac himself supports the statements of Corentin and Montcornet by intervening directly in *Le Colonel Chabert* to underline Napoleon's sympathy for the aristocracy. When Balzac describes comte Ferraud as being 'l'objet des coquetteries de l'Empereur, qui souvent était aussi heureux de ses conquêtes sur l'aristocratie que du gain d'une bataille', Balzac reiterates his point that Napoleon's weakness for the nobility extended to include the émigrés.[80]

In emphasising the successful way in which the émigrés took advantage of the opportunities offered by Napoleon, Balzac finally gives an exaggerated picture of the extent of the émigré recovery under the Empire. Emigré gains were, in fact, uneven. Resentment persisted at the same time that individual successes were achieved. In the end, Napoleon's attempt to heal the division between émigrés and 'acquéreurs' was bound to favour one side or the other. Despite what they had recovered by way of repurchase and restitution, the émigrés were far from satisfied with what they had obtained during the decade of Empire. Hence the new stridency of their demands as the weakness of Napoleon's position became more and more apparent. 'A partir de déclin de l'Empire', Gain notes, 'on voit croître l'audace et la jactance des émigrés.'[81] The degree to which the achievements of the émigrés under the Empire fell short of their aspirations can be gauged from the other half of Gain's equation, from the conclusion that, 'malgré tout, dans l'ensemble, à la fin de l'Empire, la situation des acquéreurs était plus stable que sous le Consulat'.[82]

The harsh realities of the situation facing the émigrés during the Empire are occasionally revealed by Balzac. The failure of the attacks led by the son-in-law of Mme de la Chanterie on the property of owners of 'biens nationaux' is a reminder that, as Gain points out, there were few cases of 'acquéreurs' yielding under duress to émigrés at this period. The warning addressed at the beginning of the Empire by the marquis de Chargeboeuf to émigrés seeking to win back their property from 'acquéreurs' is just as valid in 1814. 'Vous ignorez', he tells them, 'combien la position des émigrés est délicate en face de ceux qui se trouvent posséder leurs biens.'[83] While it is true that Balzac takes no account of émigré repurchase under the Empire, he creates the false impression that the losses incurred by the émigrés from the sale of a major part of their property were decisively redressed by Napoleon's restitution of their unsold property. The émigré recovery under the Empire, and Napoleon's efforts to promote it, both economically and socially, were less successful than one gathers from reading the *Comédie humaine.*

Notes

1. According to Moïse le Yaouanc, Balzac obtained his essential information about the émigré aristocracy under the Restoration from Mme de Castries and the duc de Fitz-James. See le Yaouanc's edition of *Le Lys dans la vallée* (Classiques Garnier, Paris, 1966), p. lxxx.

2. D. Greer, *The Incidence of the Emigration during the French Revolution* (Harvard, 1951).

3. A. Gain, *La Restauration et les biens des émigrés*, 2 vols. (Nancy, 1928).

4. Marcel Marion, *La Vente des biens nationaux pendant la Révolution* (Paris, 1908).

5. J. Vidalenc, *Les Emigrés Français, 1789-1825* (Caen, 1963).

6. F. Baldensperger, *Le Mouvement des idées dans l'émigration française, 1789-1815*, 2 vols. (Paris, 1924).

7. Greer, *Incidence of the Emigration*, chapter IV, 'The Social Incidence'.

8. Ibid., p. 71.

9. Ibid., chapter IV, part I.

10. The Ségur ordinance of 1781, which took its name from the War Minister responsible for it, the marquis de Ségur, required that all army officers should henceforth be of noble birth.

11. Greer, *Incidence of the Emigration*, chapter IV, part III, 'The Vocational Incidence'.

12. Ibid., p. 29. Some nobles, like the vicomte de Portenduère, had, of course, emigrated in anticipation of the Revolution. Balzac's references are not sufficiently precise to make it possible to reconstruct the pattern of the departure of his émigrés. For a concise summary of the temporal distribution of the emigration see chapter II, part III, of Greer, ibid. or, alternatively, the chapter on 'L'Emigration' in Jacques Godeschot's *La Contre-Révolution. Doctrine et Action. 1784-1804* (Paris, 1961).

13. Greer, *Incidence of the Emigration*, p. 99.

14. Ibid., p. 104.

15. Ibid., pp. 103-5.

16. Ibid., chapter V, 'Conclusion'.

17. *Le Cabinet des Antiques*, IV, 968.

18. Greer, *Incidence of the Emigration*, p. 104.

19. Gain, *La Restauration*, I, p. 37.

20. *La Muse du département*, IV, 633.

21. *Le Lys dans la vallée*, IX, 1009.

22. Ibid., p. 1002. See le Yaouanc, *Le Lys dans la vallée*, p. 458 and p. 464, where the textual variants are given concerning the date when M. de Mortsauf returned from emigration.

23. *Le Cabinet des Antiques*, IV, 673.

24. *Splendeurs et misères des courtisanes*, VI, 506.

25. *Modeste Mignon*, I, 614.

26. *Les Paysans*, IX, 152.

27. *Gobseck*, II, 962.

28. Gain, *La Restauration*, I, p. 42.

29. Marion, *La Vente des biens nationaux*, Introduction, p. vi.

30. *Les Chouans*, VIII, 1061.

31. For a discussion of this question see Marion, *La Vente des biens nationaux*, p. 157.

32. Chateaubriand mentions that, in January 1791, 'il suffisait de porter un nom *aristocrate* pour être exposé aux persécutions: plus votre opinion était

consciencieuse et modérée, plus elle était suspecte et poursuivie'. *Mémoires d'Outre-Tombe*, 3 vols. (Livre de Poche, 1973), vol. I, p. 239.

33. *Un Début dans la vie*, I, 751. The reference is misleading to the extent that, although the comte de Sérisy, who is treated as an émigré and loses his estates as a result, dies in 1794, his son survives well into the July Monarchy.

34. *Béatrix*, II, 688.

35. *Une Ténébreuse Affaire*, VIII, 522.

36. *Béatrix*, II, 650.

37. The baron du Guénic, for example, leaves his property to his sister just before he emigrates in 1802.

38. *Le Réquisitionnaire*, X, 1106.

39. *Le Curé de village*, IX, 744.

40. The factors which account for this discrepancy are examined by Marion. See Marion, *La Vente des biens nationaux*, pp. 159-61.

41. *Le Lys dans la vallée*, IX, 1010.

42. *Le Contrat de mariage*, III, 527.

43. Marion points out that relatives began to buy back property on behalf of émigrés from a very early date, 'quelquefois dès l'an II, mais plus souvent en l'an III et dans les années suivantes'. Marion, *La Vente des biens nationaux*, p. 179.

44. *Le Cabinet des Antiques*, IV, 968.

45. Marion, *La Vente des biens nationaux*, p. 379.

46. J.-H. Donnard, *La Vie économique et les classes sociales dans l'oeuvre de Balzac* (Paris, 1961), pp. 23-6. See also the work of Pierre Barbéris, *Aux Sources de Balzac. Les Romans de jeunesse* (Paris, 1965a). Barbéris identifies in Balzac's earliest novels certain themes which anticipate the historical design of the *Comédie humaine*.

47. *Les Paysans*, IX, 181.

48. *Le Contrat de mariage*, III, 527.

49. For a discussion of these examples see above, p. 27.

50. *Modeste Mignon*, I, 483.

51. Georges Lefebvre, *La Révolution Française*, 1st edn (Paris, 1957), p. 583.

52. Albert Soboul, *Précis d'histoire de la Révolution Française* (Paris, 1962), pp. 473-4.

53. Gain, *La Restauration*, I, p. 155.

54. See chapter 1, note 9.

55. *Le Cabinet des Antiques*, IV, 967.

56. *Les Secrets de la princesse de Cadignan*, VI, 990. Alternatively, the princesse de Cadignan may, of course, simply be referring to the difficulty of selling infertile and unprofitable land.

57. See note 45.

58. On this question see Gain, *La Restauration*, I, p. 42.

59. See note 39.

60. See note 53.

61. *Le Cabinet des Antiques*, IV, 973.

62. Gain, *La Restauration*, I, p. 51.

63. *Le Colonel Chabert*, III, 347.

64. Quoted by Gain, *La Restauration*, I, p. 55.

65. Ibid., 156.

66. In *Le Colonel Chabert*, Derville's clerk Boucard wrongly gives the date of the law as 'Juin 1814'. The confusion, whether that of Balzac or consciously attributed by him to his character, is presumably with the Charter, article 9 of which, in confirming the gains of the 'acquéreurs', had made no mention of returning their unsold property to the émigrés. *Le Colonel Chabert*, III, 312-13.

67. Ibid., 348.

68. *Le Lys dans la vallée*, IX, 1039.
69. Ibid.
70. Gain, *La Restauration*, I, p. 276.
71. Ibid., II, p. 420.
72. *La Muse du département*, IV, 633.
73. Gain, *La Restauration*, I, p. 59.
74. *Splendeurs et misères des courtisanes*, VI, 506.
75. *Le Cabinet des Antiques*, IV, 973.
76. Ibid.
77. *Une Double Famille*, II, 48.
78. *Une Ténébreuse Affaire*, IX, 575.
79. *La Paix du ménage*, II, 111.
80. *Le Colonel Chabert*, III, 347.
81. Gain, *La Restauration*, I, p. 86.
82. Ibid., pp. 87-8.
83. *Une Ténébreuse Affaire*, IX, 612.

3 NAPOLEON AND THE REVOLUTION

Of all the recurring characters, both fictional and historical, in the *Comédie humaine*, it is Napoleon who makes by far the record number of appearances, as a glance at the new Pléiade index will confirm.[1] As Jean Tulard observes, 'on finit par se demander si Napoléon n'est pas le héros central de cette fresque dont les autres personnages ne seraient que les comparses'.[2]

In common with Balzac's other historical characters, however, Napoleon's dramatic role is negligible. The significance which Napoleon assumes in the *Comédie humaine* is essentially ideological, in the sense that he stands at the centre of Balzac's assessment of the effect of the Revolution on the development of French society in the first half of the nineteenth century.

Balzac does more than simply contribute to the legend of Napoleon's charisma.[3] Balzac's approach to Napoleon is governed by his analysis of changing class relationships in post-revolutionary society. Napoleon is seen by Balzac as a figure whose role is shaped by the continuing struggle between bourgeoisie and aristocracy in which the shift of power towards the bourgeoisie is the decisive factor.

I

One important area in which Balzac attempts to assess Napoleon in relation to the Revolution concerns the changes in the legal system which were the work of the Consulate. The 'Code Napoléon' is a recurrent topic of discussion in the *Comédie humaine*, and the characters are frequently involved with it. Malin has a hand in drawing it up, whilst Mme Marneffe's ten months of official widowhood are stipulated by the Code. Its significance is more than anecdotal however. Balzac's references to the Code form part of his overall evaluation of the effects of the Revolution.

In his references to the 'Code Civil', Balzac concentrates almost exclusively on analysing the effects of the abolition of the 'droit d'aînesse'. It is this issue which explains almost exclusively Balzac's criticism of the 'Code Civil'. The revolutionary decrees of 1790 and 1791[4] abolishing the 'droit d'aînesse' were confirmed by article 896 of the 'Code Civil'.[5] Balzac's persistent campaign for the restoration of the 'droit d'aînesse' and its bearing on his view of Napoleon in relation to the Revolution will be examined presently. First, however, it is important to see what Balzac judges to be the effects of the abolition of the 'droit d'aînesse' on post-revolutionary society.

Let us take the secondary effects first. In *Autre étude de femme* it is the extinction of 'les grandes dames' which is attributed to the abolition of the 'droit d'aînesse'. In a lengthy debate on the social changes brought about by the Revolution, especially as they affect the position of women in society, Balzac's familiar viewpoint is expressed by de Marsay. The 'Code Civil', de Marsay argues, by confirming the abolition of the 'droit d'aînesse', completed the work of the Revolution. One of the consequences of this, he alleges, was the final disappearance of 'les grandes dames' under the Empire. The law of equal inheritance, it is claimed, by dividing property, broke up the large concentrations of wealth necessary to produce 'les grandes dames'.[6] The same argument is used on other occasions to assert that great art and intellectual distinction generally have been the victims of revolutionary egalitarianism consequent, among other things, upon the abolition of the 'droit d'aînesse'.

Much more important than such peripheral manifestations is Balzac's attack on what he sees as the effects of the abolition of the 'droit d'aînesse' on the economic position and social attitudes of the nobility. The frugal habits of Balthazar Claës are justified by the stipulations of the 'Code Civil', more specifically by the 'Titre des Successions' providing for the equal sharing of inheritance. The serious situation in which the children of noble families, daughters especially, were placed by the confirmation, under the terms of the 'Code Civil', of the abolition of the 'droit d'aînesse', is repeatedly insisted upon by Balzac. He draws attention to the harsh predicament facing the children of the nobility, threatened with ruin if they are too numerous or with extinction if too few.[7] Through Renée de Maucombe, Balzac denounces 'l'infâme Code Civil du sieur de Buonaparte, qui fera mettre au couvent autant de filles nobles qu'il en a fait marier'.[8] For Balzac the plight of the disadvantaged younger children inherent in the 'droit d'aînesse' was justifiably subordinated to the all-important need to concentrate the bulk of the family wealth in the hands of the eldest son. Therein, it was confidently assumed, lay also the surest means of maintaining the prestige of the family name which would allow its daughters to make acceptable marriages.

The duchesse de Maufrigneuse is equally critical of the 'Code Civil' for having effectively destroyed the nobility. 'Le Code Civil de Napoléon', she asserts, 'a tué les parchemins comme le canon avait déjà tué la féodalité.'[9] Of the written rights of the nobility torn up by the Revolution none is more vital for the duchesse de Maufrigneuse or more passionately defended by Balzac than the 'droit d'aînesse'. The most comprehensive and savage attack on the Napoleonic Code is, however, made by Louis Lambert. 'Le code', he announces, 'que l'on regarde comme la plus belle oeuvre de Napoléon, est l'oeuvre la plus draconienne que je sache.' More precisely, all France's ills are held to stem from the reaffirmation of the abolition of the 'droit d'aînesse'. On the one hand, it results in 'morcellement', which in turn leads to economic decline. At the same time, it is the cause of national decadence and humiliation, of the decay of art and science in France. 'La divisibilité territoriale poussée à l'infini', Lambert insists, 'dont le principe y est consacré par le partage égal des biens, doit engendrer l'abâtardissement de la nation, la mort des arts et celle des sciences.' As a result, France is leaderless and therefore weak and vulnerable. 'Vienne une invasion', he gloomily concludes, 'le peuple est écrasé, il a perdu ses grands ressorts, il a perdu ses chefs.'[10]

The many references to the 'droit d'aînesse' in the *Comédie humaine* are all part of Balzac's untiring campaign in favour of its restoration. One of the most interesting questions raised by Balzac's discussion of the 'droit d'aînesse' concerns its relevance to his view of Napoleon in relation to the Revolution. In any attempt to resolve the question the evidence of *Du Droit d'aînesse* is crucial, now that it is accepted as having been written by Balzac and as expressing, at a surprisingly early date, some important elements in Balzac's political thinking.[11] As far as Napoleon is concerned, the main interest of *Du Droit d'aînesse* lies in Balzac's assertion that Napoleon was sympathetic to the idea of restoring the 'droit d'aînesse ' and did all in his power to do so. 'Aussi', Balzac declares, 'Buonaparte connaissait-il bien l'esprit national lorsque, Empereur, il s'empressa de rétablir implicitement le droit d'aînesse, qu'imprévoyant consul il avait aboli.' Moreover, had he had his way and been given a sufficiently long period of peace, Balzac suggests, Napoleon would have reformed the 'Code Civil' in such a way as to restore the 'droit d'aînesse'. 'Le géant de la Révolution', Balzac ironically observes, 'au bout de dix ans de paix aurait réformé son Code Civil.'[12]

The second claim is mere speculation and need take up no further discussion. On the other hand, it is worthwhile examining what Balzac means when he refers to Napoleon's efforts 'de rétablir implicitement le droit d'aînesse'. In *Du Droit d'aînesse* Balzac makes it clear that he is thinking of Napoleon's creation of 'majorats'.[13] Balzac's historical accuracy is not impeccable. It was not, as he states, the 'sénatus-consulte' of 10 August 1810 which authorised the founding of 'majorats', but that of 14 August 1806. However, Balzac's argument is clear. Napoleon devised the system of 'majorats' in order to establish a new imperial aristocracy.[14] If, for reasons beyond his control, he stopped short of actually restoring the 'droit d'aînesse', the 'majorat' neverthe-less represented a conscious and significant move in that direction, for which Napoleon is to be commended.[15]

As far as it goes, Balzac's point of view is unambiguous. What Balzac omits to point out in *Du Droit d'aînesse* is that the 'majorats' were designed by Napoleon to help to create a new aristocracy sub-servient to himself but acting as a social and political force independent of both the old nobility and the bourgeoisie. Balzac's analysis therefore remains incomplete and unproductive in that it takes no account of the fundamental question of the significance of the imperial nobility in relation to the 'ci-devant' on the one hand and the bourgeoisie on the other. Balzac's preoccupation with the 'droit d'aînesse' is in fact basically misleading. Balzac's legitimism was nothing if not individual and pragmatic. No reactionary was ever less likely, one would have thought, to cling to lost causes, yet it was the same Balzac who recog-nised as unalterable the property changes of the Revolution who persisted in trying to resurrect the deadest of doctrinaire dodos, the restoration of the 'droit d'aînesse'. His persistent advocacy of the restoration of the 'droit d'aînesse', until well after the abolition of the hereditary peerage, by which time it had become a manifestly lost cause even to most of the diehard ultras, is uncharacteristic of Balzac's political flexibility, its doctrinaire tone strangely at odds with his normally realistic outlook.

Secondly, Balzac's unpragmatic urging of a return to the 'droit d'aînesse' involves him in a confused and contradictory appraisal of Napoleon in terms of the Revolution. It may help to clear the ground if one discounts some of the statements made in the *Comédie humaine*. Balzac suggests, both directly and via de Marsay, that Napoleon was unaware of the effects of the 'Code Civil'. There is in fact abundant evidence that Napoleon was aware not only of the effects produced by the 'Code Civil' in ratifying the abolition of the 'droit d'aînesse' but also of the function of the 'majorat' in countering its disappearance.[16] What is more to the point is that Balzac himself recognised the deliberate nature of Napoleon's policy and that, in *Du Droit d'aînesse*, he empha-sised Napoleon's aim of compensating for the demise of the 'droit d'aînesse' via the institution of 'majorats'.

One should be equally wary of equating de Marsay's criticism of Napoleon for failing to reintroduce the 'droit d'aînesse' with Balzac's own thinking on the matter. When de Marsay expresses his bewilderment that 'le souverain qui voulait faire balayer sa cour par le satin ou le velours de robes ducales n'a pas établi pour certaines familles le droit d'aînesse par d'indestructibles lois', he is overlooking the fact that the 'droit d'aînesse' was reestablished in certain restricted cases.[17]

The confusion which marks Balzac's reaction to the way in which Napoleon dealt with the question of the 'droit d'aînesse' arises from his ambivalent view of Napoleon in relation to the Revolution. Reinforcing his basic sympathy for Napoleon, Balzac's political pragmatism enables him to recognise that Napoleon was unable fully to emancipate himself from revolutionary influences, to do more than progressively stem the current of revolution by concessions to the clergy and the nobility. Certain revolutionary changes, such as the acquisition of 'biens nationaux' and the abolition of feudal dues and privileges, Balzac realised, were clearly irreversible. Where then did that leave the 'droit d'aînesse', whose restoration Balzac ardently and consistently advocated? How did Napoleon's failure to restore the 'droit d'aînesse' affect Balzac's view of Napoleon?

Balzac's dilemma was simple but embarrassing. The 'Code Civil', by confirming the abolition of the 'droit d'aînesse', had continued the work of the Revolution and perpetuated a revolutionary measure the consequences of which Balzac attacked with unremitting ferocity. Unlike Napoleon, Balzac was not prepared to accept the abolition of the 'droit d'aînesse', as he was the property changes and the removal of feudal privileges, as an irreversible reality. Napoleon, whom Balzac admired for his authoritarian, anti-democratic response to the Revolution, was therefore logically cast as the guarantor of the Revolution in one important respect.

The truth is that Balzac was sufficient of a realist to appreciate that the overt restoration of the 'droit d'aînesse' to the old nobility was a political impossibility for Napoleon, concerned as he was to retain his revolutionary credibility. The alliance of Balzac's political realism and his admiration for Napoleon conflict with his implied criticism of Napoleon for failing to restore the 'droit d'aînesse'. It is here that the 'majorat' comes to Balzac's rescue. Balzac's approval of the imperial 'majorat' as going a long way to compensate for the abolition of the 'droit d'aînesse' which had been confirmed in the 'Code Civil' enables him to get round the otherwise inescapable logic of having to criticise Napoleon and thus enables Balzac to maintain his esteem for Napoleon intact. The 'majorat' finally allows Balzac to get the best of both traditional and Bonapartist worlds by providing the pretext for reconciling his belief in the 'droit d'aînesse' with his cult of Napoleon.[18]

II

Napoleon's religious policy provides another important criterion by which Balzac seeks to evaluate where Napoleon stands in terms of the Revolution. In order to see the question in its true perspective, it is first of all necessary to consider Balzac's view of the social and political function of religion. The basic ideas are set out in *Le Médicin de campagne*. First, the Christian religion is seen by l'abbé Janvier as alone having the power to impose a brake on the dangerous inclinations of human nature, as a 'système complet d'opposition aux tendances dépravées de l'homme'.[19] Balzac's anti-Rousseauism is then turned to political account as Balzac emphasises that authority, to be effective, must acknowledge and seek to enhance the social utility of religion. 'La religion', he asks through his spokesman Benassis, 'n'est-elle pas la seule puissance qui sanctionne les lois sociales?'[20] Through religion, Balzac is convinced, the poor are led to accept their condition as the expression of divine will, whilst the rich are moved to seek to improve the lot of the poor.

Religion moreover, for Benassis, is the only force capable of reconciling conflicting social interests. 'Religion veut dire LIEN', Benassis maintains, 'et certes le culte, ou autrement dit la Religion exprimée, constitue la seule force qui puisse relier les espèces sociales et leur donner une forme durable.'[21] Benassis's views do not directly echo those of Balzac. For instance, his exclusive emphasis on the power of religion to effect social reconciliation overlooks Balzac's insistence on the need for authority to promote social harmony through a coherent set of policies, in which religion plays only a part, albeit an important one. Similarly Benassis omits a significant point which Balzac later stressed in *La Cousine Bette*. As well as imposing a necessary brake on Man's depraved tendencies, religion, Balzac was to underline, also acted as a salutary curb on potential abuses of authority. 'Tout pouvoir sans contrepoids', Balzac warned, 'sans entraves, autocratique, mène à l'abus, à la folie. L'arbitraire, c'est la démence du pouvoir.'[22] It was in religion that the essential 'contrepoids' was to be found.

The coherence of Balzac's thinking on the social value of religion remains unmistakable, however. Its unity lies in the case which Balzac argues for religion as providing decisive support to authority in its task of defeating subversion. The question to determine is how Balzac viewed Napoleon's efforts and achievements in this direction. To begin with, Balzac recognises the religious difficulties facing Napoleon. First, there is the problem of the continuing opposition of the priesthood after the Concordat. The abbé who succeeds the comte de Maucombe in working for David Séchard's father is atypical in rallying to Napoleon before the Concordat. A 'non-assermenté', the abbé comes out of hiding, reassured by Bonaparte's acknowledgement of the Catholic religion. A truer indication of clerical opposition to Napoleon undiminished by the Concordat is provided in *La Rabouilleuse*, where reference is made to the difficulty in finding compliant priests as late as 1806. Balzac also shows that Napoleon was not helped in his religious policy by bigotry of the kind which is denounced in the character of Angélique Bontems in *Une Double Famille*. Her religious fanaticism is attacked by Balzac partly for aesthetic reasons in that it is held to be inseparable from bad taste, but chiefly on moral and political grounds. Not only does it harm the career of her husband, Granville, but it is opposed as being inimical to the spirit of the Concordat and to the cause of social reconciliation.

In the final analysis, Balzac's verdict on the effectiveness of Napoleon's religious policy is a harsh one. Balzac's admiration for 'la supériorité politique' embodied by Napoleon is not unbounded. Of the qualifications to which it is subject, the most serious are the religious reservations. The inadequate place of religion in the imperial lycées, for example, is commented upon in *L'Envers de l'histoire contemporaine*, where Godefroid, like many children of bourgeois families under the Empire, is sent to a religious 'pension', 'par attachement à la religion un peu trop méconnue dans les lycées'.[23]

Again, as over the question of the 'droit d'aînesse', Balzac is careful not to criticise Napoleon directly. Yet the criticism is no less severe for being implied. Balzac directs it obliquely at Napoleon through the combined views of l'abbé Janvier and Benassis. It is l'abbé Janvier who contrasts the enduring force of religion with the transient power of patriotism. When Genestas tries to put in a plea on behalf of revolutionary patriotism, Benassis replies that it had run out by 1814. 'En 1814, notre patriotisme était déjà mort.'[24] It is significant that this riposte is delivered to a fervent Bonapartist by those who, like Balzac, are convinced of the need to restore religious values in society.

The implications are clear. Napoleon had missed the opportunity of replacing a jaded patriotism with the saving spirit of religion, and had thereby contributed to France's defeat and his own downfall. By failing ultimately to appreciate the social necessity of religion, Napoleon had undone his earlier valuable work under the Consulate in helping to secure an indispensable religious base for society. When he had declared the Concordat void in February 1812, one may further infer, Napoleon had shown that his *amour-propre* could, on occasion, as in his treatment of Talleyrand and Fouché, prove disastrously stronger than his political judgement.

Balzac's discretion in refraining from overtly criticising Napoleon in respect of his religious policy is as understandable as in the case of the 'droit d'aînesse'. The idol was in danger not merely of losing its gilt but of crumbling altogether. By turning away from religion, Napoleon was depriving the body politic of its oxygen. All three elements in Balzac's social concept of religion were at once undermined. The brake on human depravity was released, the curb on authority removed and the hopes of social reconciliation finally dashed. Both 'les tendances dépravées de l'homme' and 'l'arbitraire, la démence du pouvoir' were rampant and the precious 'LIEN' destroyed.

III

How then does Napoleon emerge in the *Comédie humaine* in relation to the forces of revolution and counter-revolution? Napoleon's pre-consular career constitutes, among other things, a valuable apprenticeship in repression. The victor of Toulon and fructidor is mentioned several times by Balzac for his part in suppressing another royalist rising, that of vendémiaire. Moreover, there is ample evidence in the *Comédie humaine* to indicate that Napoleon would have welcomed the opportunity to redress the anti-royalist balance by an equally severe repression of popular insurrection. It was as the appalled witness of revolutionary 'journées' that Napoleon, revolted by the spectacle of popular triumph on 20 June 1792, expressed his regret to Bourrienne at not seeing 'cette canaille' summarily swept aside.[25] Balzac refers to Napoleon's dismay at a further royal humiliation, that incurred by the capitulation of 10 August 1792. Albert Savarus, in writing to Léopold Hannequin, tells of 'ce que souffrait Napoléon . . . sur le quai des Tuileries, au 10 août, quand il voyait Louis XVI se défendant si mal'.[26] Conversely, in *Béatrix*, Balzac claims that 'Bonaparte est devenu empereur pour avoir mitraillé le peuple à deux pas de l'endroit où Louis XVI a perdu la monarchie et la tête pour n'avoir pas laissé verser le sang d'un monsieur Sauce'.[27] In this instance Balzac is contrasting Napoleon's capacity for swift and decisive repression with the fatal indecision of Louis XVI leading to the final collapse of royal authority and the installation of Republican terror. The broader picture which Balzac gives of Napoleon's pre-consular conduct reveals a deeper trend. What it shows is an authoritarian Napoleon, equally concerned to eliminate the threat to social order from both royalist and in Jacobin extremists.

This impression is confirmed by what Balzac has to say about Napoleon's behaviour during the Consulate and the Empire. Napoleon is admired by Balzac above all as an autocratic man of action with a consistent policy of repression impartially directed at removing the challenge to his authority and to national unity by Republican and royalist extremism. Napoleon's treatment of du Bousquier balances his victimisation of Birotteau. Although he is equally opposed to both counter-revolution and to a democratic extension of the Revolution, the main danger to Napoleon comes from royalist attempts to overthrow him in favour of a Bourbon restoration. In *Une Ténébreuse Affaire* it is through Fouché that Napoleon destroys the Cadoudal conspiracy of 1804. In the same novel Balzac's unqualified opposition to counter-revolution and his praise of Napoleon for successfully combating it is clearly expressed when he contrasts the inflexibility of Laurence de Cinq-Cygne and the young émigrés with the realism of M. d'Hauteserre and the marquis de Chargeboeuf in their attitude to Napoleon. Malin, himself a Bourbon double-agent, pays tribute to the effectiveness of Napoleon's policy. Its success, he believes, is based not simply on the repression of royalist conspiracies, but is equally explained by his calculated political measures, notably his overtures to the émigrés and concessions to the clergy, which are designed to pre-empt the Bourbons and to forestall counter-revolution.

Other statements made in *Une Ténébreuse Affaire* concerning the activities of pro- and anti-revolutionary factions in relation to Napoleon are conspicuously inaccurate. In suggesting, for example, that the execution of the duc d'Enghien was engineered by Talleyrand and Fouché in order to involve Napoleon irrevocably with the Revolution and thereby provoke a definitive breach with the Bourbons, de Marsay does Fouché an injustice.[28] Equally, de Marsay's hint that Louis XVIII had a personal hand in the Cadoudal conspiracy is totally without foundation.[29] Whether they reflect Balzac's own views or not, such aberrations need not divert attention from the essential features of Napoleon's policy which are outlined in the *Comédie humaine*, in response to the conflicting elements in post-revolutionary society.

In his treatment of Republicans and royalists, Napoleon appears as the defender of the Revolution only in the negative sense of resisting all attempts to bring about a Bourbon restoration. On the other hand, Napoleon's detestation of republicanism is repeatedly emphasised. It is du Bousquier's Republican past rather than his speculation on Napoleon's defeat at Marengo that causes Napoleon to remove him from the post of 'Réceveur-Général' in Alençon. Grandet, 'qui passait pour avoir porté le bonnet rouge', is dismissed by Napoleon as mayor of Saumur and replaced by a 'ci-devant'. The reason, we are told, is that 'Napoleon n'aimait pas les républicains'.[30] Finally, Blondet père, a reluctant revolutionary and mildest of punitive judges as 'Accusateur Public', is prevented from becoming 'Président du Tribunal d'Alençon' by Napoleon, 'dont l'éloignement pour les républicains reparaissait dans les moindres détails de son gouvernement'.[31] Underlying Napoleon's repression of Jacobin and royalist extremists is a more basic truth which Balzac's analysis brings out. Napoleon's actions culminate in an imperial regime in which the last vestiges of Republicanism are removed and in which the 'ci-devant' aristocracy is courted in an effort to wed it to the imperial nobility and the new dynasty.

IV

Within this broad framework of policy fundamental questions remained to be decided in the continuing flow and counter-flow of revolution and reaction, the outcome of which would determine how Napoleon finally stood in relation to the revolutionary settlement. Of these issues none was more contentious and more crucial than the unresolved conflict between 'acquéreurs' and émigrés.[32]

The continued sale of 'biens nationaux' during the Consulate and Empire was tolerated rather than actively encouraged by Napoleon, for whom it in no way conflicted with his gestures of reconciliation to the émigrés. The conviction conveyed by the *Comédie humaine* is of the irrevocability of the property changes brought about by the Revolution. Napoleon is throughout shown as recognising and acting upon this inescapable reality. Grévin's advice to Malin is based upon this conviction. He urges Malin to switch his support to Bonaparte and to inform him of the royalist plot against him. Bonaparte, Grévin is convinced, is bound to come out on top, if only because he is enough of a realist to appreciate that the regicides and 'acquéreurs' are the dominant factor in a situation governed by the irreversible acquisition of 'biens nationaux'. The Bourbons would be well advised to do the same. Sooner or later, whether they like it or not, Grévin argues, 'les Bourbons devront passer l'éponge sur tout ce que nous avons fait'. Gondreville, Grévin tells Malin, 'est le *Tiens* et la Conspiration le *Tu auras*', adding scornfully, 'La France est pleine d'acquéreurs de biens nationaux, et tu voudras ramener ceux qui te redemanderont Gonreville?'.[33] Malin's dilemma is that of an opportunist poised between opting for Bonaparte or banking on a royalist *coup* and the return of the Bourbons. The situation is also seen from the point of view of the émigrés and the non-émigré nobility, and Balzac's message is the same. When the marquis de Chargeboeuf presses Laurence and the émigrés to accept the terms of Napoleon's amnesty, his most telling argument takes the form of stressing the near-insuperable difficulties in the way of émigrés seeking to recover their property from 'acquéreurs'.

The marquis de Chargeboeuf's warning at first goes unheeded by the émigrés until, after their arrest and trial, they have effectively no other choice but to accept Napoleon's terms. Their fellow-ultras who escape the imperial police remain undeterred in their bid to regain their property and attacks on 'acquéreurs' are recorded well after the marquis de Chargeboeuf's pronouncement in 1806.[34] These attempts to reverse the *status quo* governing the transfer of landed property are the expression of a mounting frustration on the part of émigrés despairing of enlisting Napoleon's support in their claims against 'acquéreurs'. On the other hand, the faith of the peasantry in Napoleon is explained by their confidence that he is 'l'homme qui lui assurait la possession des biens nationaux'.[35] For the émigré nobility and their clerical allies, Napoleon's refusal to restore their lost land to them identified him unequivocally with the Revolution. It is the view of l'abbé Brossette that 'son sacre fut trempé dans cette idée', and accordingly Bonaparte 'est encore le roi sorti des flancs de la Révolution'.[36]

This occasion gives Balzac the opportunity to make clear his own view of the question. It is Blondet who answers l'abbé Brossette by stressing the inviolability of the transfer of 'biens nationaux'. Blondet's reasoning is the same as that used by the marquis de Chargeboeuf in advising the émigrés to come to terms with Napoleon. The expropriation of the clergy and the nobility may be regrettable, but the acquisitions of the Third Estate, including those of the peasantry, constitute an irrevocable fact which the monarchy, and by implication the clergy and the aristocracy, must accept.

For such fanatical royalist opponents of Napoleon as Mme de la Chanterie and Mlle de Cinq-Cygne it is axiomatic to regard Napoleon and the Revolution as one. To the more flexible M. d'Hauteserre, however, the benefits to the nobility of Napoleon's accession are evident enough, as the considerable improvement in the situation at Cinq-Cygne and the relaxation of restrictions on the relations of émigrés and their families amply testify. Provided he accept Napoleon's conditions, the prospects for a returned émigré under the Consulate were far from discouraging. Provided also that he did not expect any further concessions to be made in his favour by Napoleon, particularly at the expense of the 'acquéreurs'. He could, by various legal means, reasonably hope to regain his property, either by repurchase if it had been sold or by imperial restitution if it had remained unsold.[37] What he could not hope for was that Napoleon would legally compel 'acquéreurs' to restore émigré property to its former owners or that he would tolerate its illegal recovery by force. The *Comédie humaine* reveals a Napoleon who acts as the guarantor of the socioeconomic conquests of the Revolution, of the transfer of landed property as well as of the abolition of the 'droit d'aînesse' and feudal dues.

In underwriting the socioeconomic changes of the Revolution, Napoleon was not providing a blank cheque, however. The barriers to further social change were clear and formidable. This lesson is transparent in the emphasis placed by Balzac on Napoleon's basic anti-Republicanism and contempt for democracy and his unimpeded restoration of hierarchy and privilege. At the same time Balzac's account leaves one in no doubt as to the limits which Napoleon set upon 'ci-devant' aspirations. They could hope to find their place again in French society and, with Napoleon's backing, that place would be honourable if less grandiose than before. But they would have to give up their king and their privileges. They would be lucky to recover their land. And they would have to accept their imperial identity as 'une aristocratie rangée'.

Napoleon's political strategy, as presented by Balzac, is based on three interrelated factors. The supreme principle of his inviolable personal authority is made to serve two fundamental objectives. The first is to maintain the revolutionary land settlement, the second to achieve national unity by promoting social reconciliation. By insisting on the first, Napoleon was certain to secure the support of the 'acquéreurs'. The problem remained of how to win over the nobility, the émigrés especially, without antagonising the 'acquéreurs' and jeopardising the overriding aim of social harmony.

Time and again in the *Comédie humaine* it is emphasised that Napoleon is well-disposed towards the nobility, to the explicit detriment of Republicans and often to the extent of overlooking a record of hostile behaviour towards the Empire and the personal figure of Napoleon. Napoleon's pro-aristocratic leanings appear as a composite of calculated statesmanship and irrational prejudice, the outcome of which is a series of concerted policies designed to reassure an anxious and insecure nobility. There are first of all the concrete political measures, the amnesties and the religious concessions made both before and after the Concordat. Then there are the benefits of personal patronage, the chief inducements being the promise to restore a title, the offer of political appointments, removal, often unauthorised, from the émigré lists and the restitution of unsold property provided for in the 1802 amnesty.

In describing Napoleon's treatment of the nobility, Balzac indicates how important Napoleon considered it to be to disarm its opposition and to reintegrate it into French society. It is not simply that, as Villat states, compared with his rewarding of the servants of the Empire, 'l'empereur ne témoigne pas une moindre bienveillance aux nobles d'Ancien Régime qui se sont ralliés à lui'.[38] Napoleon's policy of reconciling the nobility went beyond the 'ralliés'. What Balzac points out is that, although Napoleon's main effort was directed at those returned émigrés who were willing to co-operate with him, he did not stop short of attempting to reconcile other, less tractable elements among the nobility. As *Une Ténébreuse Affaire* shows, not even émigrés conspiring to overthrow Napoleon by armed force were necessarily considered irrecoverable. Compared with his treatment of his imperial subordinates, Napoleon's behaviour towards the nobility marked a different tactic in response to a different reality. The blandishments placed before the nobility were not the rewards of vassal subservience but a systematic attempt to reduce a stubborn 'frondeur' pride.

V

How then finally does Balzac see Napoleon in relation to the Revolution? The first major task of government, Balzac was convinced, was to seek to remove social tensions in order to achieve national unity. At no time was such a policy more urgent, Balzac believed, than immediately after a revolution. It is this which he sees as the prime duty of the July Monarchy when, writing to Zulma Carraud in November 1830, he insists, 'A chaque révolution, le génie gouvernemental consiste à opérer une fusion des hommes et des choses; et voilà ce qui a fait de Napoléon et de Louis XVIII deux hommes de talent'.[39]

Napoleon and Louis XVIII are both commended for their efforts to reconcile the conflicting interests in society, in particular to induce the aristocracy to accept the irreversible changes of the Revolution. 'Le roi légitime', Balzac concludes in *Le Bal de Sceaux*, 'peut-être aussi spirituel que son rival, agissait en sens contraire. Le dernier chef de la maison de Bourbon était aussi empressé à satisfaire le tiers état et les gens de l'Empire, en contenant le clergé, que le premier des Napoléon fut jaloux d'attirer auprès de lui les grands seigneurs ou de doter l'Eglise.'[40]

At the same time, Balzac hints at the limited nature of their achievement. The comte de Fontaine may be a convert to Louis XVIII's views, 'aux idées qu'exigeaient la marche du dix-neuvième siècle et la rénovation de la monarchie', but his is a rare example.[41] The failure of Louis XVIII's aim of social reconciliation is clearly implied by Balzac's continuing attack on the majority of the Restoration aristocracy in refusing to come to terms with the reality of bourgeois wealth and the imminence of bourgeois power.

Where Napoleon is concerned, Balzac's analysis demonstrates that the ideal of fusion was basically unattainable from the start. Napoleon's success was a negative one in so far as the threat of subversive extremism was nullified through the repression of Jacobin conspiracies and the crushing of counter-revolution. The opposition of a refractory clergy and an intransigent nobility was exacerbated by errors of judgement on Napoleon's part. The annulling of the Concordat was serious enough, but the creation of the imperial nobility posed awkward problems of its own. The emergence of a new social caste, with its separate identity and divergent interests, could only antagonise the old nobility that Napoleon was anxious to reconcile, a class jealous of new rival privileges at a time when it was seeking to reassert its own. Furthermore, the relationship in which Napoleon stood to the two nobilities was an uneasy one. Ill-at-ease among the 'ci-devant', Napoleon, as Balzac frequently emphasises, had difficulty in establishing a court most of whose subjects had been his former equals or superiors. As self-appointed arbiter between the old and the new nobility, Napoleon found his authority seriously undermined by an inherent *parvenu* insecurity for which a prodigious 'volonté de puissance' scarcely compensated.

Balzac demonstrates that Napoleon's strategy of social reconciliation was nullified by the reality of bourgeois power and the refusal of the aristocracy to recognise that power, by an ultra mentality which equated 'acquéreurs' with a hated Republicanism. What ultimately destroyed Napoleon's aim of social reconciliation was that it reckoned without the new, unanswerable authority of the revolutionary bourgeoisie. Secure in its acquisition of 'biens nationaux' and enriched out of the new economic opportunities opened up by the Revolution, the bourgeoisie was in a position to dictate its own terms and to take fresh initiatives independently of Napoleon.

'La condition de l'usurpateur', Balzac wrote of Napoleon, 'est de se moquer de la Révolution qu'il confisque à son profit.'[42] Balzac's account, however, suggests that Napoleon's policies were effective only in so far as they corresponded with the essential interests of the bourgeoisie. The kidnapping of Malin, for example, is seen by Napoleon as a threat to his efforts to reconcile the 'acquéreurs' and the émigrés. Balzac makes it quite clear, however, that, for Napoleon, the recognition of the fundamental changes of the Revolution, especially the acquisitions of 'biens nationaux', was a prerequisite of any lasting settlement. The Malin affair represents, in Napoleon's eyes, 'un attentat contre ses institutions, un fatal exemple de résistance aux effets de la Révolution, une atteinte à la grande question des biens nationaux'.[43] This is entirely consistent with Lefebvre's view. 'L'action de Napoléon', Lefebvre concludes, 'n'a été vraiment efficace que dans la mesure où elle consolida et accrut la prépondérance de la bourgeoisie, parce qu'elle s'accordait, sur ce point, avec l'évolution de la nation.'[44] The Restoration aristocracy would have to prove that it was capable of learning from the lessons of the Empire. In particular, if the aristocracy was going to take the ideal of social harmony seriously, it would have to respond more readily to the possibilities of intermarriage with the bourgeoisie. Moreover, however successfully it might adapt to the new situation after 1815, any accommodation which the aristocracy might reach would be dominated by a bourgeoisie confident in the power which it had asserted under Napoleon.

It is interesting to compare Balzac's view of Napoleon with the self-assessment contained in the *Mémorial*. There Napoleon presented himself as the heir and defender of the Revolution. Apart from claiming to have extended the benefits of the Revolution to the conquered countries, Napoleon insisted that he had continued the work of the Revolution in respect of equality and the destruction of feudalism and had reinforced it by eliminating the forces disputing its changes.[45] On the question of fraternity Balzac is remarkably silent. The account of Napoleon's campaigns is unpolemical. There is no uncritical assumption of 'gloire'. Indeed one comes across the occasional hint that the cost in manpower of Napoleon's wars has been detrimental to the economy and to social stability. Nor is there any question of Napoleon being seen by Balzac as the liberator of the oppressed peoples, of their being joined by the revolutionary armies in a spirit of universal brotherhood. Of the three contributions which Napoleon claimed to have made to the Revolution, Balzac concurs only with the claim to have ratified the abolition of feudalism. Despite Napoleon's successful repression of extremist subversion, the hostility between the revolutionary bourgeoisie and the nobility defied Napoleon's efforts towards an illusory pacification of society. As for the achieving of equality, it was the last thing for which Balzac would have thanked Napoleon. Instead he chose not to take Napoleon at his word and continued to admire him for the very opposite reason.

Political liberty, which finds little place in Napoleon's self-evaluation, Balzac regarded as the price that had to be paid to ensure effective government. Therefore he welcomed Napoleon's undoctrinaire sacrifice of liberty to the priority of authoritarian rule. It is however on the issue of equality that Balzac's assessment of Napoleon in relation to the Revolution basically rests. The evidence of the *Comédie humaine* refutes Napoleon's assertion that he had perpetuated the revolutionary principle of equality by exposing the limits of such a claim. It reveals that Napoleon's egalitarian instincts went no further than the endorsement of the socioeconomic changes of the Revolution, of the dismantling of feudalism and the sale of 'biens nationaux'. Otherwise, for Balzac, everything in Napoleon's outlook and actions testifies to a systematic anti-revolutionary position in respect of equality. In *Du Droit d'aînesse*, Balzac emphasises Napoleon's hostility to equality and suggests that, given time, Napoleon would have restored even the 'droit d'aînesse'. In this view Balzac is broadly supported by Lefebvre. Whilst recognising that the restoration of the 'droit d'aînesse' was a political impossibility for Napoleon, Lefebvre nevertheless concludes that, in contrast with the popular image of Napoleon as the defender of the Revolution, 'il était devenu de plus en plus hostile à la Révolution, au point que, si le temps le lui eût permis, il aurait fini par répudier en partie l'égalité civile'.[46]

The factor which most firmly identifies Napoleon, in Balzac's eyes, with an anti-revolutionary posture is his creation of an imperial hierarchy. It accords with Balzac's permanent belief in the need for society to be based on a clearly-defined hierarchy. The conviction finds repeated expression in Balzac's writing, both in the *Comédie humaine* and in his articles. Mme de Mortsauf tells Félix de Vandenesse that the first lesson he must learn is that 'les Sociétés n'existent que par la hiérarchie'.[47] The frustration of Diard's ambition to enter the imperial nobility merely serves to confirm Balzac's belief that 'les classifications sociales toutes faites sont peut-être un grand bien, même pour le peuple'.[48] The social hierarchy of the Empire is seen as running counter to the revolutionary ideal of social democracy, the creation of the imperial court as anti-revolutionary an act as the founding of a personal dynasty. Consistent with this hierarchical trend, Napoleon's systematic anti-republicanism is viewed as complementing his deliberate flattering of aristocratic hopes of resurgence.

The Bonaparte whom we see in 1800 in *La Vendetta* and *Une Ténébreuse Affaire* has the same faith in hierarchy as the Emperor whom Laurence de Cinq-Cygne pleads with on the eve of Jena and who reviews the 'Garde impériale' in April 1813, prior to his disastrous campaign in Germany. The path to hierarchy pursued by Napoleon is firmly underlined by Balzac. In order to illustrate to Rubempré his axiom that history confirms the absence of fixed principles in face of the natural laws governing human behaviour, Herrera quotes the example of Napoleon in terms of the Revolution. 'Les Français ont inventé,' he maintains, 'en 1793, une souveraineté populaire qui s'est terminée par un empereur absolu . . . Sans-culotte en 1793, Napoléon chausse la couronne de fer en 1804. Les féroces amants de *l'Egalité ou la Mort* de 1792, deviennent, dès 1806, complices d'une aristocratie légitimée par Louis XVIII.'[49]

The reference to 1806 is particularly significant for the criterion by which Balzac judges Napoleon. It was from 1806 that the founding of the imperial nobility effectively dated, although it was not officially recognised until March 1808, when it came into being with the institution of 'majorats'.[50] Although he states the opposite of the truth, as Balzac sees it, in presenting Napoleon as pro-Jacobin during the Revolution, Herrera accurately reflects an essential feature of Balzac's view of Napoleon in relation to the Revolution. Through Herrera, Balzac reiterates his admiration for Napoleon for having turned his back on revolutionary equality by the calculated creation of an imperial hierarchy. Napoleon was right, Balzac believed, to give maximum expression to the concept of hierarchy, to encourage its every manifestation, even down to 'la question des costumes auxquels l'Empereur tenait tant et avec tant de raison'.[51]

Balzac also provides an interesting comment on the direction of the imperial regime in the period immediately preceding the Austrian marriage. In *La Paix du ménage* the opening action is set in November 1809. A more precise date, 30 November 1809, is suggested since Napoleon is mentioned as being prevented from seeing Gondreville by the quarrel with Josephine which led to their divorce on 16 December. Napoleon is shown at the height of his power, with peace between France and the coalition and the kings and princes of Europe come to pay homage. It was in April of the following year that Napoleon married Marie-Louise. The impression left by Balzac's account is that Napoleon's supremacy was accompanied by the unprecedented prestige of the imperial nobility. 'Jamais l'aristocratie française', Balzac records, 'ne fut aussi riche ni aussi brillante qu'alors.'[52] Already therefore the Empire was evolving in a sense which was confirmed and accentuated by the Austrian marriage, towards a strengthening of Napoleon's dynastic authority and an enhancement of the status of the imperial nobility.

In effect Napoleon was moving more firmly than ever away from the Revolution. By his marriage to Marie-Louise, Napoleon became the nephew of Marie-Antoinette and Louis XVI. The imperial court took on a more pronounced *ancien régime* character with increased 'ci-devant' participation. Counter-revolutionary hopes were revived and the position of the 'acquéreurs' seemed once again in question. In Lefebvre's phrase, 'le mariage autrichien hâta l'évolution qui éloignait Napoléon de la révolution'.[53] In *La Paix du ménage* Balzac pinpoints the fact which emerges from the *Comédie humaine* as a whole, that the anti-revolutionary orientation of the Empire was already well under way before the Austrian marriage.

Balzac's judgement of Napoleon's educational reforms tends to the same anti-revolutionary conclusion. They are shown to be anti-revolutionary in the sense that the recruiting of an aristocracy of talent which Louis Lambert admires as one of Napoleon's foremost achievements is sharply opposed to the egalitarian demands of social democracy. The imperial lycées were never effectively opened to the sons of the working class and peasantry but remained the prerogative of army officers and of 'petits fonctionnaires' like Bridau and Bernard-François Balzac. In his analysis of the working-class section of the population of Paris in 1814-18 in *La Fille aux yeux d'or*, Balzac refers to 'ses Napoléons inconnus'. Like the peasantry, the working class was excluded from the new educational privileges created by the Revolution.

One need not be misled by the occasional atypical statement into thinking that Balzac's view of Napoleon in relation to the Revolution is characterised by inconsistency or ambivalence. Certain characters may be regarded as speaking for themselves and not for Balzac. Goguelat and the duchesse de Laneais each see Napoleon as the embodiment of the Revolution from their respective Bonapartist and ultra extremes. Equally, Balzac's own pronouncements must be carefully examined if one is to understand their wider significance. The criticism of social injustice under the Empire is made, not in any revolutionary spirit, but with a view to promoting a more effective authoritarianism. Similarly, the coincidence of Republican and Bonapartist values which Balzac frequently draws attention to can only be properly interpreted if it is seen as an argument strengthening Balzac's attack on the failings of the Restoration aristocracy or on the ineptitude of the July Monarchy. Finally, the misgivings about Napoleon's failure to restore the 'droit d'aînesse' and to harness religion in the cause of political expediency are either mitigated by rationalisation or submerged in an overriding approval of Napoleon's achievement.

Balzac may have shared with Napoleon a concern at 'la société individualiste engendrée par la Révolution'.[54] In reality, the economic liberty enjoyed by the bourgeoisie under the Empire, in contrast with Napoleon's extinction of political liberty, ensured that the individualism which both Napoleon and Balzac deplored became the permanent driving-force of post-revolutionary society. For Balzac, however, the essence of Napoleon's response to the Revolution was that it was anti-democratic. The economic individualism of the bourgeoisie was bought with the denial of democratic liberties. The dictatorship of Napoleon found favour with Balzac because it displayed a contempt for parliamentary democracy which is echoed by Hulot when he protests that, under the July Monarchy, 'on a substitué la parole à l'action'.[55] It also met with Balzac's approval because it was just as strongly opposed to the realisation of social and economic democracy.

The *Comédie humaine* demonstrates the essential social conservatism of the Empire. It is seen as reactionary in relation to the Revolution and as conservative in comparison with the regimes that succeeded it. The latter view is expressed by the duchesse de Maufrigneuse on behalf of the Restoration aristocracy when she asserts that her class was better off under Napoleon. The same tribute to Napoleon is made by Mme Cibot in *Le Cousin Pons*. This time the point of view is that of the bourgeoisie of the July Monarchy. Indignant because Camusot's servant dresses better than herself, Mme Cibot contrasts the alleged egalitarianism of the July Monarchy with the social distinctions maintained under the Empire. 'Il n'y a plus rien de sacré', she complains, 'si Louis-Philippe ne maintient pas les rangs; . . . sous l'Empereur, . . . tout ça marchait autrement.'[56] In insisting on the social conservatism of the Empire, Balzac's characters are at one with Balzac himself and with the historians of the period.

When Herrera gives Rubempré his lesson in contemporary French history, he does more than restate Balzac's frequently-expressed conviction that democracy leads inevitably to dictatorship. He also reveals the two basic factors which finally account for Balzac's admiration for Napoleon. First, Napoleon was for Balzac the supreme example of 'l'homme supérieur' in politics. Secondly, Balzac saw Napoleon's greatest achievement as being the suspension of the threat of popular democracy inherent in the changes arising out of the Revolution. Small wonder that 'en 1800, le républicain Médal regarda la République comme flambée'.[57] The danger of popular revolution remained, and Balzac's warnings against it became more vehement as 1848 approached. Meanwhile, Balzac might take comfort in the thought that, thanks to Napoleon, the momentum of social change had been checked and that a precedent in intelligent repression existed for other post-revolutionary regimes to follow.

Notes

1. *La Comédie humaine* (ed. P.-G. Castex), 2nd Pléiade edn, XII, 1762-71.

2. Jean Tulard, *Le Mythe de Napoléon* (Paris, 1971), p. 77.

3. Maurice Descotes makes the point that, while dissociating himself from the grosser absurdities of the legend, Balzac maintained a constant admiration for Napoleon. See the chapter on Balzac in Descotes' *La Légende de Napoléon et les écrivains français du XIX*^e *siècle* (Paris, 1967), pp. 225-67.

4. The 'droit d'aînesse' was effectively abolished when the absolute equality of heirs was proclaimed on 8 April 1791.

5. For a full account of the history of the 'droit d'aînesse' and the 'majorat' see the article by P.A. Perrod, 'Balzac et les "Majorats"', *L'Année Balzacienne* (1968), pp. 211-40. Perrod's article is considered in its relevance to the Restoration in chapter 5, section VI.

6. Napoleon, de Marsay alleges, has replaced 'les grandes dames' by 'nos femmes comme il faut' through his failure to restore 'pour certaines familles le droit d'aînesse par d'indestructibles lois'. *Autre étude de femme*, III, 689.

7. 'Aujourd'hui', Balzac maintains, 'les familles riches sont entre le danger de ruiner leurs enfants si elles en ont trop, ou celui de s'éteindre en s'en tenant à un ou deux, un singulier effet du Code civil auquel Napoléon n'a pas songé.' *La Fausse Maîtresse*, II, 195.

8. *Mémoires de deux jeunes mariées*, I, 219.

9. *Le Cabinet des Antiques*, IV, 1092.

10. *Louis Lambert*, IX, 650-1.

11. *Du droit d'aînesse* was published in February 1824. Its significance in the development of Balzac's political thinking is assessed in chapter III of Bernard Guyon's work, *La Pensée politique et sociale de Balzac* (Paris, 1969).

12. *Oeuvres Complètes de Honoré de Balzac* (eds. M. Bouteron and H. Longnon), 40 vols. (Conard, Paris, 1926-63). *Oeuvres Diverses*, 38, 7.

13. Ibid. 'Les majorats', Balzac states, 'furent inventés pour récompenser une aristocratie.'

14. The historical facts relating to this question are set out on p. 69.

15. The purpose of the 'droit d'aînesse' was to ensure that the major share of the family inheritance passed to the eldest son on his father's death. The 'majorat' differed from the 'droit d'aînesse' in that, although the eldest son was similarly favoured, a specific sum was set aside in advance of the death of the head of the family in order to preserve the family wealth and title.

16. See the note in the Conard edition refuting the claim that Napoleon was not conscious of the effects of the 'Code Civil'. Vol. 4, pp. 401-2.

17. *Autre Etude de femme*, III, 689. See note 6.

18. The role of the 'majorat' in relation to the 'droit d'aînesse' under the Restoration is dealt with in chapter 5, section VI.

19. *Le Médicin de campagne*, IX, 503.

20. Ibid., 433.

21. Ibid., 447.

22. *La Cousine Bette*, VII, 233.

23. *L'Envers de l'histoire contemporaine*, VIII, 219. Balzac's reference seems a deliberate understatement. In his book, *La Vie quotidienne dans les lycées et collèges au XIXe siècle* (Paris, 1968), Paul Gerbod gives evidence of an anti-religious atmosphere in the imperial lycées which persisted well into the Restoration.

24. *Le Médecin de campagne*, VII, 504.

25. The incident is related by L. Madelin in vol. 1 of his *Histoire du Consulat et de l'Empire. La Jeunesse de Bonaparte* (Paris, 1937), p. 170.

26. *Albert Savarus*, I, 973.

27. *La Cousine Bette*, VII, 124. Jean-Baptiste Sauce was the 'procureur-syndic' of Varennes who put an end to the attempted flight of Louis XVI and his family on 20-21 June 1791, by holding them in his house until they were escorted back to Paris.

28. *Une Ténébreuse Affaire*, VIII, 694. According to de Marsay, 'Bonaparte ne semblait pas à M. de Talleyrand et à Fouché aussi marié qu'ils l'étaient eux-mêmes à la Revolution, et ils l'y bouclèrent pour leur propre sûreté, par l'affaire du duc d'Enghien'. Jean Orieux is categorical that Talleyrand, and not Fouché, bore the major responsibility for the execution of the duc d'Enghien. See Jean Orieux, *Talleyrand ou le sphinx incompris* (Paris, 1970), pp. 417-24.

29. Both Madelin and Godechot refer to the comte d'Artois' part in the Cadoudal conspiracy. Godechot makes no mention of Louis XVIII's involvement, while Madelin makes it clear that Louis XVIII thought the idea mad, ordering Cadoudal to return from France in October 1803 with the words: 'Il n'y a rien à remuer dans ce pays que des cendres'. Madelin, *Histoire du Consulat et de l'Empire*. Vol. V, *L'Avènement de l'Empire* (Paris, 1945), pp. 34-5: Jacques Godechot, *La Contre-Revolution Doctrine et Action 1789-1804* (Paris, 1961), pp. 397-400.

30. *Eugénie Grandet*, III, 1031.

31. *Le Cabinet des Antiques*, IV, 1064.

32. The question of the return and recovery of the émigrés under the Consulate and Empire forms part of chapter 2. The purpose of the present discussion is to examine Balzac's view of Napoleon in relation to the Revolution in terms of his response to the conflicting demands of émigrés and 'acquéreurs'.

33. *Une Ténébreuse Affaire*, VIII, 526.

34. For example, in the accounts of brigandage contained in *L'Envers de l'histoire contemporaine*.

35. *Les Paysans*, IX, 127.

36. Ibid.

37. The question of repurchase and restitution is considered in chapter 2.

38. L. Villat, *La Révolution et l'Empire*, 2 vols. (Paris, 1936), vol. II, *Napoléon*, p. 73.

39. Letter to Zulma Carraud, 26 November 1830. *Balzac. Correspondance générale* (ed. Roger Pierrot), 5 vols. (Paris, 1960-9), vol. 1.

40. *Le Bal de Sceaux*, I, 117.

41. Ibid.

42. The quotation can be found on p. 50 of *Pensées, sujets et fragmens* (ed. Jacques Crépet) (Paris, 1910).

43. *Une Ténébreuse Affaire*, VIII, 639.

44. Georges Lefebvre, *Napoléon*, 6th ed (Paris, 1969), p. 426.

45. E. Las Cases, *Mémorial de Sainte-Hélène*, 2 vols. (Garnier, Paris, 1961).

46. Lefebvre, *Napoléon*, p. 584.

47. *Le Lys dans la vallée*, IX, 1043.

48. *Les Marana*, X, 1071.

49. *Illusions Perdues*, V, 699.

50. See Villat, *La Révolution et l'Empire*, p. 73. Similarly, authorisation for the creation of 'majorats' had been given in August 1806.

51. *Une Ténébreuse Affaire*, VIII, 640.

52. *La Paix du ménage*, II, 95.

53. Lefebvre, *Napoléon*, p. 318.

54. The phrase is that of Lefebvre, ibid., p. 142.

55. *La Cousine Bette*, VII, 95.

56. *Le Cousin Pons*, VIII, 610.

57. Balzac, *Oeuvres Ebauchées. Le Théâtre comme il est*, 1st Pléiade edn, X, 56.

PART TWO:

THE RESTORATION

4 THE FIRST RESTORATION AND THE HUNDRED DAYS

The period of fifteen months, from Napoleon's first abdication in April 1814 to the second return of the Bourbons in July 1815, is given especial prominence in the *Comédie humaine*. Although no single novel deals specifically with the period or takes it as its principal historical theme, the references to it in the *Comédie humaine* are extremely numerous and provide an important composite picture of what is treated by Balzac as a critical phase in the history of post-revolutionary France.

A great number of Balzac's characters are directly affected by the events of the period. It is not only the marquis d'Esgrignon who lives through 'les miracles de la restauration de 1814, ceux plus grands du retour de Napoléon en 1815, les prodiges de la nouvelle fuite de la maison de Bourbon et de son second retour'.[1] It is through his description of the way in which his characters are caught up in the rapid changes of the first Restoration and the Hundred Days that Balzac demonstrates the sense of historical continuity which informs the *Comédie humaine*. In uncovering some of the fundamental forces at work during the period, Balzac reaffirms his overriding concern to examine the effects of the Revolution on French society in the first half of the nineteenth century.

The *Comédie humaine* contains many examples of loyalty to both the Bonapartist and the royalist cause. Two lessons in particular emerge from a study in the *Comédie humaine* of those characters, such as Hulot and Philippe Bridau, whose loyalty to Napoleon remains intact throughout the crisis of 1814-15. The first conclusion which it reinforces is the unprecedented degree of social mobility engendered by the Revolution and given added momentum by the Empire. The second reality, which Balzac's treatment of the first Restoration and the Hundred Days demonstrates, concerns the political consequence of that social lesson. By their unchanging support of Napoleon, vast numbers of Frenchmen of all classes, but especially those from a modest background, whether peasant, artisan or bourgeois, continued to see in Napoleon, at least up to the moment of final defeat in 1815, the firmest guarantee that the gains made in the Revolution would be preserved and its long-term aspirations finally realised.

With insignificant exceptions, the aristocracy in the *Comédie humaine* expresses its loyalty to the Bourbon cause in 1814-15 in one of two ways. Balzac's nobles either maintain the opposition to Napoleon to which they had adhered throughout the Empire, or else they abandon Napoleon for the Bourbons at the first Restoration and hold fast to their new allegiance during the Hundred Days. Among the first category, some, like the father of the duc d'Hérouville, 'revenu avec le roi en 1814',[2] choose to end their emigration on the first return of the Bourbons, or, as in the case of the baron du Guénic, at the beginning of 1814 in anticipation of Napoleon's defeat in the 'campagne de France'.[3] The baron du Guénic is fifty-one when his son Calyste is born, 'le jour même de l'entrée de Louis XVIII à Calais'.[4]

The baron du Guénic is rare among Balzac's counter-revolutionaries in having first fought the Republic as a royalist rebel before emigrating. The distinction between rebels and émigrés in their opposition to the Revolution and to Napoleon is frequently insisted upon by Balzac, as much for the period 1814-15 as for the earlier phase of counter-revolution and emigration.[5] The conviction of a section of intransigent rebels that it is a royalist's duty to fight to defend the monarchy against its enemies on the soil of France itself is articulated by the marquis d'Esgrignon when he declares that 'le roi était en France, sa noblesse devait l'entourer'.[6] It was an issue which was raised again by the Hundred Days, although in the *Comédie humaine* its renewed implications have a distinctly pragmatic character in contrast with the earlier doctrinaire assertions of the marquis d'Esgrignon.

In 1815, as during the Revolution and Empire, the majority of the aristocracy preferred to adopt an attitude of 'attentisme'. The counter-revolutionary minority could choose between rebellion and emigration. Only this time the circumstances were reversed, with the émigrés following Louis XVIII into brief exile and the rebels fighting in a country from which their king had temporarily fled. In fact, the marquis d'Esgrignon is neither a rebel nor an émigré during the Hundred Days. In 1815 he was sixty-seven and preferred the provincial retreat of the 'Cabinet des Antiques' in Alençon to the rigours of exile or armed opposition. The fact remains that, by not accompanying Louis XVIII to Ghent during the Hundred Days, the marquis d'Esgrignon acts contrary to his insistence that the place of a royalist was with his king. There was no logical reason why this should not apply as much to Louis XVIII from March to July 1815, as to Louis XVI from July 1789 to January 1793.

An interesting comparison between rebels and émigrés arises in the

Comédie humaine from the behaviour in 1815 of the baron du Guénic and the comte de Fontaine. Having returned to France just before the first Restoration, the baron du Guénic, despite his advanced years, opts to stay and fight during the Hundred Days, as he had done initially during the Revolution. He defends his native Guérande 'contre les bataillons du général Travot' and pursues his armed resistance to Napoleon to the end.[7] The decision of the comte de Fontaine to emigrate with Louis XVIII represents a startling departure from the attitude of a Vendée rebel whose stubborn independence had hitherto been the equal of that of the marquis d'Esgrignon. It is then, however, that the comte de Fontaine displays a flexibility of which the marquis d'Esgrignon is totally incapable. His emigration during the Hundred Days is the result of a calculated change of tactics which is prompted by his observation that émigrés seem to be more in favour with the Bourbons than those who have fought as rebels on their behalf. Disgusted by the 'foire aux places' of the first Restoration in which émigrés and imperial notorieties both have an important share, the comte de Fontaine leaves for Ghent 'sans savoir si cette complicité d'émigration lui serait plus propice que ne l'avait été son dévouement passé'. Balzac then hints at his motives by adding: 'mais après avoir observé que les compagnons de l'exil étaient plus en faveur que les braves qui, jadis, avaient protesté, les armes à la main, contre l'établissement de la république, peut-être espéra-t-il trouver dans ce voyage à l'étranger plus de profit que dans un service actif et périlleux à l'intérieur'.[8]

Balzac does not describe the conditions of the Ghent exile itself. Nor does he trace the route which Louis XVIII followed in the manner which one associates with Vigny and, more particularly, with Aragon.[9] Nevertheless, the references to the Ghent exiles in the *Comédie humaine* are of considerable historical interest. Whatever the truth about the conviction expressed by the marquis d'Esgrignon that it paid to be an émigré rather than a rebel in the Bourbon cause, Balzac clearly indicates that those at least who shared Louis XVIII's exile in 1815 did remarkably well from their gesture. Félix de Vandenesse's services to the exiled monarchy during the Hundred Days enable him to lay the foundations of a prestigious career under the Restoration. The comte de Fontaine's gamble in becoming a last-minute émigré proves entirely justified when, during the second Restoration, his own position and the future of his children are made secure by the grateful protection of Louis XVIII.

On the question of the relative treatment by the Bourbons of their émigré and rebel supporters, Balzac reveals little more than a discreet pro-rebel sympathy, but this is outweighed by his condemnation of armed counter-revolution, by émigrés and rebels alike, as harmful to the supreme cause of national unity. However, Balzac commits himself more fully in commenting on the motives of the Ghent exiles. While he recognises the disinterested behaviour of some, it is clear that Balzac regards the calculations of the comte de Fontaine as far from exceptional. Although the remark is attributed to an external source, there is the unmistakable stamp of Balzac's approval on the description of the comte de Fontaine as 'un des cinq cents fidèles serviteurs qui partagèrent l'exil de la cour à Gand, et l'un des cinquante mille qui en revinrent'.[10]

There are numerous examples in the *Comédie humaine* of aristocrats occupying prominent positions under the Empire who defect from Napoleon to the Bourbons at the first Restoration and uphold their new loyalty during the Hundred Days. Félix de Vandenesse does not come into this category since he is a pupil in Paris at the beginning of 1814 and is therefore not old enough to have occupied a post under the Empire when he follows Louis XVIII into exile during the Hundred Days. In showing how Félix was removed from Paris to the safety of Tours by his father in the early part of 1814 in order to escape being caught up in the fighting as the allied armies advanced, Balzac, as Moïse le Yaouanc has suggested, was almost certainly echoing his own experience.

Charles de Vandenesse, Félix's elder brother, is, however, 'employé déjà dans la diplomatie impériale' when he decides that the moment is ripe for him to switch his allegiance to the Bourbons. He is helped in his decision by the advice of his father. As Félix reveals, 'Mon père, qui pressentait le retour des Bourbons, venait éclairer mon frère'.[11] Another to do so is the comte de Sérisy, who makes it clear to Napoleon at the start of the Hundred Days that nothing can henceforth deflect him from his loyalty to the Bourbons.

All the instances which Balzac gives of a rallying to the Bourbons in 1814 concern nobles. To the civilian cases are added examples of high-ranking army officers. The comte de Soulanges is referred to as having been 'nommé pair de France en 1814, et resté fidèle aux Bourbons pendant les Cent-Jours'.[12] The most clear-cut case of an officer defecting to the Bourbons in 1814 is that of Victor d'Aiglemont. An 'officier d'ordonnance' with the rank of colonel, d'Aiglemont abandons Napoleon and offers his services to the Bourbons when the allied armies enter Paris and force Napoleon to abdicate.[13]

Having emphasised the way in which nobles who had rallied to

Napoleon reaffirmed their loyalty to the Bourbons in 1814, Balzac does not give a clear picture of their activities during the first Restoration and the Hundred Days. In referring to the comte de Soulanges and the comte de Sérisy, Balzac simply records how they persisted in their newly-declared fidelity during the Hundred Days. Too young yet to have embarked on a serious career, Félix de Vandenesse sees the first Restoration through the limited perspective of the ball at Tours at which the shoulders of Mme de Mortsauf make a greater impression on him than the presence of the duc d'Angoulême. All that one knows for certain about the royalist 'ralliés' during the first Restoration is that, as the protégé of the comte d'Artois, now 'lieutenant-général du royaume', Victor d'Aiglemont is made a general in the 'gardes du corps'. Their role during the Hundred Days is less uncertain since one is told that d'Aiglemont and both Charles and Félix de Vandenesse accompany Louis XVIII and the Bourbon court into exile. Although d'Aiglemont's contribution in Ghent is not specified, Charles de Vandenesse is mentioned as representing Louis XVIII at the Congress of Vienna, as 'envoyé récemment au congrès de Vienne'.[14] Félix, for his part, becomes the 'confidant' of Louis XVIII and is entrusted with an important mission to la Vendée.

If, finally, one considers the fortunes of those royalists in the *Comédie humaine* whose lives are directly affected by the political choices which they make in 1814-15, whether their support for the Bourbons had been consistently expressed throughout the Empire or reaffirmed only in 1814, two outstanding impressions emerge. First, the history of the Ghent exiles confirms the earlier suggestion that émigrés tended to be more generously rewarded for their services to the Bourbons than rebels.

A comparison between the two generations of royalists is interesting in this respect. Among the members of the older generation who had consistently opposed Napoleon as the heir and defender of the Revolution, the marquis d'Esgrignon had always remained a proud rebel by political conviction. The baron du Guénic, on the other hand, as a rebel who had later emigrated, turns full circle by fighting against Napoleon's armies in Brittany during the Hundred Days. In so doing, in purely material terms, he can be said to have made a tactical error, in direct contrast with the comte de Fontaine, whose decision to emigrate with Louis XVIII in 1815 proves a justified gamble when his ambitions for himself and his children are realised during the second Restoration. The same calculation on the part of the younger royalists who had rallied to the Bourbons in 1814 earns similar rewards after the Hundred Days.

Bourbon gratitude does not distinguish between talent and mediocrity in repaying the 'ralliés' of 1814 who went on to share the king's exile. While the abilities of Félix de Vandenesse are made full use of by Louis XVIII, the limited capacities of Victor d'Aiglemont are hidden behind a resourceful and devoted wife and a restored rank and title.

So far I have been concerned entirely with examples of two categories, nobles consistently loyal to the Bourbons, and those who remain faithful to Napoleon, either in a military or civilian role, throughout the Empire, the first Restoration and the Hundred Days. In addition, the *Comédie humaine* contains an outstanding case of an important minority reaction during the Hundred Days. By his behaviour in 1815, César Birotteau maintains a loyalty to the Bourbons which dates from the Revolution. Napoleon has not forgotten Birotteau's part in the royalist rising in 'vendémiaire', 1795. Having relieved Birotteau of his rank of captain in the 'Garde Nationale' earlier under the Empire, Napoleon dismisses him from his post as 'chef de bataillon' to which he had been reappointed during the first Restoration.

Birotteau's continued opposition to Napoleon in 1815 has wider implications for the political options of the commercial bourgeoisie to which he belongs. 'Durant les Cent-Jours', Balzac explains, 'Birotteau devint *la bête noire* des Libéraux de son quartier, car en 1815 seulement commencèrent les scissions politiques entre les négociants, jusqu'alors unanimes dans leurs voeux de tranquillité dont les affaires avaient besoin.'[15] Unlike Birotteau, his bourgeois colleagues are not moved by ideological considerations but by the practical concerns of business. Hitherto inclined to support Napoleon in whom they saw the defender of the revolutionary changes which had made possible their economic expansion and their social rise, the commercial bourgeoisie was more vulnerable, on Napoleon's return in 1815, to royalist arguments which acquired added economic force if they came from a 'négociant' like Birotteau. Napoleon's defeat the previous year was too close to be overlooked, and the political lessons of d'Aldrigger's ruin and du Tillet's profit during the 'campagne de France' provided a useful precedent. In the last resort, the support of the bourgeoisie in 1815 would go to whichever regime offered the best guarantee of stability and prosperity. Wars were only acceptable provided internal order was maintained and economic activity remained undisturbed. To an increasing section of the bourgeoisie during the Hundred Days the resumption of Napoleonic rule must have seemed to pose a serious threat to its essential priorities.

The political decisions made by Balzac's characters during the first

Restoration and the Hundred Days emphasise basic loyalty rather than an easy transfer of allegiance, an adherence to principles characterising their behaviour more frequently than a transparent opportunism. The result of this emphasis on steadfast loyalty is that Balzac understates the servile and cynical switches of political allegiance which were such a feature of the period 1814-15. In this respect at least, Balzac's treatment of the pattern of political loyalties in 1814-15 remains incomplete.

Economic Issues and their Political Implications

In the account which he gives of the First Restoration and the Hundred Days, Balzac confirms that he is primarily a social and economic historian, with only a secondary interest in political issues and only a peripheral concern with military matters. The overriding economic question which Balzac examines in the context of the First Restoration and the Hundred Days is that of the continuing opposition of 'acquéreurs' and émigrés.

Although the gains made by the émigrés by the law of December 1814 involved only their unsold property and were therefore not achieved at the expense of the 'acquéreurs', nevertheless the question of the rights of the 'acquéreurs' and of the counter-claims of the émigrés was very much a live issue in 1814-15. It was still, as it had always been, as much a political problem as well as an economic one.

The recognition of the property changes put into effect by the Revolution which was contained in the declaration of Saint-Ouen in May 1814, and confirmed in the Charter a month later, dealt a decisive blow to the émigrés' hopes of achieving the total recovery of their land.[16] It is Balzac's critique of the Charter of 1814 in particular that provides the clue to his assessment of the period 1814-15 in terms of the changes set in motion by the Revolution.

Balzac's view of the first Restoration and the Hundred Days reveals some fundamental contradictions. On the one hand, he approves the policy of Louis XVIII, as he was later to welcome the indemnity, as helping to eliminate social tensions by putting the royalist seal of acknowledgement on the revolutionary land settlement. This attitude totally conflicts with Balzac's unceasing denunciation of the materialism which he attributed to the Revolution and, not least, to the transfer of property which it had brought about. In sanctifying the gains of the 'acquéreurs', the first Restoration must therefore logically bear the blame for encouraging the disastrous process arising out of the

Revolution. It is precisely this, moreover, that Balzac elsewhere identifies as the consequence of the Charter of 1814. The material values enshrined in the Charter, Balzac hints in *Illusions Perdues*, have anticipated Guizot's 'Enrichissez-vous!'[17] 'Votre société', Herrera tells Lucien, 'n'adore plus le vrai Dieu, mais le Veau-d'or! Telle est la religion de votre Charte, qui ne tient plus compte, en politique, que de la propriété. N'est-ce pas dire à tous les sujets: Tâchez d'être riches?[18]

The contradictions become all the more apparent when one considers Balzac's uncompromising attack on the constitutional changes made permanent by the first Restoration. What the comte de Fontaine calls 'leur maudit système constitutionnel' is repeatedly denounced by Balzac, since it runs counter to his basic anti-democratic convictions.[19] A representative, parliamentary system was bound, in Balzac's view, to inhibit effective government, to promote mediocrity and, at the same time, to stimulate further the material appetites of the masses already encouraged by Louis XVIII's recognition, on his return in 1814, of the property won by the 'acquéreurs' in the Revolution.

What finally are the historical strengths and weaknesses of Balzac's account of the first Restoration and the Hundred Days? On the debit side, in addition to the imbalance already noted which inclines Balzac to stress loyalty to the exclusion of opportunism in response to the political changes of 1814-15, the discussion is at times confusingly imprecise. The most serious example of this tendency occurs in *La Fille aux yeux d'or*. Although de Marsay is described as walking in the grounds of the Tuileries 'vers le milieu du mois d'avril, en 1815',[20] the Hundred Days are never identified, with the result that the action unfolds in a historical vacuum. It is uncharacteristic of Balzac that history should thus be squeezed out between the sociological analysis which forms the preamble of the novel and the excess of Gothic fantasy into which it lapses thereafter.

There are also some disappointing omissions. In *La Vieille Fille*, for example, the action glides from the first to the second Restoration in such a way as to leave one in the dark on the interesting question of du Bousquier's activities in 1814-15. In general, except for financiers like Nucingen and du Tillet, these gaps affect the bourgeoisie rather than the nobility whose royalist allegiances are clearly defined. The most notable exception concerns Birotteau, who is unusual in the *Comédie humaine* in being both a bourgeois and a fervent and consistent royalist. Du Bousquier meanwhile is not alone as a leading bourgeois who has emerged during the Revolution and Empire about whom Balzac gives no information for the period of the first Restoration and the Hundred Days. It would have been interesting to know something of the behaviour in 1814-15 of, for instance, Grandet and Séchard, at a time when the fortunes and careers of individuals might be crucially affected by economic initiatives and political decisions.

One must also be on one's guard against accepting too readily any cherished critical myths concerning Balzac's handling of the period. Whatever else it may be, *Le Lys dans la vallée* is not, as Alain claimed it to be, 'l'histoire des Cent Jours vue d'un château de la Loire'.[21] The historical interest of *Le Lys dans la vallée* centres primarily on the Restoration and, to a lesser extent, on the emigration. The novel is divided evenly between the first and the second Restoration, with a brief reference to the final stages of the Empire at the beginning ('Napoléon tentait ses derniers coups')[22] and a passing mention of the Hundred Days in the middle. The Hundred Days are in fact spanned by two references which are only two pages apart. One has no sooner learned that 'les événements du 20 mars arrivèrent' than the narrative jumps straight to Napoleon's second abdication. It was on the evening of his return to Clochegourde, Félix de Vandenesse reveals, that 'j'appris les désastres de Waterloo, la fuite de Napoléon, la marche des alliés sur Paris et le retour probable des Bourbons'.[23] Félix is absent from Clochegourde for virtually the whole period of the Hundred Days, which are only faintly glimpsed through his decision to accompany Louis XVIII into exile and the Vendée mission with which he is entrusted. *Le Lys dans la vallée* is neither the history of the Hundred Days nor are the events seen from the vantage point of a Loire château.

The positive qualities which Balzac brings into play in his study of the first Restoration and the Hundred Days, the mastery of detail and the awareness of the deeper currents involved, are seen to best advantage in his social and economic analysis rather than in the military and political account. Balzac shows two realities to have been of more fundamental importance in 1814-15 than the spectacle of the succeeding regimes which sought a political solution to the basic problem which they posed. One was the extraordinary resilience of an aristocracy which saw in the first Restoration the promise of a return to its old ascendancy. The other reality was the power of a revolutionary bourgeoisie determined to protect and extend its conquests against the challenge of a resurgent nobility. The clash of these two opposing movements and its eventual outcome were to dominate the 'monarchie censitaire' and to find their historian in Balzac. It was also the essential question to which Balzac, despite the ambivalence and contradictions in which it involved him, would ultimately have to find his own personal answer.

Notes

1. *Le Cabinet des Antiques*, IV, 978.
2. *Modeste Mignon*, I, 614.
3. The baron du Guénic had returned briefly in 1813 in order to obtain the necessary papers for his marriage in Ireland.
4. *Béatrix*, II, 651.
5. The latter question is considered in chapter 5, section V.
6. *Le Cabinet des Antiques*, IV, 993.
7. *Béatrix*, II, 654. See the Pléiade note for the historical inaccuracy of this particular reference.
8. *Le Bal de Sceaux*, I, 112.
9. In *Servitude et Grandeur militaires* and *La Semaine Sainte* respectively.
10. *Le Bal de Sceaux*, I, 112. The remark is referred to as 'le mot du plus spirituel et du plus habile de nos diplomates', i.e. Talleyrand.
11. *Le Lys dans la vallée*, IX, 979.
12. *Les Paysans*, IX, 137.
13. When Balzac states that d'Aiglemont remained faithful to Napoleon 'tant que Napoléon resta debout' (*La Femme de trente ans*, II, 1072), the reference does not, of course, apply to the Hundred Days, when d'Aiglemont served the Bourbons.
14. *Le Lys dans la vallée*, IX, 1099.
15. *César Birotteau*, VI, 77.
16. In the declaration of Saint-Ouen it was affirmed that 'les propriétés seront inviolables et sacrées; la vente des biens nationaux restera irrévocable'. Article 9 of the Charter of 1814 stated that 'toutes les propriétés sont inviolables, sans exception de celles qu'on appelle *nationales*, la loi ne mettant aucune différence entre elles'.
17. Guizot's exact words were: 'Enrichissez-vous par le travail et l'épargne, et vous deviendrez électeur'. They were spoken during the campaign preceding the elections of 1846.
18. *Illusions Perdues*, V, 701.
19. *Le Bal de Sceaux*, I, 111.
20. *La Fille aux yeux d'or*, V, 1058.
21. Alain's description of *Le Lys dans la vallée* occurs in *Les Arts et les Dieux. Avec Balzac* (Paris, 1937), p. 24.
22. *Le Lys dans la vallée*, IX, 979.
23. Ibid., pp. 1098, 1100.

5 THE ARISTOCRATIC COMEBACK

Balzac's account of the Restoration aristocracy commands attention for two reasons. The first concerns its especial prominence in the *Comédie humaine*; the second is its relevance to the continuing historical debate concerning the Restoration and, in particular, the socio-economic aspects of the attempt by the aristocracy to recover its position as the leading class in French society.

The aristocracy of the Restoration has received considerable treatment in recent Balzac criticism. It is the subject of a chapter in Jean Forest's *L'Aristocratie Balzacienne*, and has figured prominently in critical contributions made during the past twenty years or so.[1] Such distinguished critics as Donnard, Guyon, Wurmser and Barbéris have, from their different ideological standpoints, all expressed a growing preoccupation with the study of the Restoration aristocracy contained in the *Comédie humaine*.

However, despite the increased interest in Balzac's analysis of the aristocracy, particularly under the Restoration, it remains under-represented as a subject of critical concern in relation to other major historical questions treated by Balzac, above all compared to his examination of the bourgeoisie. Apart from Forest's work, at best it occupies the odd chapter or is dealt with in a number of brief and scattered sections in which the various aspects are unevenly considered. Balzac in fact devotes as much attention to the decline of the aristocracy as he does to the rise of the bourgeoisie. The disproportionate emphasis given by Balzac to the aristocracy is noted by another critic, Pradalié, when he remarks that 'la noblesse joue dans son oeuvre un rôle capital qui apparaît parfois supérieur à celui qu'elle a réellement joué dans l'Histoire'.[2] This is especially true of the Restoration. A full critical evaluation of the role of the Restoration aristocracy in the *Comédie humaine* is still to be written. It is hoped that the present study, limited as it is, may go some way towards filling an important gap in Balzac criticism.

One can distinguish personal factors, both aesthetic and ideological, which help to account for Balzac's preoccupation with the aristocracy. In the first place, as Bernard Guyon points out, in terms of Balzac's 'esthétisme social', it was logical that the aristocratic instincts of the artist should have induced such a predilection on Balzac's part.[3]

Secondly, in the Marxist argument opposing Wurmser against Barbéris, one is inclined to side with Barbéris. The evidence which Wurmser assembles to support his claim that Balzac despised the aristocracy as an irrevocably doomed class is crudely selective.[4] Barbéris, on the other hand, makes an important point when he emphasises the retroactive effect of Balzac's legitimism, itself conditioned by his aversion for the bourgeoisie of the July Monarchy. The values of the aristocratic 'mal du siècle' thus acquired a renewed magic for Balzac. At the same time, Barbéris indicates how much Balzac's insight in respect of the Restoration aristocracy owed to hindsight. It was not simply that Balzac's historical outlook was more clearly defined after 1830. As Barbéris suggests, it was a relatively easier task for Balzac to describe a class whose history was irreversibly 'figé' than a bourgeoisie still fresh from its revolutionary triumphs, its precise historical character as yet undetermined.[5]

The most significant fact to emerge from recent critical appraisals of the place of the Restoration aristocracy in the *Comédie humaine* is the socioeconomic basis of Balzac's analysis. The best contributions in this area have undoubtedly been made by Donnard[6] and Barbéris,[7] particularly on the question of aristocratic landownership. It is a measure of the increased awareness of the importance of Balzac's economic analysis that it occupies a critic like Jean Forest. Insisting that his approach is neither historical nor philosophical but primarily what he calls poetic, 'Balzac accordant plus d'importance aux hommes qu'aux structures sociales', Forest does both himself and Balzac an injustice.[8] His attempted 'déhistorisation' of Balzac misfires as the historical imperatives of the *Comédie humaine* constantly impose themselves on Forest's poetic perspective. Balzac's discussion of the Restoration aristocracy emphatically confirms the socioeconomic foundations upon which his historical method rests.

I 'La Réaction Nobiliaire' and the Reconquest of Society

Although it vigorously reaffirms the primacy of ecnomic motives, Balzac's investigation of the Restoration aristocracy by no means excludes or neglects other important areas of aristocratic activity. The 'réaction nobiliaire' to which the *Comédie humaine* testifies takes in, with varying degrees of emphasis, every important aspect of Restoration society. Alongside its attempt to retrieve its economic losses, the aristocracy is shown to be reimplanted at the highest level in the army and the administration, in politics and in social life generally.

Balzac's aristocracy enjoys a monopoly of Restoration prestige and glamour. The restored social splendour centred on the 'faubourg' and palely reflected in its provincial equivalents is paralleled by the aristocratic domination of the diplomatic corps.[9] In politics, the *Comédie humaine* serves as a reminder that, as Vidalenc points out, no Restoration minister was a 'roturier'.[10]

While Balzac offers little evidence of the preponderance of nobles in the judiciary and the episcopate,[11] on the other hand there are abundant examples in the *Comédie humaine* which confirm the dominance of the aristocracy in the reconstituted Bourbon army and the 'haute administration', as expressed notably in prefectoral appointments.

The overwhelmingly 'ci-devant' character of the officer corps of the Restoration army is clearly indicated in the *Comédie humaine*. The comte de Soulanges and the comte de Sucy display a similar pattern of military achievement. After serving in the imperial armies, both had proved their loyalty to the Bourbons, the comte de Soulanges during the Hundred Days and the comte de Sucy following his return from a Russian prison camp. The comte de Soulanges is recalled to command the artillery in the war in Spain, while in the case of the comte de Sucy his military promotion is twice accompanied by an elevation in his title.

Balzac further shows that entry to the most prestigious regiments, especially the elite cavalry, was the virtual prerogative of the nobility. The majority of the noble officers mentioned by Balzac as forming part of the new Bourbon army, either through direct incorporation in 1815 or via subsequent reintegration, belong to cavalry regiments. Auguste de Maulincour, a child of the emigration who had returned at the age of eight in 1804, had rallied to the Bourbons in 1814 and followed Louis XVIII into exile during the Hundred Days. His rapid promotion under the Restoration gives him command of a cavalry regiment.

When Philippe Bridau initially refuses to join the Bourbon army, Mme Descoings tells Mme Bridau that 'on ne veut que des nobles dans la cavalerie'.[12] Yet Mme Descoings is only half right, as Bridau himself proves. The cavalry regiment of the 'Garde royale' commanded by the duc de Maufrigneuse includes, apart from its core of impeccable 'noblesse de race', the 'robin' comte de Sérisy and, most remarkable of all, the ex-'demi-solde' and Bonapartist conspirator, Philippe Bridau. The exceptional nature of Bridau's case is in itself revealing. His reintegration into the army is explained by Charles X's desire to continue Louis XVIII's policy of reconciliation with the former imperial officers.

In an attempt to minimise the social repercussions of such an initiative, non-noble officers commissioned in the 'Garde royale' were automatically ennobled. 'Sous la Restauration', Balzac notes, 'l'anoblissement devint un quasi-droit pour les roturiers qui servaient dans la Garde.'[13] Ennoblement might precede or follow the military appointment. Jeanrenaud is made baron just before receiving his commission, thanks to the influence of the marquis d'Espard. Immediately following his reinstatement in the army, Philippe Bridau becomes comte de Brambourg. However, the spectacular example of Philippe Bridau does not obscure the essential reality of the new Bourbon army which is conveyed by Balzac. The ostentatious rallying of a Bonapartist 'demi-solde' might occasionally force open the aristocratic doors, but such 'roturier' recruitment as occurred was strictly controlled in the interest of a calculated social policy. Limited admissions of this kind did nothing fundamentally to challenge the authority of the aristocracy in a commanding area of Restoration society.

The aristocracy's controlling position in the Restoration army was equalled by its grip on the 'haute administration'. As Vidalenc reveals, just as half of the intake of the 'Ecole Spéciale Militaire' came from the aristocracy, similarly, in 1829, 45 out of 86 prefects were nobles.[14] The *Comédie humaine* corroborates the historical evidence of an aristocratic preponderance in the appointment of Restoration prefects.

The vicomte de Chargeboeuf is a typical case in point. Successively 'sous-préfet' at Arcis and Sancerre, he leaves Sancerre in 1827 on his nomination as prefect elsewhere. In other instances, a prefectoral post is the reward for past services to the Bourbon cause. The marquis du Vissard, for example, is made prefect in recognition of his brother's sacrifice in the interest of the Vendée rebellion.

The Restoration prefects also included a substantial minority of imperial recruits, a special category of which is represented by comte Martial de la Roche-Hugon. A 'ci-devant' rallied to the Empire, which had made him a prefect, la Roche-Hugon remains in his post under the Restoration. Vidalenc does not specify whether he counts as nobles among the Restoration prefects only those who were free of 'parvenu' or imperial associations. If this is the case, then by adding the latter categories, one arrives at a considerably larger noble majority.

Balzac does in fact give a number of examples of such mutations. The husband of Mlle de Grandlieu, a former 'chambellan' of Napoleon, is 'préfet de l'Orne' after 1815. 'Baron de l'Empire', Sixte du Châtelet is 'préfet de la Charente' in 1821. At the same time, Balzac hints that, in order to make imperial appointments of this kind more palatable, as happened with 'roturier' officers admitted to the 'Garde royale', the recipients were often officially ennobled by the Restoration. This was made easier if the prefect happened to marry a 'ci-devant'. Du Châtelet, for instance, marries the widowed Mme de Bargeton between his appointment as prefect and being made 'comte'. Ennoblement, however, was not invariable, even if the imperial recruit combined the post of prefect with an aristocratic marriage. The husband of Mlle de Grandlieu is not ennobled and finds himself excluded from the 'Cabinet des Antiques' to which his wife has entry. An imperial record, on the other hand, if not necessarily a disqualification for office, might be a potential liability once appointed which even 'ci-devant' credentials cannot overcome. La Roche-Hugon, for example, is deposed in 1823 in favour of the ultra comte de Castéran. A parvenu taint could be even more fatal, as the comte de Chessel finds to his cost. Despite being ennobled by Louis XVIII, the comte de Chessel finds himself in and out of the Assembly and is denied the satisfaction of being made a prefect, let alone a peer.

As in the case of the army, the imperial and 'roturier' exceptions leave the overall significance of Balzac's references to Restoration prefects intact. They are entirely consistent with the findings of recent research which reveal an aristocratic majority in this important area characteristic of the nobility's domination of the 'haute administration' in general.[15]

II The Reconstruction of a Class

Unlike the monarchy from which it expected support for its aspirations, the aristocracy did not take shape again overnight with the second Restoration. The work of reconstruction was a complex and protracted process which continued throughout the reigns of Louis XVIII and Charles X. The upheaval of Revolution and Empire had shattered all semblance of a powerful and united nobility. Noble lines had died out and numbers had been considerably reduced by the rigours of emigration and revolutionary persecution. Nor was it simply a question of numerical weakening. The degenerate tendencies visible in the eighteenth century are perpetuated in the *Comédie humaine* in the ignoble careers of Peyrade and Contenson as police spies under successive regimes. Revitalisation was as imperative a need as reconstitution.

Based on the survivors and heirs of the *ancien régime* nobility, the Restoration aristocracy was redefined to accommodate an influx of totally new creations. The constitutional basis for the emergence of a revived aristocracy after 1815 was provided in the Charter of 1814. Following the decrees of 4-11 August 1789, which the National Assembly had seen as signalling the destruction of the feudal system, the law passed by the 'Constituante' on 19 June 1790 had officially abolished the hereditary nobility and all titles and coats-of-arms. Article 71 of the Charter not only reversed the revolutionary legislation when it declared that 'la noblesse ancienne reprend ses titres', it also confirmed the titles of the imperial nobility ('la nouvelle conserve les siens') and asserted the king's right to create new nobles at his discretion ('Le roi fait des nobles à volonté'). The Restoration, at a stroke, provided itself with a 'mécanisme d'anoblissement' as effective as that of the *ancien régime*.

Thus a whole climate was established in which the acquisition or recovery of noble status assumed great significance. *Ancien régime* nobles who had been incorporated into the imperial nobility presented no problem. The marquis du Rouvre had been made 'comte' and 'chambellan' by Napoleon in 1806. The comte de Sérisy was a former 'comte et sénateur de l'Empire'. 'Ci-devant' who had been stamped with the tawdry seal of imperial nobility simply resumed where they had left off in 1789, with their titles restored, provided they had given adequate proof of rallying to the Bourbons. It little mattered that the comte de Sérisy had married the widow of an imperial general. She had been a Ronquerolles anyway and the comte de Sérisy's display of loyalty to the Bourbons during the Hundred Days had been unambiguous.

For those who, like Montcornet, owed their titles to the Empire and now avidly sought admission to the Restoration aristocracy, it was a different matter. For them an aristocratic marriage was an invaluable reference. Du Châtelet's ennoblement, as we have seen, was consequent upon his marriage to Mme de Bargeton. Undeterred by the failure of his attempt to marry the daughter of his former imperial comrade-in-arms, the comte de Soulanges, Montcornet is finally rewarded for his perseverance. His marriage in 1819 to the daughter of the émigré vicomte de Troisville is a triumph for parvenu persistence over 'ci-devant' disdain. Authorised by Louis XVIII to bear the Troisville coat-of-arms, Moncornet is promised the title of marquis when he has proved himself worthy of the peerage. The promise is never fulfilled. Members of the imperial nobility might gain access to the Restoration aristocracy in the same way that 'roturiers' were recruited as officers into the army, but the terms imposed on the supplicant were clearly defined and rigorously enforced.

A further tribute to the restored prestige of the Restoration nobility is provided by the interest shown by the bourgeoisie in acquiring aristocratic status. In some cases, Balzac indicates that this did not go beyond simple affectation. The nephew of the Cruchots styles himself M. de Bonfons on the strength of his owning 'le domaine de Bonfons'. Georges d'Estourny gives himself a 'particule' from 1814. Frequently, however, bourgeois aspirations result in titled recognition. Charles Grandet is ennobled following his marriage to Mlle d'Aubrion. Baron de Villaine, a wealthy young judge from a bourgeois family, acquires his title at the beginning of the Restoration and later marries the second daughter of the comte de Fontaine. La Billardière, a former Chouan and émigré, is also made a baron by Louis XVIII. The comte d'Herbomez owes his title to the recognition by the Restoration of his brother's death in the Bourbon cause under the Empire.[16]

The career of the comte de Chessel is a model of the 'genre'. Born Durand, he had taken his wife's name after his father had made a fortune in the Revolution and had added a 'particule' as soon as it became safe to do so. His émigré past acting in his favour, he is made 'comte de Chessel' by Louis XVIII. Like the successful imperial aspirant Montcornet however, the comte de Chessel finds that the material benefits available to the parvenu aristocracy of the Restoration are strictly circumscribed.

The provisions of the Charter which were designed to facilitate the recreation of a powerful aristocracy were exploited to the full by the restored monarchy. Titles automatically reverted, often accompanied by an elevation in rank. Adrien d'Hauteserre, Polydore de la Baudraye, des Lupeaulx and the comte de l'Estorade are prominent examples in the *Comédie humaine* of nobles whose restored titles were subsequently upgraded.

Balzac's testimony in this area is of considerable interest since it highlights a particular aspect of the systematic way in which the regime took advantage of the machinery of ennoblement built into the Charter. It concerns the recovery of aristocratic status by families whose nobility had recently become extinct. In this respect, the Bourbons had a useful imperial precedent. Balzac's La Palférine, for example, comes from a family which had squandered its noble status under Louis XV. La Palférine's father had been made 'comte' by Napoleon, an imperial title inherited by his son and confirmed by the Charter.

Balzac shows a number of ways in which the practice might operate and the important historical factors involved in it. The phenomenon is dramatically illustrated in the history of the Longueville and the

Mignon families and in that of Lucien de Rubempré. The noble line of
the Longuevilles had expired with the execution of the last surviving
member of the younger branch in 1793. The future vicomte de Longueville was the son of a 'procureur' who had not troubled to purchase his
ennoblement before the Revolution. Claiming a 'particule' to which he
was not entitled, he is ennobled by Charles X after becoming a pro-
ministerial deputy and a rich landowner.

The experience of Charles Mignon is of a different kind in that it
is marked by the voluntary relinquishing of an aristocratic identity
prior to its reclamation under the Restoration. The pattern had been
set by Mignon's father, the comte de la Bastie. In order to escape the
Terror, he had become a revolutionary executioner and had disappeared
after Thermidor. Classed as an émigré, he has seen his fief sold and his
château destroyed. The family had been massacred in 1795, leaving
Charles as the only survivor. Abandoning his 'particule' in 1799, Mignon
served with distinction in Napoleon's armies. His marriage to the
daughter of the German banker Wallenrod had laid the foundation of
the fortune he made in Le Havre under the Restoration. His remarkable
recovery culminated with his ennoblement in 1829. Once again an
aristocratic marriage is decisive. When his daughter Modeste marries
Ernest de la Brière, Mignon regains the family title of 'comte' with
royal authorisation for it to pass, in the absence of a male heir, to
his son-in-law.

Lucien de Rubempré's family history shows a similar loss of noble
status, only on this occasion the attempt at recovery is unsuccessful.
Lucien's mother had been the last survivor of a family of Charentais
nobility before becoming Mme Chardon on her marriage to a 'chirurgien-
major' in the Republican armies. His social vanity flattered by his
contacts with the provincial salon of Mme de Bargeton, once in Paris
Lucien makes a calculated switch to ultra views in an effort to regain
the family title. In 1829 his prospects seem at their peak with a chance
of his marrying Clotilde de Grandlieu and becoming marquis de
Rubempré, when the revelation of his links with Vautrin leads to his
arrest and suicide in May 1830.

In examining the reconstruction of the Restoration aristocracy,
Balzac reveals the principal motives underlying the process. The aim
of re-establishing the pre-eminence of the 'ci-devant' aristocracy enjoyed
an uneasy co-existence with the policy of promoting social reconciliation via the assimilation of bourgeois and imperial elements. The former
took precedence and, when the two conflicted, priorities were made
brutally clear. Charles X and the ultras behaved increasingly as if the

Revolution had changed nothing. Blinded by the reassertion of its social and political predominance to the fact that the economic ascendancy had now passed to the bourgeoisie, the Restoration aristocracy ensured that the tragedy of revolution would be re-enacted as farce, and with the direction firmly in bourgeois hands. It is in precisely this key area that the essential interest of Balzac's analysis of the Restoration aristocracy lies, in his assessment of the realities of its economic position in relation to its overall dominance of society.

III Options and Realities

When one looks at what Balzac has to say about the Restoration aristocracy, one's immediate impression is of the sheer volume of the evidence. Every important category is discussed, although it is fair to point out that the descendants of the 'noblesse de robe' are under-represented, apart from the notable examples of comte Ferraud, Roger de Granville and the comte de Sérisy. The enormous range covered by Balzac and the massive amount of material provided fall into place, however, when one relates them to Balzac's basic economic analysis. This, in turn, is centred on three antitheses which, at various points, significantly overlap: the contrast between the émigrés and the non-émigré rebels opposed to the Revolution and the Empire; the opposing attitudes of the implacable enemies of the revolutionary settlement and of those favouring its pragmatic acceptance; and finally, the differing experience of the Parisian and provincial nobilities. The implications of these basic polarities in Balzac's treatment of the Restoration aristocracy will be examined in their relevant context in later sections of this chapter. First, however, a brief assessment is necessary of the choices with which the Revolution and its Napoleonic sequel confronted the nobility in terms of the dominant issues of post-revolutionary society.

Short of wholehearted identification with the revolutionary and imperial cause, four options were open to the nobility. It could emigrate and then decide whether to fight against the Revolution from abroad or not; it could oppose the Revolution and Napoleon from within France; thirdly, there was the possibility of going into hiding and awaiting the moment to resurface (this is the solution successfully adopted by M. de Maucombe); finally, the nobility could opt for a realistic acknowledgement of the *status quo*, especially in respect of giving its services to the Empire.

The Restoration was unlikely to be over-eager to display generosity towards aristocratic families compromised by a pro-revolutionary past. Mme Leseigneur de Rouville finds it impossible to obtain a pension under the Restoration as the widow of a 'ci-devant' killed serving in the navy of the Republic. When it came to deciding how to treat nobles involved in co-operating with the Empire, however, the situation was more delicate. Any noble who, like Maxime de Trailles, openly expressed his Bonapartist sympathies, could scarcely expect rapid promotion. The duc de Grandlieu is ostracised by the 'faubourg' because of his association with the Empire. But such cases are atypical. The 'faubourg''s hostility to the duc de Grandlieu is not permanent. He has the support of Louis XVIII even though he had affirmed his loyalty to Napoleon in 1814.[17] The nobles who chose to come to terms with Napoleon, and Balzac emphasises that the vast majority of returned émigrés did so, were 'attentistes' and not 'ralliés' in the true sense of the term, as denoting genuine commitment to the Empire. Their response was inspired by three factors. First, apart from the possibility of reaffirming their position as landowners, the Empire offered them the chance to continue or resume the professional activity which they were equipped to carry out, as magistrates, administrators and, above all, as soldiers, and without which their lives would have been an impatient void. Secondly, many of them were not unwilling to share in the patriotic achievements of the Empire. Last but by no means least, they had not given up hope that the monarchy would be restored and with it what they considered their rightful and privileged place in society. Balzac strongly suggests that the calculations of an opportunist 'attentisme' which are expressed in *Une Ténébreuse Affaire* by the marquis de Chargeboeuf and M. d'Hauteserre, were well-founded.

The *Comédie humaine* indicates that the majority of nobles who had achieved an accommodation with Napoleon had no reason to feel aggrieved by their treatment under the Restoration, whether they had served the Empire in a military or a civilian capacity. A show of support for the Bourbons, especially if it had taken the form of accompanying Louis XVIII into exile during the Hundred Days, was a useful reference, but, as the example of the duc de Grandlieu shows, all that was needed was to be clear of suspicion of any hostile or subversive intention towards the Restoration. The fortunes of the group of nobles serving in the imperial armies are particularly interesting for this reason. They include Adrien d'Hauteserre, who is characteristic of the overwhelming majority of Balzac's émigrés who reach some form of compromise with Napoleon on their return. The distinction with which the future marquis de Cinq-Cygne fights on behalf of Napoleon does not prevent his remarkable ascension under the Restoration. In civilian terms, the unbroken continuity in office of nobles who had occupied important posts under the Empire is embodied in the successful Restoration careers of the comte de Sérisy in politics, of the comte de Granville in the judiciary and of Charles de Vandenesse in diplomacy.

Balzac does much more, however, than merely outline the general character of the recovery of the aristocracy under the Restoration. His achievement can only be measured if one examines what is the area of prime concern to Balzac, the analysis of socioeconomic factors. The substantial evidence contained in the *Comédie humaine* is of particular interest in this respect in that it makes a useful contribution to the historical debate surrounding this particular question.

Balzac confirms, among other things, how the nobility took advantage of the system of royal patronage to secure prestigious and often lucrative appointments. The subject has, however, already been adequately considered by Donnard.[18] Moreover, 'la foire aux places' is not at the centre of Balzac's analysis of the economic realities affecting the Restoration nobility. For both these reasons therefore I do not propose to dwell on the question, except to point out that the traffic in royal appointments is amply illustrated in the *Comédie humaine*. Félix de Vandenesse and the comte de Fontaine are among those who benefit from royal largesse in the form of pensions and 'charges', which, Balzac hints, constituted a privilege especially favourable to the companions of the Ghent exile.

Balzac's main interest lies elsewhere, in his evaluation of the nobility's attempt to regain its important hold over 'la propriété foncière', which had been challenged by the Revolution and which it had been unable fully to reassert under the Empire. The fundamental question which is analysed in the *Comédie humaine* is the outcome of the struggle for the control of landed property in terms of the economic power of the aristocracy and its position as the dominant class in French society.

IV The Restoration and the Indemnity

(a) The Reign of Louis XVIII

In contrast with his treatment of the question under the Empire, in his account of how the émigrés fared under Louis XVIII, Balzac reverts to his normal procedure of preferring individual illustration to general statements. The result is that, instead of making unsupported and, in some cases, dubious claims, he suggests a number of interesting trends which, if not always capable of verification, nevertheless provide material for reflection.

The experience of Balzac's émigrés and their heirs under Louis XVIII is largely one of success, although it varies considerably in the extent and in the rapidity with which it is achieved. It has already been seen that émigré expectations of the first Restoration, chiefly concentrated, as they were, on the law of December 1814, authorising the return of their unsold property, are shown by Balzac to have been more handsomely fulfilled than the historical facts allow.

Balzac's description of the developments in the situation of the émigrés under Louis XVIII is notable for its variety of example and for its balance. Balzac makes it clear that some émigrés remained bitterly disappointed by what they saw as the failure of the new regime to meet their aspirations. The benefits of the royal gift are sometimes inadequate to satisfy émigré notions of income and status. The 'Liste Civile' does little to allay dissatisfaction, notably in the case of the vicomtesse de Grandlieu, while the 'charge de Grand-Ecuyer' accorded to the duc d'Hérouville fails to persuade him that he has been rescued from the indignity of inheriting only 15,000 fr. in 1819.

Other émigrés or their heirs have initial difficulties after 1815. Polydore de la Baudraye receives no immediate support for his claim to be reimbursed by his father's debtors, who had been generously subsidised by their fellow-émigré in exile. 'Après la mort de Napoléon', Balzac relates, 'il essaya de monnayer la poésie de son père', until finally, 'le vigneron perdit tant de temps à se faire reconnaître de messieurs les ducs de Navarreins et autres qu'il revint à Sancerre, appelé par ses chères vendanges, sans avoir rien obtenu que des offres de services.'[19] Polydore de la Baudraye quickly makes up for this preliminary frustration by exploiting the opportunities offered by a society which Balzac portrays as favouring the energetic, resourceful and adaptable émigré.[20]

Through the variety of examples which he gives, Balzac shows that the émigrés experienced mixed fortunes under Louis XVIII. Some of Balzac's émigrés regain little after 1815. The majority, however, achieve a substantial recovery in the period up to the indemnity. Like that of Napoleon, Louis XVIII's policy towards the émigrés, beyond the restitution of their unsold property, aimed at reintegrating them into French society. The *Comédie humaine* suggests that, in this respect, Louis XVIII furthered the work of Napoleon.[21] This can be seen from the careers under the Restoration of émigrés who had refused to compromise with Napoleon. The same émigrés who, like comte Ferraud and the comte de Fontaine, had resisted Napoleon's offers, eagerly respond to the similar initiatives of Louis XVIII.[22] In comte Ferraud's marriage to the presumed widow of Chabert there is, moreover, a hint of his latent pragmatism.

The extent to which the entire atmosphere of Louis XVIII's reign favoured émigré aspirations is indicated by an incident in *La Bourse*. The baron de Rouville had served as a naval captain on the side of the Republic and had been killed in battle fighting against the English. His widow had sought unsuccessfully to obtain a pension from the Republic and she encounters a similar refusal from the government of Louis XVIII. 'Lorsque, dernièrement', Mme Leseigneur relates, 'je la sollicitai de nouveau, le ministre me dit avec dureté que si le baron de Rouville eût émigré, je l'aurais conservé; qu'il serait sans doute aujourd'hui contre-amiral.'[23] The situation of Mme Leseigneur is ironically contrasted by Balzac with that of the comte de Kergarouët, the former commander of the baron de Rouville. 'Ses navigations terrestres', Balzac drily notes, 'à travers l'Allemagne et la Russie lui avaient été comptées comme des campagnes navales.'[24]

The resurgence of the émigrés under Louis XVIII is particularly marked in *Le Lys dans la vallée*. The Lenoncourts not only recover a large part of their property, but the duc de Lenoncourt resumes his position at court and is made a 'pair de France'. The recovery of the Mortsauf family is more modest and more discreet. M. de Mortsauf owes much to the counsel of his wife, who is determined not to ask too much of the Restoration. 'Nous profitons du bénéfice de lois', she declares, 'que nous n'avons ni provoquées ni demandées, mais nous ne serons ni mendiants ni avides.'[25] Mme de Mortsauf recognises that they are dependent on royal benevolence. During the Hundred Days the pension of 4,000 fr. granted to M. de Mortsauf during the first Restoration had been withdrawn. They had therefore counted on the Bourbons' return, for, as she tells Félix de Vandenesse, 'si le roi revient, *notre* pension reviendra'.[26] At the same time, Mme de Mortsauf insists on preserving the proud vestiges of independence. Accordingly, she induces M. de Mortsauf to refuse 'le commandement auquel il avait droit dans la Maison Rouge', preferring to rely on her father's influence at court and on Louis XVIII's promise to favour the career of her son Jacques.[27]

Balzac thus confirms that the progress made by the émigrés under Louis XVIII was facilitated by a combination of official legislation and royal patronage. At the same time, the *Comédie humaine* features another factor which contributed to the émigré recovery during this period, namely the use of litigation as a means of regaining property. In *Gobseck*, Derville wins three legal actions for the vicomtesse de Grandlieu. He recovers her shares in the Orleans canal and some property with which Napoleon had endowed various public institutions.[28] He also discovers an irregularity in the sale by the Republic of the Grandlieu house and legally enforces its return. Finally, Derville compels an almshouse by law to hand back land previously belonging to Mme de Grandlieu. 'Il chicana si bien je ne sais quel hospice', Balzac indicates, 'qu'il en obtint la restitution de la forêt de Liceney.'[29] The success of Derville's efforts on behalf of his émigré client is re-emphasised in *Splendeurs et misères des courtisanes*, where one is reminded that 'quoique revenue quasi ruinée de l'émigration, elle a retrouvé, par suite du dévouement d'un avoué, de Derville, une fortune assez considérable'.[30]

Le Colonel Chabert contains a similar instance of legal procedure designed to enable émigrés to recover their property. Again Derville is involved, and again there is reference to legal action being taken in order to force an almshouse to return property to an émigré. Derville's clerk Godeschal is preparing some papers 'dans l'affaire vicomtesse de Grandlieu contre Légion-d'Honneur' when the chief clerk Boucard gives him a document in connection with 'l'affaire Navarreins contre les hospices'.[31]

In referring to the claims of émigrés on property formerly theirs which had been acquired by almshouses, Balzac gives proof of a sense of history which is both authentic and at the same time incomplete. Gain's conclusion is that 'nous possédons peu d'exemples de biens d'émigrés affectés aux hospices et réclamés par l'ancien propriétaire ou ses descendants'.[32] In drawing attention to this rare type of émigré claim, Balzac is not concerned to indicate what the outcome of the conflict between the almshouses and the émigrés was. The historical niceties, in this instance, are not part of a general analysis from which important conclusions can be drawn. Balzac's brush-strokes need to be complemented by the fuller touches of historians. Gain found few cases of almshouses returning property to émigré litigants. 'Quant aux restitutions faites par les hospices', Gain concludes, 'nous n'en avons trouvé que peu de traces; hospices et bureaux de bienfaisance ont conservé leurs biens.'[33] In compelling an almshouse to hand back the property of Mme de Grandlieu, Derville was therefore pulling off something of a legal *coup*.

It would be churlish, however, to end this discussion of Balzac's account of the émigré recovery under Louis XVIII with a carping criticism of his treatment of what is, after all, a side issue. In what it reveals of the first decade of Restoration society, the *Comédie humaine* betrays both a detailed knowledge and a penetrating grasp. The study of the émigrés in particular enables one to appreciate the scope, precision and incisiveness of Balzac's approach.

Whatever tactical differences Balzac's émigrés may display in responding to Louis XVIII's gestures of reconciliation, with the exception of the marquis d'Esgrignon, who, in any case, is a 'faux émigré', they are all, in varying degrees, successful in re-establishing themselves in society. It is this achievement which is recognised by Mathias, the lawyer of Paul de Manerville, when he reviews the historical changes affecting the property of the aristocracy from the *ancien régime* to the present situation in 1822. 'Autrefois', Mathias concludes, 'les familles nobles avaient des fortunes inébranlables que les lois de la Révolution ont brisées et que le système actuel tend à reconstituer.'[34]

(b) The Indemnity

To return their unsold property to the émigrés was one thing. There remained the more difficult problem of finally determining the status of that part of their property which had passed into other hands as a consequence of the Revolution. Despite what the émigrés regained via repurchase, the bulk of their property was irretrievably lost. The Declaration of Saint-Ouen and the Charter had upheld the rights of the 'acquéreurs'. It was with a view to removing émigré resentment at this permanent loss that the idea of the indemnity arose.

In discussing the indemnity, Balzac concentrates on three main issues: the size of individual indemnities; the ways in which they were used by the émigrés; and the general part played by the indemnity in helping to restore the wealth, power and prestige of the émigrés. The majority of those who receive an indemnity in the *Comédie humaine* are the same émigrés whose exile and return has already been recorded by Balzac. All Balzac's 'indemnisés' are noble, whereas, in fact, the indemnity benefited other classes besides the aristocracy, just as the emigration initially attracted them.[35] Balzac thus encourages the myth of an aristocratic indemnity in the same way that he supports the notion of an aristocratic emigration.

Gain puts at some 25,000 the number who were indemnified out of a total estimate of 130,000 émigrés, or roughly one in five.[36] Normally, Balzac is careful to give a detailed account of the indemnification of individual émigrés. Very few of Balzac's émigrés are not mentioned as benefiting from the indemnity, and none actually refuses the indemnity.

The marquis d'Esgrignon stands in his usual maverick isolation. His ultra intransigence reinforced by his sense of outrage at being unjustly classified and treated as an émigré, he takes the total restitution of his property as a natural right, 'n'admettant même pas la pensée de cette indemnité qui préoccupa le ministère de monsieur de Villèle'.[37]

Gain's estimate of one indemnity for every five émigrés is grossly inflated by Balzac's approach. On the other hand, it is quite appropriate that, virtually without exception, Balzac's émigrés should be shown as accepting the indemnity. If by no means all of those indemnified were aristocrats, as Balzac's treatment suggests, few of those who were in fact refused the indemnity.

On the question of the size of individual indemnities, Balzac is not always clear. In *L'Interdiction*, for example, Popinot, who is intrigued as to the source of Mme d'Espard's annual income of 50,000 fr., tells her: 'Vous pouvez avoir des moyens fort légitimes, des grâces royales, quelques ressources dans les indemnités récemment accordées'.[38] The phrase 'quelques ressources' is inconclusive. Reflecting, as it does, Popinot's discreet curiosity, it suggests a modest amount. Otherwise, Balzac constantly emphasises the considerable financial benefits conferred by the indemnity.

Balzac's émigrés and their heirs expect much from the indemnity. Polydore de la Baudraye sees in it the possibility of recovering the money owed to him by the émigré debtors of his father. One therefore finds that 'le petit homme exigea de son Eminence (le Cardinal de Bourges) la promesse formelle de sa protection auprès du Président du Conseil, à cette fin de palper les créances sur les ducs de Navarreins et autres en saisissant leurs indemnités'.[39] In her first letter to Renée de Maucombe, Louise de Chaulieu refers to the impending indemnity law when she makes it known 'qu'on attendait une loi par laquelle on rendrait aux émigrés la valeur de leurs biens'. Her father, the duc de Chaulieu, is awaiting the indemnity in order to be able to restore his house. The amount which the duc de Chaulieu expects to receive from the indemnity is hinted at by his daughter who adds: 'Mon père recule la restauration de son hôtel jusqu'au moment de cette restitution. L'architecte du roi avait évalué la dépense à trois cent mille livres'.[40]

Emigré expectations of the indemnity are almost invariably fulfilled. The value of particular indemnities can best be judged by the use which is made of them by émigrés. The money often enables them to realise cherished projects. In some cases, it is used either to repurchase property or to make new acquisitions. In *Modeste Mignon*, there is a reference to 'Rosembray, terre récemment achetée par le duc de Verneuil avec la somme que lui donna sa part dans le milliard voté pour légitimer la vente des biens nationaux'.[41] The comte de Portenduère devotes the proceeds of his indemnity to repurchase. 'Député de l'Isère, il passait ses hivers à Paris où il avait racheté l'hôtel de Portenduère avec les indemnités que lui valait la loi Villèle.'[42]

Instead of using it for repurchase, some of Balzac's émigrés spend their indemnity on restoring or on furnishing and adorning their houses. In this respect, the duc de Chaulieu is joined by the father of the princesse de Cadignan. Ruined by the Revolution, he had recovered his fortune only to squander it. His indemnity is the object of the same irresponsible self-indulgence. 'Quand vint la loi d'indemnité', Balzac records, 'les sommes qu'il reçut furent absorbées par le luxe qu'il déploya dans son immense hôtel, le seul bien qu'il retrouva.'[43]

Above all, however, the émigrés in the *Comédie humaine* take advantage of the indemnity to reconstitute and consolidate their wealth. In this process, investment in state 'rentes' is a more attractive proposition than the repurchase or fresh acquisition of land. The house of the vicomtesse de Grandlieu is recovered for her, as we have seen, through the efforts of Derville. 'Ainsi rétablie par l'habileté du jeune avoué', it is revealed, 'la fortune de madame de Grandlieu s'était élevée à un revenu de soixante mille francs environ, lors de la loi sur l'indemnité qui lui avait rendu des sommes énormes.'[44] In *Le Bal de Sceaux*, the comte de Kergarouët is referred to as 'un vice-amiral, dont la fortune venait de s'augmenter d'une vingtaine de mille livres de rente par suite de la loi d'indemnité'.[44] Finally, Laurence de Cinq-Cygne, rather than seeking to buy back her provincial estates, prefers to live partly in the château de Cinq-Cygne on the small part of her property left over from the Revolution, and partly in the Parisian hôtel bought by her husband. At this point, Balzac makes it clear, 'sa fortune, augmentée par la loi sur les indemnités, allait à deux cent mille livres de rente, sans compter les traitements de son mari'.[46]

To what extent then does Balzac's discussion of the indemnity agree with the historical facts? First of all, Balzac exaggerates the value, both nominal and real, of the indemnity paid to individual émigrés. Even if one accepts that Balzac's émigrés fit naturally into the super-categories identified by Gain and that they therefore represent 'ces familles privilégiées auxquelles l'indemnité de 1825 avait rendu les moyens de réacquérir de la terre', a number of essential factors are left out of account by Balzac.[47] The number of Balzac's émigrés who qualify for the higher levels of the indemnity is clearly disproportionate. The average nominal value of the indemnity for the whole of France, it must be remembered, was a mere 1,377 fr.[48] Moreover, through a tendency to over-generalise in discussing the value of the indemnity, Balzac overlooks some of the finer points which have an important bearing on the issue.

Balzac's assumption that the financial expectations of the émigrés were fulfilled by the indemnity is refuted by Marion's observation that there was a discrepancy of 50 per cent between estimated émigré losses and the size of indemnities, a point which is also made by Gain when he draws attention to 'la différence de près de moitié entre le capital indemnisable et le capital indemnisé'.[49] When Louise de Chaulieu looks forward to the indemnity as a measure 'par laquelle on rendrait aux émigrés la valeur de leurs biens', she is therefore being naïvely optimistic.

Both Marion and Gain further point to a factor which was largely responsible for the uneven value of the indemnity. Article 2 of the indemnity had distinguished between property sold after 12 prairial, year III (26 May 1795) and property sold before that date. This distinction worked to the advantage of the post-prairial émigrés who more or less made up their entire losses. Many of their pre-prairial brethren, on the other hand, were less fortunate. Having lost their property mainly during the Terror, when depreciation of the currency had forced down the price of adjudication to absurdly low levels, they came off much worse than those who had emigrated later, since the amount paid in each case was based, not on the real value of the property at the time when it was sold, but on the actual price obtained.

If one recalls that the emigration reached its peak in 1793, well within the pre-prairial period, one can appreciate how, for the mass of émigrés, the indemnity brought little financial satisfaction. Balzac's émigrés, however, have every reason to be pleased with the indemnity. Gain's view is that 'le bénéfice des émigrés n'était sans doute que relatif, l'immense majorité d'entre eux, même les plus favorisés par rapport à leurs compagnons, n'ayant obtenu qu'un dédommagement inférieur à la valeur commerciale de leurs biens'.[50] This fact is entirely overlooked by Balzac.

If Balzac gives an exaggerated impression of the financial benefits which the émigrés derived from the indemnity, he is right in suggesting that they did not use it primarily to repurchase their property. On this question, Balzac is entirely in agreement with historians. Referring to the indemnity, Marion states that 'les cas où la famille anciennement propriétaire reprit alors possession de biens perdus par elle furent extrêmement rares'.[51] Gain's conclusion is identical, namely that 'le nombre des rachats a été faible'.[52]

Balzac does not, however, consider the reasons which might explain the reluctance of the émigrés to use the indemnity to buy back their property. Of the four reasons given by Gain, Balzac has nothing to say on any of them directly. He fails to bring out the essential point that the indemnity effectively gave final sanction to the transfer of property arising out of the Revolution and thereby enhanced the status of the 'acquéreurs' *vis-à-vis* the émigrés. Secondly, Balzac seems to attach no importance to the method of payment. The manner in which he refers to the size of specific indemnities suggests that, in some cases at least, Balzac is thinking in terms of a lump sum. The 300,000 fr. which the duc de Chaulieu is counting on in order to restore his house, to take just one example, could come only into this category. The indemnity was to be paid in five annual instalments. Provision was, however, made for conversion into a lump sum. Both methods were calculated to deter émigrés from using the indemnity to repurchase their property. The annuity method did not provide a ready source of capital, while the conversion option could be expected to incur a depreciation of 30-40 per cent after intermediaries had taken their share.

On the other hand, in relation to the two other points put forward by Gain, the *Comédie humaine* does offer evidence which is consistent with the conclusion of historians that the great majority of émigrés were unwilling to devote their indemnity to re-acquiring their property. A further reason for this lay in the drift of émigrés and their families and relatives from the country to the towns. In Laurence de Cinq-Cygne's preference for her Parisian 'hôtel' over her Gondreville estates, Balzac clearly illustrates this trend. Finally, the exodus of the émigrés towards the towns was accompanied by an expansion of industry, commerce and investment which, as Balzac convincingly shows, attracted émigrés and discouraged notions of repurchase.

Balzac's account of the indemnity is particularly important in that it contributes to the overall picture which emerges in the *Comédie humaine* of the measure of economic recovery which the émigrés had achieved by 1825. Although he correctly anticipates the conclusion of historians that the indemnity was not primarily used for repurchase, Balzac suggests that its economic benefits to the émigrés were far from negligible. Indeed, as we have seen, the impression which he gives of the value of individual indemnities is greatly exaggerated. Moreover, if repurchase is shown to be an exceptional product of the indemnity, Balzac indicates that it might enable an émigré to expand his existing property. With the help of 'l'indemnité qu'il reçut pour les biens de son père nationalement vendus en 1793', Polydore de la Baudraye buys the valuable Anzy estate to become 'enfin compté parmi les grands propriétaires du pays'.[53]

What Balzac has to say of the indemnity forms part of his assessment of the new economic relations of bourgeoisie and aristocracy, and more especially the émigrés, under the Restoration. On the one hand, Balzac accurately depicts the general shift of economic power from the aristocracy to the bourgeoisie and, in Grandet and du Bousquier, he provides two classic examples of bourgeois who become important landowners at the expense of the aristocracy under the Restoration. Yet the émigré aristocracy is revealed by Balzac to be anything but a spent force after 1815. While he overlooks the significance of repurchase as a factor in the émigré recovery both before and after 1815, Balzac overstates the contribution made to that recovery by restitution and by the indemnity.

The Restoration émigrés in the *Comédie humaine* do not resemble the category which is described by Marion in the following terms: 'Eux seuls, réduits à des débris de leur ancien patrimoine et aux faveurs d'un gouvernement éphémère, atteints en outre à chaque génération par le partage égal des biens, chose nouvelle pour eux, virent leur ancienne prépondérance sociale irrévocablement perdue'.[54] The evidence of Balzac's émigrés, on the contrary, is in line with the consensus of more recent historical research that the aristocracy as a whole, including the émigrés, had largely recovered its leading position as a landowning force under the Restoration, above all in terms of the highest concentrations of territorial wealth.[55] The view of an émigré aristocracy which, by the time of the indemnity, had been irrevocably deprived of its social supremacy, flies in the face of the historical facts. The monopoly of political power enjoyed by the Restoration aristocracy had its inevitable social expression. What Balzac confirms is the recovery of the economic basis on which the émigrés' share of that political and social authority necessarily rested.

The final questions which have to be examined are Balzac's view of the long-term effects of the indemnity and his overall verdict on the emigration. The right of the émigrés to recover their property is discussed on a number of occasions in the *Comédie humaine*. *L'Interdiction*, in particular, contains an interesting dialogue on the subject which offers a clue to Balzac's thinking. The justness of the émigrés' claims is queried by the marquis d'Espard. Himself an émigré, the marquis d'Espard is made to serve as the improbable spokesman of anti-émigré views purely for the purpose of ideological debate. So disturbed is he by the thought that his ancestors had originally acquired their property by violent means that he cannot rest until he has personally compensated the descendants of the family concerned.[56] 'Politiquement parlant', he asks, 'les émigrés, qui réclament contre les confiscations révolutionnaires, doivent-ils garder encore des biens qui sont le fruit de confiscations obtenues par des crimes?' The question posed by the marquis d'Espard is answered by Popinot, who argues: 'Si les gens qui possèdent des biens confisqués de quelque manière que ce soit, même par des manoeuvres perfides, étaient, après cent-cinquante ans, obligés à des restitutions, il se trouverait en France peu de propriétaires légitimes'.[57]

In this statement of Popinot can be detected Balzac's own viewpoint. The debate is relevant less to the legitimacy of the émigrés' original acquisitions than to the more immediate issue of the transfer of émigré property by the Revolution into the hands of a new category of 'acquéreurs'. Balzac is in effect arguing that if, however they may have been brought about, historical changes become firmly rooted in society, it is pointless to try to reverse them. The reality, however unpalatable, must be accepted and acted upon. It is this attitude which governs Balzac's reaction to the continuing conflict of 'acquéreurs' and émigrés.[58]

Balzac's *realpolitik* in relation to the property changes initiated by the Revolution is voiced by Blondet in *Les Paysans*. Blondet describes the peasants' conviction that the Revolution has invested them with inalienable property rights as 'une idée à laquelle 1814 a touché malheureusement et que la monarchie doit regarder comme sacrée'.[59] For Balzac, a strong monarchy and a unified nation were inseparable. He therefore saw the indemnity as the logical culmination of the Charter, as a measure which, by acknowledging an inescapable reality, promoted social harmony at the same time that it strengthened the monarchy. The indemnity thus marked the final gesture in a regrettable but irreversible process of historical change. It represented for Balzac a responsible act of statesmanship, 'qui devait consolider le trône en éteignant la fatale distinction, maintenue alors malgré les lois, entre les propriétés'.[60]

The interrelationship of aristocracy, emigration and counter-revolution constitutes one of the major historical themes of the *Comédie humaine*. In a number of respects, Balzac's treatment lacks proportion. The exclusively aristocratic character of Balzac's émigrés has already been noted. Secondly, the percentage of émigrés among Balzac's nobles is nearer to 50 per cent than to the five per cent given by Greer for the class as a whole. Thirdly, by presenting most of his émigrés as participants in armed counter-revolution, Balzac gives a false impression of the military strength of the émigrés. Vidalenc's estimate is that 'sauf de juillet à septembre 1792, le nombre des émigrés français présents sous les drapeaux, quels qu'ils fussent, sauf le drapeau tricolore, ne dépassa guère cinq mille hommes'.[61]

Vidalenc also makes the point that both supporters and opponents of the emigration had a vested interest in inflating émigré numbers. It was a tendency, he suggests, which was not confined to those who had a purely political axe to grind. 'La littérature', Vidalenc maintains, 'devait préférer, tout comme la propagande, l'aspect émouvant ou ridicule, sympathique ou inquiétant, de l'émigré défenseur obstiné, permanent, inébranlable, du trône des fils de Saint-Louis.'[62] Among French writers, none succumbed more readily to the temptation than Balzac. Equally, none matched Balzac in his understanding of the movement of contemporary history and his ability to convey the sense of that movement through his account of the emigration.

Where then does Balzac finally stand in relation to the emigration? Bernard Guyon has rightly stressed Balzac's early antipathy to the émigrés and suggested that, together with other remnants of his liberal outlook, this hostility survived Balzac's rejection of liberalism.[63] In *Les Chouans, Une Ténébreuse Affaire* and *Le Lys dans la vallée* especially, Balzac's condemnation of the émigrés is unambiguous. At times, Balzac's attitude is marked by a note of parvenu condescension. 'A l'étranger', Balzac exclaims via Herrera in *Illusions Perdues*, 'l'aristocratie, qui trône aujourd'hui dans son faubourg Saint-Germain, a fait pis: elle a été usurière, elle a été marchande, elle a fait des petits pâtés, elle a été cuisinière, fermière, gardeuse de moutons.'[64]

The émigrés are criticised by Balzac for two reasons. First, the émigrés' 'revanchiste' posture is seen as posing a threat to social order and to national unity. The second element in Balzac's critique concerns the political capacity of the aristocracy. Balzac frequently draws attention to the consequences of émigré inflexibility as proof of the failure of the aristocracy to make an intelligent appraisal of its historical role. Its inability to adapt to changing circumstances was a clear indication for Balzac that the aristocracy had shown itself incapable of ensuring effective government in a class-based society.

In the very works, however, in which Balzac attacks the émigrés most fiercely, a contrasting note is sounded. *Les Chouans* pays tribute to their disinterested idealism as well as denouncing the émigrés for fomenting civil war. At the same time that it is critical of those who collaborate with émigrés from within France, *Une Ténébreuse Affaire* does justice to the noble integrity of Laurence de Cinq-Cygne. Finally, in *Le Lys dans la vallée* two distinct attitudes are in evidence. On the one hand, M. de Mortsauf embodies all the worst features of the unrepentant émigré, above all his narrow prejudices and his total unadaptability.[65] On the other hand, Félix de Vandenesse displays in his attitude towards M. de Mortsauf a sympathetic understanding of the situation of the émigrés which he sums up by confessing: 'Je n'ai jamais senti dans mon coeur de fiel pour l'émigré, . . . je sympathise trop avec les exilés pour pouvoir les juger'.[66]

Balzac's view of the émigrés was more finely balanced than that of Félix de Vandenesse. In Balzac, sympathy coexisted with disapproval, hostility with commiseration. Alongside the harsh criticism of the émigrés, the *Comédie humaine* reveals a genuine, if more discreet admiration, for example, for 'le caractère loyal et franc des vieux émigrés'.[67] The duc and duchesse de Grandlieu are praised for 'la noblesse des maîtres dont la grande tenue aristocratique avait fini par faire oublier leur servage napoléonien'.[68] Balzac's ambivalence towards the émigrés persisted to the end. The condemnation outweighed the compassion, yet the compassion was never silenced. When, well on into the July Monarchy, doctor Poulain is tempted to emigrate, Balzac, his mind no doubt on earlier events, says his final word on the émigrés. 'Quitter la France est, pour un Français, une situation funèbre.'[69] Behind this statement lies the important historical lesson which is demonstrated throughout the *Comédie humaine*. If, by 1846, when *Le Cousin Pons* was written, the damage which the emigration had inflicted on France was now repaired, that suffered by the émigrés had proved fatal to the authority of the class to which they belonged.

V Emigrés versus Rebels

The intriguing issue which remains to be considered is Balzac's judgement of the émigrés, especially in relation to those nobles who, instead of emigrating, had opted for internal rebellion.[70] The common factor which underlies Balzac's response to the emigration is his condemnation of all the forces that made for a divided France. Thus, although he pays tribute in *Les Chouans* to the heroic idealism shown on both sides, he denounces the Chouan rebellion, in which émigrés like Montauran are involved, as contributing to 'ces temps de triste mémoire où la discorde civile avait renversé les institutions les plus saintes'.[71]

Armed rebellion, from whatever quarter and with whatever motive,

Balzac was convinced, was not the answer and could only make France's situation more tragic. At the same time, one can detect a gradation in Balzac's condemnation of counter-revolutionary violence. The more the émigrés are involved with the agents of foreign intervention, the fiercer Balzac's denunciation becomes. Those serving with Condé's army, such as M. de Mortsauf and the young émigrés in *Une Ténébreuse Affaire*, together with those who co-operate with them inside France in the manner of Laurence de Cinq-Cygne, are more strongly condemned than the nobles who, like the marquis d'Esgrignon and the comte de Fontaine, combat the Revolution from within France independently of foreign help. It is as if mere contact with foreign soil and with foreign rulers hostile to France were enough to raise the level of Balzac's indignation.

Balzac's most severe criticism is directed at those émigrés who unashamedly seek the help of foreign arms in order to crush the Revolution. The point is underlined most effectively by émigrés themselves. M. de Mortsauf draws the line at serving a foreign power. 'Ses espérances', Balzac reveals, 'toujours appointées au lendemain, et peut-être aussi l'honneur, l'empêchèrent de se mettre au service des puissances étrangères.'[72] Other émigrés, notably the comte de Kergarouët and the vicomte de Troisville, have no such scruples, the latter having been 'au service de la Russie depuis 1789'.[73] The chevalier du Halga draws the line more finely than M. de Mortsauf. Unlike the comte de Kergarouët and the vicomte de Troisville, he makes it clear that he was prepared to serve in the Russian armed forces only 'jusqu'au jour où l'empereur Alexandre voulut l'employer contre la France'.[74] The tradition of French émigrés serving in the armed forces of Russia dated from before the Revolution. As Vidalenc observes, 'Certains émigrés demeurèrent à leur tour dans l'armée russe en y poursuivant une carrière normale, jusqu'en 1814 ou plus tard'. While one accepts Vidalenc's point that the behaviour of such émigrés was the expression 'moins d'une optique que d'une curiosité, associée à tel ou tel souverain ou général', it is clear that the Revolution added a powerful political surcharge to any picaresque disposition to emigrate.[75]

The patriotic scruples of the majority of Balzac's émigrés who are engaged in violent counter-revolution are expressed by Montauran when he asks Hulot to convey his last wishes to his younger brother exiled in London. His request is that his brother should remain in the service of the king, but that he should never bear arms against France. This is a different Montauran from the émigré who had been sent by Pitt and the princes to give leadership to the Chouan and Vendée uprisings.

His changed outlook is partly the result of Marie de Verneuil's admonishing him with the words: 'Mais laissez-moi penser que vous êtes le seul noble qui fasse son devoir en attaquant la France avec des Français, et non à l'aide de l'étranger'.[76] However, Montauran is not simply responding to Mlle de Verneuil's conviction that he should fight the Revolution without enlisting foreign help. His final gesture reflects Balzac's view that armed rebellion of any kind, whether conducted from inside France or from abroad, whether undertaken independently or with foreign assistance, was never justified and essentially unpatriotic.

The point of view of the émigrés is frequently compared by Balzac with that of the non-émigré rebels. The rebel case is stated by the marquis d'Esgrignon, who bitterly resents what he regards as the preferential treatment given by the Restoration to the émigrés. 'Vraiment', he protests, 'on ne pense pas plus à nous que si nous n'existions pas', and then he adds: 'Enfin nous sommes quelque chose de mieux que les Troisville, et voici deux Troisville nommés pairs de France, un autre est député de la Noblesse'.[77]

Balzac has an undeniable sympathy for the plight of the marquis d'Esgrignon. 'En 1822', he insists, 'malgré les bénéfices que la Restauration apportait aux émigrés, la fortune du marquis d'Esgrignon n'avait pas augmenté.' 'De tous les nobles atteints par les lois révolutionnaires', Balzac claims, 'aucun ne fut plus maltraité.'[78] The adverse situation of the marquis d'Esgrignon was not principally caused, however, by deliberate discrimination on the part of the Restoration government. It arose largely from a simple economic fact. The marquis d'Esgrignon's income before the Revolution was derived almost entirely from feudal dues based on 'la mouvance de ses fiefs'.[79] When feudal dues were abolished by the Revolution, Balzac alleges, nobles in this position were totally ruined since, having so little property which could be confiscated or sold, they did not stand to gain from the reparatory measures of 1814 and 1825. In Balzac's words, 'l'ordonnance par laquelle Louis XVIII restitua les biens non vendus aux Emigrés ne pouvait leur rien rendre; et plus tard, la loi sur l'indemnité ne devait pas les indemniser'.[80]

Although most nobles drew the bulk of their income from 'rentes' and not from feudal dues, Balzac is accurate in emphasising the difficulties of this important minority of aristocrats. In so doing, he suggests another factor which reinforces the marquis d'Esgrignon's fierce sense of independence. As a 'faux émigré' whose income came overwhelmingly from feudal dues, the marquis d'Esgrignon got the worst of both worlds. This helps to explain his insistence on his rebel status and his sense of grievance which is directed at the Restoration. The experience of the duc de Navarreins is similar to that of the marquis d'Esgrignon. He also suffers from the abolition of 'la mouvance des fiefs'. His Montégnac estates, 'cette seigneurie, jadis une des plus riches mouvances du royaume', now only yield him 15,000 fr. a year.[81] There is this important difference, however, that those same estates, largely made up of forest-land, had been exempted from sale by the Revolution and thus reverted to the duc de Navarreins in 1814.

Important though dependence on feudal dues was, it need not be, as Balzac demonstrates, an unfailing cause of ruin for a noble, whether he were a rebel or an émigré. The duc de Grandlieu draws his income mainly from feudal dues, yet he survives the revolutionary crisis. Begun under the Empire, his recovery is consolidated during the Restoration. The success or failure of the desire of nobles to reintegrate themselves into society is determined by the extent to which they were prepared to modify their opposition to the changes which the Revolution had made at their expense. The straitened circumstances of the marquis d'Esgrignon are the result of his refusal to accept anything short of total restitution, which, in his case, would have involved the restoration of feudal dues. The happier experience of other nobles, émigrés and rebels alike, is explained by their readiness to come to terms either with Napoleon or with the Restoration, or with both.

In the final analysis, the question raised by the marquis d'Esgrignon when he complains that the émigrés were more favourably treated by the Restoration than the rebels who did not emigrate is only of marginal interest. Some of the evidence in the *Comédie humaine* may be taken as supporting such a claim. In contrast with the marquis d'Esgrignon, the comte de Fontaine, whose rebel pride had been equally uncompromising, abruptly changes course during the Hundred Days.[82] Like the marquis d'Esgrignon, the comte de Fontaine believes that 'les compagnons de l'exil étaient plus en faveur que les braves qui, jadis, avaient protesté, les armes à la main, contre l'établissement de la république'.[83] Instead of persisting in his intransigence, however, the comte de Fontaine makes a calculated decision to accompany Louis XVIII in his second exile. The comte de Fontaine plays Philinte to the marquis d'Esgrignon's Alceste to his decided advantage, and he and his family are rewarded, in the form of important posts and advantageous marriages, by a grateful Louis XVIII on his return. On the other hand, rebel successes are accompanied by émigré disappointments. The comte de Fontaine does better out of the Restoration because of his shrewder response to the new situation. The rebels tend to be extremist in their outlook compared with the émigrés, and their distress is proportionate to the tenacity with which they hold to their extremism. Balzac is content to express sympathy with the marquis d'Esgrignon's predicament without, however, taking sides in what could only be a sterile debate. The important fact which emerges from the discussion is that both an émigré like the duc d'Hérouville and a rebel such as the comte de Fontaine succeed only by making a radical departure from the rigid norms of their caste in a society in which the aristocracy had to adapt in order to survive.

VI The 'Droit d'aînesse' and the 'Majorat'

The lasting consequences of the abolition of the 'droit d'aînesse' are examined by Balzac in relation both to the Empire and to the Restoration.[84] If the subject of the 'droit d'aînesse' is given greater prominence in the *Comédie humaine* than the role of the 'majorat' with which it was linked, this can be explained in terms of its important place in Balzac's sociopolitical philosophy.[85] This does not mean however that the 'majorat' receives negligible treatment in Balzac's works. Indeed it figures more significantly than a recent article on the question would suggest and deserves full and careful analysis, especially in view of its direct bearing on the economic situation of the aristocracy under the Restoration.[86]

From the publication of the 1824 'brochure', Balzac advocated the restoration of the 'droit d'aînesse' with a stubborn conviction at a time when it had manifestly ceased to be a practical reality.[87] Its spokesmen in the *Comédie humaine* are numerous and varied, and the case for it is argued with particular force in *Louis Lambert, Le Curé de village* and *Mémoires de deux jeunes mariées*. Balzac deplored the abolition of the 'droit d'aînesse' from every point of view, economic, sociopolitical and moral. On the economic level, he considered that it had contributed, along with the sale of 'biens nationaux', to a disastrous process of 'morcellement'. An efficient agriculture, Balzac believed, was only possible on the basis of large concentrations of land. This, in turn, according to Balzac, had given a sharp impetus to material self-interest, to an individualism which had seriously undermined the traditional values of religion, the family and the spirit of disinterested loyalty and service to the nation. Finally, the abolition of the 'droit d'aînesse' was denounced by Balzac as having weakened the authority of the aristocracy which, ideally constituted, represented, in his view, the guarantee of a prosperous agriculture, the repository of moral values and the foundation of a unified and hierarchical social order under a legitimist monarchy.

Where the 'majorat' is concerned, Balzac's attitude is not explicitly defined as it is in the case of the 'droit d'aînesse'. He simply gives examples of its occurrence in such a way as to suggest that he regarded the 'majorat' as a useful device in countering the effects of 'morcellement', and as contributing towards the economic recovery of the aristocracy, but not to be compared with what could only be achieved by restoring the 'droit d'aînesse'.

Designed in its feudal origins to ensure 'l'indivisibilité du fief' by providing for the inheritance by the eldest son of the preponderant share of the family wealth, the 'droit d'aînesse' had been abolished by the laws of the 'Constituante' of March 1790 and April 1791, the latter having established the principle of the absolute equality of heirs. Unwilling to be identified with the restoration of an *ancien régime* institution, Napoleon ratified the abolition of the 'droit d'aînesse' in the 'Code Civil'. Napoleon's commitment to equality had nothing to do with social or economic democracy. Anxious to perpetuate titles for the imperial nobility, Napoleon reintroduced the 'majorat' by the decrees of August 1806 and March 1808.

The Restoration showed a similar disinclination to restore the more flagrant type of *ancien régime* privilege based on birth and, like Napoleon, it rejected the idea of a return to the 'droit d'aînesse' while retaining the 'majorat'.[88] The extensive use made of the 'majorat' by the aristocracy under the Restoration is confirmed by Balzac. In the range of examples which he discusses, Balzac not only displays a thorough understanding of the legal complexities involved, at the same time he reveals an awareness of the part played by the 'majorat' in the aristocracy's attempt to secure its landed wealth and to strengthen its economic power generally.

While underlining this basic economic motive, the variety of separate cases which Balzac examines takes account of a remarkable number of individual factors. Balzac demonstrates the greater diversity with which the 'majorat' was used for the benefit of the Restoration aristocracy than had been the case with the imperial nobility. For example, the dowry of his sister Louise is sacrificed to create a 'majorat' of 40,000 fr. for the marquis de Chaulieu. He is thus able to marry Madeleine de Mortsauf and later, under the July Monarchy, in consequence of his marriage, to inherit the title of his wife's maternal grandfather, the duc de Lenoncourt-Givry.

Jean de Maucombe receives on his majority 'un avancement d'hoirie' equivalent to one-third of the family fortune as a means of circumventing 'l'infâme code civil du sieur Buonaparte'.[89] In this case and that concerning the marquis de Chaulieu the interests of the daughter are sacrificed to those of the son. One is thus reminded that Balzac's advocacy of the restoration of the 'droit d'aînesse' was accompanied by his call for 'l'exhérédation des femmes', in the cause of which he recruited some improbable defenders in the *Comédie humaine*, not least the impassioned voice of Julie d'Aiglemont.

Another younger son who gains, this time fortuitously, from a 'majorat' is Maximilien de Longueville. Having given up his share of the family inheritance so that his elder brother Auguste can form a 'majorat', he has the singular mixed fortune of becoming 'vicomte et pair', as well as inheriting the family wealth, on the death of his father and brother within the space of the same year.

In the absence of a male heir, Balzac shows how a 'majorat' might benefit a son-in-law. This happens with Ernest de la Brière. On his marriage to Modeste Mignon, the 'terre de la Bastie' is reconstituted on behalf of his father-in-law, Charles Mignon. The value of 100,000 fr. in 'rentes' which it represents provides the 'majorat' which enables Ernest to call himself vicomte de la Bastie with the right to inherit his father-in-law's title.

Alternatively, a 'majorat' might be set up in anticipation of a male heir. It is for this reason that Polydore de la Baudraye creates a 'majorat' in December 1829. The ironic outcome in this case is that, although his marriage remains childless, the original 'majorat' has to be invoked to allow the illegitimate son his wife has by Lousteau to inherit the family title without complications. *Ancien régime* practices, Balzac reveals, could still prove useful even under the July Monarchy.[90]

The 'majorat', in addition, served two new important purposes under the Restoration, both of which are well illustrated in the *Comédie humaine*. They were used to create new titles and to provide the basis for nomination to the peerage. The 'parvenu' de Chessel, born Durand, is made 'comte' by Louis XVIII on the strength of a 'majorat'. The ex-'demi-solde' and Bonapartist conspirator Philippe Bridau becomes 'comte de Brambourg', taking his title from the name of the estate which embodied the necessary 'majorat'.

The king's right to appoint peers to the new 'Chambre des pairs' had been affirmed in the Charter and the hereditary peerage created by an ordinance in August of the following year. Initially, the 'majorat' had been made a requirement of the peerage, but eventually the condition was dropped in order to overcome the financial difficulty which it posed. Balzac gives several instances of the vital role played by the 'majorat' in the constitution of the peerage of the Restoration. In urging Paul de Manerville to form a 'majorat', Mathias is prompted by three considerations. First, he is concerned that his client should have maximum legal guarantees *vis-à-vis* the family of his wife-to-be, the Evangélistas. He also sees in the 'majorat' in general a measure which will help reverse the fragmentation of aristocratic property resulting from the Revolution. Finally, he calculates that the comte de Manerville's chances of a peerage are certain to be improved by the formation of a 'majorat', 'fondation qui, certes, militera dans l'esprit du gouvernement actuel pour la nomination de mon client, au moment d'une fournée'.[91] There are other similar examples. Laurence de Cinq-Cygne's Paris house is bought for her by her husband with the 'majorat' which he has formed with a view to the peerage, 'compris dans le majorat considérable institué pour l'entretien de sa pairie'.[92] The comte de Soulanges equally is anxious to increase his wealth 'pour pouvoir faire de Soulanges le majorat de sa pairie'.[93]

Balzac's references to the 'majorat' under the Restoration are an excellent example of the value and limitations of his historical testimony. On the one hand, finer distinctions are overlooked. No account is taken, for example, of the effect of Charles X's ordinance of February 1824, which made the transmission of hereditary titles conditional on the creation of a 'majorat'. The result was a sudden upsurge in the constitution of 'majorats', so that, as Perrod puts it: 'On ne demandait pas des titres pour constituer des majorats: on constituait des majorats afin d'obtenir des titres'.[94] The numerous examples which Balzac gives are taken at random. In some cases, no precise date is mentioned. Altogether they present no pattern which reflects the impact of the 1824 ordinance.

However, if some of the historical nuances are neglected, Balzac succeeds in his general purpose, which is to indicate the contribution made by the 'majorat' to the economic recovery of the aristocracy under the Restoration. In this sense the contrast between the political pamphleteer and the objective historian is illuminating. Balzac's campaign for the restoration of the 'droit d'aînesse' had already been revealed as an anachronistic futility when Villèle's proposal for its reintroduction was rejected by the 'Chambre des pairs' in 1826.[95] Villèle's argument that the aristocracy had not taken advantage of the provision in the 'Code Civil' for the 'quotité disponible' to be increased in favour of any one of the children of a family fell on largely deaf ears. Speaking for the majority of peers, the duc de Broglie denounced

Villèle's scheme as counter-revolutionary, as seeking to restore inequality and privilege.

It was not that the aristocracy had overnight become ardent defenders of the Revolution. Villèle's appeal was entirely misplaced and ignored a vital fact which allowed the peers to pose as the guardians of revolutionary change while upholding their landowning interests. Secure in their 'majorats', the nobility had no need to resurrect such an expression of *ancien régime* privilege as the 'droit d'aînesse', the more so as it stood no chance of serving their objective needs. The Restoration aristocracy showed a more intelligent awareness of the realities of its economic position than Balzac, or, for that matter, Villèle, purported to do on its behalf. The fulfilment of Rigou's prediction: 'Les majorats tomberont' was not long delayed.[96] Meanwhile, despite Balzac's strident pleading for the restoration of the 'droit d'aînesse', the lesson which emerges in the *Comédie humaine* is that the aristocracy was right in seeing in the 'majorat' the most that they could hope for, as the measure most calculated to consolidate individual fortunes and to perpetuate 'la grande propriété'.

Finally, the range of Balzac's characters who benefit from the creation of 'majorats' under the Restoration provides an important social pointer. Including, as they do, representatives of revived noble families, a bourgeois parvenu and a former champion of Bonapartism, they are not only a tribute to the resourcefulness of Balzac's historical imagination. Their experience confirms that the attempt to strengthen the power of the landed aristocracy through the device of the 'majorat' had only the limited success for which it was realistically intended. The 'majorat', as Balzac shows, benefited not merely the aristocracy, it also served the interests of a new generation whose fathers had had neither titles nor land before the Revolution.

VII 'La Propriété Foncière' – Gains and Losses

When one tries to evaluate Balzac's study of the Restoration aristocracy, one encounters two serious difficulties. First, there is the problem of the historical uncertainty which surrounds some of the basic issues of post-revolutionary society. To some extent one is still dealing with guesswork. Lamenting the fragmentary nature of the evidence and the incomplete state of research on the distribution of land before and particularly after the Revolution, Lefebvre declines to put a figure on the proportion of land owned by the nobility in 1789.[97]

Other historians have given estimates varying from 16 per cent to 25 per cent.[98] The whole question remains clouded with uncertainty. In particular, the émigré share of the total amount of land belonging to the nobility appears to be an unresolved mystery. It seems safe, however, to assume that the émigrés owned a disproportionate amount of land relative to their numbers. If the claim that 'the large proprietors were always among the fugitives' seems exaggerated, it nevertheless indicates an important tendency which is reflected in the *Comédie humaine*.[99] At the same time, M. d'Hauteserre, of whom Balzac reveals that 'ses trois mille livres de rentes viagères, sa seule ressource, l'avaient empêché d'émigrer', lends credence to the commonly accepted view of historians that the poorer nobles were the least likely to emigrate.[100]

Lefebvre queries whether the sale of émigré property was the most important factor which helped to undermine the landed wealth of the nobility. 'On peut même se demander', Lefebvre remarks, 'si c'est la vente des biens d'émigrés qui a porté le coup le plus rude à la richesse foncière de l'ancienne noblesse. La perte des droits féodaux, le malheur des temps et particulièrement l'effondrement de l'assignat ont ruiné plus d'une famille noble et l'ont obligée à vendre ses biens.'[101]

The second problem in assessing Balzac's account of the Restoration aristocracy arises from the disproportionate character of Balzac's treatment. Whereas both émigrés and rebels form important categories of nobility in the *Comédie humaine*, an obvious gap exists as far as Balzac's general picture of the Restoration aristocracy is concerned. If 95 per cent of the nobility did not emigrate, equally the majority of those who chose to remain in France did not engage in armed rebellion. The number of Balzac's rebels is as disproportionately large as that of his émigrés. The average noble whom Balzac specifically identifies as having neither emigrated nor become a rebel is a relative rarity in the *Comédie humaine*. A third distorting factor is thus added. As well as encouraging the myths of an aristocratic emigration and an émigré aristocracy, Balzac exaggerates the legend of a rebel resistance.

What then does Balzac suggest was the result of the efforts made by the Restoration aristocracy to improve on the position in which it found itself in 1815, bearing in mind the limited extent of the recovery which it had achieved thus far in relation to the losses suffered in the Revolution? In particular, what does Balzac indicate happened to the aristocracy's share of landed property under the Restoration?

Balzac gives numerous examples which underline the tendency within the aristocracy further to relinquish its land under the Restoration. This is indicated, for instance, by Charles de Vandenesse's scheme for selling the family estates. The project is successfully opposed in a legal action by his brother Félix and the aristocracy thus prevented from contributing to the 'morcellement' which Balzac saw as disastrously weakening its economic authority.

Montcornet's sale of les Aigues, which has been seen as reflecting the same trend, poses the class question in a particularly interesting light. Although not a Marxist himself, Thierry Bodin accepts the Marxist interpretation of the social conflict depicted in *Les Paysans*, in keeping with Balzac's prediction in the 'dédicace'. 'Le prolétariat est manoeuvré par la bourgeoisie contre l'aristocratie', Bodin recognises, 'au seul bénéfice du Capitalisme montant.'[102] Montcornet, however, is not a true aristocrat at all, but, as Bodin himself points out, a 'parvenu', the son of an artisan, and an individual who has been given his chance by the Revolution and Empire. In reality, Montcornet represents the first generation of the revolutionary bourgeoisie who rose from the 'couches populaires'. His ascension accelerated by military service under Napoleon, he is then ennobled by Louis XVIII. The class struggle which is waged in *Les Paysans*, at the same time that it features the growing antagonism of bourgeoisie and peasantry, also opposes conflicting factions within the revolutionary bourgeoisie for control of the important share of landed property which it now possessed.

However, the *Comédie humaine* includes a sufficient number of clear-cut cases of the sale of aristocratic property under the Restoration for it to emerge as a significant factor affecting the overall economic status of the aristocracy. Balzac is careful to make clear which sections of society benefit from these sales. Only in one instance is the purchaser unspecified. The exception concerns the marquis de Valentin, whose debts compel him to sell the last piece of land remaining in his possession, the island on which his wife is buried. It is equally rare that the relinquishment of property benefits an institution rather than an individual. There are no other examples to match the decision of the comtesse de Merret to leave her entire wealth and property to 'l'hôpital de Vendôme'.

Of the remaining sales of aristocratic estates, two are concerned with transfers within the nobility itself. Ruined by the extravagance of the duchesse de Maufrigneuse, the d'Uxelles family is forced to sell the estate and fief of Anzy in 1827 for 400,000 fr. to Polydore de la Baudraye. The 'château de Rosembray', belonging to the duc de Marigny, is acquired by the duc de Verneuil. Essentially, however, such sales are made to bourgeois purchasers. Du Bousquier becomes the richest landowner in the Orne department to the detriment of the surrounding aristocracy. The estates of the marquis de Rouvre are under increasing threat from their owner's squandering of a vast fortune, although the marquis de Rouvre manages to hold out until 1836 when he sells them to Minoret-Levrault. The marquis de Froidfond accepts Grandet's offer of ready cash in 1818 for estates worth three million, which Grandet acquires at well below their real value. It is Gaubertin who acquires the lion's share of les Aigues. Lastly, fearing that an impending revolution will have further serious consequences for the landowning nobility, the duc de Navarreins sells his Montégnac estates for 500,000 fr. to the banker Graslin in 1829. As with Grandet, the decisive factor in Graslin's case is that he is 'capable de payer immédiatement une terre considérable'.[103]

The question whether, under the Restoration, the nobility regained more land than they lost is one on which, for want of conclusive evidence, historians have been reluctant to pronounce. In showing how personal factors reinforce the effect of objective economic pressures, the *Comédie humaine* points to a further shift of landed property from the aristocracy to the bourgeoisie under the Restoration. As the references to the indemnity show, aristocratic gains tended to be in capital assets rather than in land. The Restoration is thus confirmed by Balzac as a period which underlines a fundamental reality of postrevolutionary society, namely that 'le mouvement ascensionnel de l'argent' was inseparable from 'le mouvement descendant de la propriété foncière'.[104]

Where then does Balzac finally stand in relation to the views of historians concerning the composition of 'la propriété foncière' under the Restoration? The question is one which has been the subject of a prolific debate in the past decade or so. The drain of land from the nobility continued, Balzac suggests, but it was not part of a fatal process in the way that Forster insists. Balzac's position is more finely balanced, and the *Comédie humaine* provides some interesting pointers in this important area.

The survival of the aristocracy as a potent landowning force after 1815 has been stressed by various historians. 'La grande propriété foncière', Soboul concludes, 'demeura essentiellement aristocratique.'[105] It is here that the key to the whole question lies. How big is 'grande'? Whereas Forster defines a 'grand propriétaire' as someone owning more than 100 acres, the examples which Soboul quotes for the Consulate, based on the twelve 'plus imposés' of each department, clearly imply a 'super-grande' category.[106]

The combined effect of restitutions, repurchase and fresh acquisitions, reinforced by the indemnity and the 'majorat', is to leave Balzac's aristocracy well short of realising the territorial ambitions which it had expected to be satisfied by the return of the Bourbons. Disgruntled émigrés and ruined, even more resentful rebels are familiar figures among the Restoration aristocracy in the *Comédie humaine*. If Balzac is accurate in depicting the general decline in the aristocracy's share of landed property, he leaves no doubt, however, as to the survival of the powerful landowning interests of the wealthiest and most influential section of the aristocracy, of 'la haute aristocratie terrienne'. The *Comédie humaine* offers, in particular, considerable evidence of income from land which supports the notion that this particular category of nobility retained its important hold on 'la grande propriété foncière' under the Restoration.

The significance of Balzac's indications of aristocratic income from land becomes clear when one compares them with the figures recently given by Forster. What Forster does is to take the Toulousain nobility as his model and to assess the average income in 1830 in relation to that of 1789. Emphasising that the nobility of Toulouse withstood the revolutionary changes in landownership more successfully than their counterparts in other regions, Forster shows that, in 1789, the average income of a Toulouse noble was 8,000 'livres', of which 5,000 came from land. By 1830, the respective figures had fallen to 5,200 and 4,000.[107]

In terms of Forster's claims, Balzac confirms the privileged position of the Parisian 'grandes familles'. Where the provincial nobility is concerned, however, the picture presented by the *Comédie humaine* is more complex and challenging. A number of Balzac's provincial nobles are undoubtedly poor. One has only to think of the Rastignac family and the chevalier de Valois. Yet they were already poor before the Revolution, their decision not to emigrate presumably being dictated, as in the case of M. d'Hauteserre, by their limited resources.

Otherwise, the landed income of Balzac's provincial nobility is high. His émigrés, in particular, do well by Toulouse comparisons: 30,000 fr. is a common figure. Anything approaching Forster's average of 4,000 'livres' is exceptional. The duc d'Hérouville has 15,000. Laurence de Cinq-Cygne derives 12,000 from her estates, M. de Mortsauf's two newly bought farms earn him 9,000 fr. Balzac clearly gives an inflated impression of the average income gained from land by the nobility under the Restoration. A more accurate picture emerges in *Ursule Mirouët*. This time it is a case of the impoverished urban nobility of Nemours in 1829 as opposed to the wealthy landowning aristocracy of the area. 'Les nobles de la ville sont sans fortune', Balzac explains. 'Pour tous biens, madame de Portenduère possédait une ferme de quatre mille sept cents francs de rente, et sa maison en ville.'[108] Yet Balzac makes it clear that other noble families such as the d'Aiglemonts are among the most wealthy members of the 'haute aristocratie du pays'. The example of Angoulême in the *Comédie humaine* is revealing in this sense when compared with Forster's findings for Toulouse. In contrast with the Rastignacs, whose land 'ne valait pas mille écus',[109] M. de Bargeton has an income of 10,000 'livres' from his estates, and the marquis de Pimentel 20,000 from his, a sum which, in each case, is doubled by the income of the wife. On the other hand, if Balzac tends to magnify the average landed income of the provincial nobility, he nevertheless points to an important reality which is overlooked by Forster, the survival, at the highest level, of 'la grande propriété aristo-cratique'. Either Toulouse was exceptional or Forster's averages for Toulouse must conceal some high individual incomes. It would be interesting to know, for example, the income, including the amount received from the indemnity, of Villèle.

These economic indications are confirmed by the social composi-tion of Balzac's 'notables'. Here again, the judgements of historians provide the essential yardstick. 'Plus tard', Soboul writes, 'et à une bien plus large échelle, les listes électorales de la monarchie censitaire con-firmeront – à un quart de siècle et même à un demi-siècle de la Révolution française – la persistance ou la prééminence de cette noblesse foncière de toujours.'[110] Soboul's statement raises some vital questions. What was the situation at different periods of 'la monarchie censitaire', in particular under the Restoration? Are there any meaning-ful distinctions to be drawn between the different levels contained within the 'listes électorales'?

Balzac's account is especially valuable in that it suggests some persuasive answers to these questions. There is a clear distinction in the *Comédie humaine* between the aristocratic domination of the 'cens d'éligibilité' under the Restoration and the bourgeois preponder-ance in the 'cens électoral'.[111] Just as most of his 'éligibles' are nobles, so the majority of Balzac's electors are bourgeois. In this respect, Balzac's version of events is perfectly in line with the unequivocal conclusions published by Jardin and Tudesq concerning the composi-tion of the 'corps électoral' of the Restoration: 'les classes moyennes y dominaient: au sein des collèges électoraux de département les contribuables payant de 300 F à 500 F de contribution formaient une majorité de propriétaires médiocres, et assez souvent aussi de commerçants et de petits industriels'.[112]

The distinction which Balzac makes between an electorate which was largely bourgeois and the aristocratic majority among the 'éligibles' is crucial for a clear understanding of the important divisions reflected in the social composition of 'la grande propriété foncière' under the Restoration. Above all, the confirmation which the *Comédie humaine* provides of the aristocratic domination of the highest echelons of the 'cens d'éligibilité' lends support to the view which has gained ground in recent historical discussion, namely that those noble families who had been the most powerful landowners before the Revolution were remarkably successful in maintaining their position throughout the Restoration.

Balzac thus avoids the error of some historians who have made a special study of the economic fortunes of the émigré aristocracy. In emphasising the preponderance of 'acquéreurs' over émigrés in the electoral lists of the Restoration, both Marion and Gain fail to take account of the important distinction between electors and 'éligibles'.[113] The result, in Marion's case, is that he exaggerates the increased bourgeois share of 'la propriété foncière', while ignoring the continued aristocratic command of its most important levels. 'De grandes fortunes territoriales', Marion concludes, 'ont pu s'édifier de nouveau, mais ce furent moins les leurs que celles d'industriels et commerçants enrichis.'[114] Marion is referring specifically to the émigrés. But even if one makes a strict comparison between bourgeois and émigrés, one finds that émigrés outnumber bourgeois among the 'grands notables' of 1821 analysed by Mme Soutadé-Rouger. Out of a total of 700 studied, 77 per cent were landowners, of whom 90 per cent were noble and only ten per cent bourgeois. The émigrés, who numbered 100, were thus in a clear majority over the bourgeois landowners.[115]

What Balzac shows of the experience of the aristocracy as a whole under the Restoration invites a different conclusion to that drawn by Marion, and one which has been expressed by a recent contributor to the continuing historical debate on the question. Higgs sums up the essence of his argument when he makes the point that 'the nobility of the Old Regime still figured among the most wealthy "notables" of 1820 in France'. 'The Revolution', Higgs insists, 'had shaken up the group of landowners in French society but had not displaced the old nobility from their favoured place among them.'[116] This is precisely what is revealed by Mme Soutadé-Rouger's analysis.[117] It is moreover a point of view with which the *Comédie humaine* is entirely consistent.

It is only by examining what historians have said about the division of landed property and the changes which it underwent in the period from the Revolution to the end of the Restoration that one can properly evaluate Balzac's account of the economic experience of the aristocracy. If one adds the 'super-grande' category overwhelmingly dominated by the aristocracy to the distinction made by Sée and Forster between 'la grande', 'la moyenne' and 'la petite propriété', one arrives at a more complete and accurate breakdown of landed property under the Restoration. Balzac broadly reflects Sée's view that 'la grande propriété' remained mainly aristocratic but with increasing bourgeois penetration, whereas 'la moyenne propriété' was almost entirely bourgeois and 'la petite propriété' under exclusively peasant ownership.[118] At the same time, by distinguishing the important area marked by aristocratic control of the highest strata of landed property, Balzac anticipates a view which has only recently gained ground in historical discussion of the question.

In all logic, the acknowledged pre-eminence of the aristocracy in Restoration society is inconceivable without the necessary economic base on which that supremacy depended. The 'cens' was decisively weighted in favour of 'la propriété foncière'. Tax on land was three times as high as on commerce and industry.[119] Only by retaining the largest individual holdings of land and the income which it derived from them could the aristocracy maintain its commanding presence among the 'éligibles', which was especially marked at the very highest level. Underlining the significance of 'l'enquête de l'an XI', classifying the twelve wealthiest landowners in each department, Soboul observes that 'les plus grands propriétaires fonciers appartiennent à la ci-devant noblesse'.[120] Mme Soutadé-Rouger's study confirms that the situation was essentially the same under the Restoration. The ratio of noble land to bourgeois is revealed to be remarkably similar in 1803 and 1821. Out of the 700 wealthiest 'notables' in 1821, the nobility was in a more than three to one majority over the bourgeoisie. The émigrés alone accounted for 100, not far behind the 150 bourgeois and just one more than the imperial nobility. All this against a total population of 32 million, which included some 100,000 electors and 16,000 'éligibles'.[121] The fact moreover that the non-émigré nobility were four times as numerous as the émigrés challenges the assertion referred to earlier that the biggest landowners invariably emigrated.[122]

But, it might be objected, these findings concern only the richest 700 out of a total of 16,000 'éligibles' in 1821. What do the rest show? In answer, one has only to recall the details of Villèle's defeated proposal for the reintroduction of the 'droit d'aînesse' in 1826. The motive which inspired the scheme, that of consolidating the position of the landed nobility, was identified with the 8,000 families of 'éligibles' to whom it was restricted.

Despite its incompleteness and its debatable objectivity, the historical evidence contained in the *Comédie humaine* deserves to be seriously considered, especially when it concerns such a question as the position of the landed aristocracy under the Restoration which is still surrounded by controversy. The novelist as historian may be a dubious proposition. Balzac, however, is *sui generis*. He is unique as a historical novelist not only in his account of a whole critical period in French history. His claims to rank as a historian have to do less with his range than with his method, at the heart of which is a rigorous analysis of socioeconomic factors. This method in turn gains its strength from the interdependence of analysis and illustration. The multiplicity of case-histories helps to construct a synthetic vision, which is itself heightened by the dramatisation of the 'fait divers'. With Balzac, one senses that one is in the presence of an authentic historical voice, and one to which one is compelled to listen, the more so since, as Forster acknowledges, 'even after a statistical average has been determined, individual case-histories will seem more real'.[123]

VIII The Process of Bourgeoisification

Although its share of landed property suffered a further decline from which the bourgeoisie principally benefited, the *Comédie humaine* clearly indicates that the Restoration nobility retained a tenacious grip on 'la grande propriété foncière' appropriate to its social and political predominance. Balzac none the less affirms the growing assumption of economic power by the bourgeoisie in other important areas, in commerce, finance and industry, which decisively outweighed what advantage the aristocracy derived from the retention of its land-owning authority. Instead of subscribing to the notion of the total eclipse of the aristocracy as a major landowning class, Balzac suggests that it was the bourgeoisie's control of the vital sectors of an incipient capitalist economy rather than its increasing penetration of 'la propriété foncière' that ensured its victory in the July Revolution. Indeed, what Balzac also shows is that it was the resentment caused by the aristocracy's continued manipulation of the 'régime censitaire' based largely on the ownership of land that inspired bourgeois demands for radical change in 1830.

Balzac identifies an additional factor which historians have recognised as having an important effect on the economic position of the aristocracy, namely its revised assessment of its landowning role in society.[124] This was partly in response to the failure of the ambitious expectations raised by the Restoration. It was also the case, as Balzac shows, that the Restoration aristocracy was, in the process, moving towards alternative strategies which might enable it to survive by adapting to a society in which the domination of landed property was ceasing to be the decisive factor.

Faced with the advance of the bourgeoisie in commerce, finance and industry, the Restoration aristocracy could not afford to be complacent about the position which, despite certain losses, it still held as an important landowning class. Along with a sense of its economic decline went an increasing readiness to adapt to bourgeois norms as a means of averting social extinction. This trend towards the 'embourgeoisement' of the aristocracy under the Restoration is well documented in the *Comédie humaine*.

In concentrating on the socioeconomic aspects of this development, I do not propose to go over ground which has already been more than adequately covered. For a masterly summary of aristocratic inter-marriages with the bourgeoisie in the *Comédie humaine*, for example, one need look no further than André Wurmser's concise account.[125] However, one is still left with a considerable amount of evidence which underlines the economic ascendancy of the bourgeoisie and the aristocracy's recognition of the fact. In terms of social contacts, Balzac makes it clear that, despite the persistence of entrenched ultra attitudes, there were signs that barriers were beginning to be relaxed. In Paris, salons like that of Mme d'Espard open their doors to bankers such as Nucingen and Du Tillet.

The essential change which is revealed in Balzac's analysis of the Restoration aristocracy is in the view of land as the prime source of wealth, power and prestige. The shift of economic initiative from the aristocracy to the bourgeoisie induced the aristocracy to reappraise its traditional identity as the dominant landowning force in society. The significance of this changed outlook can be judged from what Balzac reveals of the level of activity in 'la spéculation foncière' under the Restoration. The one case of aristocratic interest in this area which is given in the *Comédie humaine* concerns the chevalier du Rouvre, a considerable part of whose income of 30,000 'livres de rente' is accounted for by speculation in land. At first sight, the absence of any corresponding bourgeois involvement in land speculation may seem surprising, until one takes into account the fact that the behaviour of both aristocracy and bourgeoisie is dictated by a common reality, the switch from speculation in land to investment in 'rentes'. Grandet and Du Bousquier buy land from the aristocracy, not with a view to speculating in 'la propriété foncière' but in order to 'arrondir' their holdings of land, the capital profit from which they proceed to invest in 'rentes'.

In this preference for forms of investment other than in land, the bourgeoisie was by no means alone. The *Comédie humaine* features a number of aristocratic 'rentiers' under the Restoration, both in the provinces and in Paris. It has already been noted how certain émigrés prefer to use their indemnity for investment rather than for repurchase. Earlier still, at the very beginning of the Restoration, the landless chevalier de Valois invests his savings in the 'Grand-Livre' in successful anticipation of their rise from their low value of 56.25 fr.[126] Balzac thus illustrates an important change of economic direction on the part of the aristocracy, whereby, in Forster's words, 'the nobles of the Restoration were tending to become "rentiers" instead of landlords'.[127]

The ultimate career of Laurence de Cinq-Cygne highlights a further development which reflected and in turn contributed to the gradual abandonment by the aristocracy of its landowning role. Laurence's progression from landowner to 'rentier' is accompanied by her desertion of her estates for residence in Paris. This movement of the nobility from their territorial domains in the provinces to positions within the urban, and particularly the Parisian, aristocracy, is strongly stressed by Balzac. In addition to Laurence de Cinq-Cygne, there is the dynamic model of Rastignac. The comte de Sérisy's time is divided between the 'château de Presles' and the Chaussée d'Antin. Mlle des Touches abandons Guérande for the comforts of her Paris 'hôtel'. While other provincial nobles are gaining access to the 'faubourg', the comte de Fontaine is making his mark among the new court nobility.

The incentive for nobles to participate in bourgeois activities under the Restoration was considerable enough in the provinces, but more powerful still in Paris. The *Comédie humaine* depicts the activity of the Restoration aristocracy in several areas normally associated with the bourgeoisie. One favoured field is speculation, which takes other forms besides 'rentes'. Delbecq speculates on behalf of comtesse Ferraud in both actions on the 'Bourse' and in property. 'Delbecq', Balzac notes, 'avocat de la comtesse, ne lui avait laissé manquer aucune des chances favorables que les mouvements de Bourse et la hausse des propriétés présentèrent dans Paris aux gens habiles pendant les trois premières années de la Restauration. Il avait triplé les capitaux de sa protectrice.'[128] The vicomtesse de Grandlieu, we have already seen, is mentioned as having canal shares.[129] The chevalier du Rouvre makes his fortune out of speculation in property as well as in land. Finally, the duc d'Hérouville emphasises the departure from conventional speculation in land by his exploitation of marshland assigned to him by the 'Conseil d'Etat'. With backing from a financial consortium, the land is reclaimed for a scheme of development which lays the foundation of his successful ventures under the July Monarchy. All this is achieved, incidentally, in a manner which poses a question-mark against Jean Forest's claim that the duc d'Hérouville embodies the degeneracy of the Restoration aristocracy.[130] In visiting Le Havre in 1829 with a view to undertaking 'une affaire colossale, la mise en valeur d'un espace immense laissé par la mer, entre l'embouchure de deux rivières, et dont la propriété venait d'être adjugée par le Conseil-d'Etat à la maison d'Hérouville', the duc d'Hérouville indicates how, for a growing number of nobles, a new bourgeois identity was emerging from the ruins of an aristocratic past.[131]

'Dérogeance' is revealed to be an anachronism in face of the financial realities pressing on the aristocracy. This is clearly demonstrated by Balzac in the case of the marquis d'Espard and his wife. It is one thing for Mme d'Espard to reply haughtily to Popinot when he asks whether she has engaged in speculation and investment: '"Il n'est pas dans les habitudes des Blamont-Chauvry de faire le commerce", dit-elle, vivement piquée dans son orgueil nobiliaire'.[132] Her husband, however, is prepared to incur 'dérogeance', not, it is true, for the sake of financial gain, since his publishing venture carries with it the risk of bankruptcy. The marquis d'Espard's decision to publish *L'Histoire pittoresque de la Chine* is motivated by an eccentric monomania, but the effect is to impel him in a bourgeois direction and to perform an activity which he is aware violates the traditional values of his class. The dilemma of an aristocracy whose nominal control of society was challenged by the logic of a bourgeois economy is epitomised in the marquis d'Espard's search for a new identity and a *raison d'être*.

There is evidence of aristocratic participation in 'sociétés par actions', which as Guy Richard has shown, were an established phenomenon at the end of the eighteenth century.[133] The continued tradition of noble involvement in such companies, especially those enjoying royal protection, is recognised in the *Comédie humaine*. Des Lupeaulx is made 'commissaire du gouvernement dans une Société anonyme', while Polydore de la Baudraye is appointed 'commissaire du roi près d'une Compagnie anonyme' at a guaranteed salary of 6,000 fr.

On the other hand, Balzac does not give a single instance of an aristocrat engaged in industry. That Balzac should present no equivalent of M. de Rênal is perhaps surprising, given his remarkable grasp of economic realities. One might, for example, have expected to find some evidence of aristocratic representation in the textile industry, on the lines of the recent findings in this area, which, again, one owes to Guy Richard.[134]

Only rarely is the novelist divorced from the historian in Balzac's case. In his treatment of the Restoration aristocracy, for example, aesthetic licence takes precedence over economic analysis only in one instance. This concerns the theme of aristocratic recovery achieved via an exotic, picaresque exile. Victor d'Aiglemont, Paul de Manerville and Charles Mignon are the aristocratic counterparts of Charles Grandet, whose bourgeois rehabilitation is made possible through a period of voluntary expatriation. Otherwise, Balzac's approach remains based on a rigorous economic evaluation which extends to the question of aristocratic identification with bourgeois activities. This investigation centres around the operations of finance. Discounting the numerous examples of merely passive borrowing, one is struck by the wealth of cases involving active aristocratic participation in bourgeois finance, in addition to the investment in 'rentes' already referred to. The duc d'Hérouville is dependent on banking credit for his development plans. The vicomte de Longueville has interests in the banking firm of Palma and Werbrust. Rastignac makes a fortune out of Nucingen's speculations. The aristocracy have their preferred bankers in the Mongenod family. Finally, Charles Mignon is a banker as well as a shipowner and property owner. The exceptional factors favouring Mignon's success have been clearly identified by Maurice Regard. Le Havre, he emphasises, was unusual in attracting Parisian capital, especially from Rothschild and Laffitte. Secondly, the international trade in which Mignon engaged did not carry with it the taint of 'dérogeance'. Involved in speculation and buying up the land of his more traditional fellow-aristocrats, Mignon, as Maurice Regard underlines, had the good fortune to belong to that section of the nobility which, 'par sa nature hybride, offre des possibilités d'adaptation que la noblesse d'épée ne possédait pas naturellement'.[135]

It is important, however, to maintain a sense of perspective in discussing the bourgeoisification of the Restoration aristocracy. Although the value of land declined in relation to that of other assets under the Restoration, 'la propriété foncière' was not in fact overtaken by 'la propriété mobilière' until well into the second half of the

nineteenth century.[136] Michel Vovelle's recent study of the nobility of
Chartres confirms moreover that the aristocracy retained an important
share of landed property under the Restoration, even in some urban
areas.[137] Nevertheless, the nobility in the *Comédie humaine* accurately
express a significant trend in turning increasingly away from the ultra
precedent of M. de Mortsauf, in his refusal 'à se créer une vie indus-
trieuse . . . dans les sueurs d'un travail méprisé'.[138] In the struggle for
economic supremacy, the advantage had passed firmly to the bourgeoisie.
In the *Comédie humaine*, the aristocratic victims of bourgeois power
under the Restoration reinforce the lesson embodied by the cases of
successful adaptation. With the exception of the Mongenods, Balzac's
Restoration financiers seem to take a particular delight in ruining
their aristocratic clients. Victurnien d'Esgrignon and Savinien de
Portenduère are disastrously in debt to their financial creditors. Baude-
nord suffers in Claparon's financial crash, while Victor d'Aiglemont is
hit both by Nucingen's liquidation and by the bankruptcy of his
'agent de change', Falleix. Lastly, Philippe Bridau, now comte de
Brambourg, loses a fortune through following Nucingen and Du Tillet's
malicious advice to speculate on the likelihood of revolution being
averted in 1830.

In *Un Début dans la vie*, Balzac refers to 'le sens haineux de l'ex-clerc
de notaire qui s'amusait à prédire à la Noblesse les malheurs que la
Bourgeoisie rêvait alors, et que 1830 devait réaliser'.[139] Georges Marest's
hatred of the comte de Sérisy has profound historical implications.
The aspirations of the bourgeoisie were more than a dream under the
Restoration. In part, they had already been fulfilled at the expense of
the aristocracy. The fundamental reality of Restoration society is
conclusively demonstrated by Balzac. The economic ascendancy of
the bourgeoisie is confirmed in the *Comédie humaine* and underlined
by powerful intimations of the final defeat of the aristocracy which
was its necessary consequence.

IX Conclusion

In this appraisal of Balzac's view of the Restoration aristocracy I have
not been concerned with those aspects of the question which have
already been thoroughly examined by critics of Balzac. This is especially the case with Balzac's general critique of the aristocracy under the
Restoration, about which there is, in any case, little critical disagreement. I would only add that Balzac seems to have been less than fair to

the aristocracy in alternately demanding that, in order to survive as a class, it must take greater account of money, and attacking it for succumbing to bourgeois materialism. This confusion is the product of Balzac's ambivalent response to the rise of the bourgeoisie in post-revolutionary society. In urging the aristocracy to get the best of both worlds, material and non-material, Balzac was making demands of the aristocracy which were ill-directed. Writing after 1830, Balzac was well placed to realise that the aristocracy's options were determined by the economic realities of bourgeois power.

In giving priority to Balzac's assessment of the economic factors governing the position of the Restoration aristocracy, I have been guided by two factors. First, an economic analysis underlies Balzac's entire historical approach, in this as in all other important areas. Secondly, although more attention has been given in recent Balzac criticism to economic considerations, no systematic study has yet been undertaken of the Restoration aristocracy in the *Comédie humaine* from an economic point of view. When compared with the extensive treatment by critics of the place of the Restoration bourgeoisie in Balzac's work, the economic development of the Restoration aristocracy stands out as a historical theme which, while undoubtedly one of the most important in the *Comédie humaine*, remains relatively unexamined.

Yet the evidence of the *Comédie humaine* is enormous and its implications far-reaching. The range covered is monumental. The omissions, for example, of the industrial activity of the aristocracy, the scarcity of 'neutral' nobles who were neither émigrés nor rebels, are negligible. It is true that Balzac exaggerates certain impressions, such as the size of indemnities, and overstates some of his judgements, notably concerning the degree of 'morcellement' and the effect of the loss of feudal dues, particularly of the 'lods et ventes'. It would be astonishing if Balzac were not to leave gaps, and to exaggerate or even distort in some cases. What finally matters, however, is the remarkable accuracy of the *Comédie humaine* in anticipating historical findings. The first historian of the Restoration, Balzac is unsurpassed as the historian of the Restoration aristocracy.

Balzac's achievement can best be judged if one identifies the various questions which give proof of his authenticity. There is first the account of the reassertion of its authority by the aristocracy in all areas of Restoration society other than the strictly economic, from the episcopate and the diplomatic corps to the army, the 'haute administration' and ministerial politics. At the same time, Balzac reveals a detailed understanding of the way in which the aristocracy was reconstituted after 1815, as he does of the motives and complex workings of the 'majorat'. He also shows his awareness of the limited effects of certain measures from which the aristocracy might have expected to make significant gains, above all from the law of December 1814, and the indemnity. The massive detail which Balzac assembles never gets in the way of a lucid uncovering of basic causes, one of the most decisive of which is seen as the confirmation of the rights of 'acquéreurs' by Napoleon and in the Charter.

To complete his analysis, Balzac distinguishes the various aristo-cratic reactions to the weakening of their economic base in society. Ultra intransigence is denounced, while attention is drawn to the evidence of a movement of conscious 'embourgeoisement' on the part of the aristocracy. The transition from rural domains to urban sophisti-cation, especially to Paris, the shift of investment from land to 'rentes', the new interest in other forms of speculation, all are exposed by Balzac to emphasise the basic reality facing the Restoration aristocracy, its inescapable dependence on bourgeois finance.

Balzac is not only remarkably accurate. He can also lay claim to a certain historical originality. This quality is not only expressed in the way that his characters re-enact the processes he describes. It also emerges in a more strictly scholarly sense, through the substantial evi-dence which he offers on specific questions which continue to engage the attention of historians. In suggesting, for example, that the recovery of land by the aristocracy was achieved under the Consulate and Empire rather than during the Restoration, Balzac makes an interesting incursion into an area on which, for want of sufficient firm evidence, historians have been reluctant to commit themselves.

Balzac's most valuable contribution, however, lies in what he reveals of the survival under the Restoration of 'la grande propriété aristo-cratique'. The identification of the most eminent section of the aristocracy as being essentially involved in this process is convincingly demonstrated by joining the economic evidence of income and indem-nities with the political arguments inherent in Balzac's description of his 'notables'. The distinction which he observes between largely aristocratic 'éligibles' and predominantly bourgeois electors cuts through a confused historical terrain. The question of the economic power of the Restoration aristocracy is at the centre of the *Comédie humaine*. By reconciling the overall decline of the aristocracy with the persis-tance of the landowning power of the most privileged group within it, Balzac indicates the grounds for an objective conclusion which might flow from the clash of recent historical pronouncements on the subject.

Notes

1. Jean Forest, *L'Aristocratie Balzacienne* (Paris, 1972).

2. G. Pradalié, *Balzac Historien* (Paris, 1955), p. 39.

3. Bernard Guyon, *La Pensée politique et sociale de Balzac* (Paris, 1969), pp. 355-6.

4. André Wurmser, *La Comédie Inhumaine*, 2nd edn (Paris, 1965), pp. 445-63.

5. Pierre Barbéris, *Le Monde de Balzac* (Paris, 1973), pp. 167-8.

6. J.-H. Donnard, *Les Réalités économiques et sociales dans l'oeuvre de Balzac* (Paris, 1971). Chapter VI of Donnard's work, 'Pathologie de la Noblesse', contains some interesting observations, especially pages 145-57.

7. The sections of Barbésis's works which are of the greatest interest in this respect are as follows: *Balzac et le mal du siècle*, vol. I (Paris, 1970a), pp. 55-81; *Mythes Balzaciens* (Paris, 1972a), pp. 11-20; *Le Monde de Balzac*, pp. 163-82, 237-9.

8. Forest, *L'Aristocratie Balzacienne*, p. 16.

9. For precise details of this see Jean Vidalenc, *La Restauration* (Paris, 1968), p. 28.

10. Ibid.

11. Ibid.

12. *La Rabouilleuse*, IV, 300.

13. Ibid., p. 522.

14. Vidalenc, *La Restauration*, pp. 28-9.

15. The most important recent study is that of N. Richardson, *The French Prefectoral Corps 1814-1830* (Cambridge, 1966). It is the subject of an interesting review by Richard Cobb, which can be found in *A Second Identity. Essays on France and French History* (Oxford, 1969).

16. His brother had taken part in the renewed Chouan activity under the Empire. Arrested for his involvement with the 'Chauffeurs de Mortagne', he was sentenced and executed in 1809.

17. Louis XVIII, Balzac affirms, 'eut égard à cette fidélité lorsque le faubourg Saint-Germain en fit un crime aux Grandlieu'. *Splendeurs et misères des courtisanes*, VI, 506.

18. Donnard, *Les Réalités économiques et sociales dans l'oeuvre de Balzac*, p. 147.

19. *La Muse du département*, IV, 634.

20. Made a baron by Louis XVIII, Polydore de la Baudraye becomes 'Maître des requêtes' and is given a royal sinecure.

21. Balzac seems to have had considerable reservations about the success of Louis XVIII's social policy. Balzac's real views on the subject are occasionally expressed with incisive clarity. In *La Peau de chagrin*, for example, Balzac refers derisively to 'le fameux mensonge de Louis XVIII: *Union et oubli*', *La Peau de chagrin*, X, 95.

22. 'Quoique ruiné par les confiscations', Balzac reveals of the comte de Fontaine, 'ce fidèle Vendéen refusa constamment les places lucratives que lui fit offrir l'Empereur Napoléon.' *Le Bal de Sceaux*, I, 109.

23. *La Bourse*, I, 426-7.

24. Ibid., 435.

25. *Le Lys dans la vallée*, IX, 1040.

26. Ibid., 1103.

27. Ibid., 1040.

28. The full text reads: 'il fit encore recouvrer quelques actions sur le canal d'Orléans et certains immeubles assez importants que l'Empereur avait donnés en dot à des établissements publics'. *Gobseck*, II, 963.

29. Ibid.
30. *Splendeurs et misères des courtisanes*, VI, 506.
31. *Le Colonel Chabert*, III, 320.
32. A. Gain, *La Restauration et les biens des émigrés* (Nancy, 1928), vol. I, p. 299.
33. Ibid., II, p. 238.
34. *Le Contrat de mariage*, III, 578. Mathias is thinking primarily of the role played in this process by the 'majorat'. The 'majorat' which he persuades Paul de Manerville to insert in his marriage contract does not, however, prevent him from being ruined at the hands of his wife and mother-in-law. The 'majorat' is the subject of section VI of the present chapter.
35. On this point see Gain, *La Restauration*, vol. II, chapter XXII, section VIII.
36. Ibid., II, p. 178.
37. *Le Cabinet des Antiques*, IV, 978.
38. *L'Interdiction*, III, 465.
39. *La Muse du département*, IV, 636.
40. *Mémoires de deux jeunes mariées*, I, 200.
41. *Modeste Mignon*, I, 695.
42. *Ursule Mirouët*, III, 861.
43. *Les Secrets de la princesse de Cadignan*, VI, 982.
44. *Gobseck*, II, 963.
45. *Le Bal de Sceaux*, I, 131.
46. *Une Ténébreuse Affaire*, VIII, 685.
47. Gain, *La Restauration*, II, p. 191.
48. This question is discussed at length by Gain. See Gain, ibid., vol. II, chapter XXII, section VI, 'Valeur moyenne de l'indemnité'.
49. See Marcel Marion, *La Vente des biens nationaux pendant la Révolution* (Paris, 1908), p. 387 and Gain, ibid., II, p. 187.
50. Gain, ibid., II, p. 354.
51. Marion, *La Vente des biens nationaux*, p. 390.
52. Gain, *La Restauration*, II, p. 426.
53. *La Muse du département*, IV, 638-9.
54. Marion, *La Vente des biens nationaux*, p. 393.
55. The historical evidence concerning the territorial recovery of the aristocracy is considered in detail in section VII of this chapter. Its electoral implications are also examined in this section and, more extensively, in chapter 8.
56. The d'Espards had expropriated the Jeanrenaud family as part of Louis XIV's persecution of the Huguenots after the revocation of the Edict of Nantes.
57. *L'Interdiction*, III, 484, 490.
58. The ideological difficulties in which Balzac was involved by his pragmatic acceptance of the Revolution are considered in the concluding chapter.
59. *Les Paysans*, IX, 127.
60. *Le Cabinet des Antiques*, IV, 978.
61. Vidalenc, *La Restauration*, p. 454.
62. Ibid., p. 456.
63. Guyon, *La Pensée politique et sociale de Balzac*.
64. *Illusions Perdues*, V, 699-700.
65. In May 1836, when he was finishing *Le Lys dans la vallée*, Balzac referred to the character of M. de Mortsauf in a letter to Mme. Hanska. Moïse le Yaouanc quotes Balzac's remark: 'J'aurai élevé la statue de l'Emigration', and comments: 'Disons plutôt qu'il a fait la statue d'une certaine émigration'. Le Yaouanc, *Le Lys dans la vallée* (Classiques Garnier, Paris, 1966), pp. xiv-xvi.

66. *Le Lys dans la vallée*, IX, 1009.

67. *La Bourse*, I, 428.

68. *Splendeurs et misères des courtisanes*, VI, 507.

69. *Le Cousin Pons*, VII, 623.

70. There are, of course, numerous occasions, as in *Les Chouans*, when émigrés and rebels sink their differences and join forces in the counter-revolutionary cause. This concerted action of émigrés and rebels is noted by Maurice Regard in his edition of *Les Chouans* (Classiques Garnier, Paris, 1957), Introduction, pp. xxii-xxiii.

71. *Les Chouans*, VIII, 1205.

72. *Le Lys dans la vallée*, IX, 1008-9.

73. *Les Paysans*, IX, 152.

74. *Béatrix*, II, 668.

75. Jean Vidalenc, *Les Emigrés Français, 1789-1825* (Caen, 1963), p. 14.

76. *Les Chouans*, VIII, 1037.

77. *Le Cabinet des Antiques*, IV, 993.

78. Ibid., 977.

79. 'La mouvance des fiefs' was part of the category of feudal dues known as 'lods et ventes'. The note on p. 339 of the Conard edition of *Le Cabinet des Antiques* defines the term 'lods et ventes' as 'une redevance payée au suzerain par son vassal, à tout changement de propriétaire, d'hériter ou de tenancier'. See Conard, vol. II.

80. *Le Cabinet des Antiques*, IV, 977.

81. *Le Curé de village*, IX, 744.

82. J.-H. Donnard has revealed that the comte de Fontaine was modelled on a comte Ferrand who was a cousin of M. de Berny. See Donnard, *Les Réalités économiques et sociales dans l'oeuvre de Balzac*, pp. 74-6.

83. *Le Bal de Sceaux*, I, 112.

84. The imperial history of the 'droit d'aînesse' and of the 'majorat' is discussed in chapter 3, section I.

85. For a definition of the difference between the 'droit d'aînesse' and the 'majorat' see chapter 3, note 15.

86. P.A. Perrod, 'Balzac et les "Majorats"', *L'Année Balzacienne* (1968), pp. 211-40.

87. *Du droit d'aînesse* is contained in vol. 38 of the Conard edition, *Oeuvres Diverses*, I, 1-9.

88. The creation of a 'majorat' was made a condition of the peerage by an ordinance of August 1815. A law of April 1817 laid down the financial minimum which a 'majorat' should represent in order to qualify its beneficiary for the various titles compatible with a peerage: 30,000 fr. 'rentes' for a 'duc'; 20,000 fr. in the case of 'comtes' and 'marquis'; 10,000 fr. for 'vicomtes' and 'barons'.

89. *Mémoires de deux jeunes mariées*, I, 219.

90. For the legal history surrounding this particular use of the 'majorat' see Perrod, 'Balzac et les "Majorats"', pp. 210, 221.

91. *Le Contrat de mariage*, III, 578.

92. *Une Ténébreuse Affaire*, VIII, 684.

93. *Les Paysans*, IX, 303.

94. Perrod, 'Balzac et les "Majorats"', p. 216. In all, 306 'majorats' were created under the Restoration: 78 of them were linked with a peerage, the remaining 228 being 'hors pairie'. A further 134 came after the 1824 ordinance, which at the same time reduced the amounts required in the case of a peerage to 10,000 fr., 5,000 fr. and 3,000 fr. 'rente' respectively. See note 88.

95. Villèle's proposed measure was restricted to the 8,000 families of 'éligibles' paying at least 1,000 fr. a year in direct taxes. It was rejected by the 'Chambre des pairs' by 120 votes to 94.

96. *Les Paysans*, IX, 303. The creation of further 'majorats' was prohibited by a law passed in May 1835.

97. Georges Lefebvre, *Etudes sur la Révolution Française* (Paris, 1954). 'Répartition de la propriété et de l'exploitation foncières à la fin de l'ancien régime', pp. 201-16.

98. Georges Lizerand, 'Observations sur l'impôt foncier sous l'ancien régime', *Revue d'Histoire économique et sociale* (1958), p. 42. R. Forster, 'The Survival of the Nobility during the French Revolution', *Past and Present* (July 1967), p. 71.

99. Forster, ibid., p. 76.

100. *Une Ténébreuse Affaire*, VIII, 543.

101. Lefebvre, *Etudes sur la Révolution Française*. 'La Vente des biens nationaux', pp. 240-1.

102. Thierry Bodin, Introduction to *Les Paysans*, Pléiade, IX, 7.

103. Fearing that Polignac's ultra policies could only be disastrous, 'le duc avait envoyé son homme d'affaires à Limoges, en le chargeant de céder devant une forte somme en argent, car il se souvenait trop bien de la révolution de 1789, pour ne pas mettre à profit les leçons qu'elle avait données à toute l'aristocratie'. *Le Curé de village*, IX, 743-4.

104. The phrase 'le mouvement ascensionnel de l'argent' occurs in the opening description of the social classes in Paris in 1814-15 which is contained in *La Fille aux yeux d'or*, V, 1046.

105. Albert Soboul, *Histoire Economique et Sociale de la France* (eds. Fernand Braudel and Ernest Labrousse), 3 vols. (Paris, 1976), vol. I, p. 126.

106. Ibid.

107. Forster, 'Survival of the Nobility', pp. 82-3.

108. *Ursule Mirouët*, III, 781-2.

109. *La Maison Nucingen*, VI, 332.

110. Soboul, *Histoire Economique et Sociale de la France*, vol. III, p. 126.

111. In order to qualify as an elector, the citizen of the Restoration had to pay a minimum of 300 fr. per year in direct taxes. To be eligible to stand as a parliamentary candidate, he had to pay taxes of 1,000 fr. For an analysis of the effects of the changes in the electoral franchise under the July Monarchy see chapter 8.

112. A. Jardin and A.-J. Tudesq, *La France des notables*, 2 vols. Vol. 1. *L'Evolution générale. 1815-1848* (Paris, 1973), p. 44.

113. See Marion, *La Vente des biens nationaux*, pp. 390-3 and Gain, *La Restauration*, II, p. 426.

114. Marion, ibid., p. 393.

115. Mme Soutadé-Rouger, 'Les Notables sous la Restauration', *Revue d'Histoire économique et sociale* (1960), 1, pp. 98-110.

116. D. Higgs, 'Politics and Landownership among the French Nobility after the Revolution', *European Studies Review* (April 1971), pp. 110-11.

117. The value of the evidence uncovered by Mme Soutadé-Rouger's investigation is not diminished by the misleading conclusion which she draws when she states that the great majority of Restoration 'notables' were wealthy landowners. Most electors were, as Jardin and Tudesq have shown, bourgeois under the Restoration and, at best, 'propriétaires médiocres'. Mme Soutadé-Rouger's inference is therefore unjustified and conflicts with her basic terms of reference, which are the study of 'une couche supérieure de notables', namely the wealthiest 700 in July 1821. Mme Soutadé-Rouger, 'Les Notables sous la Restauration', pp. 98-9, 100.

118. H. Sée, *Histoire Economique de la France*, 2 vols. (Paris, 1951). Vol. II. *Les Temps Modernes (1789-1914)*, p. 119.

119. See Sherman Kent, *Electoral Procedure under Louis Philippe* (Yale, 1937), pp. 9-10.

120. Soboul, *Histoire Economique et Sociale de la France*, vol. III, p. 126.

121. Mme Soutadé-Rouger, 'Les Notables sous la Restauration', pp. 99-107.

122. Forster, 'Survival of the Nobility', p. 76.

123. Ibid., p. 82.

124. This is a point which is particularly emphasised by Forster. See ibid., pp. 82-5.

125. Wurmser, *La Comédie Inhumaine*, pp. 448-51.

126. In their readiness to invest in 'rentes' both the chevalier de Valois and du Bousquier behave in sharp contrast to the Cormon circle, whose suspicion of investment is characteristic of the provincial lack of initiative which Balzac deplores. 'Ce cénacle', Balzac reveals of the habitués of the Cormon salon, 'se refuse aux inscriptions sur le Grand-Livre.' *La Vieille Fille*, IV, 846.

127. Forster, 'Survival of the Nobility', p. 84.

128. *Le Colonel Chabert*, III, 348.

129. See note 28 .

130. Forest, *L'Aristocratie Balzacienne*, pp. 184, 218-22. This is difficult to reconcile with Forest's description (p. 283) of the duc d'Hérouville as an 'homme de génie'.

131. *Modeste Mignon*, I, 637.

132. Balzac sums up what is involved for the marquis d'Espard by his radical initiative. 'Contre les habitudes de son rang et les idées qu'il professait sur le devoir de la noblesse', Balzac states, 'il a entrepris une affaire commerciale pour laquelle il souscrit journellement des obligations à terme qui menacent aujourd'hui son honneur et sa fortune, attendu qu'elles emportent pour lui la qualité de négociant.' *L'Interdiction*, III, 464 and 447.

133. Guy Richard, 'Un Essai d'adaptation sociale à une nouvelle structure économique. La noblesse de France et les sociétés par actions à la fin du XVIIIe siècle', *Revue d'Histoire économique et sociale* (1962), pp. 484-523.

134. Guy Richard, 'Du moulin banal au tissage mécanique. La Noblesse dans l'industrie textile en Haute-Normandie dans la première moitié du XIXe siècle', *Revue d'Histoire économique et sociale* (1968), pp. 305, 506-49.

135. Maurice Regard, Introduction to *Modeste Mignon*, Pléiade, I, 463.

136. See Sée, *Histoire Economique de la France*, pp. 118-19 for a fuller consideration of this point.

137. Michel Vovelle, 'Structure et Repartition de la fortune foncière et de la fortune mobilière d'un ensemble urbain: Chartres de la fin de l'ancien régime à la Restauration', *Revue d'Histoire économique et sociale* (1958), pp. 385-98.

138. *Le Lys dans la vallée*, IX, 1008.

139. *Un Début dans la vie*, I, 863.

6 THE BOURGEOISIE OF THE RESTORATION

The Restoration provides the focal point of Balzac's historical investigation, and in his analysis the bourgeoisie and the aristocracy claim equal attention. Balzac's account of the bourgeoisie of the Restoration is comprehensive in scope; the range of bourgeois categories is vast and representative, with considerable evidence of both the Parisian and the provincial middle class. Commerce, finance and industry are treated as interrelated factors; lawyers and administrators form important groups along with intellectuals. The dominant issues which relate to the bourgeoisie, its social origins and rise, its economic activity, its further aspirations and political affiliations, all come under Balzac's scrutiny in his assessment of the Restoration.

I

Although Balzac is concerned with the liberal professions, his main preoccupation is with the economic activity of the bourgeoisie and its sociopolitical implications. Moreover, the professional middle classes and the intellectuals in the *Comédie humaine* are not isolated from their historical context. Their operations and outlook are studied in relation to the forces in post-revolutionary society to which they respond.

In the opening pages of *Les Employés* Balzac made it clear that he was concerned to write about 'ces petites révolutions partielles qui furent comme les remous de la tempête de 1789 et que les historiens des grands mouvements sociaux négligent d'examiner, quoiqu'en définitif elles aient fait nos moeurs ce qu'elles sont'.[1] Such a declaration was consistent with his frequently expressed aim to write 'l'histoire des moeurs' of contemporary French society. It does, of course, overlook the fact that no creative writer, before or since Balzac, has been more preoccupied with the question of the 'grands mouvements sociaux'. Yet it does indicate the dimensions of the historical task which Balzac set himself. In examining these changes, moreover, Balzac never failed to identify their starting-point in the Revolution.

The collective example of the 'Cénacle' in *Illusions Perdues* is of less interest than the individual cases which Balzac deals with. The function of the 'Cénacle' is moral rather than historical, concerned with its part in Lucien's crisis of values more than with the movement of contemporary society. Its political ideals are vague, we know nothing of the social background of its members and, despite Balzac's extravagant tribute to its idealism, its impact on society is of little consequence.

In contrast, the experience of Louis Lambert, Godefroid and Lucien de Rubempré is of considerable historical importance. To begin with, they are all products of a bourgeois generation which in various ways had made its mark during the Revolution. Louis Lambert was born in 1797, his father having owned 'une tannerie de médiocre importance',[2] which he had intended Louis to take over.

Lucien Chardon is the son of a former surgeon in the Republican armies who took as his wife the 'dernier rejeton de la famille de Rubempré, miraculeusement sauvée par lui de l'échafaud en 1793'.[3] Godefroid, in *L'Envers de l'histoire contemporaine*, is the 'fils d'un détaillant à qui l'économie avait fait faire une sorte de fortune'.[4] In describing Godefroid as 'confondu dans la foule des fils de la bourgeoisie qui, sans fortune faite ni distinctions héréditaires, devaient tout attendre de leur valeur personnelle ou de leurs travaux obstinés',[5] Balzac identifies him with an important group of characters in the *Comédie humaine* who confirm Adeline Daumard's point that the bourgeoisie which emerged from the Revolution to dominate the 'monarchie censitaire' had largely to make its way unaided and without any significant 'capital de départ'.[6]

Secondly, each seeks an intellectual path as a personal response to post-revolutionary materialism. Whereas Godefroid and Lucien are prepared to come to terms with society, Louis Lambert attempts to bypass it, preferring to observe it with detachment rather than becoming involved with it. Louis Lambert's assessment of post-revolutionary realities, especially of the all-importance of money, is, if anything, even harsher than that of Godefroid and Lucien. By his total intellectual commitment, Lambert pays the ultimate penalty which Godefroid and Lucien are spared by their readiness to compromise, and he is finally destroyed by the ravages of 'la pensée'.

Godefroid and Lucien are alike in having more ambition than character. Both try to achieve a short-cut to their ambition via journalism and politics, and each displays a similar political opportunism. All three reflect Balzac's own struggles and ambition, and Lambert and Lucien suffer a fate which Balzac avoided only by virtue of his superior energy and will. Personal shortcomings combine with the alienating effect of a materialist society to produce the bourgeois expression of what Barbéris has described as the manifestation of 'le mal du siècle' in Balzac's work. Only Godefroid overcomes disillusion and despair to find a spiritual *raison d'être* as a priest under the July Monarchy.

The interest of Louis Lambert, Godefroid and Lucien lies not only in their moral example but also in their historical significance. The *Comédie humaine* is characterised by the 'bourgeois conquérants' who have themselves emerged directly out of the Revolution to make a further significant advance under the Restoration. Balzac's creative instinct joins with his sense of history to suggest an interesting alternative phenomenon, that of a first-generation of intellectual 'ratés' produced by the revolutionary bourgeoisie.

II

Balzac is normally scrupulous in pinpointing the social origins of his Restoration bourgeoisie. As one has already seen, this is true of his intellectuals if less pronounced with his lawyers. In analysing the commercial and financial bourgeoisie, Balzac rarely departs from this practice, the outstanding exception being in the case of the Cointet brothers. Otherwise, there is scarcely a prominent bourgeois of the Restoration whose origins are not traced back by Balzac to the Revolution or earlier. No important section is omitted. The 'moyenne bourgeoisie' is represented by du Bousquier and Mlle Cormon. From a family long established in Alençon, his father having been a 'Lieutenant-Criminel' under the *ancien régime*, 'du Bousquier tenait le milieu entre le bourgeois et le hobereau'.[7] For all that it has similar links with the local nobility, the family of Mlle Cormon remains essentially bourgeois. 'Quoique roturière', Balzac observes, 'elle frayait avec la noblesse à laquelle elle s'était souvent alliée', adding that 'nulle bourgeoisie ne ressemblait davantage à la noblesse.'[8] On other occasions the Restoration bourgeoisie expresses a defiant confidence in its traditional class identity. Mme Minoret-Levrault takes pride in the fact that the family into which she has married can boast 'cent ans de bonne bourgeoisie'. In itself, 'cela vaut la noblesse'.[9]

The section of the revolutionary bourgeoisie from which most of Balzac's Restoration bourgeois are drawn is that of the 'petits commerçants'. Their ranks are not confined to Ragon and Birotteau. Jérôme-Baptiste Sauviat is a 'marchand forain' at the time of the Revolution,[10] and it is to this same class that Claude-Joseph Pillerault properly belongs. Balzac is inaccurate when he states that 'Pillerault appartenait à cette partie ouvrière agrégée par la révolution à la bourgeoisie'.[11] Pillerault's origins are clearly not working class but petit bourgeois since Balzac describes him as being 'autrefois marchand quincaillier à l'enseigne de la Cloche-d'Or'. Any remaining doubt is dispelled when Balzac discloses that, during the Revolution, 'ses fonds étaient engagés dans son commerce'.[12]

It is a tribute to Balzac's creative historical imagination that his Restoration bourgeoisie are shown to derive not merely from the 'petite' and 'moyenne bourgeoisie' of the Revolution but from a wide variety of social categories which between them cover virtually the whole of the revolutionary spectrum. There is the artisan Grandet who, in 1789, was 'un maître tonnelier fort à son aise, sachant lire, écrire et compter',[13] just as Montcornet, an imperial general who becomes owner of Les Aigues under the Restoration, is the son of 'un ébéniste du Faubourg Saint-Antoine'.[14] Rigou, who remains mayor of Blangy after 1815 until replaced by Gaubertin fils in 1821, is an ex-priest who married in the year I.

Jérôme-Nicolas Séchard rises from a poor background to become a member of the bourgeoisie during the Revolution itself. Illiterate, unlike Grandet, and therefore unable to become a compositor, he is originally a 'compagnon pressier' who has the good fortune to buy with his wife's savings the business of his former employer's widow for 10,000 fr. in 'assignats'. Subsequently, 'vers la fin de l'année 1819', he sells the printing-business to his son David for 30,000 fr.[15] In *Splendeurs et misères des courtisanes*, Balzac records that, on his death in March 1829, Séchard père left property worth 200,000 fr., 'assez beau déjà pour un homme qui a commencé par être ouvrier'.[16]

These cases are distinguished by three common factors. First, whatever their social origins in the Revolution, their careers show a successful rise; secondly, their ascension is uninterrupted; finally, their success is achieved directly through their own efforts and occurs within their own lifetime. Their ascension is gradual, extending from the Revolution, through the Empire, to reach fresh heights under the Restoration. In tracing their upward progress, Balzac is much more precise in respect of the Revolution than he is in relation to the Empire. One is particularly struck by the fact that so many of Balzac's Restoration bourgeoisie owe their initial success to their acquisition of 'biens nationaux'. Grandet, du Bousquier, Sauviat, Minoret-Levrault and Rigou all benefit decisively as 'acquéreurs' of Church and émigré property during the Revolution. In referring to the transitional imperial phase of the Restoration bourgeoisie, Balzac is less specific. In particular there is no evidence of 'rentier' activity on their part at this period. The picture is much more vague and one is left with a general impression of commercial consolidation, despite, in the cases of du Bousquier, Grandet and Birotteau, the adverse factor of Napoleonic victimisation.

It is only in the closing stages of the Empire that one witnesses a flurry of economic activity which is a prelude to Balzac's systematic analysis of the operations of the Restoration bourgeoisie. It is in the period 1814-15 that banking is shown as coming into its own in the *Comédie humaine*, that Nucingen and du Tillet lay the basis of their successful Restoration careers. In his treatment of the Restoration Balzac reveals the growing assertion of the bourgeoisie in commerce, finance and the beginnings of industrial expansion. It appears above all as a period of intense speculation in which fortunes fluctuate rapidly, when personal triumphs are completed and disasters suffered.

III

The *Comédie humaine* confirms the limited commercial and industrial advance which was achieved under the Restoration. According to Bertier de Sauvigny, only thirteen shares were quoted on the 'Bourse' in 1820 and this figure had risen to only thirty-eight by 1830.[17] Henri Sée distinguishes the metal industry, chemicals and the textile industry as being the only industries to have made significant progress during the Restoration prior to the general expansion of the economy during the July Monarchy, and particularly after 1840.[18] Where Balzac's treatment of the industrial activity of the period is concerned, Donnard observes that 'Balzac ne dit rien de la métallurgie et de la grande filature'.[19] Adding printing to Sée's trio of industries, Donnard concludes that 'tandis que les grandes industries chimiques et l'imprimerie prenaient un bel essor, les autres industries progressaient lentement'.[20] Finally, the marriage in 1842 of Cointet and the daughter of Anselme Popinot is seen by Donnard as symbolising the union 'des deux industries les plus prospères de cette époque'.[21]

While the evidence of the *Comédie humaine* is consistent with the emphasis placed by historians on the restricted economic growth achieved under the Restoration, Balzac nevertheless brings to light some important factors working in favour of expansion. A case in point is the development of transport and communications.

The abolition of the 'Messageries royales' in 1817 had stimulated competition in road transport. In *Un Début dans la vie*, Balzac describes how the Touchard family successfully run the transport business in the area around Paris in 1822. Balzac refers to 'les petites entreprises, menacées par des spéculateurs qui luttèrent dès 1822 contre les Touchard père et fils', and goes on to show how such firms survived the threat of being taken over by large-scale monopolies.[22] The success of Pierrotin in *Un Début dans la vie* and of Minoret-Levrault in *Ursule Mirouët* further confirms the observation made by Bertrand Gille that competition in road transport continued to flourish and to resist the general trend towards monopolisation which affected other industries, particularly during the July Monarchy.[23]

Demographic factors as well as transport are identified by Balzac as a force contributing to the economic expansion of the Paris basin under the Restoration. In *Les Paysans*, Gaubertin fils foresees the effect of the increase in the population of Paris since the end of hostilities, 'en devinant l'influence de la paix sur la population parisienne, qui, de 1815 à 1825, s'est accrue en effet de plus d'un tiers'.[24] The population of La-Ville-aux-Fayes had doubled from 4,000 in 1790 to the time of Gaubertin's term of office as mayor of Blangy from 1821. A centre for wood from the banks of the Yonne and the Seine, it had considerably increased its commercial and industrial importance as a result of the rise in the value of wood caused by the greater demands of an expanding Parisian population.

Although Balzac is chiefly concerned to identify the factors at work which are an essential prerequisite of full-scale industrialisation, at the same time he gives evidence of the limited development of capitalist industry which had taken place before 1830. In addition to Birotteau and Popinot, who are, as Donnard reminds one, 'parfumeurs fabricants' as well as 'parfumeurs commerçants', Balzac discusses in great detail the process of paper-manufacturing through the rivalry of David Séchard and the Cointet brothers.[25] On Lucien's return from Paris to Angoulême in 1821, David's future in printing seems assured since, as Balzac explains, twice as much paper is required compared with 1789 thanks to the spread of ideas and public discussion by the Revolution, a trend which Balzac elsewhere savagely denounces as being incompatible with effective government.

David's invention and the process of which it is a part are a further example of 'ces petites révolutions partielles' which Balzac saw exemplified in the growth of bureaucracy and which he considered an important object of his historical concern. The identification of the beginnings of commercial advertising also falls into this category. It is moreover characteristic of Balzac that he should associate such minor revolutions with his analysis of the 'grands mouvements sociaux'. It is a favourable moment for anyone who can invent a cheap way of making paper. The Cointets' subsequent capture of David's invention is an important step in the extension of their power. Through their diversified economic activity as printers, bankers and newspaper-owners as well as paper-manufacturers, the Cointets express the powerful advance of the provincial bourgeoisie under the Restoration. The success of a significant section of the bourgeoisie in the *Comédie humaine* is achieved during the Restoration itself. Where this is not already an accomplished fact, the basis is securely laid for its realisation in the July Revolution and under the July Monarchy.

Meanwhile Balzac's bourgeoisie continues to play an increasingly vital role in the economy and society of the Restoration. This growing participation is particularly well illustrated by the duplicated character of du Bousquier/du Croisier in *La Vieille Fille* and *Le Cabinet des Antiques*. It is du Bousquier who finances the revival of the lace and cotton industries of Alençon. His industrialisation of the Orne department is the first move towards modernising Brittany and bringing it into the mainstream of national life. This is confirmed in *Le Cabinet des Antiques* where Balzac reiterates the point he had made in *La Vieille Fille* by stating that 'en 1822, du Croisier se mit à la tête de l'industrie du département'.[26] The success of the Restoration bourgeoisie in the *Comédie humaine* is wide-ranging, embracing every important area of society and bringing with it social and political rewards. In the final analysis, however, the achievements of the bourgeoisie are accounted for by Balzac in terms of their economic activity. The particular phenomenon which the Cointets and du Bousquier underline in Balzac's analysis of the Restoration bourgeoisie is the growing importance of bourgeois finance.

IV

One of the basic reasons for the slow growth of commerce and industry under the Restoration was the lack of a system of organised credit with which to finance them. 'Un tel développement bancaire', Henri Sée emphasises, 'est un signe caractéristique des progrès du capitalisme.'[27] However, as Sée makes clear, it was a development which did not get significantly under way until after 1830 when banking put its resources more freely at the disposal of commerce and industry. The imperial impetus given to banking was largely halted under the Restoration.

Balzac's picture of the economic character of the Restoration agrees with that of historians in presenting it as essentially a period of consolidation, in contrast with the exuberant expansion for which it prepared the way under the July Monarchy.

The account given in the *Comédie humaine* of the financial bourgeoisie of the Restoration is entirely in line with the historical evidence which emphasises the restricted role of finance during the period, both in Paris and in the provinces. Of the Parisian banks which are mentioned by Balzac, that of the Mongenod brothers is particularly revealing of the behaviour of finance houses under the Restoration.

Founded in the first years of the Restoration, the Mongenod bank is atypical in its integrity and its lack of political ambitions. It also has the distinction of acting as banker to the aristocracy, of enjoying 'la confiance des premières maisons de la vieille noblesse, dont les capitaux et les immenses économies allaient dans cette banque'.[28] At the same time, the Mongenods supply credit to the government. The Mongenod bank is described as one 'qui a fait d'énormes bénéfices dans les premiers emprunts de la Restauration'.[29] On the other hand, the Mongenods, along with the Keller brothers, Nucingen and du Tillet, are only marginally involved in financing commerce and industry. 'Le crédit industriel' in particular had not yet become a widespread phenomenon. Mme Flavie Colleville, whose third son François is named after his real father, the banker Keller, is well placed to appreciate the role of Parisian finance. 'En 1820', Balzac remarks in *Les Petits Bourgeois*, 'elle regardait la banque comme la nourrice de l'industrie, le soutien des Etats.'[30] Mme Colleville's perspicacity with regard to the services of Parisian banking under the Restoration extends only to the second aspect.

Nor does organised finance at this stage show a serious interest in subsidising commerce. The credibility of Birotteau's failure to attract credit has been questioned by Maurice Bardèche.[31] Donnard, however, shows that it was perfectly plausible on both psychological and historical grounds. Each of the financiers whom Birotteau approaches has compelling personal reasons for refusing him credit, and moreover they have a common interest in seeking to take over the Madeleine speculation for themselves. More important is the fact that bankers at this period were reluctant to give credit to 'le petit commerce' at all. Adolphe Keller explains frankly to Birotteau his reasons for turning down Birotteau's request for credit. If they are employed in this way, he impresses on Birotteau, it will take five years to double 'ses fonds'. Therefore, he argues, 'il vaut mieux les faire valoir en banque'. It is little wonder then that the benign Birotteau is moved to exclaim: 'La Banque m'a toujours paru manquer à sa destination'.[32] 'En règle générale', Donnard remarks, 'les banquiers de cette époque, suivant l'exemple de la banque de France, refusaient leur service ordinaire au "petit" commerce parisien.' Donnard quotes Birotteau's complaint to this effect to Adolphe Keller and reminds one that Laffitte's 'Caisse générale du commerce et de l'industrie', with the specific aim of helping 'le petit commerce', was not founded until 1837, ironically in the same year that Balzac wrote *César Birotteau*, but too late, alas, to save 'le martyr de la probité commerciale' under the Restoration.[33] Conversely, Laffitte attributed the success of the firm of 'Perrégaux, Laffitte et Cie' under the Empire to its willingness to lend to industry. Explaining how he had doubled the profits within three years after taking over the bank on Perrégaux's death in 1808, Laffitte reveals: 'Mes moyens pour atteindre ce résultat étaient tout simples; il s'agissait de recevoir les capitaux oisifs qui venaient s'offrir et de les prêter ensuite à l'industrie qui en a toujours besoin'.[34]

In such a situation, as both Bertier de Sauvigny and Donnard stress, the possibilities open to moneylenders, with their extortionate interest rates, were enormous. What Balzac does is to exploit their economic role to invest them with broader dimensions. Gobseck is not simply a moneylender in a story which bears his name. His function is not merely narrative but historical and philosophical as well. Gobseck's horizons are international. He can explain the fall in the value of diamonds in terms of the flooding of the French market by diamond imports from Brazil since the conclusion of peace. His economic involvement occurs at the highest government level, for he makes a rich profit out of winding up the settlers' affairs in Haiti after France's recognition of the new republic in 1825. Finally, Gobseck, like Vautrin, is an important vehicle for conveying Balzac's views on human nature and society.

The absence of credit facilities was even more marked in the provinces than in Paris under the Restoration. Banking facilities were, as Bertier de Sauvigny indicates, usually assumed, not by full-time professional financiers, but by 'des notaires, les receveurs de finances, quelques capitalistes enrichis dans le négoce ou dans le trafic des biens nationaux'.[35] It was only under the July Monarchy that provincial banks appeared on a significant scale.[36] The consequent shortage of 'le numéraire' favoured the emergence, not only of moneylenders like Gobseck and Rigou, but also of financiers like the Cointets and Métivier whose lending is only one aspect of their multiple economic activity.

There are, it is true, characters in the *Comédie humaine* for whom banking is their exclusive occupation during the Restoration. Des Grassins, Grossetête and Graslin all come under this heading. Essentially however they all represent the pre-industrial banker. Des Grassins, for example, plays a subordinate financial role in relation to Grandet. It is Grandet who is the creditor and not des Grassins, who uses money borrowed from Grandet to lend it in turn at a high rate of interest. Des Grassins shares this function with Cruchet, as 'le plus riche banquier de Saumur, aux bénéfices duquel Grandet participait à sa convenance et secrètement'.[37] It is the 'bourgeois terrien' Grandet and not the banker who calls the financial tune.

The one exception to the non-participation of organised finance in Restoration industry in the *Comédie humaine* is du Bousquier, who, as we have seen, provided the credit necessary for the industrialisation of Alençon and the Orne department. Balzac's emphasis is correct and significant. For the financial bourgeoisie of the Restoration a commitment to commercial and industrial investment was a less attractive proposition than a variety of forms of speculation.

V

There are three main areas of speculation in the *Comédie humaine*, in commerce, in 'rentes' and in property. Commercial speculation takes two forms. In some cases it is concerned with the selling of products, either industrial or agricultural, often produced, as with Grandet and Birotteau, by the vendor himself. The success of Grandet's wines is explained not only by their quality but also by Grandet's shrewd control of the market, whereby his output is deliberately calculated to ensure that, when released for sale, his wines will fetch a maximum price. Charles Mignon, on the other hand, makes a fortune out of buying and selling other people's products. In his profitable two-way dealings with America, he sells silks bought cheaply in Lyon and imports raw material obtained at a low price. As a result, 'cette double opération valut un capital énorme à la maison Mignon'.[38]

The outstanding absence in Balzac's analysis of speculation during the Restoration is that of industrial shares. This omission is perfectly normal since it accords with the general view of historians concerning the restricted industrial growth of the period which was largely accounted for, as one has seen, by a lack of organised credit. Henri Sée's conclusion that, thanks to the admittedly limited expansion of industrial credit, 'il en résulte de grandes facilités pour les spéculations de Bourse, déjà assez actives sous la Restauration', is belied by the figures he cites to emphasise the insignificant rise in the number of shares quoted on the 'Bourse' during the Restoration.[39] As Donnard points out, Nucingen's mining shares of 1826 are exceptional for the time and contrast sharply with the non-industrial modes of speculation featured in the spate of plays dealing with speculation at exactly the same period.[40]

That Balzac should show virtually no evidence of speculation in industrial shares during the Restoration is further proof of his sure sense of history, of economic realities in particular. This is not a case of a happy accident working in Balzac's favour. There are in fact positive signs that Balzac was aware of the essential nature of speculation under the Restoration. Du Tillet's advice to Roguin, ruined by his passion for Sarah Gobseck, is to give him a large sum of money, 'pour être jouée avec audace dans une partie quelconque, à la Bourse, ou dans quelque spéculation choisie entre les mille qui s'entreprenaient alors'.[41] The concluding part of du Tillet's advice to Roguin was appropriate, for it was in directions other than industrial shares that Restoration speculators were primarily moved to invest.

The Restoration was the golden age of state 'rentes'. Henri Sée conclusively establishes that it was in the period 1815-20 that the basis was laid for the massive investment and speculation in 'rentes' which characterised the whole of the Restoration. Those years saw a series of concrete measures which together amounted to a rentier's charter. In April 1816, a 'caisse d'amortissement' was set up, providing 'des titres de rente dont les intérêts étaient réservés à l'amortissement de la dette'. Two years later, in order to pay off the war indemnity ahead of the term fixed, the government invited the public to subscribe to an issue of 'rentes' worth 14,600,000 fr. The invitation met with an enthusiastic response. In April 1819, a number of 'Petits Grands Livres' were created to supplement the 'Grand Livre' dating from the Revolution. By 1825, it is estimated that 145,000 subscribers had invested in the 'Grand Livre'. Finally, in 1824, 'la dette flottante' was introduced with an initial issue of 'Bons Royaux' worth 140 million.[42]

Small wonder therefore that the Restoration rentier found every incentive to invest. The supreme 'rentier' in the *Comédie humaine*, Parisian or otherwise, is Grandet.[43] For Grandet the eternal cycle of speculation revolves around the interchange of gold and 'rentes'. When he makes a profit by selling his gold at Angers, it is done with the aim of buying more 'rentes', 'en rapporter en valeurs du receveur-général sur le trésor la somme nécessaire à l'achat de ses rentes après l'avoir grossie de l'agio'.[44] In turn, his 'rentes' bought at 80 fr. and sold when they have reached a value of 115 fr., are reconverted, along with the interest made, into gold, ready at any moment to be reinvested. Grandet's advice to Eugénie is to follow the same successful method after him. His success is due to his remarkable speculative flair which gives him a decisive edge over his rivals. It is also explained by his readiness to depart from the traditional hostility to investment in the provinces. This reluctance to invest on the part of the provincial bourgeoisie is illustrated by the cautious behaviour of David and Eve Séchard. Even after their wealth has been increased by their inheritance from David's father, it is not until over a year later that they decide to invest in 'rentes' at the very outbreak of the July Revolution. 'Il concevait', Balzac notes of Grandet, 'enfin la rente, placement pour lequel les gens de province manifestent une répugnance invincible.'[45] Rather than 'l'avare de Saumur', Grandet, 'qui ne manquait pas une seule spéculation', emerges essentially as 'le spéculateur de Saumur'.

Another successful investor in the Grandet manner is du Bousquier. On marrying Mlle Cormon in 1816, he invests her savings in the 'Grand Livre' and gains as much in a year as the sum of his wife's fortune. The 'rentier' career of Birotteau, on the other hand, is clouded with ambiguity. His wife's advice to him, in December 1818, is to put aside his social and political ambitions and to devote his efforts instead to marrying off his daughter, selling his business and retiring to the countryside. To that end, she urges him, the surest means is to invest in 'rentes'. 'Si tu veux augmenter ta fortune', she tells him, 'agis aujourd'hui comme en 1793: les rentes sont à soixante-douze francs, achète des rentes.'[46] Mme Birotteau is in fact a year out in her recollection of Birotteau's 'rentier' activities under the Revolution. It was in vendémiaire, 1794, that Birotteau had exchanged 100 'louis d'or' for 6,000 fr. in 'assignats', with which he had bought 'rentes' at their current value of 30 fr., 'les paya la veille du jour où l'échelle de dépréciation eut cours à la Bourse'. Subsequently, we learn, Birotteau keenly followed 'le mouvement des fonds', so that when Ragon, demoralised by Brumaire, sold his business to his 'premier commis', Birotteau found himself 'maître à vingt ans de mille francs de rente dans les fonds publics'.[47] This is the last we hear of Birotteau as a 'rentier'. The hiatus in his holding of 'rentes' is never explained and, in the event, Birotteau prefers to ignore his wife's advice and invest in the property speculation which finally ruins him. Pillerault, on the other hand, follows precisely the opposite course to that taken by Birotteau. Unlike Birotteau,

Pillerault had not been a 'rentier' at the time of the Revolution. 'Ses fonds', one recalls, 'étaient engagés dans son commerce au moment où César employait ses économies en rentes.' He only becomes a 'rentier' on his retirement in 1814, when he invests 70,000 fr. in the 'Grand Livre'. When, in January 1819, Birotteau is about to embark on the fateful Madeleine venture, Pilleraut offers to help him by selling some of his 'rentes'. 'Voilà les rentes à quatre-vingts', he announces to Birotteau, 'je pourrais vendre deux mille francs de mes consolidés.'[48]

The details may not always be entirely clear. For example, Auguste Longueville informs Emilie de Fontaine that his brother Maximilien has made a fortune out of speculation. When he tells her that 'après avoir réuni quelques capitaux, mon frère s'est alors associé à une maison de banque; et je sais qu'il vient de faire avec le Brésil une spéculation qui peut le rendre millionnaire',[49] it is not certain what form of speculation is involved. The overall message, however, is consistent and emphatic. First of all, the constant rise in the value of 'rentes' under the Restoration which one can trace in the *Comédie humaine* is historically precise. As Henri Sée indicates, their average annual value rose from 59.35 in 1816 to 98.90 in 1824, helped by the fact that 'l'alliance avec Rothschild, qui commence en 1823, permet un cours de 89.55'. Their peak value was achieved at the very end of the Restoration. 'C'est juste avant la Révolution de Juillet', Sée observes, 'sous le ministère Polignac que les plus hauts cours furent atteints.'[50] Balzac therefore is correct in presenting the Restoration as a period rich in opportunities for the investor in government stock. It was an activity which contained inherent risks and which was bound to claim victims, not all of whom were 'rentiers'. Charles Mignon's crash in January 1826 is the outcome of the economic crisis to which Villèle's 'conversion des rentes' in the previous year had made a significant contribution.[51] More important than the failures, however, are the remarkable 'rentier' achievements under the Restoration of men like Grandet and du Bousquier. By its success in 'rentes' as in all its other economic activities, Balzac's Restoration bourgeoisie decisively strengthens its position as the increasingly dominant class in society.

The type of speculation which shares equal importance with 'rentes' in the *Comédie humaine* is speculation in property, of which Balzac provides numerous instances under the Restoration. The first signs of it are noticed by Chabert when he returns to Paris after Waterloo to find that his old house in the rue du Mont-Blanc has been sold and demolished. 'Des spéculateurs', Chabert laments, 'avaient bâti plusieurs maisons dans mes jardins.'[52] The fact that the rue de Mont-Blanc has given way to the Chaussée d'Antin is a reminder, moreover, that the financial bourgeoisie, as well as making a fortune out of speculating on the property they sold to their clients, were concerned to establish their own distinctive 'quartier' to rival the faubourg Saint-Germain.

It is this surge of house-building in Paris in the immediate post-war years that enables Delbecq, as secretary and financial adviser to Chabert's ex-wife, now the comtesse Ferraud, to triple his client's capital by shrewd speculation.[53] As well as tending to exaggerate the scope of the 'Bourse''s activities at this period, Balzac arbitrarily identifies the first three years of the Restoration as being particularly favourable to property speculators. There are other references in the *Comédie humaine*, however, which suggest that the boom in property speculation lasted longer and reached its high point somewhat later. Delphine's account of Nucingen's shady dealings in property relates to the period 1819-20. The experience of Auguste de Maulincour points in the same direction. In the spring of 1819 he narrowly escapes being killed by masonry falling from a scaffolding. In discussing this incident, in which Auguste's carriage is crushed and his valet killed, Balzac reveals that 'en ce temps-là, Paris avait la fièvre des constructions . . . En ce moment, tout le monde bâtissait et démolissait quelque chose'.[54]

This picture of widespread speculation accompanying an intense wave of building in Paris which extends well into the Restoration is emphatically confirmed in *César Birotteau*. In 1819, we are told, the price of land near the Madeleine was remarkably cheap. 'Peu de personnes', Balzac stresses, 'savent aujourd'hui combien peu valait à cette époque une toise de terrain autour de la Madeleine.'[55] Du Tillet calculates that its value will have quadrupled in three years. His confidence is fully justified since we discover that at the beginning of 1823 'les terrains situés dans le faubourg du Temple arrivèrent à des prix fous'.[56] The land on which a company is seeking to build the canal Saint-Martin is owned half by du Tillet and half by Anselme Popinot. The company is prepared to pay an enormous price for the land, the other half of which du Tillet is anxious to obtain from Popinot on its behalf. Hating du Tillet for his exploitation of Birotteau, Popinot makes him pay 60,000 fr. for the lease.[57] The Madeleine transaction, moreover, is part of a wider speculation in Parisian property extending, as Claparon announces to Birotteau, to the Champs-Elysées, 'autour de la Bourse qui va s'achever, dans le quartier Saint-Lazare et à Tivoli'.[58]

The crucial factor in the Madeleine affair is its timing. In *Les Petits Bourgeois*, Théodose de la Peyrade advises Brigitte Thuillier in 1840 to buy property in the same Madeleine area. He refers to the circumstances of 1819 out of which du Tillet had made a fortune. 'Aux environs de la Madeleine!', he exclaims excitedly, 'ce sera le coeur de Paris dans dix ans! Et, si vous saviez, on pensait à ces terrains dès 1819! . . . La fortune de du Tillet vient de là.' The failure of Ragon and Birotteau is explained as being due to the premature nature of their speculation. 'Ils spéculaient un peu trop tôt sur ces terrains-là.'[59] Du Tillet, on the other hand, timing perfectly his exploitation of Birotteau's financial naïvety, had calculated his speculation exactly right.

The question of whether Balzac committed an anachronism in situating the Madeleine speculation in 1818-19 is a valid one. Henri Sée, for example, makes no mention of speculation during this period. Indeed the strong impression given by Sée is that the expansion of the construction industry in Paris and the property speculation it gave rise to were essentially phenomena of the July Monarchy. Referring to the programme of public works initiated after 1830 by the prefect of the Seine, Rambuteau, Sée adds that, 'Aussi, s'efforce-t-on d'acquérir des maisons qu'on pense devoir être bientôt expropriées'.[60] This impression is strengthened by the extract from Stendhal's *Mémoires d'un touriste* which instances the volume of building activity everywhere evident under Louis-Philippe.[61]

The question is answered by Donnard. 'On est en droit de demander', he acknowledges, 'si le romancier n'a pas transporté sous l'Empire et la Restauration des faits économiques caractérisant le règne de Louis-Philippe.' Donnard then goes on to argue convincingly that the distinctive features of Birotteau's operations, 'vitrine attrayante, publicité bien organisée, produits scientifiquement préparés', although characteristic of the July Monarchy, already existed under the Empire and the Restoration.[62] As far as the Madeleine affair is concerned, Donnard quotes Ouvrard as assigning it in his *Mémoires* to 1824. Balzac is therefore correct, Donnard concludes, in placing the action of *César Birotteau* in 1818-19 since it was then that communications in the area of the Madeleine were developed, with a consequent rise in the value of adjoining land, in building and in speculation. The truth of the matter would seem to be that, although he is not guilty of anticipating the events of the July Monarchy in his version of the Madeleine speculation, Balzac advances it by some five or six years. This is further indicated by the investigations of Adeline Daumard.[63]

If there are any anachronisms in Balzac's account of economic activity under the Restoration, they are of a peripheral kind. A more blatant example is the attributing of Charles Mignon's second recovery to his successful participation in the opium trade which, as Donnard himself mentions without pointing to the anachronism, coincided with the middle period of the July Monarchy.[64] In the end, anachronisms of this kind, which are of a minor nature in any case, scarcely matter and should not be allowed to obscure Balzac's basic purpose and achievement. Through the evidence it provides of successful speculation under the Restoration, in commerce, in 'rentes' and in property, the *Comédie humaine* is once again witness to the continued advance of the revolutionary bourgeoisie.

VI

Le commerce doit briller et ne pas se laisser écraser par l'aristocratie.[65]

M. Lourdois, the decorator of César Birotteau who expresses this concern, need have no fear. The growing economic power of Balzac's Restoration bourgeoisie is matched by its social aspirations. Few of them are free of social pretensions in one form or another. The Parisian lawyers, Derville and Popinot, are, it is true, devoid of ambition, as are the Mongenods. They are, however, exceptions to the norm in their profession. The integrity and lack of social and political ambition of the Mongenods in particular are uncharacteristic of contemporary bankers like the Keller brothers, Nucingen and du Tillet.[66]

The social ambition of the bourgeoisie expresses itself in two ways. Either it aims to rise within the limits of its own class or else it seeks to become part of the aristocracy. The outstanding example of the first tendency is provided by Birotteau, whose ambition it becomes to 's'élever aux régions de la haute bourgeoisie de Paris'.[67] Principally, however, Balzac's attention is concentrated on provincial aspirations towards membership of the 'bourgeoisie terrienne'. In some cases the 'moyenne bourgeoisie' attempts to acquire land under the Restoration. Some are unsuccessful, like Séchard père, whose plans to marry David to a landowning widow are frustrated. Much more commonly, however, their efforts achieve success. Grandet already owns land when he acquires the estate of the marquis de Froidfond. Du Bousquier becomes the richest landowner in the Orne department. Graslin, towards the end of 1829, pays 500,000 fr. for the Montégnac lands of the duc de Navarreins. Of the three, only du Bousquier has social and political ambitions. Unlike that of Grandet, Graslin's acquisition cannot even be justified on economic grounds. The Navarreins estates are largely made up of forests and infertile plains. It is their infertility, plus the fact that they were mainly forest-land, which explains why they had escaped confiscation in the Revolution. The motivation which Graslin shares with Grandet is the desire to extend his power and reinforce his prestige through the ownership of land. Grandet, du Bousquier and Graslin all have in common the fact that their territorial gains are made at the expense of the aristocracy. They are all equally alike in their concern to remain within their class whilst strengthening their position as members of it.

One can discern in the *Comédie humaine* a simultaneous trend whereby important sections of the Restoration bourgeoisie strive to achieve some degree of assimilation with the aristocracy. The class demarcations are occasionally blurred. If Balzac is accurate in saying of Mlle Cormon's family that 'nulle bourgeoisie ne ressemblait davantage à la noblesse',[68] one might reverse the terms of the definition in respect of the Claës, of whom it could be said that 'nulle noblesse ne ressemblait davantage à la bourgeoisie'. Then there are the complex cases of Lucien de Rubempré and Maximilien Longueville, Lucien's failure to assert his spurious right to a title contrasting with Maximilien's spectacular rise.

For most members of the Restoration bourgeoisie who seek to identify themselves with the aristocracy the surest route lies in intermarriage. In the Parisian context, the marriages of Goriot's daughters under the Empire are complemented by the cynical union of Charles Grandet and Mlle d'Aubrion. In a similar spirit, the opposition to Desiré Minoret's marrying Ursule Mirouët is based on the recognition that his future depends on the choice of an aristocratic wife. 'Il fallait lui chercher une femme, une fille pauvre appartenant à une vieille et noble famille; il pourrait alors arriver à la magistrature de Paris.'[69]

Among the Restoration bourgeois who succeed in marrying into the aristocracy a special place is occupied by provincial lawyers in the *Comédie humaine*. Pierquin does so after transferring his attentions from Marguerite to Félicie Claës. Petit-Claud's triumph in marrying Mlle de la Haye is shared by the elder Cointet who had made the marriage possible. When Cointet appears at the de la Hayes wearing a diamond on his shirt-front, it is to celebrate, not only Petit-Claud's official proposal of marriage, but, more importantly, 'la vengeance du riche commerçant sur l'aristocratie pauvre'.[70] The revenge of the bourgeoisie on the aristocracy through intermarriage may be achieved by the bourgeois concerned or by his descendants in his own lifetime. Such is the case of du Croisier, who lives to see his grand-niece, Mlle Duval, marry Victurnien d'Esgrignon after 1830.

However much the circumstances may vary, the overall trend is clear. Time and again Balzac emphasises the social divisiveness of the Restoration. Whether he is describing Angoulême or Alençon, Douai, Nemours or Paris, Balzac insists on the accentuation of class divisions as the outstanding social feature of the Restoration, notwithstanding the contrasting example of the Empire and the efforts at 'amalgame' of Louis XVIII. The only significant exception is Issoudun, where, as Balzac explains, peculiar local factors had resulted in the total eclipse of the aristocracy.[71] The initiative for change comes primarily from the bourgeoisie. Where it in turn prefers to marry within its own ranks, it thereby contributes to the hardening of class lines for which the aristocracy is held chiefly responsible by Balzac. When du Croisier marries Mlle Cormon, the effect is to aggravate the division between 'la haute et la petite aristocratie, entre les éléments bourgeois et les éléments nobles réunis un moment sous la pression de la grande autorité napoléonienne'.[72]

The *Comédie humaine* demonstrates the growing challenge made by the Restoration bourgeoisie to the important vestiges of aristocratic power. Not content merely to extend its authority as a 'bourgeoisie terrienne' at the expense of the aristocracy, it sought increasingly to assimilate itself with the aristocracy on its own terms through inter-marriage. From now on, the aristocracy would despise bourgeois values at its peril. In the process, the impulsion provided by 'le mouvement ascensionnel de l'argent' helped break down the social barriers which Balzac denounced as a disastrous weakness in Restoration society. This effect was one which Balzac could be expected to welcome. Not only should it contribute to social stability and national unity. A closing of ranks between bourgeoisie and aristocracy was essential, Balzac believed, to combat the threat of popular subversion inherent in the triumph of bourgeois values. The price was a difficult one for Balzac to accept but one that would have to be paid. If society were to be defended against the barbarous masses, it would be led not, as Balzac would have pre-ferred, by an enlightened and resurgent aristocracy, but by a bourgeoisie confirmed by the Restoration as the true heir of the Revolution.

VII

It is rare that the Restoration bourgeoisie in the *Comédie humaine* are apolitical. There are those who, like Grandet, Mongenod, Derville and Goriot, show no desire to participate in Restoration politics, but they are outnumbered by their politically-minded and, in some cases, politically active counterparts. The latter, to a man, are all royalists in one sense or another. This is true even of Pillerault, whose political opinions are wrongly described by Balzac as being 'celles de l'extrême gauche'. Pillerault is a left-of-centre liberal bourgeois, a faithful reader of *Le Constitutionnel*, not opposed in principle to the restored monarchy but concerned, like the 'acquéreurs', to defend the gains of the Revolution. Alarmed by the power of the Jesuits and the views of the comte d'Artois, 'il tenait à ses droits, à la liberté, aux fruits de la révolution'.[73]

However, what matters are the distinctions in the nature of their royalism. In *Les Employés* Baudoyer is quoted by a ministerial journal as proof that 'de tout temps, la haute bourgeoisie fut royaliste'.[74] The *Comédie humaine* reveals this to be nothing more than wishful government thinking, although the example of Ragon and Birotteau proves that 'partisans du trône et de l'autel' could be found within the 'moyenne' as well as in the 'haute bourgeoisie'. Birotteau never wavers in the fanatical royalism which had earned him the distinction of being wounded by Bonaparte on the steps of the church of Saint-Roch in vendémiaire, 1795. With Ragon he embodies 'la bourgeoisie grave et sérieuse, à moeurs économiques, à idées respectueuses envers la noblesse, dévouée au souverain et à l'église'.[75] One of the chief spokesmen of the 'parti prêtre' in Angoulême is the elder Cointet. This does not prevent him, however, from becoming a minister and 'pair de France' under the July Monarchy.

The unqualified royalism of Ragon and Birotteau is a distinct minority phenomenon among Balzac's Restoration bourgeoisie. The majority tendency is represented by liberals who stand for a constitutional monarchy, who are opportunist in their dealings with the clergy where not openly anti-clerical, and who are in fierce competition with the aristocracy. Some become ultras in anticipation of the impending triumph of reaction. This is the case with Lucien de Rubempré, whose expedient switch of loyalties is inspired by Coralie's implausible prediction of the discrediting of liberalism and Villèle's coming to power in 1822. Or liberal tactics may vary. Always tantalisingly short, like Vinet in *Pierrette*, of a few decisive electoral votes, du Bousquier stands as an official royalist candidate whilst secretly retaining his liberal sympathies and contacts.

Of the general liberal movement of the Restoration bourgeoisie Balzac leaves one in no doubt. The younger Cointet and Petit-Claud mark the success of liberalism in Angoulême as does du Bousquier, with more devious equivocation, in Alençon. It is du Bousquier whose political involvement suggests the important realignment which was to culminate in the July Revolution, 'cette fatale opinion qui sans être vraiment libérale, ni réellement royaliste, enfanta les 221'.[76] Closely linked with Parisian finance through his banker, François Keller, du Bousquier is presented as a precursor of the 'royalistes doctrinaires' who were to play a vital part in the final crisis of the regime.[77] Balzac therefore commits an anachronism when de Marsay refers to the 'royalistes doctrinaires' in his letter to Paul de Manerville at the end of *Le Contrat de mariage*. De Marsay is writing in 1827 whereas the 'royalistes doctrinaires' only emerged as a political force in reaction against the Polignac ministry in 1829-30.[78]

Such occasional errors on Balzac's part do nothing finally to detract from the impression of the growing political power of the Restoration bourgeoisie which is conveyed by the *Comédie humaine*. Qualifying as landowners for the 'cens', they constantly reinforced the number of electors guaranteed to vote in the liberal cause.

Balzac's analysis is both broad and perceptive of important political nuances. In particular, the 'royalistes doctrinaires' whom du Bousquier foreshadows, led by Royer-Collard, were to become 'le parti de la résistance' of the early period of the July Monarchy, under first Casimir Périer and then Guizot, and identified with 'la politique du juste milieu' so despised by Balzac. Meanwhile, the *Comédie humaine* accurately charts the progress of the Restoration bourgeoisie towards its total domination of society. Having consolidated its wealth, it was now in a position to translate its social ascendancy into undisputed political mastery.

VIII

Balzac's attitude to the bourgeoisie of the Restoration provides an important clue to his social and political thinking. If the future of French society was to be entrusted neither to an effete aristocracy nor to the unthinkable 'peuple', where then did that leave the bourgeoisie in Balzac's view? The truth is that Balzac found it difficult to forgive the bourgeoisie, liberals and 'royalistes doctrinaires' alike, for having helped overthrow the elder branch of the Bourbons. No matter how they might perform when in power after 1830, their treasonable irresponsibility in deposing the last legitimist king of France made them, for the time being at least, politically untouchable for Balzac.

Political exclusion was one thing, economic approval was quite

another. Balzac's political reaction to the Restoration bourgeoisie
reveals a complete dichotomy with his economic views. The attack on
'morcellement' and 'la petite culture' complements Balzac's plea for
the free circulation of the money supply. Both are recurrent notions
at the root of his socioeconomic philosophy. Grandet and du Bousquier
both succeed and are admired for two reasons. They not only become
'grands propriétaires'; each makes an important departure from the
established norm whereby 'pour la province, la richesse des nations
consiste moins dans l'active rotation de l'argent que dans un stérile
entassement'.[79] Balzac, on several occasions, reiterates his plea for the
greater mobility of capital as a prerequisite of the economic development of France as a whole. In *Les Employés*, for example, the Minister
refers to the need to 'animer le mouvement de l'argent dont l'immobilité
devient, en France surtout, funeste par suite des habitudes avaricieuses
et profondément illogiques de la province qui enfouit des tas d'or'.[80]
The obvious gainer, if such policies were pursued, could only be the
'bourgeoisie terrienne'. It is, moreover, this same class which emerges
in the *Comédie humaine* as the ascendant force in Restoration society,
its wealth increasingly expressed in political terms through its prominent
role in the 'régime censitaire'.[81]

As Balzac's outlook became more marked by the repercussions of
1830, so the novels dealing with the Restoration show the force of his
contempt for the July Monarchy. The Restoration bourgeoisie thus
incurs the venom of hindsight and the savagery of an apocalyptic
vision. 'Cet élément insocial créé par la Révolution', Balzac prophesies
in *Les Paysans*, 'absorbera quelque jour la Bourgeoisie, comme la
Bourgeoisie a dévoré la Noblesse.'[82] 'Le temps est gros de révolutions',
Corentin similarly announces in *Splendeurs*.[83] These predictions were
made with full experience of the final triumph which the bourgeoisie
had savoured. The implications for Balzac were clear. The class whose
ascension Balzac's economic views favoured are revealed to be the
advancing force in French society under the Restoration. The future,
even more than the present, belonged to the Grandets, the du Bous-
quiers and the Cointets. Sooner or later Balzac would have to swallow
his political aversion for the bourgeoisie and recognise, as any share-
holder in the 'Chemins de fer du Nord' would have to, that it constituted
the only effective defence against the threat of popular democracy.

Notes

1. *Les Employés*, VII, 906.
2. *Louis Lambert*, XI, 589.
3. *Illusions Perdues*, V, 140.
4. *L'Envers de l'histoire contemporaine*, VIII, 219.
5. Ibid., 220.
6. Adeline Daumard, *La Bourgeoisie Parisienne de 1815 à 1848* (Paris, 1963), p. 272.
7. *La Vieille Fille*, IV, 826.
8. Ibid., 847.
9. *Ursule Mirouët*, III, 845.
10. *Le Curé de village*, IX, 643.
11. *César Birotteau*, VI, 119.
12. Ibid., 118.
13. *Eugénie Grandet*, III, 1030.
14. *Les Paysans*, IX, 151.
15. *Illusions Perdues*, V, 126.
16. *Splendeurs et misères des courtisanes*, VI, 665.
17. G. de Bertier de Sauvigny, *La Restauration* (Paris, 1955), p. 312.
18. H. Sée, *Histoire Economique de la France*, 2 vols. (Paris, 1951). Vol. II, *Les Temps Modernes (1789-1914)*, pp. 153-60. See also the article by François Crouzet, 'French Economic Growth in the Nineteenth Century Reconsidered', *History* (June 1974), pp. 167-79.
19. J.-H. Donnard, *Les Réalités économiques et sociales dans l'oeuvre de Balzac* (Paris, 1971), p. 278.
20. Ibid., p. 271.
21. Ibid., p. 270.
22. *Un Début dans la vie*, I, 734.
23. Bertrand Gille, *Recherches sur la formation de la grande entreprise capitaliste, 1815-1848* (Paris, 1959b), p. 70.
24. *Les Paysans*, IX, 304.
25. Donnard, *Les Réalités économiques et sociales dans l'oeuvre de Balzac*, p. 255. The firm of Protez and Chiffreville, with which Birotteau is associated from 1813, is a reminder that 'l'industrie des produits chimiques' developed under the Empire.
26. *Le Cabinet des Antiques*, IV, 980.
27. Sée, *Histoire Economique de la France*, p. 228.
28. *L'Envers de l'histoire contemporaine*, VIII, 232.
29. Ibid., 276.
30. *Les Petits Bourgeois*, VIII, 42.
31. Maurice Bardèche, 'Balzac et Flaubert', *L'Année Balzacienne* (1976), pp. 9-29.
32. *César Birotteau*, VI, 214-15. Quoted by René Guise in his Introduction to *César Birotteau*, Pléiade, VI, 33.
33. Donnard, *Les Réalités économiques et sociales dans l'oeuvre de Balzac*, pp. 283-4.
34. Jacques Laffitte, *Mémoires* (ed. Paul Duchon) (Paris, 1932).
35. Bertier de Sauvigny, *La Restauration*, p. 311.
36. Henri Sée mentions as an exception the bank founded in 1818 in Bordeaux by the shipowner Balguerie-Stuttenberg. Sée, *Histoire Economique de la France*, p. 228.
37. *Eugénie Grandet*, III, 1032.
38. *Modeste Mignon*, I, 487.

39. Sée, *Histoire Economique de la France*, p. 229. See also note 17. Sée's figures differ slightly from those given by Bertier de Sauvigny. According to Sée, seven shares were quoted in 1816, compared with 42 in 1826.

40. Donnard, *Les Réalités économiques et sociales dans l'oeuvre de Balzac*, p. 320. In his article 'Qui est Nucingen?', *L'Année Balzacienne* (1960), pp. 135-48, Donnard persuasively suggests that Nucingen was a composite creation, based on Fould, Humann, Ouvrard and Girardin, and not, as was previously assumed, a simple reflection of Rothschild.

41. *César Birotteau*, VI, 87.

42. Sée, *Histoire Economique de la France*, pp. 110-14.

43. For an account of speculation in 'rentes' in Paris under the Restoration see Daumard, *La Bourgeoisie Parisienne de 1815 à 1848*, part III, chapter III, section II, 'La Psychologie des possédants'.

44. *Eugénie Grandet*, III, 1121.

45. Ibid., 1150.

46. *César Birotteau*, VI, 43-4.

47. Ibid., 57-8.

48. Ibid., 121.

49. *Le Bal de Sceaux*, I, 159.

50. Sée, *Histoire Economique de la France*, pp. 112-13. See also the article by Eugene B. Dubern, 'La Rente Française chez Balzac', *L'Année Balzacienne* (1963), pp. 251-68. Dubern concludes that Balzac's account is both accurate and perceptive, faithfully reflecting the uninterrupted increase in the value of 'rentes' from 1815 to 1848.

51. Rejected in 1824, Villèle's scheme for the conversion of 'rentes' was made law in the following year in order to provide the means of financing the indemnity awarded to the émigrés. From five per cent, the interest on 'rentes' was reduced to give the option of 4½ per cent at 'pair' or 3½ per cent at 75.

52. *Le Colonel Chabert*, III, 332.

53. Ibid., 348. See also pp. 127-8 above.

54. *Ferragus*, V, 822-3.

55. *César Birotteau*, VI, 90.

56. Ibid., 295.

57. The price of land continued to rise. As Balzac confirms, 'les terrains de la Madeleine commençaient à s'élever à des prix qui présageaient les valeurs exorbitantes auxquelles ils atteignirent en 1827'. Ibid.

58. Ibid., 240.

59. *Les Petits Bourgeois*, VIII, 133.

60. Sée, *Histoire Economique de la France*, p. 230.

61. Quoted by Sée, ibid., p. 226.

62. Donnard, *Les Réalités économiques et sociales dans l'oeuvre de Balzac*, p. 254.

63. See Daumard, *La Bourgeoisie Parisienne de 1815 à 1848*, pp. 427-31. Mlle Daumard also has some interesting things to say in this section about commercial speculation under the Restoration and about the limited role of 'la haute banque parisienne' in financing industry.

64. Donnard, *Les Réalités économique et sociales dans l'oeuvre de Balzac*, pp. 326-7.

65. *César Birotteau*, VI, 141.

66. 'Loin d'ambitionner la pairie', Balzac emphasises, 'comme les Keller, les Nucingen et les du Tiller, les Mongenod restaient éloignés de la politique et n'en savaient que ce que doit en savoir la banque.' *L'Envers de l'histoire contemporaine*, VIII, 232-3.

67. *César Birotteau*, VI, 77.

68. *La Vieille Fille*, IV, 847.

69. *Ursule Mirouët*, III, 954.

70. *Illusions Perdues*, V, 654.

71. *La Rabouilleuse*, IV, 362.

72. *Le Cabinet des Antiques*, IV, 979.

73. *César Birotteau*, VI, 119.

74. *Les Employés*, VII, 1033. The term 'royaliste' is used here in the sense of 'ultra'.

75. *César Birotteau*, VI, 226.

76. *La Vieille Fille*, IV, 922.

77. The group of 221 deputies issued a manifesto as a vote of censure on the speech from the throne in March 1830. Of their original number, 202 were re-elected in June 1830, and were among the 219 deputies supporting Louis-Philippe.

78. See the note on pp. 444-5 of vol. 7 of the Conard edition. Also Bertier de Sauvigny, *La Restauration*, pp. 586-8.

79. *La Vieille Fille*, IV, 914.

80. *Les Employés*, VII, 1114.

81. The whole question of the 'notables' is the subject of chapter 8.

82. *Les Paysans*, IX, 49.

83. *Splendeurs et misères des courtisanes*, VI, 559.

PART THREE:

THE JULY MONARCHY

7 THE JULY REVOLUTION

The Continuing Class Analysis and the Road to Legitimism

Balzac is only incidentally concerned with either the causes or the details of the Revolution. 'Pour les hommes du siècle, les hommes d'avenir', he wrote in April 1830, 'ce n'est pas dans les détails qu'ils étudient la révolution, c'est dans son ensemble, c'est dans ses résultats.'[1] What essentially interests him are its effects on French society in the first half of the nineteenth century. It is against the background of this continuing historical analysis, with its starting-point in the Revolution, that Balzac's judgement of each successive regime is made. The *Comédie humaine* essentially examines first the swaying fortunes of the continuing conflict between bourgeoisie and aristocracy under the Empire and the Restoration. Then Balzac analyses the effects of the July Revolution and the affirmation of bourgeois power under the July Monarchy which victory in 1830 made possible.

The central notion in Balzac's indictment of the Revolution, that the cult of materialism was inseparable from the revolutionary conquests of the bourgeoisie, is already clearly stated in Balzac's writing before the *Comédie humaine*. The key-note in Balzac's appraisal of the changes brought about by the Revolution is first sounded in 1822 with the sustained attack on the bourgeois worship of money which is developed in *Jean Louis*. In the *Mémoires de Sanson*, a wine-merchant's wife sums up what Balzac insisted were the exclusive values of her class: 'L'essentiel est que ça rapporte; l'argent, c'est tout. L'argent est toujours propre, d'où qu'il vienne'.[2]

Although its basic features are therefore discernible in what he wrote before 1830, Balzac's social and political thinking was profoundly affected by the impact of the July Revolution and by his experience of the July Monarchy. Yet, on the eve of the July Revolution, Balzac's interest in politics seemed to have deserted him. 'J'en suis arrivé', he wrote to Victor Ratier on 21 July, 'à regarder la gloire, la Chambre, la politique, l'avenir, la littérature comme de véritables boulettes à tuer les chiens errants et sans domicile, et que je dis: "La vertu, le bonheur, la vie, c'est six cents francs de rente au bord de la Loire".'[3] The prospect of a blissful 'rentier' retreat had seemingly replaced the determination to conquer Paris through his pen and through the ballot-box which he had first expressed to his sister Laure in September 1819.[4] Balzac remained in Touraine throughout the July Revolution and only broke his silence on the events with the publication of the *Lettres sur Paris*, the first of which appeared in *Le Voleur* on 30 September.

Thereafter, the critique of 1830, at first tentative and ambiguous, evolved into a comprehensive political philosophy centring around a systematic attack on the Revolution of 1789. The most important year in the context of this development is 1832. Besides the proclamation of legitimism which was contained in *Le Départ* at the beginning of the year, 1832 produced two other important political statements in two articles, the 'Essai sur la situation du parti royaliste' and 'Du Gouvernement moderne'.[5] It was also the year in which Balzac set out his political views in two major novels, *Louis Lambert* and *Le Médecin de campagne*.

However, before looking more closely at the novels which were composed in the first flush of Balzac's legitimism, it is important to trace the process whereby Balzac arrived at such a viewpoint in the period 1830 to 1832, and especially in so far as it affects his attitude to the Revolution.

In referring to the articles which Balzac wrote during this period, one has to proceed with considerable caution. Bruce Tolley has revealed that a significant proportion of the articles previously thought to have been written by Balzac in 1830-1 were wrongly attributed to him.[6] Therefore all the articles identified by Tolley as falsely or dubiously assigned to Balzac have been discounted. On the other hand, the *Lettres sur Paris* have been confirmed as the work of Balzac by Bernard Guyon, a conclusion which is accepted by Tolley.[7]

The *Lettres sur Paris* display, at first sight, a series of uncertainties, contradictions even, on Balzac's part. Yet the overall direction which they indicate is clear. The unconvincing protestations of constitutionalism give way to a growing insistence on the need to find authoritarian solutions. This trend is particularly marked in Letters XV and XVI, which betray the outrage felt by Balzac at witnessing the sacking of Saint-Germain l'Auxerrois,[8] although it can be detected in the earlier *Lettres sur Paris* and in the two letters which Balzac wrote to Zulma Carraud in November 1830.[9] The tone of superficial liberalism which characterises some of Balzac's remarks, rather than, as Pierre Barbéris claims, initially expressing the democratic hopes inspired by the July Revolution, may be seen as the anti-bourgeois gesture of a reactionary responding to the principle of 'The enemy of my enemy is my friend'.[10]

A more consistent line of thought begins to emerge in April-May

1831, when the failure of Balzac's electoral ambitions underlined Amédée Faucheux's warning about the danger of belonging to no political group.[11] Balzac's inherent Bonapartism found its populist appeal echoed in the more acceptable language of legitimism, which welcomed its uneasy convert in January 1832. *Le Départ* thus crystallised an evolution in Balzac's political outlook whose origins can be traced in what he wrote before 1830. Balzac thereby confirmed his fundamental hostility to the Revolution, which the July Revolution intensified and enabled him to articulate more clearly and more systematically.

The legitimist bottle contains some familiar wine dating from before 1830. The view of society based on a class struggle expressing at a human level the inequalities governing the natural, animal world; the identification with the rich in their eternal combat with the poor; the advocacy of repression to defeat attempts to subvert the natural order of society; the attack on revolutionary egalitarianism as a genetic absurdity and a social danger. These are the basic articles of faith which constantly recur in the expressions of Balzac's social and political philosophy both before and after 1830. The question which one now has to consider is what evidence there is of the impact of this ideological response to the July Revolution in the *Comédie humaine* itself.

It is in this context that *La Peau de chagrin* assumes a unique significance. Published in fragments between December 1830 and May 1831, *La Peau de chagrin* coincided almost exactly with the appearance of the *Lettres sur Paris*. The comparison which they offer provides the first important indication of Balzac's reaction to the July Revolution and to his experience of the first ten months of the July Monarchy.

In *La Peau de chagrin*, Balzac's attack on the July Revolution is made in two ways, via a discussion at a dinner party given by Taillefer and in the form of a tirade delivered by Blondet. The argument which is developed on both occasions is that the transfer of power from the aristocracy to the bourgeoisie which was finally confirmed in the July Revolution has exclusively benefited a new ruling elite of bankers, lawyers and journalists. The main target are the journalists, who represent for Balzac not merely the triumph of 1830 but the corrupt material values of 1789. 'Le journalisme', Balzac alleges, 'c'est la religion des sociétés modernes.'[12] For journalism one can read money. Two years later, in *Eugénie Grandet*, Balzac was to use almost identical terms to denounce the replacing of religion by money as the peculiar achievement of the Revolution.

One cannot therefore accept Pierre Barbéris's interpretation of *La*

Peau de chagrin as expressing Balzac's disenchantment with a July Revolution which had failed to fulfil its democratic expectations.[13] When Balzac asks the question who is to blame 'si le libéralisme devient La Fayette?',[14] it only makes sense if it is seen as a derisive accompaniment to the urging of an authoritarian alternative to a disastrous situation which had seen one banker succeed another as 'président du Conseil'.[15] The liberal, democratic ideals of the Revolution, reaffirmed in 1830, Balzac never tired of insisting (because they ignored the natural laws on which human society rested) were unattainable and could lead only to disillusionment or corruption. Balzac's illiberalism in *La Peau de chagrin* is unmistakable. The whole tone of the work is anti-constitutional. 'La conséquence immédiate d'une constitution est l'aplatissement des intelligences', Balzac maintains. By the consistent ferocity of its onslaught on egalitarianism, *La Peau de chagrin* establishes itself as an anti-revolutionary text. 'Les individualités', Balzac warns, 'disparaissent chez un peuple nivelé par l'instruction.'[16]

Because of what it reveals of Balzac's thinking 'au lendemain de 1830', *La Peau de chagrin* is a political document of great interest. It contains all the notions essential to Balzac's critique of the July Revolution as the logical and disastrous outcome of 1789. They are best summed up in the sympathetic portrait of Raphaël de Valentin's former teacher, Porriquet. Dismissed from his chair shortly after the July Revolution, 'le bonhomme', Balzac explains, 'voulant un gouvernement fort, avait émis le voeu patriotique de laisser les épiciers à leurs comptoirs, les hommes d'état au maniement des affaires publiques, les avocats au Palais, les pairs de France au Luxembourg'.[17] The charge of Carlism levelled at Porriquet already provided a discreet announcement of *Le Départ*.

The two novels written by Balzac in 1832 express, in different ways, the ideological position which he had stated in *Le Départ*. In *Louis Lambert*, the familiar extension of the concept of struggle is made from nature to society, which is distinguished by 'son contrat entre les forts contre les faibles'.[18] This leads Balzac to present an analysis of the Restoration in which the impact of the July Revolution can clearly be felt. The action in *Louis Lambert* covers the period 1812 to 1824, so that Balzac is unable to refer directly to the July Monarchy. Instead he offers a view of the Restoration which is coloured by his reaction to the July Revolution and which he interprets in terms of the effects of 1789.

Revolutionary principles are again ridiculed, but what is more interesting is Balzac's interpretation of the effects of the economic changes introduced by the Revolution. The abolition of the 'droit d'aînesse', the sale of 'biens nationaux' and the consequent division and redistribution of land are claimed to be responsible for the disasters afflicting the whole of post-revolutionary society. At the root of it all, Balzac reiterates his condemnation of the Revolution for having elevated money to its present unprecedented status. 'Ici', he reflects on the Restoration, 'le point de départ en tout est l'argent.'[19] *Louis Lambert* is a comprehensive 'cahier de doléances', inspired by Balzac's alarm at the direction of events since 1830 and directed at the lasting consequences of the Revolution.

Le Médecin de campagne amplifies the views outlined in *Louis Lambert*. Although, unlike *Louis Lambert*, it is principally concerned with expounding a practical political philosophy, *Le Médecin de campagne* also has its point of departure in an analysis of the Revolution. It is the Revolution, Benassis asserts, which has caused 'les catastrophes de nos quarante dernières années'.[20] Monarchy, patriotism and religion have all been seriously damaged, if not destroyed. A disastrous individualism has replaced the non-material values which, before the Revolution, gave purpose and unity to the nation. The society which Balzac recommends in order to arrest the drift towards social chaos and national humiliation is one based on religion, the family and privilege. It is this emphasis on religion which constitutes the new element in Balzac's thinking as expressed in *Le Médecin de campagne*.

In terms of class conflict, the effect of the July Revolution, Balzac believed, had been to replace the struggle between bourgeoisie and aristocracy, which had been finally decided in favour of the bourgeoisie in 1830, by a growing confrontation involving the bourgeoisie and the masses. In *Le Médecin de campagne*, democracy and universal suffrage are opposed because of a fear of their subversive consequences. At the same time, the Catholic religion is upheld for its social utility, as being the religion best calculated to avert revolution by making the masses resigned to their conditions.

For Balzac as for du Bousquier, 'l'avènement de la branche cadette était le triomphe de la Révolution',[21] in the sense that the July Revolution completed the bourgeois conquest of society which had been launched with the important victories gained from 1789 to 1793. What was for du Bousquier 'la plus savante application des principes de 1793', signified for Balzac, however, a catalogue of disasters, 'la Pairie sans hérédité, la Garde nationale qui met sur le même lit de camp l'épicier du coin et le marquis, l'abolition des majorats réclamée par un bourgeois-avocat, l'Eglise catholique privée de sa suprématie, toutes les inventions législatives d'août 1830'.[22] It is this consecration of bourgeois power by the July Revolution that Balzac identifies in the incisive phrase which is contained in *La Cousine Bette*: '1830 a consommé l'oeuvre de 1789'.[23]

Notes

1. This statement appears in a review (7 April 1830) by Balzac of the *Esquisses dramatiques du gouvernement révolutionnaire de France aux années 1793, 1794 et 1795* by P.-C. Ducanel. *Oeuvres Diverses* III, 40, 294-6.

2. *Oeuvres Diverses* I, 38, 242.

3. *Correspondance générale*, vol. I.

4. 'Je remarque', Balzac had written to Laure, 'que les littérateurs sont les gens que l'on recherche le plus volontiers dans les crises politiques. Ainsi, *si je suis un gaillard*, je puis avoir encore autre chose que la gloire littéraire.' *Correspondance générale*, vol. I.

5. Written in October 1832, *Du Gouvernement moderne* was intended for publication in *Le Rénovateur*, but in fact it only came to light when it was published by the vicomte de Lovenjoul in 1900. It is included in vol. 39 of the Conard edition, *Oeuvres Diverses*, II, 526-38. The *Essai sur la situation du parti royaliste* appeared in *Le Rénovateur* on 26 May and 2 June 1832. It can be found in *Oeuvres Diverses*, II, Conard, 39, 545-56.

6. See Tolley's articles: 'Three Articles Wrongly Attributed to Balzac', *Modern Language Review* (1960), pp. 85-7; 'Balzac et "la Caricature"', *Revue d'histoire littéraire de la France* (January-March 1961), pp. 23-35 (Tolley's conclusion (p. 33) is that 'il est probable qu'il ne collabora pas à ce périodique après la fin de 1830'); 'Balzac and the "Feuilleton des journaux politiques"', *Modern Language Review* (1962a), pp. 504-17.

7. See Bernard Guyon, *La Pensée politique et sociale de Balzac* (Paris, 1969), pp. 757-8.

8. The church was ransacked on 14 February 1831 by a mob incensed at the holding of a mass to commemorate the assassination of the duc de Berry in 1820.

9. The first letter has no precise date; the second was written on 26 November 1830. *Correspondance générale*, vol. I.

10. Barbéris sums up the significance of the *Lettres sur Paris* in terms of Balzac's reaction to the July Revolution and the opening period of the July Monarchy in the phrase: 'De septembre 1830 à mars 1831, Balzac va nous montrer, nous faire vivre, la naissance et la mort d'un espoir'. *Balzac et le mal du siècle*, 2 vols. (Paris, 1970a), vol. II, p. 1271.

11. In reply to Balzac's request that he should support his proposed candidature in Tours, Amédée Faucheux impressed on Balzac that 'dans les temps où nous sommes il faut se dessiner franchement sous la bannière d'un parti'. Letter of 1 May 1831. *Correspondance générale*, vol. I.

12. *La Peau de chagrin*, X, 93.

13. Barbéris insists that 'Balzac a été, en 1830, un homme du Mouvement'. The turning-point which was reached in the course of the *Lettres sur Paris*, Barbéris goes on to argue, culminated in the disenchantment with the July Revolution which is expressed in *La Peau de chagrin*. *Balzac et le mal du siècle*, vol. II, p. 1281.

14. The quotation from *La Peau de chagrin* prefaces chapter IX of Barbéris's

Balzac et le mal du siècle, vol. II, pp. 1417-1613. It can be found in vol. X of the Pléiade edition, p. 105.

15. Laffitte was 'président du Conseil' from 2 November 1830 to 12 March 1831. His successor, Casimir Périer, died a victim of the cholera epidemic on 16 May 1832.

16. *La Peau de chagrin*, X, 103.

17. Ibid., 218-19.

18. *Louis Lambert*, XI, 650.

19. Ibid., 647.

20. *Le Médecin de campagne*, IX, 506.

21. Ibid.

22. *La Vieille Fille*, IV, 928.

23. *La Cousine Bette*, VII, 151.

8 'LES NOTABLES'

That Balzac is a political novelist seems self-evident. Yet it is an assumption which calls for a thorough examination if its real significance is to be grasped. One has to account for a disconcerting fact, namely Balzac's remarkable indifference to political events and to party politics. In terms of the latter, it has been emphasised by a number of critics, notably by Wurmser[1] and by Pierrot.[2] As for the great events themselves, one finds only passing, if frequent references to 1789 and 1793, to Thermidor, Brumaire and the two Restorations. The Hundred Days are seen more mistily through the vaporous veils of Clochegourde than Alain's facile 'boutade' would suggest.[3] The revolutions, the great 'journées' are 'les grandes absentes' of the *Comédie humaine*. There is no 'Chronique de 1830' in Balzac's repertoire, nor is there one for 1789, while 1848 falls just outside his creative compass. No Bonapartist conspiracy disturbs the somnolence of Grandet's Saumur.[4] Goriot's death takes precedence over the assassination of the duc de Berry.[5] Private drama, however humble, has more appeal for Balzac than public events, however dramatic. Individual passion takes priority over the collective occasion. Whatever else it may be, Balzac's history is not 'l'histoire événementielle'.[6]

One can only understand Balzac's disregard of political events and alignments if one appreciates that the political 'dehors' are subordinated in his historical analysis to consideration of the socioeconomic 'dessous'. Indeed it is this insistence on the primacy of economic causality which governs Balzac's entire approach to society. This is demonstrated in what, at first sight, might seem to be an exception to the norm, in the extraordinary place which is taken up in the *Comédie humaine* by discussion of the 'cens' and of 'la notabilité'. Balzac's preoccupation with 'les notables' is consistent, however, with the basic outlook which underlies his historical method. He is concerned to show how the socioeconomic changes which occurred under the Revolution and Empire were expressed in the shifting structure of political authority from 1815 to 1848. Through his assessment of the 'cens' and, in particular, through his account of the electoral system of the July Monarchy, Balzac attempts to answer two fundamental questions. First, he examines the political consequences of the transfer of economic power from the aristocracy to the bourgeoisie. Secondly, Balzac considers the various antagonisms, both socioeconomic and political, which emerged within the victorious bourgeoisie itself.

I The Working of the Electoral System

(a) The Acquisition of Eligibility

In his account of the way in which the electoral system of the 'monarchie censitaire' worked, Balzac is a contemporary witness of unique interest. Sherman Kent remains the one historian to have made a thorough study of the question, but despite his occasional enlivenment of the investigation by reference to individual examples, Kent's analysis, by its very method, tends to be of a statistical nature. It is for this reason, and also because it bears the authentic mark of first-hand experience, that Balzac's testimony is so valuable. Not only does Balzac illuminate an area of historical interest which, apart from Kent's work, remains largely unexplored. In addition, although it cannot pretend to be systematic, Balzac's evidence more than compensates for this in its extraordinary richness of dramatic illustration and its remarkable mastery of detail. The historical significance of the *Comédie humaine*, based on the analysis of the fundamental long-term effects of the Revolution, is thereby greatly enhanced.[7]

In his description of the electoral system of the 'monarchie censitaire', Balzac's most original contribution undoubtedly consists in his treatment of the acquisition of eligibility.[8] First of all, it is an important issue which is not covered even by a specialist historian such as Kent. Moreover, the acquisition of eligibility was a major preoccupation of Balzac during the greater part of the July Monarchy, from 1831 to 1846. It must have been cause for bitter reflection on Balzac's part, for example, to realize that his father would have qualified comfortably as an 'éligible' had he lived to see the law of 1831.[9] There is, on the surface at least, a paradoxical imbalance in Balzac's treatment of 'l'éligibilité' over the whole period of the 'monarchie censitaire'. What accounts for the striking fact that, although the major part of the *Comédie humaine* deals with the Restoration, in discussing the particular question of the 'cens', Balzac concentrates so heavily on the July Monarchy? There are two kinds of reasons, both interrelated. In the first place, Balzac had barely begun writing the *Comédie humaine* when the July Monarchy came into existence, so that any question which had a profound impact on his life at this decisive moment in his creative maturity was certain to find an important and lasting place in his work. The second factor is a political one. Born in the year of Brumaire, Balzac only became an elector at the very end of the Restoration. Had the electoral provisions of the Restoration not been changed by the law of 1831, Balzac would have had to wait until 1839 to be old enough to be 'éligible', quite apart from the awkward question of the fiscal qualification. As it was, a whole new field of political ambition seemed to Balzac to have been opened up to him by the changes in the electoral franchise introduced by the July Monarchy.

One is familiar with the history of Balzac's electoral fiascos, and I do not propose to dwell unnecessarily on the question of his own political ambitions, except to point out one important fact which has a direct bearing on his treatment of 'l'éligibilité' in his work. Despite his attempts to get himself elected in 1831 and 1832, doubts have been expressed whether Balzac was in fact an 'éligible' at this period at all.[10] One need not take at its face value the publicity accompanying the appearance of the 'Enquête sur la politique des deux Ministères' in April 1831, which stated that the article was written by 'M. de Balzac, électeur, éligible'.[11] When Balzac announced in a letter to baron de Pommereul, 'Je suis, par la nouvelle loi, devenu tout-à-coup éligible et électeur', is it not possible that he meant 'éligible' by age and only elector financially?[12] This is certainly what is indicated by his telling Mme Hanska in January 1833 'Je suis éligible depuis la nouvelle loi qui nous reconnaît hommes à trente ans'.[13] In the circumstances, how Balzac came to entertain serious parliamentary ambitions in 1831 and actually to offer himself as a candidate in 1832 must, for lack of evidence, remain a mystery. One can only speculate, but one's suspicions are strengthened by the knowledge that, for the rest of his life, Balzac was desperately concerned to acquire eligibility, as his correspondence amply testifies. What is more interesting is the way in which Balzac's personal experience, his ambitions, tensions and frustrations, finds its way into the *Comédie humaine*. The quest for eligibility is, as we shall see later, the outstanding example of a political theme in the *Comédie humaine* which derives its force from Balzac's own efforts in that direction. The prominent place taken up in his work by 'l'éligibilité', the intensity of the passions aroused in the characters whom it affects, are the expression of Balzac's direct involvement in the electoral process of the July Monarchy.

After fluctuating in his political aspirations between 1832 and 1836, Balzac says nothing more on the subject in his correspondence until 1842. For the next four years, the concern to achieve eligibility was to become something of an obsession with Balzac, after which everything was subordinated to the aim of marrying Mme Hanska and the search for a Paris house worthy to receive her.

It is not surprising therefore that what was a subject of such pressing concern to Balzac over a long period should find expression in his work. With its impassioned source in Balzac's personal experience, the acquisition of eligibility was to provide a recurrent theme in the *Comédie humaine*. The intensity with which it is treated and the vital role which it plays in the lives of many of Balzac's characters are a clear indication of the importance which Balzac had himself attached to becoming an 'éligible'. There is no other topic in the whole of the *Comédie humaine* which communicates a greater sense of immediate involvement on Balzac's part than the problem of acquiring eligibility. A further proof of this is the fact that the composition of two of the novels in which the theme is most prominent, *Les Petits Bourgeois* and *Albert Savarus*, is contemporary with its recurrence in Balzac's reappraisal of his political ambitions. In contrast, it is significant that there is not a single example in the *Comédie humaine* of a 'non-censitaire' seeking to become an elector. This strengthens the case for believing that Balzac was an elector from the time of the law of April 1831. The same factors explain why, apart from the case of des Lupeaulx and, initially, that of Savinien de Portenduère, Balzac discusses the question entirely in the context of the July Monarchy and not that of the Restoration.

Balzac gives a wealth of examples to show that, in order to enable someone to become an 'éligible', three principal means were employed which, by their nature, were often closely interrelated. The acquisition of eligibility, Balzac demonstrates, was in many cases dependent on the acquisition of three important assets: land, a house and a wife.

The experience of Camusot de Marville shows how the forfeiting of an important piece of land could involve the loss of eligibility. Camusot de Marville's dilemma is a cruel one. In opting for a long-term solution, he has to be prepared to sacrifice his immediate political interests. When his entire fortune and that of his wife are spent on buying 'la terre de Marville' to give as a dowry to their daughter so that she can marry Popinot's son, 'la cession de tous les biens à leur fille entraînait la suppression du cens d'éligibilité pour le président'.[14] The estate is acquired in 1844 and the marriage which its acquisition makes possible takes place the following year. In describing the process whereby Camusot de Marville recovers his lost eligibility, Balzac displays the full measure of the creative ingenuity on which his historical method rests. It is Mme Camusot de Marville who asks her father-in-law Camusot for 'cent mille francs en avance d'hoirie, afin d'acheter un petit domaine enclavé dans celui de Marville, et rapportant environ deux mille francs net d'impôts'.[15] When Camusot declines the request for help, the situation is saved by Fraisier, who arranges to buy some land adjoining the Marville estate. Camusot de Marville's eligibility is thus restored and he is elected deputy for the neighbouring district in the following year, 1846, thanks to 'l'habile homme à qui elle doit non seulement l'acquisition des prairies de Marville et du cottage, mais encore l'élection de monsieur le président, nommé député à la réélection générale de 1846'.[16]

The importance of 'le foncier' in conferring eligibility, this time under the Restoration, is revealed by Balzac with the same inventiveness that he employs in the case of Camusot de Marville when he explains the precarious start to the political career of des Lupeaulx. Because of his debts, des Lupeaulx is unable to buy back the land, presumably confiscated from an émigré father, which is necessary to give him the 'cens d'éligibilité'. The problem is solved when his debts are paid by Gobseck and Gigonnet in return for his support of the 'Congrégation' candidate Baudoyer against Rabourdin in the bid to succeed La Billardière as 'chef de division' in the Finance Ministry. The way to des Lupeaulx's eligibility is now clear, but the political rewards are not immediately forthcoming. He has first to make way for a minister to take the electoral seat which he has his eye on. Des Lupeaulx's impatience is finally rewarded, however, and he is a deputy before the July Revolution.[17]

More numerous than the purchases of land are the initiatives in house buying which are undertaken with the same purpose of acquiring eligibility. The three characters directly involved in this process in the *Comédie humaine* are Thuillier, Marcas and Albert Savarus. It is La Peyrade who tells Thuillier: 'Pour être éligible, il faut payer le cens, et vous ne le payez pas'.[18] He therefore suggests to Brigitte, as the financial power behind her brother, that she buy a house in Thuillier's name that will ensure 30-40,000 fr. each year in rents on a capital outlay of 150,000 fr. The electoral advantage of such a move is not explained by Balzac in this case, but as it formed such an important part of his own experience, it was something which he must have been well aware of. As well as yielding profitable rents, the purchase of a house could be expected to make a significant, perhaps even decisive contribution to the 'cens d'éligibilité' through what its owner would have to pay in direct taxes. (The advantage of house-purchase was that it helped to qualify for eligibility by virtue of the amount of land tax which was imposed on the house.)

Confirmation of this is provided in Colin Smethurst's remarks about *Jérôme Paturot*, a work by Louis Reybaud. Jérôme's father tells him how he can hope to become an elector when he enters the family business as a retail 'bonnetier'. 'Dès le lendemain', he informs Jérôme, 'tu es électeur; tu payes 310 francs de patente et de personnel, plus 405 francs de foncier pour la maison qui t'appartient'.[19] As well as demonstrating the way in which the electoral franchise was weighted in favour of landed wealth, Balzac points to a further significant trend, in the sense that the preference for buying houses rather than landed property marks the beginning of the transfer of investment from land to urban property and 'le mobilier' which was a consequence of the bourgeois ascendancy.

In Marcas's case, the purchase of a house is associated with two other important factors which were instrumental in securing eligibility. One is a propitious marriage, about which more will be said in a moment. The other is the value of an influential political patron. 'Pauvre et ne pouvant se faire élire', Marcas becomes secretary to a minister, 'dans l'espoir que son protecteur le mettrait en position d'être élu député'. Promoting the minister's cause through his journalism, Marcas looks to his protector to enable him to become an 'éligible'. In the first place, he hopes for a loan from him with which to buy the sort of house in Paris which will ensure his eligibility. 'Marcas', Balzac makes it clear, 'ne souhaitait pas autre chose que le prêt nécessaire à l'acquisition d'une maison à Paris, afin de satisfaire aux exigences de la loi.'[20] Secondly, by obtaining an important post through the minister's protection, Marcas calculates that he will be able to make a marriage of the kind which will doubly guarantee that he will be an 'éligible'. 'Marcas', Balzac explains, 'avait compté sur une place pour obtenir par un mariage l'éligibilité tant désirée. Il avait trente-deux ans, il prévoyait la dissolution de la Chambre.'[21] Twice let down by his protector, Marcas on each occasion helps to bring down the government of which he is a member through the power of his journalism.

In neither the case of Thuillier nor in that of Marcas is it finally clear whether eligibility is achieved or not. The unfinished state of *Les Petits Bourgeois* leaves Thuillier a 'conseiller municipal' but short of becoming a deputy. Marcas's death, in January 1838, equally leaves the question unresolved, but with the evidence suggesting that his ineligibility is never overcome. In dealing with the similar ambitions of Albert Savarus, however, Balzac shows the efforts towards attaining eligibility having a successful outcome, but one which is in turn the prelude to ultimate frustration in the attempt to get elected.

Although too young to have been an 'éligible' under the Restoration, Savarus resents even more the fact that he missed the chance of securing the fiscal basis of his eligibility before 1830. 'Pourquoi n'avais-je que trente-trois ans', he laments to Léopold Hannequin, 'et comment ne t'ai-je pas prié de me rendre éligible?'[22] Now eligible by age, he is still relying on Hannequin to enable him to achieve the financial qualification. He then indicates how Hannequin could have helped him earlier and can help him now. 'D'ici à quelques mois', he writes to Hannequin, 'j'aurai trouvé dans Besançon une maison à acheter qui puisse me donner le cens. Je compte sur toi pour me prêter les capitaux nécessaires à cette acquisition.'[23] This aim is realised in 1834. 'Il avait acheté, soi-disant pour rendre service à un négociant embarrassé dans ses affaires, au mois d'octobre 1834, et avec les fonds de Léopold Hannequin, une maison qui lui donnait le cens d'éligibilité.'[24] It would seem, from Savarus's behaviour, to have been common practice to conceal one's electoral motive when buying a house for that purpose, to the extent perhaps of using a 'prête-nom' to avert suspicion.

The tactic adopted by Thuillier, Marcas and Savarus of buying a house with a view to obtaining eligibility bears the clear imprint of Balzac's own experience. The first evidence that Balzac seriously contemplated a similar course of action is contained in his correspondence with Amédée Faucheux in 1832. Referring to a house which Balzac had expressed an interest in buying, Roger Pierrot comments, 'Il s'agit d'une acquisition en Touraine en vue d'obtenir le cens d'éligibilité'. Reinforcing the doubts he expresses earlier about Balzac's claims to 'éligible' status at this period, Pierrot adds: 'Balzac a plusieurs fois songé à acheter une propriété en Touraine sans jamais pouvoir réaliser son rêve'.[25]

For the next decade or so one hears no more from Balzac on the subject until, in 1842, the year, significantly enough, in which *Albert Savarus* was written, it recurs with even greater insistence. The first reference occurs in a letter to Mme Hanska of 5 January 1842. 'Je veux avoir mon cens d'éligibilité', he tells Mme Hanska, 'et être de la prochaine législature, c'est tout notre avenir', then adds: 'il me faudrait de quoi acheter une maison à ma mère, à qui je dois 40,000 fr. d'ailleurs, afin d'avoir le cens d'éligibilité.'[26] While Balzac's mother was a more substantial reality than Savarus's 'négociant', Balzac was no doubt thinking of the electoral benefit of such an action rather than expressing a concern to redeem in this way his unpaid debt to his mother. Thereafter, Balzac talks only about buying a house for himself as a means of acquiring eligibility. In a letter to Mme Hanska of January 1844, he announces his intention of moving from les Jardies to a house in Paris, 'pour me donner le cens'.[27] The previous month he had told Mme Hanska that the taxes he paid on les Jardies fell short of the 500 fr. required to qualify for the 'cens d'éligibilité'. 'Les Jardies', he revealed, 'payent plus de deux cents francs de contribution.'[28] He longs to be able to tell the 'académiciens' that he has no debts, owns his own house and pays the 'cens de l'éligibilité' (sic).

In this same letter, Balzac hints at another possible means of ensuring his eligibility when he reveals that 'mon beau-frère me propose un moyen de me faire cent écus de contributions directes en me passant la gérance d'un pont'. Balzac's continued ineligibility is proof that Surville's suggestion never came to anything. Meanwhile, unlike des Lupeaulx, Balzac is not worried that his debts will prevent his becoming 'éligible'. Two-thirds of his total debts of 150,000 fr., he reassures Mme Hanska, 'sont dus à 5 personnages qui ne me feront aucun chagrin, qui ne m'empêcheront pas d'être propriétaire et de payer le cens d'éligibilité'.[29] Three weeks later, he re-expresses the same serene confidence to Mme Hanska. 'En 8bre de cette année', he predicts, 'je pourrai être propriétaire et posséder une maison qui me donnera le cens d'éligibilité.'[30]

Perhaps, in his more despairing moments, Balzac may have thought of adopting the device used by one of his characters in order to become 'éligible'. Or, alternatively, Vinet's illegality may have helped Balzac to sublimate a dangerous temptation. How is it that this 'petit avocat de province' manages to qualify as an 'éligible' under the Restoration at all? Vinet owes the fact that he is able to oppose Tiphaine in the election for Provins in 1826 to the extra-legal expertise of his solicitor, Maître Cournant. It is Vinet, Balzac discloses, 'à qui monsieur Cournant avait procuré le cens par l'acquisition d'un domaine dont le prix restait dû'.[31] Balzac does not indicate whether Vinet manages to become legally 'éligible' before his election for Provins in 1830. What is more important is that he has put his finger on an electoral abuse which is identified by Bertier de Sauvigny. In order to ensure that a potential candidate qualified to stand for election under the Restoration by paying the necessary 1,000 fr. in direct taxes, it was not unknown for his supporters to acquire a house on his behalf by an act of purchase which might be either genuine or fictitious. The way in which Balzac describes Vinet's case points to a fictitious acquisition in which the solicitor plays a key part, of the kind referred to by Bertier de Sauvigny. 'un des moyens les plus courant', Bertier de Sauvigny reveals, 'est de procéder à l'achat fictif d'immeubles suffisamment imposés; en même temps que l'acte de vente, le notaire établit une contre-lettre secrète qui annule l'acte officiel.'[32]

One knows that in the end Balzac's efforts to acquire eligibility via the purchase of a house did not materialise. The idea arose again in November 1845. If he can buy the house in the 'place Royale' which he has his eye on, he tells Mme Hanska, 'ce serait à la fois *le logement*, du *revenu* et *le cens*'.[33] Finally, as the 1846 elections approached, Balzac wrote to Mme Hanska to assure her that 'Il ne faut plus trouver que 225 fr. d'impôts, et la moindre maison, une maison de 40,000 fr. à Paris me donnerait le cens'.[34] This is the last one hears on the subject from Balzac. Nor did anything come of another idea he flirted with which was conceived with the same end in view, that of a calculated marriage. Balzac at least persisted in pursuing the house which would give him eligibility, but Eléonore de Trumilly seems to have had no successor. What matters in each case, however, is that both options and the objective which they were designed to achieve found significant expression in the *Comédie humaine*. As well as being an important factor in the rise of Balzac's 'censitaires', marriage, as Balzac indicates, could play a crucial role in the acquisition of eligibility.

Marcas, it will be recalled, considered a favourable marriage as a necessary step towards eligibility along with the purchase of a house. Marriage also figures prominently in the calculations of other aspiring 'éligibles' in the *Comédie humaine*. It acquires a particular attraction, for example, for Lousteau when his ineligibility prevents him from taking up Mme de la Baudraye's invitation to stand as Opposition candidate in Sancerre in 1836. Thus, when Mme Schontz suggests that he marry Cardot's daughter, he is quick to see the merits of the proposal. His debts, that electoral millstone around the neck of Balzac, and of des Lupeaulx and La Peyrade, would be paid off and he would have 12,000 fr. 'de rente' into the bargain. Moreover, for the brother-in-law of a deputy in Camusot, a father-in-law like Cardot would have valuable political connections. Nothing seems impossible to Lousteau, given such a marriage. 'Si je paie le cens', he tells Cardot, 'si je suis propriétaire de mon journal au lieu d'en être un rédacteur, je deviendrai Député comme tant d'autres!'[35]

Almost without exception, those who aim to become 'éligibles' through a helpful marriage are disappointed. Lousteau is no more successful than Marcas in this respect. Fraisier's failure is of an altogether more pathetic and grotesque kind. His great ambition is to become a 'juge de paix' of the eighth 'arrondissement'. Mlle Tabareau,

Fraisier tells himself, 'est propriétaire du chef de sa mère d'une maison à la place Royale; je serai donc éligible'.[36] As in the case of Marcas, the dual tactic is envisaged of an advantageous marriage and the acquisition of a house, with the difference that Fraisier contemplates combining the two at a stroke, whereas Marcas considers the two expedients separately.

The result in all three cases is the same in the sense that the mere turning over in the mind of such projects is enough to inspire unlimited faith in a distinguished political career ahead. The mood and tone of Fraisier are those of Balzac writing to Mme Hanska about his electoral hopes from 1842 to 1844. Fraisier, Balzac comments, 'se voyait un des rois du quartier, il dominerait les élections municipales, militaires et politiques'.[37] Alas for Fraisier, the sequel is more humiliating than it was for Balzac. Mme Camusot de Marville fails to fulfil her side of the bargain in return for Fraisier's providing the means of her husband's eligibility when she persuades Fraisier that he can do better than Mlle Tabareau. There is no mention of Fraisier's ever marrying, in fact. Even without Mme Camusot de Marville's fastidious interference, any potential wife, Mlle Tabareau or otherwise, would have found an insuperable barrier to marriage, and thereby to Fraisier's dreams of eligibility, in Fraisier's persistent 'ozène'.[38]

The importance which marriage might assume in the search for eligibility is highlighted by the contrasting attitudes of two pairs of characters. The first antithesis, which involves the characters more directly through their link with the same woman, concerns Simon Giguet and Maxime de Trailles in relation to Cécile Beauvisage. The second, unlike the first, is an entirely involuntary contrast as far as Balzac is concerned. It arises out of the independent thinking on the social and political implications of marriage of Désiré Minoret and Savinien de Portenduère.

With no regular income or property, de Trailles' political prospects seem hopeless. 'Sans propriété, il n'avait jamais pu consolider sa position en se faisant nommer député.' Nor has he the position or influence which would make the peerage a practicable alternative. 'Puis, sans fonctions ostensibles, il lui était impossible de mettre le couteau sous la gorge à quelque ministère pour se faire nommer pair de France.'[39] It is Rastignac who suggests that the effective means of solving his problems lies in marriage. As there is no hope of a debtor and 'roué' like de Trailles finding a suitable wife in Paris, especially among the aristocracy, Rastignac advises him to think in terms of marrying the daughter of an ambitious provincial manufacturer who would be only too eager to have a noble as his son-in-law. Moreover, Rastignac urges, the death of Charles Keller, whom Grévin had intended to marry to his grand-daughter, gives de Trailles a unique opportunity. Sent by Rastignac to Arcis in 1839 to press the campaign of the government candidate, de Trailles persuades the Beauvisages of the advantages of Cécile's marry-ing him rather than Simon Giguet. Now eminently 'éligible', de Trailles wastes no time in becoming deputy for Arcis.

For Simon Giguet, the situation is quite different. When he expresses the view that 'Aujourd'hui, la grande fortune, c'est le pouvoir', Giguet is speaking as an 'éligible' who is a candidate in the forthcoming election.[40] There is no question, as with de Trailles and the other instances already discussed, of marriage being seen as the prerequisite of eligibility. On the contrary, Giguet's hoped-for marriage to Cécile Beauvisage, though recognised as being essential to his political career, is considered to be dependent on his being elected deputy. The parents of the richest heiress in the Aube department would not settle for anything less, unless, of course, the prospective son-in-law happened to have a title.

If one compares the attitudes of Savinien de Portenduère and Désiré Minoret, the same kind of antithesis emerges, centring around the relationship of marriage and political ambition. The parallels with the opposition of de Trailles and Simon Giguet are striking. The noble-bourgeois contrast is reinforced by the 'éligible'-'non-éligible' distinction in both cases. During his spell in prison, Savinien has had time to give serious thought to his future. When he leaves prison in 1829, he has become convinced of the need to marry the daughter of a rich bourgeois. His motives are not financial but political. For Savinien, a bourgeois marriage is regarded as an indispensable means of achieving eligibility. He tells himself that he is prepared to marry a peasant's daughter, provided she is rich enough, 'tout en cherchant à me marier avec une jeune personne qui me donne l'éligibilité'.[41] De Marsay plays the role of mentor to Savinien, and also to Victurnien d'Esgrignon, in the way that Rastignac does in the case of de Trailles. When de Marsay proposes the toast, 'A la fille d'argent!', Savinien responds with enthusiastic conviction.[42]

At exactly the same moment, in September 1829, Désiré Minoret is being given the opposite advice. Goupil tells him: 'Ta femme doit être une d'Aiglemont, une mademoiselle du Rouvre, et te faire arriver à la députation'.[43] At this time, under the electoral provisions of the Restoration, neither Savinien nor Désiré was old enough to be an elector, let along an 'éligible'. Indeed, even when the age limit was lowered in 1831, Désiré would still have to wait until 1835 and Savinien until 1837 before they became 'éligibles' by age. The difference, however, is that Désiré is an 'éligible' in the financial sense, whereas Savinien is not. The distinction is a vital one, as we have seen in discussing the relative positions of Simon Giguet and de Trailles, in so far as it accounts for the opposing view which the two of them have of marriage in relation to their political future. Savinien specifically refers to his intention of acquiring eligibility through marriage. For an 'éligible' like Désiré, on the other hand, marriage provides the means of ensuring both that he becomes a deputy and that he advances in his career. Désiré and his entourage never abandon their conviction that 'Il fallait lui chercher une femme, une fille pauvre appartenant à une vieille et noble famille; il pourrait alors arriver à la magistrature de Paris. Peut-être pourraient-ils le faire élire député de Fontainebleau.'[44]

The contrast is not only with Savinien, but also with Simon Giguet. Like Désiré, Giguet is also an 'éligible', but they differ in their social appraisal of marriage. Giguet has a bourgeois marriage in view, whereas Désiré can see advantages only in having an aristocratic wife. It is interesting to see the consequences of this in terms of their contrasting expectations. Giguet is in no doubt that the Beauvisages will insist that he become a deputy before they consent to his marrying Cécile. Désiré is no less convinced that an aristocratic family, especially an impoverished one, will scarcely be in a position to impose conditions of this kind. At the same time, he calculates that the prestige and influence of an aristocratic marriage will further both his political and his professional ambition in helping him to be elected deputy and appointed magistrate in Paris.

The whole weight of the evidence in the *Comédie humaine* concerning the acquisition of eligibility points in one direction, to the reality of bourgeois power under the July Monarchy. Everything confirms the weakening of the economic base of the landed aristocracy, and with it the surrender of its social and political authority. Only the Parisian nobility retains sufficient prestige to dazzle the 'grande bourgeoisie provinciale' into matrimony and into taking the risk of inheriting a dubious decadence. The Portenduères, on the other hand, reveal the precarious plight of the 'petite noblesse de province', hard hit by emigration and vulnerable in relation to both the urban bourgeoisie and the 'haute aristocratie du pays'. Even the latter has to give way before the bourgeois advance, as the marquis du Rouvre's sale of his estates to Minoret-Levrault testifies. The behaviour of Savinien's mother is also revealing in this respect. When she finally relents and agrees to Savinien's marrying Ursule Mirouët in 1837, her change of heart is perhaps inspired less by Savinien's threats of suicide than by two more compelling facts. Savinien becomes 'éligible' by age in the year of his marriage to Ursule, which would guarantee his financial eligibility. Moreover, Ursule had just been given the Rouvre estates by Minoret-Levrault, where Mme de Portenduère could live in more prestigious retirement.

It is the 'grande bourgeoisie' which increasingly calls the tune, enjoying a dominance which extends to determining the patterns and terms of marriage. The political outcome in the case of both Désiré and Savinien is far removed from their original expectations. Neither, in fact, becomes a deputy, although Savinien's marriage to Ursule makes him an 'éligible'. Désiré meets with a premature death in an accident, while Savinien chooses to put domestic happiness before his political ambition. He is content with being 'conseiller-général' of the Seine-et-Marne, and there is talk of his being made a peer. As for becoming deputy, 'il avait déjà deux fois décliné les honneurs de la députation, il préférait faire le bonheur de sa femme à toutes les chances de la vie politique'.[45]

The ultimate fate of Désiré and Savinien is less important than the historical perspective which emerges from their contrasting assessment of marriage in relation to their view of a changing society. The July Revolution only strengthens them in the conviction which they had expressed in 1829. The direction of the July Monarchy was to prove the noble right in seeing the future as belonging to the bourgeoisie, and the bourgeois wrong in overestimating the surviving power of the aristocracy. Intermarriage between bourgeoisie and aristocracy is just one aspect, though an important one, of the effort to achieve eligibility through marriage. Whether the means employed in the attempt to become an 'éligible' by marriage, the acquisition of a house or the purchase of land, they point towards the same conclusion in underlining the supremacy of the 'grande bourgeoisie' under the July Monarchy.

(b) The Process of Becoming Deputy

In *Les Petits Bourgeois* Balzac shows how experience of municipal elections could be made to serve as a valuable rehearsal for election as deputy. While Thuillier is marking time, 'en attendant d'atteindre l'éligibilité', La Peyrade urges him to turn the interval to useful account. The first step is to become 'conseiller général'. 'Un jour', he assures him, 'vous serez le député de l'arrondissement, quand on réélira la Chambre, et cela ne tardera pas.'[46] Since 1834, the 'électeurs censitaires' of Paris had enjoyed the automatic right to vote in municipal elections.[47] The key to being elected, at both municipal and at national level, La Peyrade insists, is to be sure of the support of those who control the electorate. The votes won in municipal elections, La Peyrade claims, will help to elect Thuillier deputy. 'Les voix qui vous auront nommé au conseil municipal', he tells Thuillier, 'vous resteront quand il s'agira de la députation.'[48] Thuillier follows La Peyrade's advice to the letter and is elected, in April 1840, as councillor for the seat made vacant by the death of Popinot.

Mlle Daumard has remarked upon the considerable number of Parisian 'conseillers généraux' who left their municipal functions immediately after the July Revolution in order to pursue a career as deputy. 'Très vite', Mlle Daumard observes, 'la composition du Conseil général se modifia. Bien des personnalités qui avaient accepté, au lendemain de la révolution, de gérer les affaires de Paris et de la Seine, donnèrent leur démission au bout de quelques mois: nommés députés par les départements, elles se consacrèrent à la politique générale.' She then draws the general conclusion that 'à partir de la Monarchie de Juillet, les milieux supérieurs se détournaient des fonctions munici-pales'.[49] Thuillier aims to follow the same path along which the 'éligible' Minard has already made a significant advance. Some of Balzac's 'notables' go further and end up as deputy after starting out in politics at local level. Dionis had been mayor of Nemours after the July Revo-lution. Among the Parisian deputies in the *Comédie humaine*, Crevel, Camusot and Cardot fils are all examples of the value of a spell in municipal office as a stepping-stone towards becoming deputy.

Balzac was well aware, from his personal contacts, especially with someone like Girardin who was both a newspaper owner and a deputy, of the power of publishing, and of journalism in particular, to influence political events, including the election of deputies. He draws attention, for example, to the habit of sending free copies of political newspapers to attract electoral votes when he refers to Nucingen's 'bourg-pourri, où le journal fut envoyé gratis à profusion'.[50] Again it is La Peyrade who impresses on Thuillier the need to publish a substantial political work in order to improve his chances of being elected deputy, to the extent of helping Thuillier compose a publication of Saint-Simonian tendencies.

The press, Balzac demonstrates, has the power to make and to destroy political careers and reputations. We have seen how Marcas is twice able to bring down a ministry by the power of his articles. None is more alive to the political force of journalism than Nathan. His founding of a political journal is inspired by the reflection that 'la Presse avait été le moyen de tant de fortunes faites autour de lui'. Academic journalism may be just as effective as the political variety, since Nathan has seen 'des faiseurs d'articles passés au Conseil-d'Etat, des professeurs pairs de France'.[51] If Nathan finally fails in his ambition to become deputy, it is not through the political impotence of journalism, but simply because he is crushed by an overwhelming coalition of financial and political interests.

The manipulation of the electorate which Balzac describes at municipal level in *Les Petits Bourgeois* is repeatedly revealed to be the determining factor in the outcome of elections for deputy. A major factor in du Bousquier's decision to marry Mlle Cormon concerns the electoral influence of her salon. 'Du Bousquier avait calculé', Balzac indicates, 'que les personnes qui le hantaient possédaient cent trente et une voix au Collège électoral.'[52] Massin and Dionis have a decisive influence over the electors of Nemours in 1830. Poupart and Fromaget play a similar role in Arcis in 1839. It is for this reason that Mme Camusot de Marville pays tribute to Fraisier. 'Camusot sera député', she explains, 'car en lâchant ce Fraisier dans l'arrondissement de Balbec, il nous obtiendra la majorité.'[53] Finally, the 27 'gros bonnets' present at Savarus's election meeting each controls six votes. Moreover, Savarus claims to have the support of 'l'un des personnages les plus influents aux élections'. 'Sûr de son succès', Balzac enlarges, 'il attendait avec impatience la dissolution de la Chambre. Il avait conquis, parmi les hommes du juste-milieu, l'un des faiseurs de Besançon, un riche entrepreneur qui disposait d'une grande influence.' Balzac ironically conveys Savarus's premature scenting of victory, based on the conviction that he has the influential electors on his side. 'Mes voix à moi', he tells the duchesse d'Argaiolo, 'celles du vicaire-général, celles des gens que j'obligerai et celles de ce client, assurent déjà mon élection.'[54]

Balzac gives a lively description of the various meetings that were held as part of the process of electing a deputy. There was first the adoption meeting. At municipal level, Thuillier's nomination is approved at a 'dîner de la candidature'. It is at the meeting which he calls in order to have himself adopted as Opposition candidate in Besançon that Savarus decides to take the bourgeois electors into his confidence about his legitimist past. His bold initiative is justified as 'le commerce de Besançon fit de l'avocat Savaron de Savarus son candidat'.[55] It was the task of the local committee to approve the choice of candidate, and the meeting was often held in a private house. Over fifty electors are present, for example, at the stormy meeting held in the house of Simon Giguet's aunt, Mme Marion, which results in Giguet's being chosen as Opposition candidate in Arcis.[56]

Once the rival candidates had been nominated, the next stage in the proceedings took the form of the 'réunion préparatoire', which brought the electors and the various candidates together. As well as providing an electoral platform, this meeting served as the primitive forerunner of modern opinion polls by sounding out the voting intentions of the electors in advance. It is the evidence of this preliminary meeting which enables the abbé de Grancey to make a pessimistic forecast of Savarus's chances which is confirmed by events.

Balzac also emphasises what historians have noted concerning the enormous advantage enjoyed by the government party through its control of the electoral administration. The 667,000 'fonctionnaires' of the July Monarchy, and especially the 203,000 employed by the Ministry of the Interior alone, provided the government with the ideal machinery with which to influence the course of the elections, the more so as they were guaranteed immunity against charges of corruption. Casimir Périer's circular to prefects in 1831 was an open incitement to 'fonctionnaires' to use their authority in favour of government candidates.

There are two ways in which this manipulation of the elections by the government is shown to operate in the *Comédie humaine*. The first concerns the timing of the elections. Those of July 1831 were the first to be held under the July Monarchy and the only ones whose date was prescribed by law. The rest were fixed by the cabinet. The government party could thus exploit the element of secrecy to its advantage. It was a device which the Opposition had good reason to complain of, and its resentment is echoed in *Albert Savarus* in the observation that 'le Ministère choisit son terrain en choisissant le moment de la lutte'.[57]

A similar tactic was used by the government in deciding the local place where the elections should be held. At the same time, pressure was put on suspect electors, usually by the threat of dismissal or of blocked promotion, to prove themselves 'probes et libres'.[58] However, the most effective electoral weapon which the government had at its disposal via its control of the administration lay in the power of prefects to influence events. Opposition electors were sometimes prevented from voting by prefects and sub-prefects withholding the admission-card which had to be obtained in advance in order to gain access to the polling station. At election time, contacts between ministers and prefects became assiduous. It frequently happened that the government itself chose a candidate and recommended him to the local prefect, perhaps adding that the prefect's future career might depend on the help he gave to the candidate.

The *Comédie humaine* contains two classic examples of this kind of prefectoral intervention for or against a particular candidate. Savarus's hopes are effectively destroyed when the prefect, informed of Savarus's legitimist background by a jealous Rosalie, arranges the switch of 30 pro-Savarus votes to the 'député sortant', M. de Chavoncourt. When de Trailles is sent to Arcis by Rastignac to further the cause of the government candidate, he carries with him a message addressed to the 'préfet de l'Aube'. In turn, the latter conveys via de Trailles a letter to Antonin Goulard, 'sous-préfet d'Arcis', instructing him to give full support to the ministerial candidate. Sherman Kent quotes an actual case of this happening in 1846 as proof, among other things, that 'Balzac possessed second sight in addition to his other extraordinary abilities'. This tribute to Balzac's historical gifts is the more remarkable as it comes from a historian of repute who has made an authoritative study of the electoral system of the July Monarchy. 'Here as in a hundred other works', Kent concludes, 'Balzac fills the historian with a sense of despair. His accuracy and comprehension give the present-day researcher that hollow feeling he sometimes experiences when he finds another to have covered his subject, and covered it better than he.'[59]

Balzac also helps to throw some light on two features of the electoral system of the 'monarchie censitaire', one of which has now totally disappeared, whereas the other has survived, with modifications, to the present day. It is no longer possible for a parliamentary candidate to stand in more than one constituency at a time. At that period, however, there was theoretically no limit to the number of districts in which a candidate could try his luck. Laffitte, for example, stood in seven constituencies in 1837. Although there is no manifestation of this practice in the *Comédie humaine*, Balzac does refer to it in his correspondence. Writing to Mme Hanska in July 1846, and still hopeful of becoming 'éligible', in time to be a candidate in the elections which were less than a month away, Balzac rejoiced in the thought that 'Si Lamartine est nommé à Paris, il aurait le siège de Mâcon à lui pour moi'.[60]

On the other hand, there is mention in *Albert Savarus* of the system of 'ballottage'. Article 54 of the electoral law of 1831 required that, in order to be elected, a candidate should receive at least one-third of the votes of the registered electors and a half of those actually voting.

Eighty-two per cent of successful candidates were in fact elected in the first round. In the event of a third ballot, the electors, as in the second round under today's system, had to choose between the two leading candidates. In the case of a tie, the older candidate was elected. Before it becomes clear that Savarus's chances are negligible, l'abbé de Grancey confidently forecasts that he will be elected after a 'ballottage'. 'Vous n'étiez pas encore nommé', he tells Savarus, 'mais vous étiez maître de l'élection par le ballottage.' It might even, he hints, go to a third ballot. 'Nous aurons plusieurs scrutins, et vous arriverez par un ballottage.'[61]

All of this, the planning, the campaigning, the technicalities of the electoral system of the July Monarchy, Balzac describes in considerable detail over a wide range of his works. What brings it to life, however, is the way in which Balzac dramatises the tensions and intrigue inseparable from parliamentary elections in a series of fierce personal rivalries in the competition to become deputy. We are frequently reminded, for example, of the clash between Tiphaine and Vinet in Provins, Vinet having avenged his defeat by two votes at the hands of his legitimist opponent in 1826 by his victory in 1830.

The electoral battle opposing Nathan and du Tillet claims a considerable amount of attention in *Une Fille d'Eve*. Having formerly supported du Tillet through his journalism, Nathan decides to stand against him in the elections of June 1834. Nathan's cause becomes hopeless when the combined forces of finance and politics join against him. By involving Nathan in debt, du Tillet totally discredits him as a candidate. As a result, 'l'homme célèbre n'eut pas plus de cinq voix dans le collège où le banquier fut élu'.[62]

Important though they are, the rivalries of Tiphaine and Vinet, and of du Tillet and Nathan do not form the dominant interest of the novels in which they are discussed. In *Albert Savarus* and in *Le Député d'Arcis*, on the other hand, electoral struggles are at the centre of Balzac's preoccupations. Savarus's chances of victory depend on two issues. First, he has to overcome the handicap of a legitimist past in his attempt to attract the liberal vote of Besançon. It is not this problem which is his undoing so much as the more immediate question to which it is related, that of trying to reconcile the conflicting class interests of Besançon. La Peyrade and Thuillier have a much easier task in attracting the homogeneous support of the 'petits bourgeois censitaires' of Paris in *Les Petits Bourgeois*, whereas Savarus's defeat is determined well in advance of his dramatic withdrawal on the eve of the election by his failure to get the best of both electoral worlds, the legitimist-clerical and the liberal bourgeois.

In *Albert Savarus* we know the outcome of the electoral campaign in Besançon. 'Le lendemain, monsieur de Chavoncourt fut nommé d'emblée à une majorité de cent quarante voix', and Savarus becomes a monk instead of a deputy.[63] This is not the case with *Le Député d'Arcis*, which, in its unfinished state, leaves the result of the 1839 election in Arcis unspecified. As it stands, the novel has a misleading title. *Une Campagne électorale* would be more accurate.[64] The electoral intrigue which is exposed in *Le Député d'Arcis* reinforces the historical significance of the novel. 'La campagne électorale', Jardin and Tudesq note of the elections of 1839, 's'était déroulée dans un climat d'intrigues, de pressions, voire de corruption qui déconsidéra le régime.'[65]

(c) The Privileges of Parliamentary Office

Just as the acquisition of eligibility was often a difficult process, so election as deputy was not always an automatic and painless business. What was it therefore, apart from mere considerations of prestige, that made the office of deputy so attractive? What powers and benefits did it bring with it?

One of the important attractions of holding a parliamentary seat was that, in most cases, a deputy could combine his political functions with one or more separate appointments which, more often than not, he owed to the influence of his post. The electoral law of 1831 had clearly defined the rules covering 'l'incompatibilité', that is the ban which prohibited certain important categories from holding simultaneously the post of deputy. Those which were totally 'incompatibles' comprised the 'préfets, sous-préfets' and 'receveurs des finances' ('receveurs généraux' and 'receveurs particuliers'). Relative 'incompatibilité' was enforced on army generals, 'procureurs généraux' and 'procureurs du Roi', 'directeurs des contributions (direct and indirect), des domaines, de l'enregistrement, des douanes'.[66]

The qualification of 'relative' contained an important exemption. It was possible, as Tudesq recalls, under the provisions of the electoral law of 1831, for a deputy to be a 'fonctionnaire' at the same time, provided that he represented a parliamentary district outside his area of administrative competence.[67] It happens that none of Balzac's deputies under the July Monarchy is a 'fonctionnaire'. However, one of his provincial deputies is a 'magistrat' of a significant kind. Vinet, who is elected deputy for Provins in 1830, is appointed 'procureur général' after 1830. Tudesq does not mention that 'l'incompatibilité' was only relative in relation to certain grades of 'magistrat' as well as to some levels of 'fonctionnaires'. The 'magistrats' exempt from 'l'incompatibilité' were, as we have just seen, 'procureurs généraux' and 'procureurs du Roi'. Balzac does not suggest that Vinet was benefiting from this exception, but the circumstances of Vinet's career are perfectly consistent with an awareness of this particular historical refinement.

The ruling on 'l'incompatibilité' was quite arbitrary since those who held posts of equal standing in other professions, or even, as in the case of 'magistrats', in certain branches of the same profession, were not affected by it. Camusot de Marville, for example, can be deputy for Jarente and at the same time 'président de la cour Royale de Paris' without the slightest complication. As an 'avocat', Simon Giguet would not be subject to 'l'incompatibilité' in the event of his being elected deputy for Arcis. If, like Vinet, he were to become 'procureur général' or, alternatively, 'procureur du Roi', he would still be able, thanks to the escape-clause of 'relative incompatibility', to continue as deputy. Either way, the post of deputy would be perfectly compatible with his legal career, as Mme Marion unwittingly acknowledges when, in attempting to convince Mme Beauvisage of the advantages of a marriage between Cécile and her nephew, she flatters their desire to live in Paris. 'Qui sait', she insinuates, 'si le député d'Arcis n'y sera pas fixé par une belle place dans la magistrature?'[68]

Under the July Monarchy, the ruling on 'l'incompatibilité' resulted in some extraordinary efforts to circumvent it. Kent describes, for instance, the unique case of M. Hello, who had been approved as the official government candidate for Ploërmel in Le Morbihan in 1837. M. Hello had resigned his post as 'procureur général' at the 'Cour Royale de Rennes' in order to be eligible to fight the election. However, his resignation was only five months old, one month short of the minimum period stipulated by the law on 'l'incompatibilité'. His ineligibility was duly exposed by the opposition candidate four days before the convocation of the electoral college. The following day a fire destroyed the electoral lists at the 'sous-préfecture'. A sympathetic prefect ordered the election to be postponed for a month. Though finally able to stand, M. Hello was defeated in the election.[69]

Perhaps even the conservative voters of Ploërmel were displeased at such transparent electoral trickery. Although Balzac has nothing direct to say on 'l'incompatibilité', he was no doubt aware of the resentment caused by the exemptions which it allowed. Indeed, the demand for the enforcement of 'l'incompatibilité' became one of the prominent demands in the campaign for electoral reform which grew in strength under the July Monarchy. In two other areas, however, Balzac offers a considerable amount of evidence of aspects of the parliamentary system which did much to discredit the regime. The first deals with the abuses and corruption frequently identified with the exercise of a deputy's functions. The second is concerned with the economic involvement of deputies. Needless to say, the two were often closely associated.

Election as deputy is often seen in the *Comédie humaine* as essential to promotion at the highest level in certain professions. Once a Parisian vacancy arises, the deputies vie with one another to secure it, as Balzac emphasises in *Le Cousin Pons*. 'La vacance probable d'une des vingt-quatre perceptions de Paris cause une émeute d'ambitions à la chambre des députés! Ces places se donnent en conseil, la nomination est une affaire d'Etat.'[70] This is especially true of the top posts in the Parisian magistrature. Désiré Minoret and Simon Giguet both view their eleva-tion from provincial obscurity to the status of leading Parisian magis-trates as inseparable from their election as deputies. The thinking of Mme Camusot de Marville is identical when she asks her father-in-law 's'il pouvait fermer à son fils aîné le chemin aux honneurs suprêmes de la magistrature, qui ne seraient plus accordés qu'à une forte position parlementaire'.[71]

Deputies, as Balzac frequently stresses, often used their position in order to obtain a variety of lucrative posts and appointments. In some instances, the practice is so taken for granted that the benefits auto-matically come the deputy's way without his having to solicit them. Victorin Hulot, for example, is given some valuable briefs by the normally incorruptible War Minister, the prince de Wissembourg, in order to help him to pay his father's debts. The price of such ministerial favours was generally a pledge of political support on the part of the recipient, and one can assume that the prince de Wissembourg was exceptional in assuring Victorin that the gesture involved no sacrifice of his political independence.

Balzac views such a system of privilege as encouraging the spread of corruption. The abuses which are revealed are as widespread at deputy as at ministerial level. It is Hulot who complains to the prince de Wissembourg about the systematic grabbing of the most lucrative administrative posts by deputies. 'Vous connaissez les principes des quatre cents élus de la France', he protests. 'Ces messieurs envient toutes les positions . . . et pour eux veulent nos places quand les appointements sont de quarante mille francs?' It is these same deputies, Hulot continues, who are responsible for the low salaries of all but the highest posts in the magistrature, many of which are occupied by deputies in any case. 'Qu'attendre de gens', Hulot asks, 'qui paient aussi mal qu'elle l'est la magistrature?'[72] The mere fact of being a deputy was invaluable from every point of view. It not only conferred privileges but, like the 'fonctionnaires' who enjoyed immunity from prosecution in cases of electoral irregularity, a deputy would find his status extremely useful if he were to commit any serious indiscretions. This time it is Hulot who has the lesson spelled out to him by the prince de Wissembourg, when he makes him realise that he has no means of protection against the consequences of his misconduct. 'Ah!', he regretfully points out to Hulot, 'tu n'es pas député, mon ami.'[73]

In order to continue to enjoy the favours of a system from which they were the first to benefit, it was essential that the deputies should ensure their survival in office by the most effective means at their disposal. Balzac reveals the considerable resourcefulness which the deputies displayed in achieving this object. To avoid having to seek re-election, for example, it was possible for a deputy to obtain immunity in certain circumstances. This is shown by the device employed by du Bruel. 'De Bruel fut nommé député', Balzac discloses, 'mais auparavant, pour n'être pas soumis à la réélection, il se fit nommer Conseiller-d'Etat et directeur.'[74]

The two outstanding abuses associated with parliamentary office were the 'bourgs-pourris' and nepotism. In the case of the first, the motive was the election and retention in office of the deputy himself. In the second instance, the aim was to ensure that a desirable nominee or successor be elected as deputy. Both these forms of electoral corruption are abundantly documented in the *Comédie humaine*.

The law of 1831 increased the number of parliamentary districts from 430 to 459. The great disparities which they revealed in size, population, wealth and voting strength created an electoral imbalance favourable to the government party. The ministerial majority was guaranteed by the fact that it required fewer votes to elect a deputy in the small rural constituencies where the government's strength lay and which at the same time were more vulnerable to corrupt pressures. The figures given by Duvergier de Hauranne in his 1847 pamphlet are the clearest possible indication of the way in which the system discriminated against the Opposition.[75]

Number of Electors per Constituency	Government Deputies	Opposition Deputies
Less than 400	113	59
400-800	133	93
Over 800	30	31

Duvergier de Hauranne's figures also vividly underline the limited size of the total electorate and, in particular, the excessively small number of electors in the government-held seats. With 248,000 electors spread over 459 seats in 1846, that meant an average of only 540 electors per constituency. France, critics were quick to point out, was creating 'bourgs-pourris' at a time when England was abolishing them.

These facts are accurately reflected in the details of the voting in elections in the *Comédie humaine* for the whole period of the 'monarchie censitaire'. They explain, for example, the small size of the electorate of Besançon, less than 400 in fact, as described in *Albert Savarus*.[76] They also account for the derisory number of votes that a candidate might obtain, Nathan's five votes against du Tillet reminding one of Balzac's score of seven at Chinon in 1832. Not surprisingly, therefore, many elections were closely fought, as Tiphaine's victory over Vinet by a margin of two votes in 1826 indicates.

Balzac refers specifically on several occasions to the existence of 'bourgs-pourris'. We have seen how, in 1846, he had expressed the hope that one of the seats for which Lamartine was standing would revert to himself if Lamartine were elected elsewhere. It is no doubt the same Mâcon constituency that Balzac had in mind four years earlier when he had mentioned, again to Mme Hanska, that 'Lamartine a un bourg-pourri pour moi'.[77] In the *Comédie humaine* itself, the outstanding example of a 'bourg-pourri' is the district represented by Nucingen from 1824 to 1834, 'une espèce de bourg-pourri, un collège à peu d'électeurs'.[78] In describing the 'bourg-pourri' of Sancerre, Balzac gives a clear idea of how the seat was controlled by a handful of powerful electors. When she is looking for an Opposition candidate, Mme de la Baudraye draws her support from local 'notables' resentful at the way their constituency has become a 'bourg-pourri' faithfully returning the government deputy in perpetuity. 'L'Arrondissement de Sancerre', Balzac records, 'choqué de se voir soumis à sept ou huit grands propriétaires, les hauts barons de l'Election, essaya de secouer le joug électoral de la Doctrine, qui en a fait son bourg-pourri.'[79]

The prevalence of 'bourgs-pourris' was a further incitement to the other major abuse of nepotism. For example, the official reason for Beauvisage's support of Giguet's candidature in Arcis is that he wants to put an end to Arcis's being a 'bourg-pourri' and one in which a flagrant case of nepotism seemed about to be perpetrated with the nomination of Charles Keller as candidate to succeed his father.[80] Under the Restoration, Leclercq had intended to hand over his seat of deputy for La Ville-aux-Fayes to his father-in-law Gaubertin. Similarly, though this time the transfer operates within a profession and not within a family, it is Nucingen who ensures that his deputyship passes to his fellow-banker du Tillet.

Once a deputy had, by one means or another, guaranteed his stay in office for a significant period of time, the material rewards which thus came within his reach fully justified his exertions. What finally made the post of deputy an enviable one was that, in addition to the lucrative posts and contracts which deputies had access to, the possibilities of profitable involvement in the economic sphere took on a new dimension from the moment of their election.

No 'incompatibilité', however flimsy, hindered deputies in their pursuit of economic activities nominally outside their parliamentary sphere of duty. Deputies were always to be found among the 'régents de la Banque de France' and the number of those represented on 'conseils d'administration' ran into three figures under the July Monarchy. Balzac captures this important trend by showing that it was mainly identified with the outstanding sector of economic growth in the 1840s, the development of railways.

The participation by deputies in the railway boom which characterised the second half of the July Monarchy is reflected in the career of Crevel. Crevel's position as deputy is important to him only in so far as it enables him to make the necessary business contacts. Instead of being the director of a railway company like Gaudissart, Crevel is a speculator who makes much of his money out of investing in the new railway enterprises.[81] He speculates on behalf of Bette and Mme Marneffe as well as for his own benefit. He tells Mme Marneffe: 'Je vous ai doublé depuis deux mois vos économies dans l'Orléans', and he has 1,000 shares of his own in the Paris-Versailles line.[82]

Balzac is here writing with an authenticity born of painful first-hand experience. Having persuaded Mme Hanska to invest in the 'Chemins de fer du Nord', he was perpetually tormented by the fluctuations in the value of the shares, particularly during the terminal crisis of the regime from 1846 to 1848, as the anguished tone of his letters to Mme Hanska at this time reveals. Like Balzac, Crevel is quick to take advantage of the boom in railway construction which began in the early 1840s, only with happier results than anything Balzac experienced. The law of June 1842, providing for the systematic creation of a national railway network, had rapid early success. The Paris-Orleans and the 'rive droite' of the Paris-Versailles lines in which Crevel speculates were among several to be opened in 1843.[83]

At the same time, Crevel's speculation in railways indicates an important phenomenon increasingly associated with the later stages of the July Monarchy, the collusion between government circles and business interests. Crevel has bought shares in the Paris-Versailles line for 125 fr. each. He confidently predicts that their value will rise to 300 fr. because of the projected joining of two lines, of which he has foreknowledge through his political contacts at a high level. The situation as described by Balzac in discussing the affairs of Crevel precisely anticipates the conclusion expressed by Tudesq in referring to 'les projets de voies ferrées, parfois véritables marchandages entre l'administration, les députés, les électeurs et le ministère'.[84]

Balzac was fully alive to the connection between business interests and the world of politics, and in particular to the important role played by deputies in linking the two. It is Bixiou who, in 1845, reveals that 'l'adjudication du Chemin sera positivement ajournée à la Chambre'.[85] The date of Bixiou's remark is important since it marked a delicate moment in the struggle to win control of the development of French railways. The law of 1842 had established a compromise between the government's backing of state direction and the interests of private investment represented by the deputies. Bixiou's disclosure, moreover, confirms the success which the deputies had in resisting the proposals for state intervention.[86]

In a letter which he wrote to Mme Hanska in April 1836, Balzac gives proof both of his own desire to be involved in profitable ventures and of his awareness of the financial power of deputies. Again it is the transport system which is at the centre of interest, only this time it is not railways but canals. It would appear that the project referred to by Balzac of a canal from Nantes to Orleans, which had been approved earlier in the year, never in fact materialised, presumably because the sponsors of the scheme were unable to attract sufficient capital. The collapse of the project was a particular blow to Surville, to whom the contract had been given. Balzac's hopes of making a *coup* out of it were dashed at the same time. His idea had been to borrow money to buy a 'concession' in the company belonging to a deputy, M. de

Villevêque, and then to resell it at a profit to Rothschild. Balzac's reaction: 'C'est surtout dans la guerre politique que l'argent est le nerf' effectively sums up the degree of inter-involvement between finance and politics which marked the latter part in particular of the July Monarchy.[87]

As the nature and extent of the extra-parliamentary activities of deputies gradually came to light, the regime began to lose its credibility. As Jardin and Tudesq have remarked, 'La construction des chemins de fer à la fin du règne donne au régime son caractère de collusion entre le monde des affaires et celui de la politique'.[88] In exposing the network of corruption embracing politicians, financiers and the 'haute administration', the Teste case contributed to the growing disenchantment with which the voters tended to regard their elected representatives. The campaign for electoral reform became more powerful and when the blocking of its limited demands coincided with the economic crisis of 1846-7, the revolutionary consequences of such an impasse could not be long delayed.

II The Ideological and Historical Implications of Balzac's Account of 'les Notables'

(a) Balzac's Critique of the Elective Principle and the Parliamentary System

In dealing so comprehensively with the 'notables' of the 'monarchie censitaire', Balzac was doing more than simply recording a contemporary phenomenon, as an exercise in historical analysis. The central position which the question takes up in the *Comédie humaine* is a measure of the importance which it assumed in relation to Balzac's social and political philosophy.

In *Le Député d'Arcis*, Balzac defines his aim in the novel as follows: 'Cette scène est écrite pour l'enseignement des pays assez malheureux pour ne pas connaître les bienfaits d'une représentation nationale, et qui, par conséquent, ignorent par quelles guerres intestines, aux prix de quels sacrifices à la Brutus, une petite ville enfant un député!'[89] Although the exposure of the brutal realities of electoral campaigns is the main theme of *Le Député d'Arcis*, Balzac is more concerned in his work as a whole to attack what he sees as the disastrous farce of parliamentary government. There is a strong suggestion of this in *Le Député d'Arcis*, where Balzac denounces the sham of a parliament 'où les chambres et les ministres ressemblent aux acteurs de bois que fait jouer le propriétaire du spectacle du Guignolet, à la grande satisfaction des passants toujours ébahis'.[90]

Les Comédiens sans le savoir also contains a satirical account of the Chamber of Deputies, in which the cynical posturings of the deputies are paraded for the benefit of the naïve provincial Gazonal. Léon de Lora's question to his cousin Gazonal: 'Qu'il y ait un député de plus ou de moins à gauche ou à droite, cela te met-il dans de meilleurs draps?',[91] sums up Balzac's contempt for a system which puts the interests of its members before the welfare of those who have elected them and before the needs of France as a whole. The emphasis, as in the examples already discussed in *La Cousine Bette*, is on the corruption which Balzac regards as inseparable from a parliamentary form of government. When Jardin and Tudesq conclude their discussion of the complicity between financiers and politicians with the remark: 'Non qu'il s'agisse d'une nouveauté mais le régime parlementaire et censitaire y prédispose', they make a judgement which Balzac would have been the first to applaud.[92]

The attack on the parliamentary system forms part of Balzac's general indictment of the 'régime censitaire'. Balzac repeatedly expresses his opposition to the financial criteria of the 'cens', although, as we shall see in a moment, Balzac was capable of modifying his views on the question if self-interest required him to do so. 'L'argent autrefois n'était pas tout', Bianchon argues in *La Cousine Bette*, 'on admettait des supériorités qui le primaient. Il y avait la noblesse, le talent, les services rendus à l'Etat; mais aujourd'hui la loi fait de l'argent un étalon général, elle l'a pris pour base de la capacité politique.'[93] Balzac makes the same point through the statement of Savinien de Portenduère. 'Aujourd'hui on ne vous demande pas si vous êtes un Portenduère', he protests; 'si vous êtes brave, si vous êtes homme d'Etat, tout le monde vous dit: Combien payez-vous de contributions?'[94]

The consequences of making electoral qualification solely dependent on money are, in Balzac's view, wholly disastrous. The first price to be paid is the elimination of genuine talent which is unsupported by wealth. This criticism, which is implicit in the comments on Savinien's ineligibility, is reiterated by Bianchon. 'Certains magistrats', he complains, 'ne sont pas éligibles. Jean-Jacques Rousseau ne serait pas éligible!'[95] The inevitable corollary of this was the promotion of mediocrity. '*Le gouvernement constitutionnel*', Balzac wrote to Mme Hanska in January 1843, 'est le gouvernement des sots, la déification du sot, le triomphe des sots!'[96] The tendency, which historians have pointed to, was to prefer local nonentities to talented outsiders. This situation is illustrated on several occasions by Balzac. It is to oppose the representative of the 'juste-milieu' in Sancerre that Mme de la Baudraye tries to persuade Lousteau and Bianchon to stand as Opposition candidates. 'Cette idée', Balzac reflects, 'était extrêmement avancée pour la province, où, depuis 1830, la nomination des notabilités de clocher a fait de tels progrès que les hommes d'Etat deviennent de plus en plus rares à la Chambre élective.'[97]

Just as money kept out ability, so youth was excluded in favour of an inept gerontocracy. As Marcas explains, 'En France, la jeunesse est condamnée par la légalité nouvelle, par les mauvaises conditions du principe électif, par les vices de la constitution ministérielle. En examinant la composition de la chambre élective, vous n'y trouvez point de député de trente ans.'[98] Political power became self-perpetuating at the same time that it remained in a few hands. What one finds in the *Comédie humaine* concurs entirely with the conclusion of Jardin and Tudesq: 'Qu'il s'agisse de l'administration ou des municipalités, les mêmes hommes se perpétuent et ont tendance à monopoliser les avantages du pouvoir'.[99]

Balzac's critique of the 'régime censitaire' is unqualified. Its disastrous effects, he believed, extended to every area of national life. Among its more intimate repercussions, it was, Balzac alleged, obsession with the 'cens' which had killed the charm of conversation. 'Les gens du monde', he lamented, 'causent aujourd'hui beaucoup trop chevaux, revenus, impôts, députés pour que la conversation française reste ce qu'elle fut.'[100] Balzac's dissent from the 'régime censitaire' is inspired by a rejection of the elective principle as such. The essence of Balzac's thinking had been expressed in the assertion contained in the *Lettres Russes* in 1840. 'Gouverner, c'est savoir choisir les capacités. L'élection ne choisit que les médiocrités.'[101] As in politics, so in art. The political assumptions apart, Balzac's attack on what he saw as the degeneration of the 'Salon' after 1830 anticipates Zola's assault in his 'Salons' on the jury-system which operated in the 1860s. In both cases, talent is upheld against mediocrity, and the enemy is a privileged group of self-appointed arbiters of artistic standards. The decline of art, Balzac was convinced, was symptomatic of the folly of the elective principle in general, of 'cette cruelle maxime à laquelle la société doit ces infâmes médiocrités chargées d'élire aujourd'hui les supériorités dans toutes les classes sociales; mais qui naturellement s'élisent elles-mêmes, et font une guerre acharnée aux vrais talents. Le principe de l'Election, appliqué à tout, est faux, la France en reviendra.'[102] 'Si vous saviez', he wrote to Mme Hanska in 1847, 'à quels hommes l'élection est descendue en France! et par qui nous sommes non pas *gouvernés*, mais administrés!'[103]

Balzac's critique of the 'régime censitaire' and of the elective principle in general has finally to be considered in relation to his social and political philosophy. Although it is the July Revolution and the July Monarchy which bear the brunt of Balzac's attack,[104] his argument is ultimately directed at the Revolution and the Charter of 1814. While Balzac refrains from making the point himself, the fact is that the constitutional basis of the 'monarchie censitaire' was the work of Louis XVIII. 'Le roi se trouve pris entre les deux chambres', Balzac regretted, 'comme un homme entre sa femme légitime et sa maîtresse.'[105] In expressing his conviction that the important alliance between king and aristocracy had been impaired by the constitutional obligation imposed on the king to defer to an elected lower house, Balzac on this occasion at least omitted to acknowledge that this was a state of affairs which dated from 1814.

It was after all the Charter of 1814 which established the electoral basis of the 'régime censitaire'. The Charter of 1830 merely reaffirmed the provisions of its predecessor by annulling Charles X's third Ordinance,[106] while the electoral law of 1831 did no more than extend a suffrage whose principles had been laid down seventeen years earlier. The original Charter was in turn a recognition of the notion of elected representation inherent in, if strictly limited by, the Revolution. Indeed it was one of the features of the campaign for electoral reform under the July Monarchy that it appealed to the principles of 1789 and 1830.[107] A liberal demagogue like Simon Giguet, for example, tells his election meetings: 'Pour moi, le progrès, c'est la réalisation de tout ce qui nous fut promis à la révolution de Juillet, c'est la réforme électorale'.[108]

The idea of any extension of the suffrage was anathema to Balzac, so convinced was he of the enormous damage already caused by even so severely restricted a franchise. It is therefore all the more surprising to find Balzac making a rare proposal for electoral reform. 'L'électeur', he urged in 1831, 'étant le principe du député, doit seul offrir des garanties. Il payera un cens, tiendra au sol, à la science ou à l'industrie. Le député ne saurait être soumis à aucune exigence d'éligibilité. Il doit être citoyen français, avoir 25 ans, et n'être frappé d'aucune incapacité.'[109] Balzac's recommendation is significant for two reasons. The first is its date, occurring as it does in a letter of 26 February 1831. It was therefore written at a time when Balzac was 'inéligible' by age. When that obstacle was removed two months later by the law of

April 1831, one hears nothing more from Balzac on the need to lower the age limit of eligibility to his original suggestion of 25, although the financial qualification, as we have seen, continued to be an embarrassment to Balzac's political ambitions and one which he was anxious to see legally removed.

The other interesting feature of Balzac's proposals is that they are in contradiction with his refusal to admit any form of elective system. A devastating answer to the inconsistency of Balzac's proposed reforms is given by Marcas, who speaks with the authentic voice of Balzac when he affirms that 'On aurait pu mettre la majorité à vingt et un ans et dégrever l'éligibilité de tout espèce de condition, les départements n'auraient élu que les députés actuels, des gens sans aucun talent politique, incapables de parler sans estropier la grammaire, et parmi lesquels, en dix ans, il s'est à peine rencontré un homme d'Etat'.[110]

There are other more serious and more fundamental flaws in Balzac's social and political thinking which are revealed in his discussion of the elective basis of the 'régime censitaire'. Take, for example, his reiterated view that the political application of the elective principle had engendered a fatal 'individualisme'. La Peyrade acts as Balzac's spokesman in this respect when he claims that 'l'élection, étendue à presque toutes les fonctions, a fait pénétrer les préoccupations de l'ambition, la fureur d'être quelque chose à des profondeurs qu'elles n'auraient pas dû agiter'.[111] No one better embodies this self-seeking spirit than La Peyrade's protégé, Thuillier, and Balzac's conviction of the social threat which it posed is evident from the terms in which La Peyrade's warning is expressed.

Philosophically, Balzac's denunciation of 'l'individualisme' clashes with his cult of 'l'homme supérieur', which, in the context of the July Monarchy, could find its political embodiment only in his despised bourgeois democrat. It was one thing for Balzac to dismiss the principle of political election as utopian, to assert that 'l'élection n'est possible que dans les sociétés où tous les individus sont égaux ou également éclairés'.[112] It was an altogether different matter when it came to proposing clear, concrete alternatives to the existing system. The 'bourgeoisie censitaire' of the July Monarchy, while ill-inclined to extend political rights to the rest of the middle class, was equally unprepared to dismantle, as the logic of Balzac's argument demanded it should, the system of limited franchise on which its authority was based. Balzac could express his dissatisfaction in his creative work, in *Le Député d'Arcis*, for example, where, he announced, it was his intention to 'faire le portrait du *bourgeois-homme politique*', to write 'l'histoire de cette hideuse bourgeoisie qui mène les affaires'.[113] For all his tirades against the sectional self-interest and the mediocrity which he insisted were inseparable from an elected system of government, Balzac would have to look for a solution within a bourgeois order of society.

'Le gouvernement produit par les institutions d'août 1830', Balzac wrote in the *Lettres Russes* in 1840, 'est inférieur au gouvernement monarchique.'[114] Seven years later the July Monarchy was still in existence when he complained that the ravages of the elective system in France were such that 'c'est à dégoûter d'un pays'. More significantly, Balzac saw fit to add, 'Enfin, l'Europe est folle de bourgeoisie. On ne peut pas se mettre en travers de son siècle.'[115] An authoritarian way out of the elective impasse had to be found and it could only lie in a bourgeois and not in a legitimist direction. As the later novels of the *Comédie humaine* and the contemporary letters to Mme Hanska show, it was increasingly to a 'césariste' solution, 'le pouvoir fort dans la main d'un seul', that Balzac looked in an effort to resolve the tensions between his political convictions and the realities of post-revolutionary society.[116] When it came to an urgent choice between a bourgeois democracy and the threat of popular revolution, Balzac could not afford to hesitate, and the 'régime censitaire' which he loathed could not be too repressive.

(b) The Historical Value of Balzac's Account

In attempting to assess the authenticity of Balzac's treatment of 'les notables', let us first consider the debit side. First, there is the point which was noted at the outset regarding the imbalance in Balzac's approach. Because Balzac's own political preoccupations were confined to the July Monarchy, the Restoration figures much less prominently than the later period, with the result, in particular, that the electors who are shown before 1830 are thinly represented.

Another and more serious qualification has to be made under this heading. It concerns the disproportion evident in the professional composition of Balzac's 'notables'. Certain groups of 'censitaires' are featured in the *Comédie humaine* to the detriment of others. The 'professions libérales' dominate the 'professions économiques'. 'Fonctionnaires', 'employés' and 'magistrats' crowd out the 'propriétaires médiocres' and the 'boutiquiers', not to mention the virtually non-existent industrialists. Although this is a matter of emphasis rather than one of distortion, it does result in an unbalanced projection of the social character of the 'notables' which is in inverse proportion to the historical reality.

It would be astonishing if, given both the range and the depth of Balzac's discussion of the subject, some things were not left out. Some of these omissions are of minor consequence. There is no mention, for example, of the device of 'dégrèvement' which the government resorted to on several occasions both before and after 1830 in order to reduce the number of Opposition voters.[117] A more intriguing point concerns the right of widows (and of divorcees) to credit their male heirs, beginning with the eldest son, with their taxes. Already in force under the Restoration, this dispensation was confirmed by the law of 1831. It might have helped towards Savinien de Portenduère's eventual eligibility, and one wonders if it might not have been a factor in Balzac's case, when, for example, he thought of buying his mother a house in order to become 'éligible' in January 1842.[118] It would be unreasonable, however, to make too much of such omissions, and there is, finally, only one significant aspect of the whole question which Balzac overlooks. He has nothing specific to say about the different modes of tax assessment used in determining the 'cens', and it is only implicitly that the bias in favour of 'le foncier' can be appreciated from a reading of the *Comédie humaine*.

It is rare that Balzac makes an obvious error. The only clear-cut mistake occurs when Balzac mentions that Anselme Popinot had twice been elected deputy for the IVe 'arrondissement' before 1830. Born in 1797, Popinot would not have been 'éligible' under the Restoration, nor would he have been able to continue as deputy under the July Monarchy until the age limit of eligibility was lowered from 40 to 30 by the law of April 1831.

On other occasions, Balzac shows an indifference to historical precision which can scarcely be justified on the grounds of creative inventiveness. While the liberty which Balzac took in creating a fictional constituency in *Arcis* in 1839 may be of no consequence,[119] one finds it difficult to understand why Balzac should have been so casual with regard to the accuracy of some of his election dates. All the internal indications make it impossible, for instance, for the election in Besançon which is described in *Albert Savarus* to have been held, as happened in reality, in June 1834, or for that in *Arcis* to have taken place in March 1839. In both cases, the context is so clearly defined as to suggest a later election date.

Balzac is also guilty of another kind of confusion, this time in respect of the social composition of his 'censitaires'. Although the imprecision is only marginal in relation to the overall clarity of the picture provided by the *Comédie humaine*, nevertheless it has to be recognised that the demarcation between 'électeur' and 'éligible' is not always clear in some individual cases. In particular, some electors show all the signs of being 'éligibles' as well. Nor does Balzac establish which of his characters become 'censitaires' at either level as a result of the law of 1831.

Finally, in examining the deficiencies in Balzac's presentation, one has to consider the question of distortion. First of all, there is the tendency to oversimplify his bourgeois categories, to polarise the opposition of interests in terms of 'petite' versus 'grande bourgeoisie'. This means that the 'moyenne bourgeoisie' and the vital position which it occupied on either side of the 'électeur'-'éligible' division is not taken sufficiently into account. It is sufficient to study the remarkable analysis of the divisions in the social hierarchy of Paris in 1814-15 which forms the preamble of *La Fille aux yeux d'or* to appreciate that Balzac had an acute understanding of the different levels within the bourgeoisie.[120] It is all the more surprising therefore that the awareness of class nuances which Balzac demonstrates on this particular occasion should not have been equally expressed in his analysis of the 'notables' of the 'bourgeoisie censitaire'.

A further significant distortion arises out of Balzac's view of the degree of democratisation of the electorate. Detesting the 'régime censitaire' and the elective principle on which it was based, Balzac was the last person to approve of proposals for the extension of the suffrage. The one exception arose, as we have observed, when it was a question of his own political emancipation. Just as he advocated the removal of any financial qualification for 'éligibles', so he protested at the exclusion from the 'cens' of those 'capacités' who, like himself, were alone equipped, in his view, to supply France with the talented political leaders which it needed.

There is an ironic affinity between Balzac's aristocratic contempt for a regime dominated by 'épiciers', to borrow his favourite term of anti-bourgeois abuse, and the liberal demands for the incorporation of the 'capacités' into the electorate. No one would have greeted with more delight than Balzac Altaroche's poem which appeared in *Le Charivari* in 1838.

Toi t'es écrivain ou savant
Sans le sou . . . Ça se voit maintenant
Ton voisin qui vend d'la réglisse
Ou de la saucisse
Est un vrai jocrisse
Seul il a l'droit électoral
V'la c'que c'est qu' l'ordre légal[121]

It is at this point that the implausible alliance of liberal and reactionary breaks down. There is already a hint of polemical exaggeration in *Le Charivari*'s caricature of the 'petit commerçant' who is now an automatic elector. Mlle Daumard's emphasis on the high proportion of bourgeois 'non-censitaires' in Paris under the July Monarchy is a sufficient corrective to this kind of fallacious assumption.

Balzac, however, goes even further than this in his distortion of the extent to which the 'notables' of the July Monarchy had become democratised. In *Les Comédiens sans le savoir*, Bixiou makes the claim that 'un garçon de restaurant est électeur-éligible'. Beneath the surface of provocative 'boutade' which is an essential part of Bixiou's character, the remark occurs in the context of a serious analysis of the effects of economic concentration, whereby 'les petits métiers' are being taken over by the 'boutiquiers'. Marius, a fashionable hairdresser, is grotesquely magnified by Bixiou into a 'grand commerçant' enjoying 'le monopole de la vente des cheveux en gros'.[122]

In the previous year, 1844, Balzac had developed a similar economic argument in *L'Hôpital et le Peuple* and accompanied it with the same kind of comment on the changing character of the electorate. 'Devenir électeur, éligible, député, ministre comme le premier fabricant venu', Balzac had exclaimed. Even 'le premier fabricant' might have difficulty with the 'cens d'éligibilité'. As for the other categories whose political horizons Balzac insists are unlimited under the July Monarchy, 'le savetier', 'le recarreleur de souliers', 'le crémier', while, as Mlle Daumard has shown, they formed the majority of the Parisian electorate after 1830, they were no more likely to be 'éligibles' than Bixiou's 'garçon de restaurant' could hope to be an elector.[123] The essential difference was between a 'garçon de restaurant' and a 'restaurateur'. Referring to the Parisian electorate of 1842, Mlle Daumard emphasises that 'les petites et les moyennes entreprises dominaient'. They included 'tous les boutiquiers de l'alimentation, bouchers, charcutiers, boulangers, . . . des limonadiers, des restaurateurs'.[124]

In this sense, Flaubert is a more reliable and objective witness than

Balzac. In *L'Education Sentimentale*, Deslauriers gives his reason for resigning from his post as 'maître-clerc'. 'Comme si j'allais me gêner', he explains to Frédéric Moreau, 'pour de pareils cocos, qui vous gagnent jusqu'à des six et huit mille francs par an, qui sont électeurs, éligibles peut-être.'[125] Flaubert's tone is noticeably more cautious, particularly in respect of the fluid frontier separating 'électeurs' and 'éligibles'. Flaubert despised the bourgeoisie as much as Balzac. Unlike Balzac, however, Flaubert was not swayed by ideological prejudice in referring to the 'censitaires' of the July Monarchy. Moreover, he was writing from the standpoint of a later generation which could look on the electoral passions of the July Monarchy with a certain detachment. Balzac's contempt for the bourgeoisie was exceeded only by his hatred and fear of the masses. It was the interaction of the two which inspired him to magnify the degree of 'morcellement' resulting from the Revolution and to attribute the myth of a revolutionary peasantry to its acquisition of land from a rapacious 'bourgeoisie terrienne'. It was the combination of the same two factors which led Balzac to exaggerate the democratisation of the 'cens' under the July Monarchy.

To balance these defects, what positive qualitites can one detect which demonstrate the historical value of Balzac's account of the 'notables' of the 'monarchie censitaire'? The consistent and at times astonishing accuracy of detail has already been noted. Beyond this, there are solid grounds for concluding that Balzac displays genuine historical originality in his discussion of the question. In pointing, in particular, to the survival of 'la grande propriété aristocratique' under the Restoration, Balzac anticipates the conclusions of recent historical research.

Moreover, Balzac reveals some aspects of the activities of the 'notables' which no historian, for lack of concrete evidence, could have illuminated. One thinks particularly of the brilliant evocation of what was involved in the effort to acquire eligibility.[126] But Balzac not only brings to light. He also brings to life. The account of the 'censitaires' in the *Comédie humaine* is proof of the value of Balzac's contribution as a contemporary witness of the important developments which transformed French society in the first half of the nineteenth century. No other literary testimony approaches that of Balzac in its unique blend of richness of experience, a sense of history and power of creative reconstruction.

Above all, Balzac's treatment of the 'notables' reaffirms Balzac's understanding of the forces making for change in post-revolutionary society and, in particular, of the continuing impact of the Revolution on the Restoration and the July Monarchy. This awareness is expressed by Balzac's emphasis on the ascension of important revolutionary categories to the position where they became 'grands notables' of the 'monarchie censitaire'. The contribution which Balzac makes to an understanding of post-revolutionary society is not to be measured, however, in statistical terms or even in what he suggests about the composition of social classes and professional groups. Its interest lies in his faithful registering of contemporary attitudes to the changes arising from the Revolution, above all to traditional notions of status challenged by the acceleration in social nobility. Faced with a bourgeoisie united in its affirmation of its new power, the aristocracy in the *Comédie humaine* is divided between the desire to retain its values and the urgent search for a fresh identity.

Mlle Daumard makes out a convincing case for her conclusion that the pace of social mobility was appreciably quicker before 1815 than in the generation that followed.[127] While showing nothing that indicates disagreement with Mlle Daumard's thesis, Balzac adds an important dimension to it. Balzac's revolutionary bourgeoisie lay the foundations of their wealth and authority during the Revolution and Empire, but their rise does not stop at 1815. It continues significantly and without interruption during the Restoration and, in many cases, notably that of his 'négociants-députés', achieves its final consecration under the July Monarchy.

Notes

1. André Wurmser, *La Comédie Inhumaine*, 2nd edn (Paris, 1965). Wurmser rightly insists that it is not for what it reveals of the 'parti-prêtre' that Balzac's account of the Restoration is most memorable.
2. Roger Pierrot makes the observation that 'Balzac n'était pas l'homme du juste milieu. La faune politique de la monarchie louis-philipparde ne l'a jamais intéressé. Il est frappant de voir dans la *Comédie humaine* qu'il n'est pratiquement jamais question (ou très directement) du personnel de la monarchie de Juillet.' *Europe* (Colloque Balzac) (January-February 1965), p. 243.
3. See p. 85 of chapter 4, with particular reference to note 21.
4. The abortive Bonapartist insurrection in Saumur took place in December 1821, just ten months before the death of Grandet's wife.
5. The absence in *Le Père Goriot* of any reference to the assassination of the duc de Berry, which occurred on 13 February 1820, exactly a week before Goriot's death, and the anachronisms which Balzac commits in relation to it, are dealt with in an article by Jean Gaudon, 'Sur la Chronologie du *Père Goriot*', *L'Année Balzacienne* (1967), pp. 147-56. Balzac's realism, Gaudon concludes, is characterised by 'l'indifférence . . . envers les contingences'.
6. Jean-Louis Bory explains this feature of Balzac's treatment of history by

reference to the aesthetic convictions expressed in the *Avant-Propos*, whereby the obtrusive presence of historical characters is regarded as prejudicial to fictional 'vraisemblance'. *Balzac* (Hachette, Paris, 1959), chapter IV, 'Balzac dévoile le dessous des cartes' (pp. 95-135).

7. For a historian's involuntary tribute to the value of Balzac's method see chapter 5, note 123.

8. The electoral basis of the 'monarchie censitaire' was laid by the Charter of 1814. The franchise was limited to males of 30 or over paying a minimum of 300 fr. per year in direct taxes. For the right to be an 'éligible' and to stand as a parliamentary candidate, the requirement was for 1,000 fr. in direct taxes and a lower age limit of 40. The law of April 1831, which was the first and last act of electoral reform of the July Monarchy, lowered the 'cens d'électorat' to 200 fr. and the 'cens d'éligibilité' to 500 fr. The respective age-limits were reduced to 25 and 30 by one of the 'lois organiques' designed to strengthen the revised Charter in 1830.

9. In his Introduction to *Eugénie Grandet* (Classiques Garnier, 1965a), facing p. 11, P.-G. Castex reproduces the document showing Jean de Margonne as the leading 'éligible' in the Indre-et-Loire in 1807, with Balzac's father in ninth place on the strength of the 778 fr. which he paid that year in direct taxes.

10. 'En 1831', Roger Pierrot concludes, 'Balzac, semble-t-il, était loin de payer de tels impôts. Il n'était imposé au titre de la cote mobilière que pour 31,55 fr.' Pierrot's view is expressed in a note on p. 513 of vol I of the *Correspondance générale*. Balzac's certificate of enrolment as an elector is contained in the Collection Lovenjoul, A.379, Fol.185.

11. *Oeuvres Diverses*, II, Conard, 39, 346-68.

12. The letter is dated 26 April 1831. *Correspondance générale*, vol. I.

13. The date of the letter is 'fin janvier, 1833'. *Lettres à Madame Hanska*, (ed. Roger Pierrot), 4 vols. (Paris, 1971), vol. 1.

14. *Le Cousin Pons*, VII, 660.

15. Ibid.

16. Ibid., 763.

17. Mme Meininger suggests that the character of des Lupeaulx was based on Joseph Lingay, 'maître des Requêtes' and secretary to the 'Présidence du Conseil' during the July Monarchy. See the article by Mme Meininger, 'Qui est des Lupeaulx?', *L'Année Balzacienne* (1961), pp. 149-84.

18. *Les Petits Bourgeois*, VIII, 85.

19. Quoted by Smethurst in his introduction to *Le Député d'Arcis*. Pléiade, VIII, 709.

20. *Z. Marcas*, VIII, 842-3.

21. Ibid., 843.

22. *Albert Savarus*, I, 972.

23. Ibid., 976.

24. Ibid., 985.

25. Pierrot's note relates to a letter from Amédée Faucheux to Balzac dated April 1832. *Correspondance générale*, vol. I.

26. *Lettres à Madame Hanska*, vol. 2.

27. Letter of 20 January 1844.

28. Letter of 14 December 1843.

29. Letter of 1 January 1844.

30. Letter of 23 January 1844.

31. *Pierrette*, IV, 96.

32. Bertier de Sauvigny, *La Restauration* (Paris, 1955), p. 400.

33. Letter of 27 November 1845. *Lettres à Madame Hanska*, vol. 3.

34. Letter of 6 July 1846.

35. *La Muse du département*, IV, 740.

36. *Le Cousin Pons*, VII, 694.

37. Ibid.

38. *Le Petit Robert* gives as a definition of 'l'ozène': 'Ulcération de la muqueuse nasale, dont le principal symptôme est l'exhalaison d'une odeur fétide'.

39. *Le Député d'Arcis*, VIII, 806.

40. Ibid., 727.

41. *Ursule Mirouët*, III, 877.

42. Ibid., 866.

43. Ibid., 811.

44. Ibid., 954.

45. *Les Méfaits d'un procureur du roi*, *Oeuvres Ebauchées*, 1st Pléiade edn, X, 1071.

46. *Les Petits Bourgeois*, VIII, 84.

47. In addition to the 'électeurs censitaires', from 1834 the municipal electorate of Paris included Parisian electors in the provinces, retired army officers with a pension of at least 1,000 fr. and some 'capacités'.

48. *Les Petits Bourgeois*, VIII, 84.

49. Adeline Daumard, *La Bourgeoisie Parisienne de 1815 à 1848* (Paris, 1963), part III, chapter III, section II, pp. 538, 540.

50. *Une Fille d'Eve*, II, 312. Donnard points out that this detail was inspired by the charges made against Girardin in the 1839 elections. J.-H. Donnard, *Les Réalités économiques et sociales dans l'oeuvre de Balzac* (Paris, 1971), p. 342.

51. *Une Fille d'Eve*, II, 312.

52. *La Vieille Fille*, IV, 853.

53. *Le Cousin Pons*, VII, 668.

54. *Albert Savarus*, I, 980.

55. Ibid., 998.

56. Kent's account of this meeting suffers from a number of inaccuracies, especially the statement that the meeting was held in a room let by a 'restaurateur'. Sherman Kent, *Electoral Procedure under Louis Philippe* (Yale, 1937), pp. 170-1.

57. *Albert Savarus*, I, 995.

58. Kent, *Electoral Procedure*, chapter IX.

59. Ibid., p. 115.

60. Letter of 6 July 1846.

61. *Albert Savarus*, I, 996, 1002.

62. *Une Fille d'Eve*, II, 382.

63. *Albert Savarus*, I, 1007.

64. Or the title which Balzac originally had in mind, 'L'Élection en Province 1838'. The reference is preserved in the Collection Lovenjoul, Cote A.55, fol.B.

65. A. Jardin and A.-J. Tudesq, *La France des notables*, 2 vols. Vol. I. *L'Evolution générale. 1815-1848* (Paris, 1973), pp. 152-3.

66. These details are given by Jean Lhomme, *La Grande Bourgeoisie au pouvoir. 1830-1880* (Paris, 1960), p. 29.

67. In defining relative incompatibility, the law stated that government officials 'ne pourront être élus députés par le collège électoral d'un arrondissement compris en tout ou en partie dans le ressort de leurs fonctions'. Quoted by François Julien-Laferrière, *Les Députés Fonctionnaires sous la monarchie de Juillet* (Paris, 1970), p. 163.

68. *Le Député d'Arcis*, VIII, 794.

69. See Kent, *Electoral Procedures*, chapter VI.

70. *Le Cousin Pons*, VII, 643.

71. Ibid., 660.

72. *La Cousine Bette*, VII, 341.

73. Ibid., 312.

74. *Un Prince de la Bohème*, VII, 836.

75. Quoted by Kent, *Electoral Procedures*, chapter III.

76. Colin Smethurst has proved the accuracy of Balzac's figures by revealing that Besançon had 365 electors in 1842, while Bar-sur-Aube had 392. 'Balzac and Stendhal: Electoral Scenes' in *Balzac and the Nineteenth Century. Studies in French Literature, presented to Herbert J. Hunt* (Leicester, 1972), p. 113.

77. Letter of 5 January 1842.

78. See note 50.

79. *La Muse du département*, IV, 631.

80. Smethurst underlines the authenticity of Balzac's account in this respect when he points out that there was an attempt in the 1842 elections to unseat the government deputy for Bar-sur-Aube, in order to rid the constituency of the reputation of being a 'bourg-pourri'. Despite these efforts, M. Armand, the deputy in question, received 90 per cent of the votes in the election. See the introduction to *Le Député d'Arcis*, Pléiade, VIII, 711-12.

81. The affinities which link Crevel with Véron, the owner of *Le Constitutionnel*, are analysed by Mme Meininger in the Introduction to *La Cousine Bette*, Pléiade, VII, 47-9.

82. Ibid.

83. Neither the 'rive droite', financed by Rothschild, nor the shorter 'rive gauche', for which the money was put up by Fould, was financially successful. The 'rive gauche', which was hit by a disaster in May 1842, was even less viable than the 'rive droite', and the two were merged in 1846 in an attempt to make them profitable.

84. A.-J. Tudesq, 'L'Attraction Parisienne sur le recrutement parlementaire à la fin de la monarchie de Juillet', *Politique* (July-September 1958), p. 275.

85. *Les Comédiens sans le savoir*, VII, 1182.

86. For a reliable account of the development of railways in France during the 'monarchie censitaire' see chapter III of A.L. Dunham's *La Révolution Industrielle en France. 1815-1848* (Paris, 1953). Appendix II contains some useful information about the financial aspect, including the part played by Rothschild.

87. Letter to Mme Hanska of 30 April 1836.

88. Jardin and Tudesq, *La France des notables*, p. 212.

89. *Le Député d'Arcis*, VIII, 724.

90. Ibid., 286-7.

91. *Les Comédiens sans le savoir*, VII, 1199.

92. Jardin and Tudesq, *La France des notables*, p. 212.

93. *La Cousin Bette*, VII, 428.

94. *Ursule Mirouët*, III, 884.

95. *La Cousine Bette*, VII, 428.

96. Letter of 23 January 1843. In the same year, in the preface to part III of *Illusions Perdues*, Balzac speaks with equal derision of 'la plaisanterie qu'on nomme le gouvernement constitutionnel, et qui a pour base la perpétuelle intronisation de la médiocrité!', Pléiade, V, 120.

97. *La Muse du département*, IV, 631.

98. *Z. Marcas*, VIII, 847.

99. Jardin and Tudesq, *La France des notables*, p. 164.

100. *La Fausse Maîtresse*, II, 199.

101. *Oeuvres Diverses*, III, Conard, 40, 332.

102. *Pierre Grassou*, VI, 1101.

103. Letter of 2 August 1847.

104. In *La Vieille Fille*, for example, the protest of the 222 deputies in March

1830 against the ultra policies of Charles X and Polignac is seen as marking the day when 'la lutte se précisa entre le plus auguste, le plus grand, le seul vrai pouvoir, la *Royauté*, et le plus faux, le plus changeant, le plus oppresseur pouvoir, le pouvoir dit *parlementaire* qu'exercent des assemblées électives'. *La Vieille Fille*, IV, 922-3.

105. *Ursule Mirouët*, III, 884.

106. The third Ordinance sought to limit the vote to the wealthiest 25 per cent of the existing electors.

107. The change demanded was, to quote Mlle Daumard, 'conforme à l'esprit de la Charte de 1830 et aux principes de 1789'. Daumard, *La Bourgeoisie Parisienne de 1815 à 1848*, p. 614.

108. *Le Député d'Arcis*, VIII, 741.

109. *Correspondance générale*, vol. I.

110. *Z. Marcas*, VIII, 848.

111. *Les Petits Bourgeois*, VIII, 107.

112. *Catéchisme Social, Oeuvres Diverses*, III, Conard, 40, 708.

113. Letter to Mme Hanska of 21 December 1842.

114. *Oeuvres Diverses*, III, Conard, 40, 332.

115. Letter to Mme Hanska of 2 August 1847.

116. Letter to Mme Hanska of 22 January 1843. This development in Balzac's political thinking is examined, in terms of his reaction to the 1848 revolution, in Chapter 10.

117. 'Dégrèvement' involved lowering the amount of direct taxes paid annually by an elector sufficiently to disqualify him from the franchise.

118. See note 26.

119. Balzac himself openly admitted to the invention when he confessed that 'la Ville d'Arcis-sur-Aube n'a pas été le théâtre des événements qui en sont le sujet. L'Arrondissement d'Arcis va voter à Bar-sur-Aube, il n'existe donc pas de député d'Arcis à la Chambre.' Quoted by Colin Smethurst in 'Balzac and Stendhal: Electoral Scenes', p. 113.

120. The passage in question can be found in vol. V of the Pléiade edition, pp. 1041-52.

121. Quoted by Kent, *Electoral Procedures*, pp. 53-4.

122. *Les Comédiens sans le savoir*, VII, 1187.

123. The full quotation from *L'Hôpital et le Peuple* can be found in the *Oeuvres Ebauchées*, 1st Pléiade edn, IX, 1081.

124. Daumard, *La Bourgeoisie Parisienne de 1815 à 1848*, pp. 41-2.

125. *L'Education Sentimentale. Flaubert. Oeuvres II*, Pléiade (Paris, 1952), p. 142.

126. In this sense, Balzac's study of the 'notables' requires one to qualify Donnard's judgement that the political analysis in the *Comédie humaine* lacks the acuteness of the economic investigation. Donnard, *Les Réalités économiques et sociales dans l'oeuvre de Balzac*, p. 351.

127. See Daumard, *La Bourgeoisie Parisienne de 1815 à 1848*, p. 286.

9 THE ECONOMIC EXPANSION

I The Aristocratic Options and their Limits

The July Revolution had placed the relationship of bourgeoisie and aristocracy on a new basis. Faced with a regime which was symbolised by the appointment of bankers as its first two 'présidents du Conseil', the aristocracy had two realistic choices, for one can consider the abortive counter-revolutionary *coup* of the duchesse de Berry in 1832 as an ill-considered aberration. It could either affect 'le silence du mépris' or it could come to terms with the July Monarchy with greater or less enthusiasm.

If, rather than opt for 'l'émigration à l'intérieur', legitimist nobles chose to remain where they were after 1830, they might mark their disaffection in various ways. Balzac shows the form which some of these reactions might take. They could resign, in the manner of baron Lecamus and his fellow-magistrates in Besançon. Baron Lecamus subsequently chooses the path of spiritual withdrawal from a society which he finds intolerable by becoming a member of the 'Frères de la Consolation'. The response of baron Bourlac is similar. Removed from office and victimised by the July Revolution, he finds in intellectual retreat the means of individual salvation.

For the more remote representatives of the provincial nobility it is as if nothing had happened in 1830. In Guérande, the baron du Guénic, the chevalier du Halga and Mlle de Pen-Hoël form 'les chefs du petit faubourg Saint-Germain de l'arrondissement, où ne pénétrait aucun des membres de l'administration envoyé par le nouveau gouvernement'.[1] In Paris, where the effect of the July Revolution was virtually to suspend 'salon' life until 1833, the legitimists meet at the house of the princesse de Cadignan and at the winter 'hôtel' of Laurence de Cinq-Cygne, 'l'une des sommités aristocratiques, et dont le salon était inabordable pour la bourgeoisie et les parvenus'.[2]

However, although Balzac takes account of the importance of the legitimist opposition to the July Monarchy, he correctly shows it to have been a minority response on the part of the aristocracy. Accordingly, the emphasis in the *Comédie humaine* is placed on those former legitimists who, relieved that the ravages of 1789 had not been repeated, find it in their interest to rally to the July Monarchy. Some bourgeois legitimists, such as Philippe Bridau, Albert Savarus and Nathan, have already been mentioned in other contexts. If one adds to them the numerous aristocratic examples mentioned by Balzac, one has a clear picture of the behaviour and motives of the majority of legitimists when confronted with the reality of a regime which, in theory, embodied all to which they had previously been opposed.

The cynical opportunism which characterises the switch of allegiance to the July Monarchy by most of Balzac's 'ralliés' is displayed by du Bruel and the comte de l'Estorade. Both du Bruel and his wife, the former dancer Tullia, had been fervently attached to the elder branch of the Bourbons before 1830, du Bruel having resigned his post as 'chef de bureau' immediately after the July Revolution. After some initial reluctance, their adjustment takes place gradually. Du Bruel finally puts his loyalty to the July Monarchy beyond all doubt by helping to put down a riot as 'chef de bataillon' in the National Guard, for which he is rewarded with the title of 'comte' and election as deputy.

When Mme Marie Gaston criticises the comte de l'Estorade for serving the July Monarchy, it is the 'comtesse' who justifies his actions. The arguments which she candidly expresses are those of material self-interest. The need to bring up three children matters more than loyalty to the deposed monarchy. 'Pour rester fidèle à la branche aînée et retourner dans ses terres', she reasons, 'il ne fallait pas avoir à élever et à pourvoir trois enfants.' 'Ne devions-nous pas vivre de notre place', she asks, 'et accumuler sagement les revenus de nos terres?' Financial necessity has overcome legitimist scruples. 'Ces sages calculs' the comtesse de l'Estorade emphasises, 'ont déterminé dans notre intérieur l'acceptation du nouvel ordre de choses.' Legitimists, she makes it clear, do not believe in doing things by halves, whether it is in defending a principle or in betraying it. 'Du moment où l'Estorade prêtait serment', she concludes, 'il ne devait rien faire à demi.'[3]

One of the remarkable features of *Béatrix* is that it offers an unparalleled range of aristocratic responses to the July Revolution. As opposed to the ultra attitude already referred to are the more flexible reactions of Mlle des Touches, the marquise de Rochefide and Calyste du Guénic. Mlle des Touches has no problems in adapting to the new order of society. Her salon, which has been in existence since 1817, is among the first to re-open after the July Revolution. With its easy mingling of aristocracy, intellectuals and diplomats, it embodies a continuity of civilised values which takes the political transition in its stride and regards doctrinaire party divisions as a vulgar irrelevance.

The acceptance of the July Monarchy by the marquise de Rochefide is of a nebulous kind. Balzac suggests that, when 'Béatrix alla de 1830 à 1831 passer la tourmente à la terre de son mari', her concern had been simply to survive rather than to express dissent. On her return to Paris, she became convinced that the July Monarchy was less a political revolution than 'une révolution morale', so much so that she absorbed herself in all that was intellectually modish in the first few years of its existence. 'Elle prit', Balzac remarks with a malice which is as misogynist as it is illiberal, 'une part intellectuelle aux nouvelles doctrines qui pullulèrent durant trois ans, après Juillet, comme des moucherons au soleil, et qui ravagèrent plusieurs têtes femelles.'[4]

With Calyste du Guénic, the recognition of the changes brought about by the July Revolution involves a denial of his family, but not of his class. When he exclaims, 'Que m'importe la race des du Guénic par le temps où nous vivons!' he is thinking not just of his passion for Béatrix but of his future as a noble in a bourgeois-dominated society. In order to survive, he believes, the aristocracy must renounce the discredited values represented by the du Guénics, which are responsible, Calyste realises, for 'l'insuffisance de mon éducation à une époque où les nobles doivent conquérir une valeur personnelle pour rendre la vie à leur nom'.[5]

The question of aristocratic attitudes to the July Monarchy figures prominently in the *Comédie humaine*. The opponents are featured in judicious proportion to the majority of 'ralliés'. Among the latter, bourgeois ex-legitimists are found along with nobles, and although a pragmatic self-interest is the dominant motive which inspires the change of loyalties, Balzac never loses sight of the important personal factors, moral and intellectual as well as material, which enter into the reckoning.

Balzac had been quick to see the direction that the aristocracy would have to take after the July Revolution. The *Comédie humaine* confirms the judgement which Balzac made when the new regime was barely six months old. 'L'aristocratie se rapproche tous les jours de la nouvelle dynastie', Balzac noted in February 1831, 'et moins que jamais son opposition est à craindre.'[6] The aristocracy had two principal means of cutting its losses and of consolidating its weakened position under the July Monarchy. Neither was entirely new. Each had existed to a limited but increasing extent before the Revolution. What was new was the incentive given to both courses of action by the adverse situation in which the aristocracy found itself after 1830.

(a) Intermarriage

There was the possibility of intermarriage with the bourgeoisie. Under the Restoration, both bourgeoisie and aristocracy in the *Comédie humaine* tend to marry strictly within their class.[7] At the same time one sees signs that this insistence is beginning to break down. Du Bousquier only marries Mlle Cormon 'faute de mieux'. 'Il avait tenté tout d'abord', it emerges, 'd'épouser mademoiselle Armande, la soeur d'un des nobles les plus considérés de la ville.'[8] This change is particularly evident in the habits of the younger generation. The comte de Fontaine, for example, had insisted on marrying the daughter of a poor noble family rather than countenance a bourgeois marriage, however rich. His three sons, however, all marry into bourgeois families, while his two elder daughters marry 'anoblis' of the Restoration. His youngest daughter Emilie, true to her father's example, refuses to consider a bourgeois marriage. The ironic consequences of her rejection of Maximilien Longueville in favour of the comte de Kergarouët are clearly intended by Balzac to emphasise the anachronistic folly of ultra inflexibility, the repercussions of which, he believed, extended beyond marriage to prejudice the entire position of the aristocracy in French society. In addition, there are what one might call the Chargeboeuf idiosyncrasies, only in their case it is the wealthy bourgeois himself who marries an aristocratic heiress. It is Vinet who marries Mlle de Chargeboeuf, of the richer branch of the family, and sets the precedent for Rogron to marry Bathilde de Chargeboeuf in 1828.

The fact is, however, that Balzac shows more bourgeois-noble marriages for the July Monarchy than for the Restoration. This is particularly evident in the case of deputies. Rastignac marries Mlle Nucingen in 1838, and de Trailles becomes the husband of Cécile Beauvisage in 1841. Ten years earlier, du Tillet had married the younger daughter of the comte de Granville. The marriage of Savinien de Portenduère, who had once had serious thoughts of becoming a deputy himself, and Ursule Mirouët takes place in 1837. In suggesting that marriages between bourgeois and nobles became more common after 1830, Balzac indicates that the futility of ultra disdain had been effectively exposed by the July Revolution. The reality of bourgeois power was there for all to see, and the aristocracy now had no other choice than to come to terms with it. And if that meant marrying their sons to the daughters of the 'vile bourgeoisie', so be it. It is this rationale which is epitomised by Mme de Portenduère's capitulation to the previously unthinkable step of Savinien's marrying Ursule Mirouët.

The advice which the duchesse de Maufrigneuse gives to Victurnien d'Esgrignon is to abandon the traditional preference of his class for marrying within the nobility and to marry a bourgeois heiress. The gist of her argument to the young d'Esgrignon is that the future belongs to the bourgeoisie, which can only strengthen its present position and translate its challenge to the aristocracy into undisputed mastery. It is only a matter of time, she believes, before bourgeois wealth is matched by bourgeois power, and that outcome cannot be long delayed. Balzac's hindsight finds expression in the prescience of his character. 'Vous serez bien plus nobles que vous ne l'êtes', the duchesse de Maufrigneuse tells the d'Esgrignons, 'quand vous aurez de l'argent.'[9]

For all Balzac's reservations about the bourgeoisie of the July Monarchy, the bourgeois triumph of 1830 induced Balzac to reappraise the realities of the situation and to redefine the attitudes and measures appropriate to it. The shift in Balzac's position towards a pragmatic legitimism involved him in a radical critique of the Restoration aristocracy. If a reconciliation of bourgeoisie and aristocracy were to be achieved, it would be on terms considerably less favourable to the aristocracy than it could have obtained when its authority was still intact under the Restoration. In particular, intermarriage with the bourgeoisie, which ultra intransigence had disdained, was no longer a tactical means of maintaining supremacy but an urgent necessity for survival. After 1830, Balzac was convinced that social harmony, national unity and the future of the nobility were dependent on a greater degree of movement between the bourgeoisie and the aristocracy, and that in this necessary *rapprochement* intermarriage had an important part to play. Intermarriage was now clearly in the interests of both bourgeoisie and aristocracy and could make a valuable contribution to the social reconciliation which, for Balzac, was the prerequisite of national unity and revival.

(b) Economic Competition

As an alternative to intermarriage, unless the two options chanced happily to coincide, the aristocracy could accept the economic challenge and compete in areas of activity essentially dominated by the bourgeoisie. One saw in an earlier chapter that Balzac gives examples of aristocratic participation in the economy of the Restoration, particularly in various forms of speculation.[10] He also indicates that this trend continued after 1830, deriving renewed incentive from the July Revolution and becoming more diversified in keeping with the general development of the French economy under the July Monarchy. The *Comédie humaine* contains a great deal of evidence which enables one to measure the success or failure of these attempts.

In 1826 Couture had predicted: 'Avant peu, vous verrez l'Aristocratie, les gens de cour, les Ministériels descendant en colonnes serrées dans la spéculation'.[11] In fact, as Balzac shows, the entry of the aristocracy into various fields of speculation had already begun when Couture's remark was made, but it was the impact of 1830 which, if it did not produce an army of aristocratic speculators, gave fresh impetus to the movement.

The voluntary transfer of investment from 'le foncier' to 'le mobilier', and especially to 'rentes', is expressed in the decisions taken by the widowed baronne de Macumer in the first few years of the July Monarchy. 'J'ai vendu mon hôtel', she reveals in a letter to the comtesse de l'Estorade in October 1833, 'j'ai vendu Chantepleurs et les fermes de Seine-et-Marne.' The bulk of the proceeds of these sales and the 1,200,000 fr. inherited from her husband has been invested in 'rentes'. The financial gain has been considerable, as she goes on to indicate, 'soixante mille francs de rentes au lieu de trente que j'avais en terres'.[12] 'La noblesse aujourd'hui c'est 500,000 fr. de rentes ou une illustration personnelle', Balzac wrote in 1835.[13] The aristocracy of the July Monarchy who appear in the *Comédie humaine* are more distinguished by their 'rentes' than by their intellectual qualities.

Couture's prediction is confirmed by Balzac's account of economic activity under the July Monarchy. When de Trailles first arrives in Arcis in the middle of the electoral campaign of 1839, he is thought to be a noble engaged in business. For Achille Pigoult, this is nothing new. 'Dans ce moment-ci', he claims, 'les grands noms, les grandes familles, la vieille et la jeune pairie, arrivent au pas de charge dans les commandites!' His following comment betrays a mingling of gratification at the humbling of the aristocracy and the condescension of a member of the liberal professions towards his fellow-bourgeois who earn their money from speculation. 'Mais n'est-ce pas démoralisant', he asks, 'de voir les noms des Verneuil, des Maufrigneuse et des d'Hérouville accolés à ceux des du Tillet et des Nucingen dans des spéculations cotées à la Bourse?'[14]

There are, in fact, signs that Balzac came to see that the aristocracy had no option but to compete financially with the bourgeoisie. The attack on the aristocracy in *La Duchesse de Langeais* for selling its land in order to be able to invest and speculate was dictated by Balzac's recent commitment to legitimism. It was in the first phase of his legitimist 'conversion', for example, that Balzac had insisted, in October 1832, in *Du Gouvernement moderne*, that 'un Pair de France, ayant des rentes inscrites, était un contresens, que la Restauration a laissé malheureusement subsister'.[15]

Experience of the July Monarchy was enough to induce a significant change in Balzac's attitude. In relation to 'la triple aristocratie de l'argent, du pouvoir et du talent' which Balzac had identified in the *Traité de la vie élégante* in 1831, the options had now shrunk to exclude the aristocracy from any real prospect of power.[16] From now on, Balzac made it clear, the aristocracy had a straight choice between money and talent. Of 'la naissance' there is no more mention. The *Comédie humaine* keeps step with this development in Balzac's vision of the aristocracy. The disdainful Mme de Portenduère can no longer afford to despise money and finally consents to Savinien's marrying Ursule Mirouët. Mlle des Touches speaks with the authentic voice of Balzac when she urges that 'aujourd'hui la noblesse a plus que jamais besoin de la fortune'.[17]

Balzac's perceptiveness goes beyond the identification of an important aristocratic initiative. In describing the activities of the duc d'Hérouville in particular, Balzac reveals an accurate understanding of economic realities under the July Monarchy as well as the qualities of a social historian. Josépha explains to Hulot why she has abandoned him for the duc d'Hérouville. The house in which the duc d'Hérouville has installed her has cost 600,000 fr. Josépha's account of the way in which the duc d'Hérouville has made his money contains an incisive commentary on some of the important economic developments of the July Monarchy. 'Le duc a mis là', she reveals, 'tous les bénéfices d'une affaire en commandite dont les actions ont été vendues en hausse', and then adds: 'Pas bête, mon petit duc! Il n'y a que les grands seigneurs d'autrefois pour savoir changer du charbon de terre en or.'[18]

Josépha's contribution allows Balzac to make three important points, and all the more effectively as the risk of a tedious lecture is avoided by the mocking tone of the character's intervention and by the incongruous choice of spokesman. First, Balzac underlines the voluntary 'embourgeoisement' of an important section of the aristocracy. Moreover, his grasp of economic matters is equally sound. Josépha's interview with Hulot takes place in 1838, and the date is significant. French coal production doubled under the July Monarchy and, especially before 1840 and the rush to invest in railway shares, was a tempting field of investment for speculators like the duc d'Hérouville. Finally, Josépha twice refers to the importance of 'commandites'. 'Pourquoi n'as-tu pas inventé de commandite?', she taunts Hulot.[19] Once again, Balzac's sureness of touch serves him well, for 'commandites' remained for a long time a more popular form of financial association than the 'sociétés anonymes par actions' which required government authorisation.[20]

Balzac thus establishes the limited success which the aristocracy achieved in its efforts to counter the bourgeois domination of society, either by marrying into the bourgeoisie or by competing with it in the economic field. To complete the picture, one now has to examine what the *Comédie humaine* reveals of the continued advance of the bourgeoisie at the expense of the aristocracy.

The most obvious area in which the bourgeoisie gained directly from the aristocracy was in the acquisition of land. Its rise in value fom 700 fr. per hectare under the Restoration to 1,300 fr. per hectare in 1846 meant that land remained an attractive form of investment. The process which began with the confiscation and sale of 'biens nationaux' continued long after 1815 and, as we have seen in the study of the 'notables', Balzac illustrates its extension both under the Restoration and the July Monarchy. At the same time, Balzac reminds one that the bourgeois erosion of the economic strength of the aristocracy extended to urban property as well. Gréven acquires 'l'hôtel Beauséant' in 1831, the same year in which 'l'ancien hôtel de Maulincour' is bought by Elie Magus. The 'pavillon' which Victorin Hulot buys in 1834 is what is left of the 'hôtel' of the Verneuil family. The baronne de Macumer, it has been noted, sells her 'hôtel' along with her country property and estates. The princesse de Cadignan suffers the same experience. Combined with her personal extravagance, the effects of the July Revolution have seriously undermined the princesse de Cadignan's fortune and social position. As a result of her husband's leaving France with Charles X, 'les revenus du majorat avaient été saisis'. Formerly, 'une des reines de Paris', she now lives in 'un petit hôtel, à un rez-de-chaussée d'un prix modique'. The number of her servants has been cut from thirty to two, and she now has to be content with five rooms and some 12,000 'livres de rente'. The most interesting revelation concerns her former house, 'un immense hôtel qu'aucune fortune ne pouvait habiter, et que le marteau des spéculateurs a démoli'.[21]

No one understood more clearly than Balzac the truth that the supremacy of the bourgeoisie was inseparable from the decline of the aristocracy, and it is a message which is emphatically spelled out in the *Comédie humaine*. It is characteristic of Balzac's class-centred view of history, with its starting-point in the conflict of aristocracy and bourgeoisie in the Revolution, that the most forceful expressions of the power of the bourgeoisie under the July Monarchy should be addressed to its aristocratic victims. It is Balzac himself who sums up the lesson for her class which is contained in the experience of the marquise de Rochefide. 'Le monde auquel elle appartenait n'ayant pu se reconstituer pendant le triomphe inespéré des quinze années de la Restauration, s'en irait en miettes sous les coups de bélier mis en oeuvre par la bourgeoisie.'[22] It is left to Nathan, in his indictment of Félix de Vandenesse, to affirm 'le triomphe de la classe moyenne, la nouvelle force des sociétés, temporaire ou durable, mais réelle'.[23]

II Towards a Capitalist Economy

(a) Commerce: the Example of Gaudissart

The *Comédie humaine* is far from offering a complete and balanced picture of the bourgeoisie of the July Monarchy. Industry, especially 'la grande industrie', is almost entirely absent. Moreover, Balzac chooses to concentrate on the financial bourgeoisie to the detriment of commerce and industry. It would be wrong therefore to expect to find in the *Comédie humaine* a comprehensive account of economic developments under the July Monarchy. What Balzac does give, on the other hand, is an indication of certain basic trends, but his most original contribution consists in illuminating specific activities and phenomena by reference to single characters or groups of characters. The study of 'la spéculation et la conjoncture' is an outstanding example of the second category. The best single case-study is centred around the early career of Gaudissart.

'Une des plus curieuses figures créées par les moeurs de l'époque actuelle', Gaudissart is partly treated by Balzac as the mythological expression of 'l'homme supérieur', sharing a place in the contemporary gallery occupied, among others, by Grandet and Vautrin. Important though this aspect is, it is less significant finally than the socioeconomic analysis to which it is linked. The early retirement of the majority of Balzac's 'négociants' leaves Gaudissart to dominate the commercial stage of the July Monarchy in the *Comédie humaine*. The essential interest of *L'Illustre Gaudissart* lies in what it reveals of an important economic development which marked the early part of the July Monarchy in particular, namely the commercial exploitation of the provincial market for the products of an expanding Parisian industry, 'des grands dignitaires de l'industrie parisienne au profit desquels trottent, frappent et fonctionnent ces intelligents pistons de la machine à vapeur nommée Spéculation'.[24]

Balzac is accurate in emphasising the diversified nature of Gaudissart's activities, at a time when 'l'indifférenciation' had not yet given way to specialisation in the profession of 'commis-voyageur' as in other branches of the economy. This has been recognised by a number of critics such as Guyon and Faillettaz, but these same critics are wrong when they state that Gaudissart abandons his traditional commercial role after 1830 in favour of new forms of selling.[25] 'Qu'emporte-t-il en effet dans sa valise?', Guyon insists 'Non plus ces "Articles-Paris" que proposaient aux îlotes de la province ses prédécesseurs de la Restauration!'[26] Admittedly, the text is inconsistent or at best misleading. 'Jusqu'en 1830', Balzac explains, 'l'illustre Gaudissart était resté fidèle à l'*Article-Paris* . . . , après août et octobre 1830, il quitta la chapellerie et l'Article Paris, laissa les commissions du commerce des choses mécaniques et visibles pour s'élancer dans les sphères les plus élevées de la spéculation parisienne.'[27] Although there is no further mention of hats, Balzac contradicts his earlier statement by showing that 'l'Article-Paris' is still very much Gaudissart's concern.[28] After setting off on his annual provincial tour in April 1831, Gaudissart writes to Jenny Courand from Blois. Among other things, he tells her: 'L'Article-Paris va son petit bonhomme de chemin . . . J'ai placé cent soixante-deux châles de cachemire Ternaux à Orleans.' He explains that he already earns, from 'mes Articles-Paris', 8-10,000 fr. per year.[29]

This figure, he hopes, will be increased to a total of 20-30,000 fr. by two new commercial initiatives. The first is the selling of insurance policies. There is no doubt about Gaudissart's success in this area. 'L'Assurance sur les Capitaux va très-bien', he announces to Jenny, 'j'ai de Paris à Blois, placé près de deux millions.'[30] It is a more difficult matter, however, when it comes to selling newspaper subscriptions, which Balzac defines as a form of speculation specifically created by the July Revolution. The Republican *Le Mouvement* falls on stony, conservative ground in the provinces, while the more advanced ideas of the Saint-Simonian *Le Globe* are enough to frighten off potential subscribers.

Bernard Guyon has questioned Balzac's authenticity in respect of the insurance side of Gaudissart's activities, and is sceptical about 'ces compagnies d'assurances qu'il affirme avoir été en pleine effervescence au lendemain de Juillet'.[31] The historical facts, however, tend to support Balzac. Bertrand Gille shows that most of the large insurance companies had come into existence under the Restoration, particularly in the period from 1816 to 1820.[32] The theory has also been advanced that the wave of fires whic a swept France in the first half of 1830 was the work of the agents of insurance companies anxious to promote their business.[33] Their foundations thus laid, the new companies would find an ideal climate for expanding their activities in the economic crisis which marked the first year of the July Monarchy.

(b) Industrial Development

The accuracy of the description of economic developments in *L'Illustre Gaudissart* has been confirmed by critics of such varying tendencies as Guyon, Donnard and Wurmser. At the same time, there is a danger of making out an exaggerated case, from a study of the novel, for the stage of economic advance achieved in France by 1831. It is a tendency which is manifested in Bernard Guyon's assessment of *L'Illustre Gaudissart*.[34] Referring to the early period of the July Monarchy which is characterised by Gaudissart's activities in 1831, Guyon concludes that 'c'est alors que naquit vraiment, que prit son véritable "essor", le grand capitalisme'.[35] In making this judgement, Guyon anticipates the 'take-off' of the French economy by a decade. It is now generally agreed that it was only after 1840 that industrial expansion began on a significant scale, and then only in certain limited sectors, notably in the metal industry, coal and textiles.[36] It is true that Guyon qualifies his error when he describes the *Comédie humaine* as 'l'étude de cette conquête, de ses débuts du moins et de certains de ses effets: économiques, politiques, sociaux ou psychologíques'.[37] However, Guyon overlooks another vital factor in attributing to the initial period of the July Monarchy which is covered in *L'Illustre Gaudissart* developments which only occurred after 1840. It is now generally accepted that one of the most important reasons for the slow growth of the French economy in the first half of the nineteenth century was the lack of a system of organised credit. Financiers were traditionally reluctant to lend to commerce and industry, especially to smaller firms seeking long-term credit.[38] It was only with the creation of an expanded railway network in the 1840s that industrial investment began in a systematic way and not until the Second Empire that France acquired a fully developed structure of credit facilities. Guyon is therefore premature when he states that 'La "haute banque" . . . est en plein essor. Sous son impulsion, les entreprises industrielles et commerciales se multiplient; elles modernisent leur matériel, développent leur potential, accroissent leurs débouchés.'[39] The reference which Guyon makes elsewhere to Gaudissart as the 'héraut du capitalisme naissant' is much nearer the mark.[40]

Given these historical limitations, what evidence does the *Comédie humaine* give of industrial activity under the July Monarchy? To begin with, there is one obvious and serious gap. The 'gros industriel' is missing.

Faillettaz puts forward a plausible argument when he applies Stefan Zweig's thesis that Balzac was working on a dwindling 'expérience vécue' after 1840 to explain Balzac's failure to take adequate account of French industrialisation in the latter part of the July Monarchy.[41] Whatever the reason may be, the fact is that Balzac is silent on the beginnings of 'la grande industrie' and its specific characteristics: mechanisation, concentration and integration.[42] The *Comédie humaine* gives only an occasional glimpse of what Sée defines as the essential economic reality marking the July Monarchy, 'le passage du capitalisme commercial au capitalisme industriel'.[43] The two exceptions, coal and railways, are treated by Balzac in terms of the impetus which they gave to investment and speculation, and discussion of them is therefore deferred until the following section.

What Balzac does show is that, in a number of important respects, French industry under the July Monarchy still had not progressed beyond the 'ancien régime économique'. Balzac emphasises the backwardness of French industry, especially in relation to the achievements realised by England. Writing in 1842 in *Valentine et Valentin*, he compares the history of gas-lighting in Paris and London. 'L'historien des moeurs', he declares, 'ne doit-il pas faire observer que la ville de Londres fut éclairée au gaz en dix-huit mois et qu'après quinze ans une seule moitié de Paris est en ce moment éclairée par ce procédé miraculeux. La rue des Marais fait partie de la moitié qui conserve le hideux réverbère.'[44] (Balzac's sense of civic grievance was justified. As historians have pointed out, the first gas companies were set up in London in 1808 and in the large towns in 1820. Having to import a third of its coal from England and Germany for conversion into gas, France was a generation behind England in providing its streets with gas lighting.[45])

The industrial activity which Balzac describes under the July Monarchy displays many of the features of a retarded economy. There is first of all the survival, on a significant scale, of domestic industry. The 'bonneterie', to which Arcis owes its prosperity and which is typified by Beauvisage's enterprises, is organised on the same domestic basis throughout the whole of Champagne. Its character is concisely summed up by Balzac as follows. 'La campagne, dans un rayon de dix lieues, est couverte d'ouvriers dont les métiers s'aperçoivent par les portes ouvertes quand on passe dans les villages. Ces ouvriers correspondent à des facteurs, lesquels aboutissent à un spéculateur appelé fabricant.'[46] He also explains that it is the 'fabricant' himself who sells directly to Parisian 'négociants' and retailers, but does not mention that he supplied the workers with machinery and raw materials. Balzac's account is supported by the study of Bertrand Gille who, while pointing to the disappearance of domestic industry in certain sectors, makes it clear that it persisted in another important industry in Champagne, in textiles. Gille quotes the case of a M. Hanriot, 'drapier de Reims', who had three-quarters of his work force scattered in surrounding country areas.[47]

The precise nature of Beauvisage's activity has been indicated by Professor Hunt. It is not the case, however, as Professor Hunt states, that Beauvisage was engaged in this form of manufacture in 1839, for he had in fact sold his business on becoming mayor of Arcis in 1830.[48] The difference of date is important. The French textile industry remained diffuse and rural in character until well on into the July Monarchy and it was only in 1835 that the number of textile workers in factories exceeded those working in their own homes.[49] The important point which Beauvisage's example demonstrates is the slow pace of industrialisation in France, even in its most advanced sectors such as textiles.

It is through Beauvisage, moreover, that a second factor is revealed which accounted for France's industrial backwardness. Beauvisage belongs to the era of pre-specialisation or 'indifférenciation'. Both he and Minard are 'fabricants-négociants', just as Birotteau and Popinot are 'fabricants-commerçants' under the Restoration. Neither is an 'industriel' in the sense of the full-time manufacturer who already existed in some industries and whose monopolisation of industrial production was to become a recognised feature of a fully-developed capitalist economy later in the century.

The third indicator of a retarded industry which Balzac associates with the July Monarchy is provided by Gaudissart. When Gaudissart continues to sell 'l'Article-Paris' after the July Revolution, he changes from hats (perhaps manufactured in Beauvisage's 'fabriques' and passed on to the commercial front line by the Parisian 'négociants' with whom both Beauvisage and Gaudissart deal?) to 'châles de cachemire Ternaux'.[50] Unable as yet to produce its own machine tools and responding to the demands of a restricted domestic market, French industry still concentrated on luxury or semi-luxury goods, especially in textiles. Historians have identified the tendency in a way which brings out Balzac's mastery of economic detail. 'De 1815 à 1847', Mlle Daumard notes, 'une évolution se fit sentir dans la fabrication parisienne qui, de plus en plus, tendait à s'orienter vers les produits de luxe ou les articles "de goût".' The trend was most marked, Mlle Daumard adds, in 'les châles fantaisie' and 'cachemires'.[51] As if this were not sufficient tribute to Balzac's historical precision, Henri Sée supplies an even more meticulous point of reference in confirming the specialist manufacturer identified by Balzac. After mentioning that laws passed in 1820 and 1822 had kept out Indian silks and 'cachemires', Sée then explains that 'à Paris, à Lyon, à Nîmes, grâce à Ternaux, on commence à fabriquer des cachemires imitant les cachemires de L'Inde'.[52]

(c) Finance: Investment and Speculation

If both commerce and industry suffer from serious gaps in Balzac's review of economic life under the July Monarchy, the same cannot be said of his treatment of the world of finance. It is Balzac's 'rentiers', speculators and financiers who, through their activities at all levels, dominate the society of Louis-Philippe as it is described in the *Comédie humaine*.

Where 'rentes' are concerned, it is first necessary to explain the immediate historical background and, in particular, the factors which would be likely to determine the choice between investment and speculation. In 1825, Villèle's proposed conversion of the 'rentes sur l'Etat' had given 'rentiers' the option of exchanging their five per cent holdings for an equivalent alternative at three per cent. That few took up the option is seen by Mlle Daumard as proof that the majority of 'rentiers' preferred steady investment to risky speculation, for, as Mlle Daumard explains, 'le 3% était par excellence la valeur de jeu, celle qui se prêtait le mieux à l'agiotage. Si les bourgeois parisiens, fortunés ou modestes, préféraient le 5%, c'est qu'ils achetaient des fonds publics pour les conserver et non pour spéculer.'[53] The five per cent 'rente' was, as Gille puts it, one of the 'valeurs de tout repos', whereas the three per cent was 'la valeur favorite des spéculateurs'.[54] Both forms of 'rente' are much in evidence in the *Comédie humaine*, and the distinction between routine investment and calculated speculation is often emphasised.

Only exceptionally does Balzac present a character who invests exclusively in 'rentes' at five per cent. The one case where this is suggested concerns Cousine Bette. Bette, we discover, 'possédait . . . un petit capital de cinq à six mille francs que Crevel lui faisait paternellement valoir'.[55] Otherwise, the five per cent either gives way to the three per cent or is combined with some other form of investment. Brigitte Thuillier, who represents both these patterns, has profitably invested in the 'Grand Livre' from 1814. When, at La Peyrade's suggestion, she sells her five per cent in 1840, she reinvests at three per cent the capital which she has left after buying a house as investment-property with the proceeds. Mme Marneffe, on whose behalf Crevel both invests and speculates in railways, is referred to as having 32,000 fr. in 'rentes', more than two-thirds of which comes from sources, including presumably 'rentes sur l'Etat', other than railway shares.

This tendency on the part of Balzac's characters to change from five per cent to three per cent is not fortuitous. That Balzac was fully aware of the advantage of switching to the three per cent 'rente' is proved by references to the question in his letters to Mme Hanska in 1844-5. When he was trying to persuade Mme Hanska to provide him with the capital with which to invest in property in Paris, Balzac urged her: 'Ceci . . . n'est pas *spéculer*, c'est *placer*. Ne confondons point. C'est jeter une somme dans un coin où elle se trouve décuplée.'[56] In terms of 'rentes', Balzac had expressed his regret that Mme Hanska had no investments in Paris, where there were 'des placements sûrs, réalisables à toute heure, et sur lesquels il n'y a rien à perdre, tout en profitant des variations'. If Mme Hanska continues to show a lack of interest, then he will advise Mme Borel, who is already obtaining a return of 1,200 fr. on a half-yearly investment of 12,000 fr. at five per cent, to change to three per cent, since 'notre 3% est à 86; il y a donc encore 14p. à gagner avant qu'il atteigne le pair, puisque notre 5 est à 120f.'[57]

The diversified nature of individual investment under the July Monarchy is demonstrated by the example of Brigitte Thuillier and of Mme Schontz. In addition to her successive investment in 'rentes' at five and three per cent, Mlle Thuillier makes considerable gains by other means, notably from moneylending and from rents on the house which her own shrewd management and the advice of La Peyrade enable her to buy. Finally, she has a further source of income from her shares in the 'Banque de France'. Mme Schontz also invests both in 'rentes' and in the 'Banque de France'. She declares her interest in the first when she lets it be known, in answer to rumours of her wealth, 'qu'au taux des rentes, trois cent mille francs donnaient douze mille francs'. Her shares in the second are invested for her by Arthur de Rochefide. 'En gentilhomme qu'il était', we learn, 'Rochefide plaça ses six cent mille francs en actions de la Banque, et il en mit la moitié au nom de mademoiselle Joséphine Schiltz.'[58] Balzac gives other instances of investment in 'la haute Banque parisienne'. Mme de la Chanterie and Godefroid are both clients of the Mongenod bank, Mme de la Chanterie's account being of the order of 1,600,000 fr. It is on Thaddée Paz that Adam Laginski relies for a profitable investment. 'Il nous a placé cent mille francs chez Rothschild', Laginski discloses.[59]

The values of a society in which the holding of 'rentes' conferred especially important privileges are expressed with remarkable critical detachment by Bianchon. 'J'ai précisément assez de rentes sur le grand-livre', he announces, 'pour aimer cette vie étroite, l'existence avec les soies, les cachemires, les tilburys, les peintures sur verre, les porcelaines, et toutes ces petites merveilles qui annoncent la dégénérescence d'une civilisation.'[60]

Apart from these cases which largely involve 'rentes', the financial activity which is discussed by Balzac is concentrated on three areas: investment and speculation in industrial shares; speculation in property; and speculation, almost exclusively in 'rentes', which is directly motivated by the assessment of a political or economic crisis.

This analysis undoubtedly reflects Balzac's preoccupation with his own investment plans at the time. Apart from his shares in the 'Nord', in the same year, 1845, Balzac had ideas of investing in various projects, in property, a 'haut fourneau' in Belgium, even in whaling. It is for this reason that the subject of investment and speculation is particularly prominent in *Les Parents Pauvres*.

As for industrial investment and speculation, only two industries, coal and railways, are involved, and their discussion is limited to the two novels of *Les Parents Pauvres*. The situation which is described by Balzac is altogether more eventful than that indicated by Mme Schontz when she tells de Trailles that, at the idea of marrying her, Fabien du Ronceret 'est resté, comme les eaux-de-vie dans le Bulletin de la Bourse, très-calme'.[61] The extraordinary attraction which the new mining companies had for the industrial investor in the 1830s is underlined by Bertrand Gille, who observes that 'la période 1835-1839 présente une sorte de révélation de l'industrie houillère pour le public. Les sociétés les plus invraisemblables attirent les capitaux, les actionnaires se précipitent en foule vers cette nouvelle source de richesse.'[62] The link between coal and railways was a vital one. As the essential source of power it was coal which made the expansion of railways in the 1840s possible. The interdependence of the two industries is demonstrated in masterly fashion in *La Cousine Bette*. The duc d'Hérouville's speculation in coal shares belongs to the early part of the novel where the action takes place before 1840. Crevel's dealings in railway shares occur in the boom period of the 1840s with which the greater part of *La Cousine Bette* is concerned. The historical lesson receives added force from the way in which Balzac dramatises its human impact. It is their share in two of the commanding sectors of a developing economy which enables the duc d'Hérouville and Crevel to control the favours of Josépha and

Mme Marneffe and deny them to a Hulot whose erotomania takes no account of economic necessity.

Apart from the duc d'Hérouville's interest in coal, the evidence which the *Comédie humaine* provides of industrial investment and speculation under the July Monarchy is entirely concerned with railways. In his impatience at the slow growth of the French economy, Balzac at times failed to do justice to the part played by railways. The pessimistic forecast expressed in *Valentine et Valentin*, that 'il en sera pour les chemins de fer comme du gaz'[63] was made in the same year in which the Chamber of Deputies gave its approval for the beginnings of a systematic rail-network for the whole of France.[64] Of all the social categories of the July Monarchy none is more underrepresented in the *Comédie humaine* than the railway passenger, for not a single one is to be found in Balzac's novels.

On the other hand, the *Comédie humaine* or, more precisely, *Les Parents Pauvres*, contains a great deal of information about investment and speculation in railways in the 1840s. In this, as in other respects, the work reflects the man. Balzac was interested in railways more for what they offered the speculator than for what they achieved for the traveller. In *Le Cousin Pons*, Camusot finds a plausible pretext for refusing Mme Camusot de Marville's request that he purchase an estate to enable his son to regain his eligibility. 'Le vieillard se disait entraîné dans les chemins de fer au delà de ses moyens.' He intimates, however, that he will be able to provide the money at a later date from an anticipated *coup* in railway shares. 'Et il remettait cette libéralité, de laquelle il reconnaissait d'ailleurs la nécessité, lors d'une hausse prévue sur les actions.'[65] In the same novel, Elie Magus advises Mme Cibot to invest the money obtained from Pons in railways. 'Achetez des actions du chemin de fer d'Orléans', he urges her, 'elles sont à trente francs au-dessous du pair, vous doublerez vos fonds en trois ans!' His advice is based on personal experience, for, as he tells Rémonencq, 'J'y ai placé mes pauvres petites économies . . . c'est la dot de ma fille'.[66]

Whether they are concerned with 'rentes' or with industrial shares, Balzac's investors are almost without exception speculators, the pure investor being as rare as the full-time speculator.[67] The situation of the July Monarchy was more favourable to speculation than that of the Restoration. The number of firms whose shares were quoted on the 'Bourse' rose from eight in 1816 to 42 in 1826 and to 88 in 1836, after which they increased dramatically to reach 260 by 1841.[68] Sixty-eight coal companies were formed between 1835 and 1838, with a capital of 142 million. The 1840s saw a corresponding proliferation in railway companies, accompanied by a similar wave of speculation.

The dual role of investor and speculator is seen most clearly in the activities of Crevel. As well as having 1,000 shares of his own in the Paris-Versailles company, Crevel also invests in the Orleans line on behalf of Mme Marneffe. Mme Marneffe's various 'rentes' include an investment of 10,000 fr., 'somme de ses gains dans les affaires de chemin de fer depuis trois ans'.[69] It is Crevel who persuades Mme Marneffe to sell her 'rentes' at a profit, and under his guidance she quickly acquires an expert knowledge of the workings of the 'Bourse'. Crevel meanwhile continues on a career of speculation which derives an important advantage from his contacts in high places. 'J'ai mille actions de Versailles', he confides to Mme Marneffe, 'rive gauche achetées à cent vingt-cinq francs, et elles iront à trois cents à cause d'une fusion des deux chemins, dans le secret de laquelle j'ai été mis.'[70]

Balzac was not the only novelist to have identified the economic features of the July Monarchy which are related in the *Comédie humaine*. In *L'Education Sentimentale*, for example, M. Dambreuse includes coal-investments among his wide range of business activities, while Frédéric Moreau has more reason to be satisfied with his shares in the 'Nord' than Balzac ever did. But Balzac is unique among contemporary writers both in the wealth of material which he provides and for the penetrating analysis which arises out of his account. These qualities are demonstrated in what one has just seen of Balzac's references to 'rentes' and industrial shares and, in particular, in his emphasis on the interrelatedness of investment and speculation. They are no less apparent in Balzac's handling of the two remaining economic aspects on which he concentrates, speculation in property and speculation undertaken with a view to profiting from a specific period of national crisis.

Property speculation is an important factor in the lives of a number of Balzac's characters under the July Monarchy. Some are only indirectly affected by it. The princesse de Cadignan's former 'hôtel', for example, is demolished by speculators anxious to build on the site thus made available. Although her prosperity contrasts with the reduced circumstances of the princesse de Cadignan, Mlle des Touches presents a similar case. 'Elle vendait sa maison de la rue du Mont-Blanc', we are told, 'de laquelle quelques spéculateurs offraient deux millions cinq cent mille francs.'[71] Others, however, are more directly involved. The house which Victorin Hulot acquires in 1834 and which is all that remains of the former splendour of the Verneuil 'hôtel' is bought together with two others built by a speculator. The rents from the property are certain to rise appreciably because of developments peculiar to the Parisian economy after 1840, but it will be several years before the speculation pays off. 'Si les spéculations en maisons à Paris sont sûres', Balzac reflects, 'elles sont lentes ou capricieuses, car elles dépendent de circonstances imprévisibles.' In fact, it takes ten years for the commercial potential of the area to be developed. As Balzac explains, 'le boulevard se nettoya, s'embellit avec tant de peine, que le Commerce ne vint étaler là qu'en 1840 ses splendides devantures, l'or des changeurs, les féeries de la mode et le luxe effréné de ses boutiques'. Victorin's property reaches its peak value in March 1843. 'La spéculation se réalisait à huit ans d'échéance', Balzac concludes, 'l'élévation continue des loyers, la beauté de la situation, donnaient en ce moment toute leur valeur aux deux maisons.' To this is added a further favourable factor in the transfer of the business centre of Paris to that area at exactly the same period. As Balzac comments, 'les appartements acquéraient du prix par le changement du centre des affaires, qui se fixait alors entre la Bourse et la Madeleine, désormais le siège du pouvoir politique et de la finance à Paris'.[72]

The outstanding example of property speculation under the July Monarchy is represented by the combination of La Peyrade and Brigitte Thuillier. As in the case of Victorin Hulot, the speculation takes the form of buying with a view to profit, not from reselling but from the accumulation of rents. The property which La Peyrade advises Brigitte to buy is on the same site as that which, as La Peyrade reminds her, had ruined Birotteau and made du Tillet rich twenty years earlier.[73] Now is the moment for Brigitte to make a fortune, especially as the ideal property is available. In order that she may have the capital with which to buy the house, La Peyrade persuades Brigitte to sell her 'rentes', which are now at their maximum value. When the purchase is made, La Peyrade tells her: 'Vous possédez un immeuble qui, dans cinq ans, vaudra près d'un million. C'est un coin de boulevard!'[74] This is just one of several forms of investment and speculation by which Brigitte creates the necessary financial basis for the pursuit of the social and political ambitions of her brother Jérôme. In turn, this particular example of property speculation and, more especially, speculation in 'rentes' are examined by Balzac in their relationship to 'la conjoncture', to specific moments of crisis, both political and economic, in the life of the July Monarchy.

(d) Speculation and 'la Conjoncture'

Balzac's preoccupation with the theme of speculation and 'la conjoncture' reveals a remarkable continuity. At both extremities of the Consulate and Empire, as the *Comédie humaine* reveals, the crises of Brumaire and 1814-15 had witnessed a marked upsurge in speculation. The pattern is maintained during the July Monarchy, when speculation is invariably linked by Balzac to 'la conjoncture'. Again, Balzac concentrates his attention on two years of crisis, on 1830-1 and on 1840.

The crisis which immediately followed the July Revolution and was to last well into 1831 was serious enough to bring commercial and financial life to a virtual standstill. It was a period in which the value of 'rentes' and shares fell drastically and in which banks for a time had to suspend payments. The crisis claimed some notable victims, none more so than Laffitte, and its tremors are clearly felt in the *Comédie humaine*. The two firms which engage Gaudissart to sell their products do so because they are worried about 'la baisse des affaires' immediately after the July Revolution. Cérizet and his partner Georges d'Estourny are both ruined by the first shock-wave of the Revolution, d'Estourny being described as 'un joueur trop habile, dont les fonds, en Juillet 1830, ont sombré de compagnie avec le vaisseau de l'Etat'.[75] Graslin's disaster is typical of the many bankruptcies which were a feature of the economic crisis provoked by the revolutionary upheaval. 'En août 1830', Balzac records, 'Graslin, surpris par les désastres du commerce et de la banque, y fut enveloppé malgré sa prudence.'[76]

Such a situation of turbulence, which was marked by a rapid fall in the value of 'rentes' and shares, provided a perfect terrain for the speculator. The principles for the speculator to observe are neatly summed up by Donnard. On the one hand, there is the negative policy of avoiding unnecessary losses, which is summed up in the 'Bourse' axiom, 'vendre au son du canon, acheter au son du clairon'. It will be recalled how Nucingen had turned to his advantage his foreknowledge of the outcome of Waterloo.[77] In contrast, the ruin of d'Aldrigger in 1814 and that of Couture in 1840 is explained by their failure to obey the first half of the 'Bourse' proposition.

Its lessons are dramatically spelled out in *Une Ténébreuse Affaire*, where Philippe Bridau meets with disaster in his attempt to speculate on the political crisis of 1830. Reassured by the Ordinances, he gambles on an increase in the value of shares and does not sell. A major factor in his decision is his confidence in Nucingen and du Tillet, whose advice has helped him to make a fortune out of speculation up to that point. Correctly anticipating revolution and a consequent fall in share prices, Nucingen and du Tillet sell at the right moment and deliberately provoke

Bridau's ruin by encouraging him to make a disastrous speculation in buying just before the outbreak of the July Revolution.

The more positive form of speculation based on an assessment of 'la conjoncture' is embodied in the precept 'vendre ses rentes à la hausse, les racheter à la baisse'. 'L'essential', Donnard emphasises, 'est de connaître a temps les événements politiques qui peuvent influer sur la cote.'[78] Professor Castex has drawn attention to Grandet's extraordinary flair for detecting movements in financial values and, in particular, his timely switch from five per cent 'rentes' to three per cent.[79] 'La haute Banque' was particularly noted for its quickness off the mark in this respect.[80]

The most effective demonstration of this kind of activity is provided by Balzac in relation to the crisis of 1840, the full implications of which will be studied in a moment. Meanwhile, Balzac shows that, when the 'clairon' succeeded the 'canon' in 1830, great profits were to be made by speculators confident that the return to political stability would be quickly followed by an upsurge in economic activity.

Those who benefit materially from speculation in the period 1830-1 and from the general economic effects of the July Revolution outnumber the victims who are their contemporaries in the *Comédie humaine*. Both Brigitte Thuillier and the baronne de Macumer obtain their house in the exceptional circumstances that followed immediately on the Revolution. Mlle Thuillier acquired her house cheaply thanks to the decline in the value of property in the Latin quarter caused by the movement of population, which was accentuated by the July Revolution, from 'la rive gauche' to 'la rive droite'. The baronne de Macumer has a country house built with a view to her marriage to Marie Gaston. 'L'acquisition', she informs the comtesse de L'Estorade, 'a été faite pendant les mouvements qui ont suivi la révolution de Juillet.'[81]

In particular, all the cases of speculation which Balzac quotes during the economic crisis of 1830-1 are an unqualified success. Without exception, they are concerned with 'rentes' and not with 'Bourse' shares. Characters as socially divergent as Poupillier and Laurence de Cinq-Cygne both make a considerable profit out of speculation carried out in the first months of the July Monarchy in anticipation of a recovery in the value of 'rentes'. The only difference is that Poupillier speculates on his own behalf, whereas Laurence de Cinq-Cygne's investments are made for her by M. d'Hauteserre.

The most spectacular gains in the period 1830-1 are made via the classic device of the speculator, the purchase of 'rentes' at three per cent when their value has fallen with a view to reselling after their anticipated recovery. The baronne de Macumer and Mme Graslin both invest at three per cent at precisely the same moment. 'J'ai mis un million dans le trois pour cent', Mme de Macumer writes to the comtesse de l'Estorade, 'quand il était à cinquante francs, et me suis fait ainsi soixante-mille francs de rentes.'[82] In contrast to her husband, who died a financial victim of the July Revolution, Mme Graslin, within three months of his death in April 1831, has invested her fortune through Grossetête, 'dans celui des fonds français qui présentait les plus grands advantages, le trois pour cent alors à cinquante francs'.[83]

If Mme Graslin and the baronne de Macumer wait twelve months before buying 'rentes' at three per cent, Mme de Watteville and doctor Minoret invest in them earlier, before the end of 1830. Mme de Watteville, we are told, 'avait mis dans le trois pour cent ses économies en 1830'.[84] Doctor Minoret acquires his three per cent 'à la faveur des troubles politiques', when, according to Balzac, their value had fallen to 45.[85] Balzac is inaccurate on this point, since the three per cent never fell as low as 45 at this period. From 79 it dropped to 58 before the end of 1830, to reach a record low-point in March 1831, at the time of the downfall of Laffitte. By April, it was back to 62 again. The fact remains that, among Balzac's speculators in 'rentes' during the economic crisis of 1830-1, it is those who buy early who make the greatest gains, since they benefit from a greater discrepancy between the purchase price and the price at which they resell. Conversely, those who, like the baronne de Macumer and Mme Graslin, wait until the summer of 1831, make a smaller profit because of the higher price which they have to pay for the three per cent 'rente' which had by then regained much of its value.

Between the crisis of 1830-1 and 1840 Balzac gives only one other instance of the financial repercussions of broader events in society. It concerns the circumstances in which Adam Laginski acquires his house in 1834. In discussing the factors involved in the transaction, Balzac shows a remarkable understanding of the interaction of economic and political realities in determining property values. Laginski acknowledges to his wife that he has bought the house with the profit Thaddée Paz has made for him by selling his 'rentes'. In the same novel, *La Fausse Maîtresse*, two additional facts are mentioned. The house had originally been part of 'l'hôtel d'un fournisseur, un des Crésus de la Révolution, mort à Bruxelles en faillite après un cen dessus-dessous de Bourse'. It had then become the property of an English opium-dealer, whose widow had decided to sell it cheaply at the time of the 1834 riots in Paris. 'A cause des émeutes', Balzac indicates, 'le prix de cette folie ne monta pas à plus de onze cent mille francs', before adding: 'La pudique veuve ordonna de vendre le scandaleux immeuble au moment où les émeutes mettaient en question la paix à tout prix.'[86]

On another year of economic crisis and speculation during the July Monarchy, 1837, Balzac has little to say, apart from the reference to the fall in the value of the shares in Claparon's bank from 1,000 to 40. However, Donnard has pointed to the impact of 1837 on Balzac's creative work, both *César Birotteau* and *La Maison Nucingen* being written in that year. The emphasis in the *Comédie humaine* is placed at a different point of historical tension, at a moment of crisis in which the interdependence of the political and economic aspects of the regime is brutally exposed.

After the period 1830-1, the second demonstration of 'la spéculation et la conjoncture' concentrates on the crisis of 1840. Couture is the unhappy victim of his miscalculations in 1840. 'Couture se laissa pincer sa caisse', Bixiou remarks in *Un Homme d'affaires*.[87] A fuller explanation of Couture's disastrous experience is given in *Béatrix*. 'La fausse alerte de 1840 rafla les derniers capitaux de ce spéculateur qui crut à l'habileté du 1er mars.'[88] Couture pays the same price for his faith in Thiers as D'Aldrigger does in 1814 for his belief in the invincibility of Napoleon.[89] Having bought 'rentes' when their value was high, he is then panicked into selling them at a loss when they fall as a result of the 'fausse alerte' produced by the signing of the Treaty of London in July 1840, by England, Russia, Prussia, Austria and Turkey.

Other speculators appraise the political situation more correctly. Calculating that Thiers' bellicose bluff would be called over his support for Mehemet Ali in Egypt, they speculate accordingly and are rewarded when the 'rente' recovers after Thiers' replacement by Guizot in October of that year. Mme Schontz, for example, is the guiding force behind Arthur de Rochefide's successful speculation on the outcome of the political crisis of 1840. 'Elle entra dans le maniement de la fortune de son Arthur, elle lui fit acheter des rentes en baisse avant le fameux traité de Londres qui renversa le ministère du 1er mars.' Drawing the lesson of Couture's failure, 'Aurélie, le voyant en mauvaise veine, fit jouer . . . Rochefide en sens contraire'.[90] Polydore de la Baudraye is another who profits by speculating 'à la baisse' in 1840, only in his case it is the rarer 4½ per cent 'rente' and not the three per cent which is involved. When its value falls, he invests 1,200,000 fr., the total of his father-in-law's succession.[91]

The most masterly timing in speculation in 1840 is the work of La Peyrade. His warning to Brigitte Thuillier: 'Mais vienne un événement

politique, et les rentes, toutes les affaires tombent', is soon fulfilled
by events. His advice to Brigitte is to sell her five per cent while they
are at their maximum value before the political crisis breaks. 'Les
rentes', he argues, 'peuvent-elles aller plus haut qu'elles le sont aujourd'
hui? Cent vingt-deux! c'est fabuleux, il faut se hâter.'[92] This assessment
of the situation by La Peyrade is made in April 1840. Three months
later, the signing of the Treaty of London causes an immediate fall in
the 'rente'. Having followed La Peyrade's advice and sold her 'rentes',
Brigitte is now persuaded by La Peyrade to reinvest her capital in two
ways, confident that 'le ministère du 1er mars va tomber'.[93] The first
is the purchase of a house, since the value of property has also slumped
because of the uncertain political situation. The fall in the 'rente' has
in turn forced down the price of houses. 'Cette déroute financière',
Balzac recalls, 'influa sur les immeubles de Paris de la façon la plus
fâcheuse, et tous ceux qui se trouvaient en vente se vendirent en baisse.'
The second form of reinvestment is one which has been noted in an
earlier context, the buying of 'rentes' at three per cent. Balzac describes
the dramatic drop in their value caused by the political crisis. 'De juillet
à la fin d'août, les rentes françaises, effarouchées par la perspective
d'une guerre à laquelle s'adonna un peu trop monsieur Thiers, tombèrent
de vingt francs, et l'on vit le trois pour cent à soixante.'[94] Brigitte is
thus able to achieve a rare *coup* for herself and her brother. She buys
'rentes' at three per cent when they are at their lowest value and can
anticipate a handsome profit from reselling when a return to political
normality allows them to rise again. At the same time, she acquires as
investment-property a magnificent house at less than a fifth of what
it had cost to build.

Balzac's analysis of the economic effects of the political crisis
of 1840 is impeccable. He does not, however, take into account an
important economic factor which had a direct bearing on the fall in
house prices in Paris in 1840. Gille mentions how, in 1826 and 1839,
both years of economic crisis, construction work came to a halt. Land
that had been bought was not built on and houses that had been built
remained unsold.[95] In acquiring her house so cheaply in 1840, Brigitte
was profiting from a doubly favourable 'conjoncture'. The low price
of property was, in the first place, the consequence of a slump in the
building industry whose effects carried over from the previous year.
Prices were then, as Balzac shows, reduced still further by the unstable
political climate of the summer of 1840.

III   The Economic Analysis: its Implications and Limitations

The account which Balzac gives of the financial structure of the July Monarchy presents an uneven picture. Where he excels is in the area with which he was most familiar, the description of its day-to-day workings and, above all, in his astonishing knowledge of its various levels. Bertrand Gille pays tribute to this quality of Balzac when he recognises that 'c'est peut-être Balzac qui nous a le mieux décrit tout ce monde grouillant de petits intermédiares . . . , le milieu des commerçants pratiquant l'escompte à titre occasionnel'.[96] But not even this compliment of a specialist historian does justice to Balzac's penetrating analysis of the financial society of the July Monarchy, which is most concisely expressed in the description of the 'quatre couches de la finance parisienne' in *Les Petits Bourgeois*: 'En haut, la maison Nucingen, les Keller, les du Tillet, les Mongenod; un peu plus bas, les Palma, les Gigonnet, les Gobseck; encore plus bas, les Samanon, les Chaboisseau, les Barbet; puis, enfin, après le Mont-de-Piété, ce roi de l'usure, un Cérizet!'[97] What is so striking about this description is its emphasis on the hierarchical structure of Parisian finance, with its clearly-defined yet interrelated strata. Vauvinet, for example, is referred to as 'le valet du requin'.[98] The ruling predator in this case is du Tillet, who also is responsible for enabling Gigonnet to ruin Nathan by lending to him at 25 per cent. Balzac's analysis reflects, in all its essentials, his conviction that human society reproduced the hierarchy which natural inequalities gave rise to in the animal species.

Against this, it has to be pointed out that Balzac fails to draw the important conclusion from his analysis, the fact which is stressed by all historians of the period, namely the lack of an organised system of credit which was largely responsible for the slow growth of the French economy. The lesson emerges only implicitly, for example in the reliance on usury for want of established credit facilities, and in the multifarious activities of a financier such as Nucingen. Only very occasionally is there a hint that Balzac has grasped the nature of the problem, for instance in a couple of isolated references in *L'Envers de l'histoire contemporaine*. When M. Bernard has difficulty in finding financial backing for his book, Mme de la Chanterie explains that the 'Banque de France' refuses to lend to publishing firms because it considers them too risky. The Mongenod bank, though distinguished from others by its integrity, is typical in lending to the state rather than to commerce and industry. This attitude still persists under the July Monarchy. When Mme de la Chanterie asks for a loan to save a 'négociant' from bankruptcy, Louis Mongenod replies: 'On ne confie pas seize cent mille francs au commerce'.[99] Otherwise, one looks in vain for evidence that Balzac was aware of what was a serious weakness in the French economy in the first half of the nineteenth century.

This failure on Balzac's part has a wider significance, for it can only properly be assessed as part of his overall response to the July Monarchy, which is in turn related to his view of the Revolution of 1789. The arguments which Balzac advances, notably in *Le Curé de village*, to account for France's economic backwardness betray his incorrigible hostility to the Revolution and, by diverting his attention from the real issues, lead him, as Roger Fayolle has indicated, to propose unreal solutions.[100] It was not primarily, as Balzac persisted in maintaining, the greed of the bourgeoisie and peasantry for land resulting from their acquisition of 'biens nationaux' which prevented the circulation of the capital needed for investment in commerce and industry. Traditional distrust of investment certainly did not help, but the fact was that, until the second half of the nineteenth century, France did not develop the rational organisation of credit which was the condition of uninhibited economic growth. Given Balzac's anti-revolutionary convictions, perhaps the only kind of argument which would have made him alive to the fact is that recently developed by Morazé who maintains that it was the failure to develop a national credit system in the eighteenth century which was a major cause of the Revolution.[101]

Finally, when one attempts to evaluate Balzac's reaction to the emerging capitalist society of the July Monarchy, one sees that what criticism is expressed is limited to either moral or aesthetic objections. Under the moral heading, Mme du Tillet denounces the dealings of financiers such as her husband in the following terms: 'Les assassinats sur les grandes routes me semblent des actes de charité comparés à certaines combinaisons financières'.[102] In *La Cousine Bette*, Josépha condemns 'ces froids banquiers sans âme, qu'on dit vertueux et qui ruinent des milliers de familles avec leurs rails'.[103] In *Les Petits Bourgeois*, Balzac feels it is his duty as a historian to record that 'cette infâme spéculation n'est pas un fait exceptionnel'.[104] Or, alternatively, the argument assumes an aesthetic tone, when, for example, in *Les Petits Bourgeois* and *La Fausse Maîtresse*, Balzac deplores the architectural degradation of Paris which he sees as a consequence of the Revolution and the especial achievement of the bourgeoisie of the July Monarchy.

The moral misgivings and the aesthetic laments never form part, however, of a systematic critique which questions the economic credo of the July Monarchy as such. Balzac's attitude to the bourgeoisie of the July Monarchy is finally one of pragmatic acceptance, as his 'Nord' fixation demonstrates. Considering the distorting effect of his anti-revolutionary position, Balzac's economic analysis of the July Monarchy is remarkably perceptive. However, its prescriptive value is undermined from the start by his inability to see the need for a fully developed system of credit as the prerequisite of genuine capitalist expansion. Balzac's outlook reveals a marked imbalance between his political and his economic thinking. Faced with the growing threat of a popular challenge to the new bourgeois society, Balzac was able to envisage an authoritarian political solution which would guarantee the interests of a bourgeoisie he detested. What he was incapable of doing was to visualise how that society could become as efficient in economic management and performance as in the art of political repression.

Notes

1. *Béatrix*, II, 668.
2. *L'Envers de l'histoire contemporaine*, VII, 254.
3. *Mémoires de deux jeunes mariées*, I, 372-3.
4. *Béatrix*, II, 717.
5. Ibid., 791 and 729.
6. *Lettres sur Paris*, no. XIV, 10 February 1831. *Oeuvres Diverses*, II, Conard, 39, 126.
7. This question is briefly discussed on p. 155. For an account of the marriage patterns involving bourgeoisie and aristocracy in the eighteenth century see Franklin Ford, *Robe and Sword. The Regrouping of the French Aristocracy after Louis XIV* (Harvard, 1953), pp. 142-5.
8. *La Vieille Fille*, IV, 277.
9. *Le Cabinet des Antiques*, IV, 1092.
10. See chapter 5, section VIII and the anticipatory remarks concerning Balzac's view of the economic role of the aristocracy under the July Monarchy which are contained in the Conclusion of the same chapter.
11. *La Maison Nucingen*, VI, 374.
12. *Mémoires de deux jeunes mariées*, I, 359.
13. Letter to Alcide de Beauchesne, July or August 1835. *Correspondance générale*, vol. II.
14. *Le Député d'Arcis*, VIII, 790.
15. *Du Gouvernement moderne*, *Oeuvres Diverses*, Conard, II, 39, 555.
16. *Traité de la vie élégante*, *Oeuvres Diverses*, Conard, II, 39, 160.
17. *Béatrix*, II, 842.
18. *La Cousine Bette*, VII, 122.
19. Ibid.
20. For the history of these two types of finance companies see Bertrand Gille, *Recherches sur la formation de la grande entreprise capitaliste. 1815-1848* (Paris, 1959b), p. 34.
21. *Les Secrets de la princesse de Cadignan*, VI, 949-53.

22. *Béatrix*, II, 716-17.

23. *Une Fille d'Eve*, II, 350.

24. *L'Illustre Gaudissart*, IV, 563.

25. Bernard Guyon, *L'Illustre Gaudissart* (Classiques Garnier, Paris 1970); Emmanuel Faillettaz, *Balzac et le monde des affaires* (Lausanne, 1932).

26. Guyon, ibid., Introduction, p. xxx.

27. *L'Illustre Gaudissart*, IV, 565-6.

28. The confusion is aggravated by Gaudissart's distinguishing 'le châle' from 'l'Article-Paris'. 'Si je perds le châle', he tells Jenny Courand, 'je reviens à mon Article-Paris et à la chapellerie.' *L'Illustre Gaudissart*, IV, 571.

29. Ibid., 573 and 570.

30. Ibid., 573.

31. Guyon, *L'Illustre Gaudissart*, p. xxxiii.

32. Bertrand Gille, *La Banque et le crédit en France de 1815 à 1848* (Paris, 1959a), p. 191.

33. Frederick B. Artz, 'La Crise des assurances en 1830 et les Compagnies d'assurances', *Revue d'histoire moderne* (March-April 1929), pp. 96-105.

34. In the Garnier edition referred to in note 25.

35. Ibid., p. xxxi.

36. For a comprehensive statement of this view see J.-A. Lesourd and C. Gérard, *Nouvelle Histoire Economique*, vol. I, *Le XIXe siècle* (Paris, 1976).

37. Guyon, *L'Illustre Gaudissart*, p. xxxii.

38. The implications of this for Balzac's discussion of the Restoration bourgeoisie are examined in chapter 6.

39. Guyon, *L'Illustre Gaudissart*, p. xxxii.

40. Bernard Guyon, 'Balzac héraut du capitalisme naissant', *Europe* (January-February 1965), pp. 126-41.

41. Faillettaz, *Balzac et le monde des affaires*, part I, chapter III.

42. For a discussion of concentration and integration see Gille, *Recherches sur la formation de la grande entreprise capitaliste*, chapters II, III.

42. H. Sée, *Histoire Economique de la France*, 2 vols. (Paris, 1951). Vol II. *Les Temps Modernes (1789-1914)*, p. 165.

44. *Oeuvres Ebauchées*, 1st Pléiade edn, XI, 70.

45. See Lesourd and Gérard, *Nouvelle Histoire Economique*, chapter V.

46. *Le Député d'Arcis*, VIII, 749.

47. Gille, *Recherches sur la formation de la grande entreprise capitaliste*, p. 45.

48. Herbert J. Hunt, *Balzac's Comédie humaine*, 1st edn (London, 1964), pp. 408-9.

49. See A. Jardin and A.-J. Tudesq, *La France des notables*, 2 vols. (Paris, 1973). Vol. I, *L'Evolution générale. 1815-1848*, chapter 8.

50. *L'Illustre Gaudissart*, IV, 573.

51. Adeline Daumard, *La Bourgeoisie Parisienne de 1815 à 1848* (Paris, 1963), p. 441.

52. Sée, *Histoire Economique de la France*, p. 156.

53. Daumard, *La Bourgeoisie Parisienne de 1815 à 1848*, p. 505.

54. Gille, *La Banque et le crédit en France de 1815 à 1848*, part III, chapter I, section 3, p. 263.

55. *La Cousine Bette*, VII, 199.

56. Letter to Madame Hanska of 3 April 1845.

57. Letter to Madame Hanska of 28 December 1844.

58. *Béatrix*, II, 904 and 901.

59. *La Fausse Maîtresse*, II, 232. Laginski also reveals how Thaddée Paz has enabled him to acquire his house by shrewdly speculating in 'rentes' on his behalf.

'C'est lui qui m'a trouvé cet hôtel pour presque rien', Laginski tells his wife. 'Il a vendu mes rentes en hausse, les a rachetées en baisse, et nous avons payé cette baraque avec les bénéfices.' Ibid., 209.

60. *Echantillon de causerie française, 1832-44, Oeuvres Diverses*, II, Conard, 39, 482.

61. *Béatrix*, II, 922.

62. Gille, *Recherches sur la formation de la grande entreprise capitaliste*, p. 65.

63. *Oeuvres Ebauchées*, 1st Pléiade edn, XI, 70.

64. By the terms of the law of 1842, the state was to provide the infrastructure, which essentially involved the acquisition of land and the building of stations, while the rest, notably the track, rails and general management, was open to bids from private firms.

65. *Le Cousin Pons*, VII, 660.

66. Ibid., 678.

67. Faillettaz makes the point that Mercadet in *Le Faiseur* is the only example in the whole of Balzac's work of a speculator by profession or 'coulissier'. Faillettaz, *Balzac et le monde des affaires*, part I, chapter II, section 8.

68. The figures are those given by Sée, *Histoire Economique de la France*, chapter VII.

69. *La Cousine Bette*, VII, 253.

70. Ibid., 286. Balzac's reference is entirely authentic: the two branches of the Versailles line were joined in 1846. See chapter 8, note 83.

71. *Béatrix*, II, 838.

72. *La Cousine Bette*, VII, 366-7.

73. *Les Petits Bourgeois*, VIII, 133. The involvement of Birotteau and du Tillet in the Madeleine speculation in 1819 is examined on pp. 151-2.

74. Ibid., 153.

75. *Un Homme d'affaires*, VII, 781.

76. *Le Curé de village*, IX, 746.

77. The account of Nucingen's speculation on Napoleon's defeat at Waterloo is given by Blondet in *La Maison Nucingen*, VI, 338. Balzac also refers to the similar legend surrounding Nathan Rothschild in *Les Paysans*, IX, 224. For the historical details see Saint-Paulien, *Balzac Napoléon et l'empire de la Comédie humaine* (Paris, 1979), p. 305.

78. J.-H. Donnard, *Les Réalités économiques et sociales dans l'oeuvre de Balzac* (Paris, 1971), p. 300.

79. P.-G. Castex, 'L'Ascension de Monsieur Grandet', *Europe* (January-February 1965b), pp. 247-63.

80. See Gille, *La Banque et le crédit en France de 1815 à 1848*, part I, chapter I, section 2 ('La Banque étrangère à Paris'), for an account of Rothschild's and the Fould family's activities in this field.

81. *Mémoires de deux jeunes mariées*, I, 368.

82. Ibid., 359.

83. *Le Curé de village*, IX, 747.

84. *Albert Savarus*, I, 921.

85. *Ursule Mirouët*, III, 903.

86. *La Fausse Maîtresse*, II, 201. On 13 April 1834, the day following the suppression of riots in Lyon, serious rioting broke out in Paris. With Thiers as Minister of the Interior, the army commanded by Bugeaud put down the rising which ended, after two days, with the massacre of the rue Transnonain on 14 April.

87. *Un homme d'affaires*, VII, 782.

88. *Béatrix*, II, 905.

89. D'Aldrigger's misfortunes are described in *La Maison Nucingen*, VI, 359-60, along with Nucingen's forthright comments on the ineptitude of his former employer.

90. *Béatrix*, II, 905.

91. The 4½ per cent 'rente' which was offered as an alternative to the three per cent option in Villèle's conversion of the 'rente' in 1825 proved even less attractive to investors than the three per cent.

92. *Les Petits Bourgeois*, VIII, 134.

93. Ibid., 161.

94. Ibid., 140.

95. See Gille, *La Banque et le crédit en France de 1815 à 1848*, pp. 335, 343.

96. Ibid., p. 71.

97. *Les Petits Bourgeois*, VIII, 120.

98. *La Cousine Bette*, VII, 179.

99. *L'Envers de l'histoire contemporaine*, VIII, 233.

100. Roger Fayolle, 'Notes sur la Pensée politique de Balzac dans "Le Médecin de campagne" et "Le Curé de village"', *Europe* (January-February 1865), pp. 303-23.

101. Charles Morazé, *Les Bourgeois Conquérants* (Paris, 1957). Morazé's conclusion is that 'la monarchie a sombré pour n'avoir pu ni su organiser le crédit en France' (p. 123).

102. *Une Fille d'Eve*, II, 287.

103. *La Cousine Bette*, VII, 358.

104. *Les Petits Bourgeois*, VIII, 144.

10 THE 1848 REVOLUTION

I The New Class Struggle and the Search for a New Solution

In attacking the July Revolution as the logical outcome of 1789, Balzac was insistent that the damage did not stop at 1830. The great threat to which he drew attention was that to which he believed all the effects of the Revolution ultimately contributed, namely the rise of popular forces eager to inherit the materialism engendered by the Revolution and sanctified by 1830. The redivision of wealth resulting from the Revolution, Balzac was convinced, could only act as an incentive to the natural cupidity of the masses. The bourgeoisie had set a fatal precedent, as was strikingly demonstrated by the action of bourgeois 'acquéreurs' in reselling to peasant bidders. The alarm is clearly sounded in 1833 in *Eugénie Grandet*. After identifying 'le seul dieu moderne auquel on ait foi, l'argent dans toute sa puissance', Balzac then poses the sombre question: 'Quand cette doctrine aura passé de la bourgeoisie au peuple, que deviendra le pays?'[1]

It is from 1840 in particular that Balzac's warnings become more insistent, his attack on the Revolution as the source of France's recurrent problems more intransigent. 1840 itself witnessed a systematic restatement of Balzac's analysis of the July Revolution. Balzac's journalism, fuelled by the deepening crisis of the Thiers ministry, achieves a new level of invective in the exposure of the alleged evils of constitutional government in the *Lettres Russes*, *Sur les Ouvriers* and the *Lettre sur Sainte-Beuve*. There is now no trace of the ambivalence which had induced Balzac to praise the Charter of 1814 in the essay on Louis XVIII three years previously.[2] The 'monstruosités de la Haute Banque'[3] are eclipsed by the advance of the masses. *Les Paysans* is conceived as a work of protest, 'dirigé contre le peuple et la démocratie'.[4] The economic side of the argument is taken up in *Le Curé de village*, in which Clousier, Grossetête and l'abbé Bonnet in turn indict the July Revolution for giving final expression to the changes of 1789.

As he became increasingly preoccupied with the threat of popular disorder, Balzac's pronouncements reveal the search for a political answer to the problem. The urging of autocratic solutions grows in force in keeping with Balzac's conviction of the inevitability of future revolution. Immediately after the July Revolution, Balzac had at first ruled out the likelihood of a fresh outbreak of revolution. In 1831, in the *Traité de la vie élégante*, Balzac had declared that 'une révolution populaire est impossible aujourd'hui', unless it were provoked 'par le froid mépris de la classe intelligente'.[5] The events of June 1832, however, convinced Balzac otherwise. His sister Laure records how, watching the funeral procession of general Lamarque from her window, Balzac had remarked: 'Il y a une révolution dans ces mines-là'.[6] By the early 1840s, in *Les Paysans*, Balzac is prophesying the inevitable defeat of the bourgeoisie in its revolutionary struggle with the masses, while identifying 'le Communisme, cette logique vivante et agissante de la Démocratie'.[7]

Balzac's pessimistic prognosis alternates with the search for a form of government which will prevent the masses from seizing power. To ensure that this does not happen, Balzac repeatedly urges that the present constitutional form of bourgeois democracy, which is clearly inadequate to the task, must be replaced by some form of dictatorship. There had been a hint of this in Louis Lambert's lament for lost leadership, which had been echoed in the same year in *Le Médecin de campagne* by Benassis's faith in 'le grand homme qui nous sauvera du naufrage vers lequel nous courons'.[8] In 1839, it is d'Arthez who, in *Les Secrets de la princesse de Cadignan*, expresses his attachment to 'le magnifique gouvernement d'un seul, qui, je crois, convient plus particulièrement à notre pays'.[9] After 1840, such statements become the dominant note in the expression of Balzac's political faith. In *Sur les Ouvriers*, Balzac looks towards some 'vigoureux génie de domination, un de ceux qui font les 18 brumaire et les 13 vendémiaire',[10] while l'abbé Bonnet, in *Le Curé de village*, calls upon God to provide 'un homme providentiel, un de ces élus qui donnent aux nations un nouvel esprit'.[11]

II Balzac's Response to the 1848 Revolution

This then was the direction of Balzac's political thinking when his apprehensions of further revolution were confirmed by the events of February 1848.[12]

Having left France for the Ukraine in September 1847, Balzac remained with Mme Hanska at Wierzchownia until the end of January 1848. He returned to Paris on 15 February, just a week before the outbreak of the revolution. He was thus present in the capital at the time and able to witness events for himself. This accounts for the different manner of Balzac's reaction to 1848 compared with 1830.

In 1830, Balzac was staying in Touraine with Mme de Berny when Charles X was overthrown, and his silence on the July Revolution was only broken when the *Lettres sur Paris* began to appear in the September.

In 1848, on the other hand, Balzac's feelings were conveyed 'sur le vif' in the letters which he wrote to Mme Hanska. Composed for the most part either on the day of the events described itself or on the day following, they transmit a general sense of revolutionary excitement as well as the immediate impact which the revolution of February 1848 had on Balzac personally. Thereafter, if the testimony diminishes in intensity, particularly at the time of the June repression, on which Balzac reported to Mme Hanska from Saché, its interest persists. The letters which Balzac addressed to Mme Hanska between February and June 1848, are of great significance in that they represent a final statement of Balzac's political convictions at a moment of crisis both in his own life and in the history of France.

To see these developments in their correct perspective, however, one has to relate them to a process which, on both the personal and the national level, dates from the decisive turning-point of 1846-7. This period was a critical one for Balzac in every sense. It not only marked the end of his creative activity with the composition of *Les Parents Pauvres*. It also saw the end of his serious political ambitions. The elections of 1846 were the last to be held under the July Monarchy and the failure of his hopes of being nominated a candidate concluded for Balzac a sorry chapter of electoral frustrations going back to 1831. Meanwhile, Balzac was increasingly preoccupied with plans for his eventual marriage to Mme Hanska. Closely allied to this, for after all it was Mme Hanska who provided the necessary funds, there developed an obsession with investment, which was especially marked from the moment when Balzac acquired his shares in the 'Chemins de fer du Nord' in September 1845. In turn, the economic crisis of 1846-7 had a direct effect on Balzac's investments, as the feverish tone of his letters to Mme Hanska at this period testifies. Coinciding with the blocking of moderate demands for electoral reform, the economic crisis announced the revolution of 1848, which provoked Balzac's final reappraisal of his political position.

Before looking at the Hanska letters of February–June 1848, it is important to assess what evidence there is of Balzac's evolving outlook in the period 1846-7 in *Les Parents Pauvres*. There are two reasons for doing so. First, there are signs in both novels, but particularly in *Le Cousin Pons*, that in the closing phase of the July Monarchy Balzac was becoming aware of the growing importance of the working class in French society. There is a new concern with working-class conditions, especially in the description of 'le peuple des fabriques' and of 'la cité Bordin, le faubourg Saint-Antoine en miniature' in *Le Cousin Pons*.

Most remarkable of all is the account, unique in the *Comédie humaine*, of the living conditions of a working-class family, the Topinards. With an income of 900 fr. per year, they live in a cramped space on the sixth floor of an 'immeuble'. To make matters worse, their rent is increased by counting an attic as a full room. 'Cette pièce', Balzac explains, 'donnée comme chambre de domestique, permettait d'annoncer de logement de Topinard, comme un appartement complet, et de la taxer à quatre cent francs de loyer'. One is immediately struck by the close parallels between this scene and Zola's picture of the Parisian working class under the Second Empire which is contained in *L'Assommoir*. An excessive proportion of the family income has to be spent on rent in both cases. Overcrowding and oversized families go hand in hand. One detail in particular anticipates Zola's Lalie. Emphasising the role of the eldest child in working-class families, Balzac remarks that 'dans beaucoup de familles de la classe inférieure, dès qu'un enfant atteint à l'âge de six ou sept ans, il joue le rôle de la mère vis-à-vis de ses soeurs et de ses frères'.[13]

In relation to Zola, however, the differences are more important than the resemblances. One need not be misled by what appears to be a sympathy for the working class on Balzac's part. If Zola's attitude to the working class is marked by a profound ambivalence, the rare expressions of compassion which the awareness of working-class conditions inspires in Balzac have to be seen in the context of the socio-political philosophy into which they fit. The reference to the area of 'la Petite-Pologne', part working-class, part 'bohême', in *La Cousine Bette* gives a truer indication of Balzac's view of the place of the working class in society. In that instance, Balzac had counted on property speculation to force out, by raising the level of rents, the existing undesirable population.

It is true that Balzac distinguishes between a 'lumpenproletariat' and working-class families like the Topinards, 'pauvres mais honnêtes', just as Zola polarises working-class values between Goujet and Bijard. However, what sympathy Balzac may occasionally have felt for the victims of social injustice is negated by a political ideology based on the premise of natural inequality. Whether the argument takes a specifically class form or is expressed in the more general terms of rich versus poor, the outcome is the same. Balzac has undeniable sympathy for such social innocents as Goriot, Pons and Schmucke and, in expressing it, he transposes the argument onto a class level. When commenting on Schmucke's grief at the death of Pons, Balzac makes the point that, because of their wealth, the rich can soften even the impact of death. 'Partout, et en toute chose', he concludes, 'éclate à Paris l'inégalité des conditions, dans ce pays ivre d'égalité.' Referring again to the effect of bereavement, he goes on to elaborate on the class implications of economic inequalities. 'En ceci', Balzac reflects, 'comme dans la répartition des impôts, le peuple, les prolétaires sans aide, souffrent tout le poids de la douleur.'[14]

'Homo duplex. Res duplex.' The epigraph of *Les Parents Pauvres* might serve as a reminder not only of the duality of human nature but also of the divided nature of human society. To complement the increased interest in the working class which is apparent in *Le Cousin Pons*, *La Cousine Bette* indicates the remaining options open to the bourgeoisie in facing the problem of how to contain the working class whose demands posed a growing threat to the survival of the July Monarchy.

Balzac leaves no doubt in *La Cousine Bette* of his conviction that a regime which entrusts its political interests to the cynical materialism of a Crevel and his pale provincial image Beauvisage, or to the more youthful mediocrity of a Victorin Hulot, does so at its peril. For a hint of the future direction of society it is necessary to look beyond the representatives of the Louis-Philippard bourgeoisie to those who embody the values of an earlier generation and a different form of government. Hulot d'Ervy's contribution to the riposte addressed by Balzac to a regime in terminal crisis is limited but significant. In his detestation of parliamentary government, Hulot expresses a basic article of Balzac's political faith.

Hulot's elder brother, the comte de Forzheim, is a republican who had rallied to Napoleon and who retains his republican beliefs under the July Monarchy. In the values of the comte de Forzheim is reflected an affinity of Bonapartist and republican convictions which converge in a common identification with the cause of the working class. 'N'a pas qui veut, le peuple à son convoi', Balzac comments in referring to the crowds at the comte de Forzheim's funeral.[15]

It is significant that, in his search for a political solution, Balzac should have responded to those tendencies which made a special appeal to the masses. The one requirement was that the appeal be made 'd'en haut'. It was partly for this reason that Balzac had been attracted to legitimism, and it helps to explain his persisting Bonapartist sympathies.

Balzac had praised Napoleon for his efforts to reconcile the conflicting interests of bourgeoisie and aristocracy in the struggle to decide the final balance of the revolutionary settlement. Now that the social conflict had changed to a new form in the tension which opposed the bourgeoisie and the masses, it was essential, in Balzac's view, that a similar *rapprochement* be achieved.

All sections of society, including the working class, are represented at the funeral of the comte de Forzheim, 'l'Armée, l'Administration, la Cour, le Peuple', even the legitimist aristocracy in the person of Montauran's younger brother.[16] The paternalistic concern with the interests of the working class was an important element in Louis Napoleon's political campaign under the July Monarchy. At the same time, the capacity of Bonapartism to switch from a benevolent paternalism to a repressive authoritarianism was a valuable quality in a period of economic crisis and social unrest which threatened to produce a society unfit for Balzac and Mme Hanska to live in, and one in which his author's rights and his investments might be at risk.

Such then was the state of Balzac's political thinking when he left Paris to join Mme Hanska in September 1847. The unswerving attachment to absolutism was reaffirmed in the *Letter sur Kiew* which Balzac wrote a month after his arrival in the Ukraine.[17] The letters addressed to Mme Hanska between February and June 1848 reveal how that thinking was affected by the series of revolutionary events which began a week after Balzac's return to Paris on 15 February 1848.

Writing to Mme Hanska on 20 February, while certain that France was 'à la veille d'une révolution', Balzac felt reassured as to its outcome by the fact that 'Rotschild achète des rentes'.[18] The events of the next few days were to prove Balzac as complacent in his political judgement as Rothschild in his financial calculations. On the immediate outbreak of revolution, Balzac had looked to Louis-Philippe to suppress it. 'Louis-Philippe doit en finir avec la République', he recorded at 10 a.m. on 23 February. By 11 o'clock that same evening, Balzac regarded the anti-republican cause as lost. Unable to contemplate living under a republic, he is anxious to get his passport ready in order to leave again for the Ukraine. Already he has seen enough to feel more than ever convinced of the need for absolutism. 'Ma doctrine de l'absolutisme gagne tous les jours', he concluded.[19] Now that the July Monarchy had shown itself incapable of saving the situation, the only question that remained to be decided was what form of absolutism would be most effective.

On the following day, 24 February, Balzac personally witnessed the sacking of the Tuileries. His reaction, as expressed to Mme Hanska, recalls the prediction which Balzac had made at the beginning of the July Monarchy when similar events had enabled him to detect the rumblings of further revolution.[20]

Two days of revolution had been enough, Balzac wrote, to reduce France to a state of anarchy. The situation was doubly threatening for Balzac personally. In the first place, it meant 'plus de recettes littéraires', with the closing of the theatres and the suspension of publishing and bookselling. It also spelled disaster for investors since, in Balzac's view, the setting up of a republic was bound to lead swiftly to national bankruptcy.[21] Balzac's fears were justified. The value of shares in the 'Nord', which had already caused Balzac acute distress, fell to a quarter of what they had been worth on the eve of the revolution. Balzac's forecast of a similar drop in the value of the 'rente' also proved correct. When the 'Bourse' reopened on 7 March, the 5½ per cent had fallen from 111.60 to 97.50 and the 3½ per cent from 77.50 to 58, the latter eventually slumping to as low as 32.

The Republic was proclaimed on 26 February. A week later, Balzac announced to Mme Hanska that the only answer to the Parisian masses was the bayonet.[22] Throughout early March, Balzac's letters to Mme Hanska are dominated by the prediction of impending civil war, which is remarkably precise in its accuracy. The fighting would begin, Balzac insisted, by June at the latest.[23] Meanwhile, Balzac must look to his own future. His republican candidature in the April elections, officially announced in the *Profession de foi politique*, was only a smokescreen to conceal his real preoccupations.[24] For the authentic 'Profession de foi politique' one has only to read the letters to Mme Hanska which were written at the same time. His absolutist convictions, Balzac confessed to Mme Hanska, 'm'éloignaient de toute chance pour l'Assemblée.[25] The real motive behind such a move which, on the surface, denoted acceptance of the republicanism which Balzac passionately detested, was to ensure that no difficulties would be put in his way when it came to leaving France to rejoin on her native soil the aristocratic representative of a ruthless autocracy.[26]

When the moment was approaching for the fulfilment of Balzac's prophecy of civil war by June, a new note is introduced into the letters to Mme Hanska. As the crisis of the Republic intensifies, Balzac is increasingly concerned to know what new regime will emerge from the inevitable renewal of social conflict. In the days immediately leading up to the June repression, a legitimist outcome seems more likely to Balzac than a Bonapartist solution. If Louis-Napoleon does come to power, Balzac states on 15 June, it will be only for a brief spell which will be the prelude to the rule of Henri V. Five days later, legitimism is seen as the only possibility. 'Henri V', Balzac declares, 'qui était toujours, dans mes convictions, sans aucun espoir est redevenu possible, il n'y a plus que ce dénouement-là.'[27]

The June 'journées' were enough, it appears, to sweep away Balzac's last-minute resurgence of faith in a return to legitimism. On 25 June, when the armed struggle in Paris was at its height, there is no mention of Henri V. Balzac's authoritarian convictions remain unshaken, however. Something on Tsarist lines, he tells Mme Hanska, is needed to save France. For Balzac, the lesson of the events from February to June 1848 has been to underline the necessity of a Bonapartist form of government. 'Tout ce qui nous arrive depuis 4 mois', Balzac concludes, 'est un horrible plaidoyer en faveur du régime Napoléonien.'[28]

In September 1848, Balzac returned to the Ukraine to marry Mme Hanska. When he came back to France in May 1850, he was a dying man for whom the political affairs of his country were no longer a matter of supreme importance. The letters which he wrote to Mme Hanska from February to June 1848, therefore, represent Balzac's political testament. Together with the evidence of *La Cousine Bette*, they indicate a reaffirmation of Balzac's Bonapartist tendencies at a period of acute national crisis. A Bonapartist regime is finally envisaged by Balzac as the only effective means of dealing with a dangerous new alignment of social forces which is rigorously defined in class terms.

The discussion, as is invariably the case in Balzac's historical analysis, leads back to 1789. Balzac's view of the history of the July Monarchy, the view which serves as the basis of his critique of the revolution of 1848, is consistently clear. After the confirmation of its revolutionary gains in 1830, the bourgeoisie, fresh from its victory over the aristocracy, had found itself confronted with the challenge of the masses. If Balzac's interpretation takes little account of the internal divisions within the bourgeoisie and overlooks the alliance of its unenfranchised sections with the popular forces which made the 1848 revolution possible, he recognises that, now that universal suffrage has reunited the warring factions within the bourgeoisie, its immediate struggle is with a working class determined to achieve social and economic parity with it. In a letter to Anna Mniszech of March 1848, Balzac stated this view in the clearest possible terms when he spoke of 'cette croisade des prolétaires contre les bourgeois. Forcément, dans peu de temps, les bourgeois seront d'un côté, les prolétaires de l'autre, et le problème ainsi posé, c'est la guerre civile.'[29]

Louis-Philippe and Guizot, Balzac argued, had failed to avert a republic, first by committing errors of political judgement and secondly by applying inadequate measures of repression. Louis-Philippe's mistake, Balzac claimed in the *Lettre sur le travail*, had been to identify himself exclusively with the sectarian materialism of the bourgeoisie. Balzac's argument is disingenuous, to say the least. 'Le commerce, la bourgeoisie repue, . . . la plus trompeuse de toutes les forces', were more strongly established than ever after their savage triumph in June 1848.[30] Moreover, the parallels with the Empire were compelling. It had required a Bonaparte to defend the revolutionary conquests of the bourgeoisie against both an aristocratic reaction and the danger of a further extension of economic democracy. The Second Republic had its Cavaignac to crush the popular threat, but summoned a Bonaparte to attempt the ensuing task of social reconciliation. In each case, the bourgeoisie was willing to pay the price for the defence of its interests by abandoning a republic for an imperial dictatorship. Balzac's final identification with the bourgeoisie was affirmed unambiguously immediately after the June days. In answer to a request for a performance of the theatrical adaptation of *Les Petits Bourgeois*, Balzac refused on the grounds that it would be improper to see the bourgeoisie publicly pilloried on stage just when it had made such vital sacrifices in order to save civilisation.[31]

Had Balzac lived to see Louis-Napoleon's seizure of power, there can be little doubt that he would have welcomed the event as the most effective political answer that had yet been found to counter the democratic momentum of 1789. Several years earlier, in *Sur les Ouvriers*, Balzac had looked to someone capable of realising a new Brumaire to rescue France. 'Il faut un Bonaparte industriel', Balzac urged in the *Lettre sur le travail*, 'et, à la République, un organisateur.'[32] If there was no Bonaparte to take over industry, there was an obvious candidate ready to assume the direction of the Republic. Balzac's reticence is the result not of any doubts of principle, but simply stems from an awareness that Louis-Napoleon would be 'la parodie de l'Empire'.[33]

Neo-Bonapartism offered for Balzac the rare advantage of being a populist form of authoritarianism which guaranteed bourgeois interests and at the same time caught the social and nationalist imagination of the masses. The plebiscite by which Louis-Napoleon was elected would have been calculated to strike Balzac as particularly ingenious in combining the reality of autocratic government with a harmless gesture of popular consultation. It was Guizot who defined the appeal of Louis-Napoleon in the following terms: 'C'est beaucoup d'être à la fois une gloire nationale, une garantie révolutionnaire et un principe d'autorité'.[34]

It is precisely this brand of eclectic pragmatism represented by Louis-Napoleon which emerges as the final statement of Balzac's political ideology in the letters addressed to Mme Hanska from February to June 1848. For Balzac there was still hope that the full democratic consequences of the Revolution could be averted by the survivor of the one truly effective anti-revolutionary dynasty.

Notes

1. *Eugénie Grandet*, III, 1052, 1102.
2. See *Oeuvres Diverses*, III, Conard, 40, 172.
3. Preface to *Splendeurs et misères des courtisanes*, VI, 427.
4. Letter to Mme Hanska of 11 October 1844.
5. *Oeuvres Diverses*, II, Conard, 39, 162.
6. Laure Surville, 'A une amie de province', 12 June 1832.
7. *Les Paysans*, IX, 141. Referring to the peasantry, Balzac predicts: 'Cet élément insocial créé par la Révolution absorbera quelque jour la Bourgeoisie, comme la Bourgeoisie a dévoré la Noblesse'. Ibid., 49. Balzac thus reaffirms the myth of a landowning peasantry brought into existence by the Revolution.
8. *Le Médecin de campagne*, IX, 430.
9. *Les Secrets de la princesse de Cadignan*, VI, 970.
10. *Oeuvres Diverses*, III, Conard, 40, 411.
11. *Le Curé de village*, IX, 820.
12. Mme Meininger underlines Balzac's perspicacity in this respect when she reminds one that de Tocqueville was alone among contemporary historians in anticipating the 1848 revolution. Introduction to *Les Comédians sans le savoir*, Pléiade, VII, 1151.
13. *Le Cousin Pons*, VII, 751-2.
14. Ibid., 723.
15. *La Cousine Bette*, VII, 353.
16. Ibid.
17. The *Lettre sur Kiew* was written at Wierzchownia in mid-October.
18. All the letters to Mme Hanska which are referred to in this chapter are contained in vol. 4 of the *Lettres à Madame Hanska* (ed. Roger Pierrot), 4 vols. (Paris, 1971).
19. Letter of 23 February 1848.
20. See p. 243 and also chapter 7, note 8.
21. Letter of 25 February 1848.
22. Letter of 2 March 1848.
23. Letters of 6, 10 and 12 March 1848.
24. Published on 18 March 1848, the *Profession de foi politique* can be found in the *Oeuvres Diverses*, III, Conard, 40, 681-2, which gives incorrect dates for its composition and publication.
25. Letter of 30 April 1848. In the elections held on 23 April, Balzac obtained only a handful of votes.
26. 'C'est là ce qui me permet de partir si je ne suis pas élu', Balzac wrote to Mme Hanska on 18 March, the same day that the *Profession de foi politique* was published.
27. Letter of 20 June 1848.
28. Letter of 25 June 1848.

29.   Letter of 8 March 1848.

30.   The *Lettre sur le travail* is undated, but it was written some time after February 1848. It is contained in vol. 40 of the *Oeuvres Diverses*, III, in the Conard edition. This particular reference occurs on p. 685.

31.   The incident is quoted by Anne-Marie Meininger in her Introduction to *Les Petits Bourgeois*, Pléiade, VIII, 20.

32.   *Lettre sur le travail. Oeuvres Diverses*, III, Conard, 40, 690.

33.   The phrase is used by Balzac in a letter to Mme Hanska of 15 June 1848.

34.   Quoted by Jean Lhomme, *La Grande Bourgeoisie au pouvoir. 1830-1880* (Paris, 1960), p. 154.

11 CONCLUSION

Balzac's Ideological Relationship to the Revolution

(a) The Philosophical Basis of Balzac's Critique of the Revolution

Balzac's social and political views stem from his conviction of the immutability of certain basic natural laws to which human beings, no less than animal species, are subject. This was to be the premise of the *Avant-Propos*, but Balzac had arrived at this viewpoint long before 1842. In the *Traité de la vie élégante*, which appeared in October-November 1831, Balzac drew the social conclusions of the law of biological necessity and expressed them in the notorious phrase: 'Un homme placé au dernier rang de la société ne doit pas plus demander compte de sa destinée qu'une huître de la sienne'.[1] The fixed place occupied by individuals in the social scale follows logically for Balzac from the divisions observed in nature. Balzac did not allow himself to be embarrassed by the contradictions in which his determinism, social as well as biological, involved him, with, for example, his faith in an omnipotent deity. Their social and political consequences in terms of Balzac's vision of the Revolution were, however, profound and they will be considered in detail in the final assessment of this conclusion.[2]

Balzac's determination is characterised by a pre-Darwinian emphasis which, as the *Catéchisme Social* makes clear, owes much to the influence of Hobbes.[3] The axiom 'la nature ne laisse vivre que les forts', sums up Balzac's thinking in the *Catéchisme Social*.[4] The Darwinian implications of Balzac's position are acknowledged, if somewhat reluctantly, by Wurmser when he comments in respect of Balzac's notion of 'l'homme supérieur': 'C'est déjà tout le parti que la bourgeoisie tirera de Darwin et de la notion de la sélection naturelle'.[5] It is from this determinist starting-point that Balzac proceeds to construct the social and political system which is set out in such statements as the *Avant-Propos* and the *Catéchisme Social* and which is consistently expressed in the *Comédie humaine*.

Balzac's belief that zoological structures provided a valid model for the study of human society reinforced his experience of the history of post-revolutionary France to determine his concept of class. One of the more remarkable achievements of Balzac is to have anticipated, in their broader formulation at least, the basic notions of Darwin and Marx.

When Zola resumed the debate a generation later, he had the advantage of writing with the *Communist Manifesto* and the *Origin of Species* as his points of reference. It is his class-based approach to society which governs Balzac's entire view of the Revolution. Writing at the end of 1830, for example, Balzac interprets the Revolution in the following terms: 'En 1789 . . . , la lutte qui existe dans toute société entre ceux qui possèdent et ceux qui n'ont rien, entre les privilégiés et les prolétaires, s'est réveillée avec une fureur sans example'.[6] Although this particular analysis is more appropriate to 1848 than to 1789, its significance lies in the insistence that class conflict lay at the heart of the Revolution. In *Ursule Mirouët*, Balzac identifies the class factors involved in the Revolution more accurately when he observes: 'Le lacis de la noblesse, embrassé par le lacis de la bourgeoisie, cet antagonisme de deux sangs protégés, l'un par des institutions immobiles, l'autre par l'active patience du travail et par la ruse du commerce, a produit la révolution de 1789'.[7] In *Jean Louis*, which dates from 1822, Courottin's weighing-up of his prospects is based on his calculation of the likely shift of power from the aristocracy to the bourgeoisie.

Like Courottin, Balzac was not simply concerned with making a dispassionate analysis of class relations in post-revolutionary France. From the start, as early as 1825 in *Le Code des gens honnêtes*, Balzac made it clear which side he was on, with the strong against the weak, with the rich against the poor. This is particularly the case in *Gobseck*, where the view is expressed that 'l'homme est le même partout; partout le combat entre le pauvre et le riche est établi, partout il est inévitable; il vaut donc mieux être l'exploitant que d'être l'exploité'.[8] The occasional outburst against privilege and social injustice, such as one finds in *La Vie de château*, and the odd approval of revolutionary retribution are inspired by what Balzac sees as gratuitous ultra excesses of the kind which is destined to provoke social subversion. In the last resort, the *status quo*, Balzac insists, must be defended at all costs, preferably with an intelligent sense of responsibility but if necessary, if all else fails, with ruthless repression. Society cannot be condemned, Balzac maintains, because of the activities of a Nucingen nor invalidated by the suffering of the 'canuts' of Lyon. As Couture argues, 'Attaquer la liberté commerciale à cause de ces inconvénients, ce serait attaquer la Justice sous prétexte qu'il y a des délits qu'elle ne punit pas, ou accuser la Société d'être mal organisée à cause des malheurs'.[9]

It was, in the first instance, because he believed that they were in fundamental conflict with the laws of nature that Balzac denounced the ideals of the Revolution. They are either dismissed as inherently unattainable or, in some cases, dangerous, or else Balzac claims that they have been perverted by those who spoke and acted in their name. The basic principles of the Revolution are repeatedly assailed in a persistent campaign which culminates in the massive indictment which is contained in a letter written to Mme Hanska in April 1848. For Balzac, the effects of the February revolution are the inevitable fulfilment of the grandiose slogans of 1789. 'Nous avons la *liberté* de mourir de faim', Balzac reflects, 'l'*Egalité* dans la misère, la fraternité de Caïn.'[10] In *Sur les Ouvriers*, liberty is rejected as being irreconcilable with the prior demands of social order. In the *Catéchisme Social*, 'le libre arbitre' is condemned as the prime cause of revolution, the most insidious of the 'préjugés philosophiques' in the sense that it has engendered 'la liberté politique'.[11] Finally, Balzac finds the ultimate absurdity of liberty in its extinction at the hands of the revolutionary forces that created it. 'Une extrême liberté tue la liberté', he concludes. 'Voilà la maxime la plus vraie que nous aient léguée les révolutions.'[12]

Fraternity, in the form of 'l'humanitarisme' or 'la philanthropie', is also fiercely attacked. Balzac's especial fury is concentrated, however, on the doctrine of equality. The *Essai sur la situation du parti royaliste* presents equality as a dangerous nonsense, as being, like liberty, incompatible with effective government. At best, it is seen by Balzac as a utopian ideal. 'Vouloir, au nom d'une égalité chimérique et impossible', Balzac states in the *Catéchisme Social*, 'au nom des souffrances du prolétariat, changer les Etats, les Sociétés' is absurd, since to seek to do so is, Balzac reiterates, to ignore the natural laws which make the existence of a social hierarchy inevitable.[13]

Equality is also held responsible by Balzac for the death of the intellect, since it precludes the formation of exceptional intelligence on which cultural achievement depends. 'L'esprit', it is argued in *La Fausse Maîtresse*, 'veut du loisir et certaines inégalités de position. Des égaux n'ont plus besoin de finesse, ils se disent alors tout *bêtement* les choses comme elles sont.'[14] Inequality and privilege are, Balzac is convinced, essential to great art. Without large individual fortunes, cultural mediocrity cannot be avoided. What Balzac views as the current cultural malaise is traced to its source in the Revolution. 'Il n'y a plus de grands seigneurs ni de rois absolus qui pourraient récompenser noblement les hommes de lettres. La révolution de 1793 a tout changé.'[15] One need, of course, look no further than the example of Balzac himself to see the fallacy of this particular argument, to appreciate that the inequalities of a bourgeois society were not necessarily inimical to the emergence of a remarkable culture, even if its greatest artists were ungenerously rewarded.

Balzac's social pessimism leads him to question the value of individual behaviour in the Revolution. If not unrealisable, revolutionary ideals are depicted as being easily corrupted. Examples of disinterested idealism and of selfless patriotism are matched by cases of cynical self-seeking, flawless probity is answered by callous betrayal. For every Niseron there is a Rigou, a Pillerault has his counterpart in du Bousquier. Where Niseron is concerned, Balzac is sceptical, not of 'ce sublime républicain', but of the adequacy of isolated instances of idealism, 'qui rendrait la république acceptable s'il pouvait faire école'.[16] The purchase and resale of 'biens nationaux', profiteering in conditions of acute shortage and lucrative dealings in military supplies are common activities among a significant proportion of the Republican figures in the *Comédie humaine*. Endemic in all revolutions, corruption, Balzac believed, had found in the French Revolution a particularly favourable soil. 'Les révolutions populaires', he concludes, 'n'ont pas d'ennemis plus cruels que ceux qu'elles ont éléves.'[17]

(b) Contradiction and Reality

(i) The Tensions in Balzac's Ideology. Balzac's attitude to social change is marked by a basic ambivalence. In two recent articles comparing Balzac with Scott, D.R. Haggis has suggested that both novelists responded to the revolutionary transformation of their respective societies by subordinating a lingering attachment to *ancien régime* values to a realistic acceptance of changed circumstances.[18] Where Balzac is concerned, Haggis's conclusion is entirely justified, but it is important to examine the process whereby Balzac arrived at such an adjustment and, in particular, to consider the conflicting reactions to the Revolution which provide the dominant feature of his political ideology.

The ambivalence arises essentially from Balzac's divided attitude to class values. On the one hand, an admiration for bourgeois vitality, industry and success is balanced by Balzac's contempt for the materialism, vulgarity and philistinism of the bourgeoisie. On the other hand, an infatuation with magnanimity, distinction and refinement vies with misgivings about the inflexibility of the aristocracy, its failure of will and its political incapacity. In the end, Balzac's political realism overcame his aesthetic reticence, but not without a struggle. It was only in the second half of the July Monarchy, as Balzac came to see the bourgeoisie as the only effective defence against the advance of the masses, that the solution which Haggis refers to can be said to have been achieved.

Balzac exhibits a wide range of mixed responses to the fundamental issues in post-revolutionary society. Some of these tensions, notably the clash between Balzac's condemnation of social injustice and his insistence on the need for repression, have already been noted. Basically, however, Balzac's ambivalence revolves around two antitheses, each related to the other, progress in opposition to reaction and hierarchy conflicting with social movement.

In the first case, Balzac is primarily concerned with the impact on the provinces of the expansion of economic activity in Paris and with the transmission of the values associated with it. Balzac's analysis is distinguished by its consistently ambivalent character. Reservations about the price paid for modernisation alternate with Balzac's impatience with fossilised attitudes and economic stagnation. Provincial simplicity is frequently preferred to Parisian sophistication. Social progress is often questioned, at the same time that resistance to change is welcomed. In *Les Chouans*, the denunciation of provincial backwardness is distinctly ambiguous, just as the tribute paid to du Bousquier's achievement in industrialising Alençon is double-edged. 'Alençon lui doit', Balzac remarks, 'son association au mouvement industriel qui en fait le premier anneau par lequel la Bretagne se rattachera peut-être un jour à ce qu'on nomme la civilisation moderne.'[19] The balance is finely drawn, but in the final analysis Balzac's view is that the economic advantages of revolutionary progress to the provinces are less important than the erosion of traditional values at the contact of Parisian ideas. Religion is seen as the victim of modernisation, liberty as the price of equality. All of Balzac's nostalgia for a vanquished past, as well as his aversion for the doctrines of the ideologues, are expressed in Sabine de Grandlieu's reflections: 'Ah! la noble et sublime Bretagne, quel pays de croyance et de religion! Mais le progrès la guette, on y fait des ponts, des routes; les idées viendront, et adieu le sublime. Les paysans ne seront certes jamais si libres ni si fiers que je les ai vus, quand on leur aura prouvé qu'ils sont les égaux de Calyste, si toutefois ils veulent le croire.'[20]

Balzac's defence of hierarchy has to contend with the disruptive force of revolutionary individualism. The effect of this is that the conflict between the insistence on the need for hierarchy and the recognition of the necessity of social movement, instead of being resolved, is driven to breaking-point. Tensions degenerate into contradictions. Individualism, for example, at different moments is claimed both to have been frustrated and encouraged by the Revolution.

More seriously, the attack on individualism is negated by Balzac's notion of 'l'homme supérieur' and his admiration for the dynamic success of individual bourgeois, which, in turn, are at odds with Balzac's contempt for bourgeois materialism.

If a society based on hierarchy and privilege was to survive, Balzac insisted, it must promote the accession of talented individuals from its lower levels. This was necessary, Balzac argued, for two reasons. First, such a process of renewal was the only effective safeguard against degeneracy. Secondly, by encouraging the ascension of such elements, the likely leaders of any future revolution would be neutralised. Balzac's scheme founders on the sacred monster which he saw as the supreme idol worshipped by the society that had emerged out of the Revolution. Sacrosanct, omnipotent, money proves to be the decisive factor. 'Le mouvement ascensionnel de l'argent', anarchic and uncontrollable, breaks through Balzac's defence of a society founded on privilege and class, both disrupting its hierarchy and destroying its unity.[21]

(ii) Balzac and Counter-revolution. The difficulty of reconciling the insistence on social hierarchy with the need for a degree of mobility within it is reflected in Balzac's attitude to counter-revolution. For Balzac, the July Revolution was an event of greater magnitude than it was for Casimir Périer.[22] It involved, in Balzac's view, more than a mere change in the head of state. It is true that there is the occasional suggestion that 1830 was a 'révolution manquée', for example in the reference to 'le grand vice du replâtrage social de 1830' in *Béatrix*. This, however, does not mean that Balzac regarded the July Revolution as being of negligible consequence, any more than it lends credence to Pierre Barbéris's claim that Balzac's hostility to the July Monarchy reflected his disquiet at the failure of the regime to fulfil the democratic hopes raised by 1830. Balzac's consistent view of the July Revolution was, as we have seen, that it completed a disastrous process of bourgeois domination which had begun in 1789. This is confirmed by the determination of Fabien du Ronceret to climb on the bourgeois bandwagon to which the 1830 Revolution had given a decisive impetus. 'Aussi comptait-il l'exploiter à son profit', Balzac comments, 'en suivant l'exemple des finauds de la bourgeoisie.'[23]

Balzac was quick to recognise, however, that the bourgeois victory of 1830 was total and irreversible. His vision of a restored elder branch of the Bourbons working in harmony with a neo-aristocracy of 'intelligentiels' was short-lived and unconvincing. Any reluctance Balzac might have about accepting the vulgar realities of a bourgeois society was put aside as the threat of popular revolt intensified. In Balzac, the 'rentier' proved more powerful and more relevant than the 'mondain'. As early as 1832, in the *Essai sur la situation du parti royaliste*, Balzac had urged the acceptance of the new order of society in terms which, despite their vagueness, undermine the logic of his legitimism and put a question mark against his critique of the July Revolution and, indeed, of the Revolution itself. The determination which governs Balzac's scientific outlook finally pervades his view of history. An implicit faith in the power of the 'libre arbitre' to act on the historical process is temporarily suspended as Balzac acknowledges that the changes which began in 1789 and which were extended by the July Revolution are irrevocable. Balzac's language in fact takes on a note of violent insistence in emphasising the need to accept the 'fait accompli' of both Revolutions. 'Là où une révolution a successivement passé dans les intérêts et dans les idées', he insists, 'elle est inattaquable; il faut l'accepter comme un fait.'[24] This is equally true of 1830 as of 1789. 'Les barricades de juillet', Balzac concludes, 'ont eu lieu; l'homme politique doit les accepter comme un fait.'[25]

The rejection of counter-revolution as a practicable option which Balzac had strongly voiced in the *Essai sur la situation du parti royaliste* is frequently expressed in the *Comédie humaine*. In *Une ténébreuse affaire*, the debate over counter-revolution is represented by the opposing attitudes of Laurence de Cinq-Cygne and M. d'Hauteserre. It is the cautious neutrality of M. d'Hauteserre which is preferred to the impassioned interventionism of Laurence. Even before 1830, Balzac had identified the Chouan rebellion with 'ces temps de triste mémoire où la discorde civile avait renversé les institutions les plus saintes'.[26] But counter-revolution is opposed for another reason than that it divides the nation. Like the Revolution itself, counter-revolution is considered dangerous by Balzac, because, by enlisting the support of a section of the masses, it increases the risk of popular disturbances. 'Les Chouans sont restés', Balzac warns, 'comme un mémorable exemple du danger de remuer les masses peu civilisées d'un pays.'[27] Counter-revolution is rejected as being counter-productive.

It is at this point that the contradictions in Balzac's outlook become apparent. At the same time that he rules out counter-revolution as a realistic response to the changes imposed in 1789 and 1830, Balzac looks back nostalgically on the *ancien régime* as an age of lost values and as a model of political wisdom. However emphatic Balzac's pragmatic acceptance of revolutionary change may be, it is almost lost sight of in the ceaseless and systematic attack on the Revolution which is the dominant historical note in the *Comédie humaine*.

In attempting to resolve this impossible dilemma, Balzac involved himself in recurrent inconsistency. While stressing that the effects of 1789 and 1830 were irreversible, he persisted, for example, in campaigning for the revival of some of the more obsolete features of the *ancien régime*, notably the 'droit d'aînesse'. It does not matter in the end that Balzac did not believe that the total restoration of the *ancien régime* was either possible or desirable. Few, if any, of the leading counter-revolutionary thinkers included it in their programme either.[28] What is important is that the logic of counter-revolution, in some form or other, is inherent, right up to his final 'césariste' orientation, in Balzac's vehement and unrelenting denunciation of virtually all that the Revolution stood for.

This fundamental contradiction in Balzac's political thinking clearly emerges if one takes a systematic look at some of the remarks made in the contributions to the new Pléiade edition. André Lorant, for example, draws attention to the admiration expressed by l'abbé Bonnet and Gérard for Charles X, Polignac and the Ordinances of 1830.[29] Lucienne Frappier-Mazur, for her part, quotes Balzac's plea in the 'Essai sur la situation du parti royaliste': 'le parti royaliste . . . doit accepter le combat dans les termes où il est posé par le dix-neuvième siècle', and refers to Balzac's concern 'de concilier avec son désir d'un pouvoir fort le sens de l'évolution historique'.[30] The essential point which needs to be emphasised, however, is that Balzac's political despair arose precisely out of his sense that the force and direction of post-revolutionary change seemed to preclude the creation of the strong form of government which he advocated.

Although Balzac was careful to dissociate himself from the extremist faction among the legitimists, it would be a mistake to dismiss too lightly, as some critics have tended to do, the identity of views which links Balzac with such traditionalist thinkers as De Maistre and Bonald, in whom the ultras found the ideological justification of their material ambitions.[31] If, in Balzac, a social realism tends to replace the theocratic sanctions which De Maistre and Bonald apply to their critique of the Revolution, Balzac's affinities with Bonald in particular are undeniable.

At the basis of their thinking is the shared conviction that class divisions and social hierarchy are inevitable, given, in Bonald's phrase, 'la passion naturelle de s'élever au-dessus des autres et les inégalités naturelles de corps et d'esprit'.[32] The outlook of Balzac and Bonald is also identical in respect of the social function which they ascribe to religion. 'La société religieuse', Bonald reasons, 'se joint à la société politique pour réprimer les volontés dépravées de l'homme ou ses passions.'[33] In the *Avant-Propos*, Balzac introduces the same argument in remarkably similar terms when he refers to Christianity, the Catholic religion especially, as 'un système complet de répression des tendances dépravées de l'homme'.[34] Ten years earlier, in 1832, following closely on Balzac's rallying to the legitimist cause, l'abbé Janvier had described the Christian religion as 'un système complet d'opposition aux tendances dépravées de l'homme'.[35]

Finally, it is in Bonald that one finds clearly stated the fundamental notion which unites Balzac's view of human nature with his social and political system of thought. The outcome of the struggle for dominance which can be observed throughout nature, Bonald argues, is the emergence in human society of the superior individual. 'La nature est avare d'hommes supérieurs', he affirms, 'elle sème avec profusion les hommes médiocres. L'homme vraiment supérieur aux autres hommes, celui que la nature fait naître pour remplir ses vues sur la société, s'élève toujours de lui-même, et malgré tous les obstacles, à la place que la nature lui assigne; car, s'il avait le même besoin que les autres hommes de la faveur des circonstances ou du secours de l'éducation, il ne leur serait pas supérieur.'[36] Here, in essence, is a formulation of the essential attributes of Balzac's 'homme supérieur', of the qualities of leadership that were needed, Balzac believed, if France was to be saved from the egalitarian mediocrity implanted by the Revolution.

One can understand therefore why Balzac should have paid tribute to Bonald in the *Avant-Propos*. Balzac makes it clear where he stands ideologically in relation to the Revolution when he declares: 'Je me range . . . du côté de Bonald, au lieu d'aller avec les novateurs modernes'.[37] This self-confessed affinity with Bonald is all the more significant as it immediately follows Balzac's insistence on the social function of religion as an indispensable instrument of repression.

Any criticism which Balzac has to make of the *ancien régime* is based on purely moral grounds. Otherwise, Balzac considered it to be superior, in all essential respects, to the society produced by the Revolution. First, there was the question of manners and taste. The occasional moral chidings are insignificant when compared with Balzac's enthusiasm for the sense of elegance which graced the *ancien régime* cult of sensual pleasure. Secondly, in contrast with the exclusive materialism which Balzac saw as the pernicious legacy of the Revolution, the *ancien régime*, he believed, had a concern for non-material values which distinguished it from those which had succeeded it. This often-repeated argument of Balzac is effectively summed up by Bianchon when he claims that 'l'argent autrefois n'était pas tout, on admettait des supériorites qui le primaient. Il y avait la noblesse, le talent, les services rendus à l'Etat; mais aujourd'hui la loi fait de l'argent un étalon général.'[38] Finally, in a political sense, everything in the *Comédie humaine* indicates that the ideal kind of society which Balzac approved of was one based on an authoritarian monarchy, a systematic hierarchy and aristocratic privilege, of which the *ancien régime* provided a model.

Balzac's vision of a modernised version of the *ancien régime* was as utopian as the revolutionary ideals which were the constant object of his ridicule. The July Monarchy was dominated by the affirmation of bourgeois power and by growing evidence of the rise of the masses. Faced with these urgent realities, Balzac abandoned legitimism in his search for a dictatorial solution. Counter-revolutionary dreams of salvaging, if not of restoring, the past from the grasp of a victorious bourgeoisie gave way to anti-revolutionary prescriptions designed to defend bourgeois society against the new class enemy.

Much has been written about the alleged revolutionary implications of Balzac's appraisal of the effects of the Revolution. Where Marxist critics make such claims, they only do so by ignoring completely the fact that Balzac's critique of the Revolution is consistently made from a reactionary viewpoint and by attributing to Balzac conclusions favourable to their own political presuppositions but which are the opposite of those which stand out in virtually all that Balzac wrote. This technique is well illustrated by the two propositions on which André Wurmser relies. The first, the distinction between 'l'homme et l'oeuvre', is groundless. The two are essentially one, as the remarkable concordance between the *Comédie humaine* on the one hand and the articles and correspondence on the other serves to show. Only by the arbitrary waving of a doctrinaire wand can the evidence be forced in a revolutionary direction, and it is Antonio Gramsci's dictum, 'la vérité est révolutionnaire' which provides Wurmser and, by implication, other Marxists, with the convenient device.[39]

Non-Marxist critics, such as Donnard and Guyon, have no inhibitions about recognising that a great writer may be a reactionary. Donnard's emphasising of the resemblances between Balzac's political ideology and that of Maurras is much more in keeping with the facts.[40] Once the contradictions in Balzac's thinking have been taken into account, Balzac clearly emerges, not as a revolutionary, but as an unrepentant authoritarian. To adapt Hugo's verdict in the 'discours funèbre', Balzac belongs to 'la forte race des écrivains réactionnaires'. 'Qu'on le veuille ou non.'[41]

Notes

1. *Oeuvres Diverses*, II, Conard, 39, 157.
2. Although the emphasis in Balzac's scientific determinism is on the biological aspect, Balzac occasionally invokes the authority of the physical sciences in order to expose the absurdity of post-revolutionary developments. In attacking the growth of bureaucracy under the Restoration, for example, he affirms that 'la loi contraire est un axiome écrit dans l'univers: il n'ya a d'énergie que par la rareté des principes agissants'. *Les Employés*, VII, 908.
3. The date of the composition of the *Catéchisme Social* is uncertain. It is accepted, however, that it was probably written between 1840 and 1848. It can be found in *Oeuvres Diverses*, III, Conard, 40, 691-708.
4. Ibid., 694.
5. André Wurmser, *La Comédie Inhumaine*, 2nd edn (Paris, 1965), p. 607.
6. *Lettres sur Paris*, no. 10, 31 December 1830. *Oeuvres Diverses*, II, Conard, 39, 106.
7. *Ursule Mirouët*, III, 783.
8. *Gobseck*, III, 969.
9. *La Maison Nucingen*, VI, 377.
10. Letter of 21 April 1848.
11. *Oeuvres Diverses*, III, Conard, 40, 697.
12. *Enquête sur la politique des deux ministères*, April 1831. *Oeuvres Diverses*, II, Conard, 39, 361.
13. *Oeuvres Diverses*, III, Conard, 40, 692.
14. *La Fausse Maîtresse*, II, 199.
15. *Procès de la Société des Gens de Lettres contre le Mémorial de Rouen*, 25 October 1839. *Oeuvres Diverses*, III, Conard, 40, 263.
16. *Les Paysans*, IX, 222.
17. Ibid., 286.
18. D.R. Haggis, 'Scott, Balzac, and the historical novel as social and political analysis: "Waverley" and "Les Chouans"', *Modern Language Review* (January 1973), pp. 51-68; 'Fiction and Historical Change: "La Cousine Bette" and the lesson of Walter Scott', *Forum for Modern Language Studies* (October 1974), pp. 323-33.
19. *La Vieille Fille*, IV, 928.
20. *Béatrix*, II, 851.
21. *La Fille aux yeux d'or*, V, 1046.
22. 'Non, Monsieur', Casimir Périer replied to Odilon Barrot, 'il n'y a pas eu de Révolution en juillet, il y a eu seulement un changement dans la personne du chef de l'Etat.'
23. *Béatrix*, II, 905. In recognising 'le grand vice du replâtrage social de 1830', du Ronceret restates Balzac's fundamental conviction that the July Revolution was the logical culmination of the bourgeois victories of 1789 and 1793. Ibid.
24. *Essai sur la situation du parti royaliste*, *Oeuvres Diverses*, II, Conard, 39, 522.
25. Ibid., 534.
26. *Les Chouans*, VIII, 1205.
27. Ibid., 919.
28. For a concise account of the leading theorists of the counter-revolution, see Jacques Godechot, *La Contre-Révolution. Doctrine et Action. 1789-1804* (Paris, 1961). In his Introduction (p. 2), Godechot states, 'très peu, parmi eux, songeaient à rétablir "l'Ancien Régime" sans rien y changer'.

29. Introduction to *Le Curé de village*, Pléiade, IX, 633-4.

30. Introduction to *Les Chouans*, Pléiade, VIII, 871.

31. This is the view taken, for example, by Bernard Guyon, *La Pensée politique et sociale de Balzac* (Paris, 1969), p. 496.

32. The *Théorie du pouvoir politique et religieux* comprises the first two volumes of the complete works of Bonald in the Le Clere edition (Paris, 1854). This particular quotation occurs in vol. I, p. 184.

33. Ibid., p. 171.

34. *Avant-Propos*, I, 12.

35. *Le Médecin de campagne*, IX, 503.

36. Bonald, *Théorie du pouvoir politique et religieux*, vol. I, p. 184.

37. *Avant-Propos*, I, 13.

38. *La Cousine Bette*, VII, 428.

39. Wurmser, *La Comédie Inhumaine*, p. 708.

40. J.-H. Donnard, *La Vie économique et les classes sociales dans l'oeuvre de Balzac*, p. 450-4.

41. Hugo's actual words were: 'L'auteur de cette oeuvre immense et étrange est de la forte race des écrivains révolutionnaires. Qu'on le veuille ou non.'

BIBLIOGRAPHY

The compilation of a bibliography related to a study of 'Balzac and the French Revolution' confirms the serious gaps which remain in the historical evaluation of Balzac's work. No full-length analysis has yet been attempted of the *Comédie humaine* in terms of a specific period, let alone of the whole of post-revolutionary society. Revolution and Empire, the Restoration and the July Monarchy still await the commitment of, to use Louis Chevalier's distinction, both 'balzaciens historisants' and 'historiens balzacisants'. The most ambitious works of synthesis have been achieved by Marxist critics such as Wurmser and Barbéris. To Barbéris in particular must go the credit for having stimulated by his remarkable output a whole fresh awareness of the historical dimensions of the *Comédie humaine*. Indeed, Barbéris's contribution can be measured by the frequency of his appearances in this bibliography.

At the same time, three important sources are available, which are valuable both for their general contribution to Balzac scholarship and criticism and for the concern which they show with the historical aspects of Balzac's work. Two of them, *L'Année Balzacienne* and the Classiques Garnier series, are long-established. Thanks to the excellent introductions contained in the new Pléiade edition of the *Comédie humaine*, an invaluable third source of scholarly information and critical insight has now been added.

I Balzac's Life and Work

(a) Editions of Balzac's Works

Balzac. *Correspondance générale* (ed. Roger Pierrot), 5 vols. (Paris, 1960-9)
La Comédie humaine (ed. M. Bouteron), 1st Pléiade end, 11 vols. (Paris, 1951-65)
―――― (ed. P.-G. Castex), 2nd Pléiade edn, 12 vols. (Paris, 1976-81). Volume I contains a valuable introduction by Professor Castex entitled 'L'Univers de la "Comédie humaine" ' (pp. ix-lxxvi)
Jean Louis, edn of 'les Bibliophiles de l'Originale' (Paris, 1961).
Letters à Madame Hanska (ed. Roger Pierrot), 4 vols. (Paris, 1971).
Oeuvres Complètes de Honoré de Balzac (eds. M. Bouteron and H. Longnon), 40 vols. (Conard, Paris, 1926-63). The *Oeuvres Diverses*, I-III, comprise volumes 38-40 of this edition.
Romans de jeunesse, vols. 29-37 of the edn of Roland Chollet. *Honoré de Balzac.*
Oeuvres (Cercle du Bibliophile, Paris, 1965)

(b) Biographical and Critical Studies

Bardèche, Maurice, *Une Lecture de Balzac*, 2nd edn (Paris, 1970)
——— , *Balzac* (Paris, 1980)
Hunt, Herbert J., *Balzac's 'Comédie humaine'*, 2nd edn (London, 1964)
Marceau, Félicien, *Balzac et son monde*, 5th edn (Paris, 1955). pp. 11-13 contain useful tables listing side by side the date of composition of each work and the date of the action covered by it
Maurois, André, *Prométhée ou la vie de Balzac*, 2nd edn (Paris, 1974)

(c) Miscellaneous

Bardèche, Maurice, 'Balzac et Flaubert', *L'Année Balzacienne* (1976), pp. 9-29
Crépet, Jacques (ed.), *Balzac, Pensées, sujets, fragmens* (Paris, 1910)
Lotte, Fernand, *Dictionnaire biographique des personnages fictifs de la Comédie humaine* (Paris, 1952)
Pommier, Jean, 'Naissance d'un héros: Rastignac', *Revue d'Histoire littéraire de la France* (1950), pp. 192-209
Tolley, Bruce, 'Three Articles Wrongly Attributed to Balzac', *Modern Language Review* (1960), pp. 85-7
——— , 'Balzac et "la Caricature"', *Revue d'Histoire littéraire de la France* (January-March 1961), pp. 23-35
——— , 'Balzac and the "Feuilleton des journaux politiques"', *Modern Language Review* (1962a), pp. 504-17

II Works of General Historical Interest

Baldensperger, F., *Le Mouvement des idées dans l'émigration française, 1789-1815*, 2 vols. (Paris, 1924)
Bertaut, Jules, *Le Faubourg Saint-Germain sous l'Empire et la Restauration* (Paris, 1949)
Bouloiseau, Marc, *Etude de l'émigration et de la vente des biens des émigrés* (Paris, 1963)
Chalmin, P., *L'Officier Français de 1815 à 1870* (Paris, 1957)
Chateaubriand, François, *Mémoires d'Outre-Tombe*, 3 vols. (Livre de Poche, Paris, 1973)
Cobban, Alfred, *A History of Modern France*, 3 vols., vol. 2, *1799-1871*, 2nd edn (London, 1965)
Crouzet, François, 'French Economic Growth in the Nineteenth Century Reconsidered', *History* (June 1974), pp. 167-79
Daumard, Adeline, *La Bourgeoisie Parisienne de 1815 à 1848* (Paris, 1963)
Duguit, Léon and Monnier, Henri, *Les Constitutions et les principales lois politiques de la France depuis 1789*, 6th edn (Paris, 1943)
Dunham, A.L., *La Révolution Industrielle en France. 1815-1848* (Paris, 1953)
Flaubert, Gustave, *L'Education Sentimentale. Oeuvres II.* Pléiade (Paris, 1952)
Forster, Robert, 'The Survival of the Nobility during the French Revolution', *Past and Present* (July 1967), pp. 71-86
Gerbod, P., *La Vie quotidienne dans les lycées et collèges aux XIXe siècle* (Paris, 1968)
Gille, Bertrand, *La Banque et le crédit en France de 1815 à 1848* (Paris, 1959a)
——— , *Recherches sur la formation de la grande entreprise capitaliste, 1815-1848* (Paris, 1959b)
Higgs, David, 'Politics and Landownership Among the French Nobility after the Revolution', *European Studies Review* (April 1971), pp. 105-21

Jardin, A. and Tudesq, A.-J., *La France des notables*, 2 vols., vol. I, *L'Evolution générale, 1814-1848* (Paris, 1973)

Laffitte, Jacques, *Mémoires* (ed. Paul Duchon) (Paris, 1932)

Lesourd, J.-A. and Gérard, C. *Nouvelle Histoire Economique*. Vol. I, *Le XIXe siècle* (Paris, 1976)

Lhomme, Jean, *La Grande Bourgeoisie au pouvoir. 1830-1880* (Paris, 1960)

Madelin, L., *Fouché*, 2 vols. (Paris, 1903)

Morazé, Charles, *Les Bourgeois Conquérants* (Paris, 1957)

Orieux, Jean, *Talleyrand ou le sphinx incompris* (Paris, 1970)

Puy de Clinchamps, P., *La Noblesse* ('Que Sais-je?', Paris, 1959)

Richard, Guy, 'Du moulin banal au tissage mécanique. La Noblesse dans l'industrie textile en Haute-Normandie dans la première moiteé du XIXe siècle', *Revue d'Histoire économique et sociale* (1968), pp. 305-38, 506-49

Sée, Henri, *Histoire Economique de la France*, 2 vols., vol. II, *Les Temps Modernes, 1789-1914* (Paris, 1951)

Soboul, Albert, *Histoire Economique et Sociale de la France* (eds. Fernand Braudel and Ernest Labrousse), 3 tomes, tome III (Paris, 1976) Vol. I, livre I, *La Révolution Française, 1789-1815*

Tudesq, A.-J., 'Les listes électorales de la Monarchie censitaire', *Annales* (April-June 1958), pp. 277-88

Vidalenc, Jean, *Les Emigrés Français, 1789-1825* (Caen, 1963)

Villat, L., *La Révolution et l'Empire*, 2 vols. (Paris, 1936)

Vovelle, Michel, 'Structure et Répartition de la fortune foncière et de la fortune mobilière d'un ensemble urbain: Chartres de la fin de l'ancien régime à la Restauration', *Revue d'Histoire économique et sociale* (1958), pp. 385-98

Zeller, G., 'Une notion de caractère historico-social: la dérogeance', *Cahiers Internationaux de Sociologie* (January-June 1957), pp. 40-74

Zola, Emile, *Les Rougon-Macquart*, Pléiade, 5 vols. (Paris, 1960-7)

III Balzac in Relation to the Period 1789-1848

Alain, *Les Arts et Les Dieux. Avec Balzac* (Paris, 1937)

Andréoli, Max, 'La Politique rationnelle selon Balzac', *L'Année Balzacienne* (1980), pp. 7-35

Auerbach, Erich, *Mimesis* (Princeton, 1968), contains an appraisal of Balzac in chapter 18, 'In the Hôtel de la Mole' (pp. 454-92); and a discussion of the French realist novel in chapter 19 on 'Germinie Lacerteux' (pp. 493-524)

Balzac (Collection 'Génies et Réalités') (Paris, 1959): chapter III by Gilbert Sigaux, 'Balzac enfant et père du Siècle' (pp. 65-93); chapter IV by Jean-Louis Bory, 'Balzac dévoile le dessous des cartes' (pp. 99-135); chapter VI by Jean Duvignaud, 'L'homme d'affaires joue et perd' (pp. 169-94)

Barbéris, Pierre, 'Les Mystères de la Dernière Fée' *L'Année Balzacienne* (1964), pp. 139-55

——— , *Aux Sources de Balzac. Les Romans de jeunesse* (Paris, 1965a)

——— , 'Balzac et la démocratie', *Europe* (January-February 1965b)

——— , 'Balzac, le baron Charles Dupin et les statistiques', *L'Année Balzacienne* (1966), pp. 67-83

——— , 'La Pensée de Balzac: histoire et structures', *Revue d'Histoire littéraire de la France* (January-March 1967), pp. 18-54

——— , *Balzac et le mal du siècle*, 2 vols. (Paris, 1970a)

——— , *Balzac: une mythologie réaliste* (Paris, 1971)

——— , *Mythes balzaciens* (Paris, 1972a)

——— , *Le Monde de Balzac* (Paris, 1973)

———, 'Réalisme et symbolisme dans *Wann-Chlore*' (Paris, 1974)

———, 'La Province comme langage romanesque.' La dramatisation dans la constitution du héros balzacien', *Stendhal et Balzac II*, Actes du VIIIe Congrès International Stendhalien, Nantes, 27-29 May 1971 (Nantes, 1978), pp. 129-41

Bellos, David, 'Du nouveau sur Balzac "écrivain révolutionnaire"', *L'Année Balzacienne* (1969), pp. 280-91

Bertaut, J., 'Balzac et la duchesse d'Abrantès', *La Revue de Paris* (January 1949), pp. 129-39

Bolster, Richard, 'Was Balzac a Revolutionary?', *French Studies* (January 1965), pp. 29-33

Bonald, L. de, *Théorie du pouvoir politique et religieux*, 2 vols., Le Clere edn (Paris, 1854)

Bruhat, Jean, 'Balzac et la classe ouvrière française', *Europe* (Colloque Balzac) (January-February 1965), pp. 74-90

Butler, Ronnie, 'Historical Dimensions of the *Comédie humaine, Bourgeoisie and Aristocracy under the Revolution and Empire*', *European Studies Review* (April 1975), pp. 147-70

———, 'Les Emigrés dans *la Comédie humaine*', *L'Année Balzacienne* (1978), pp. 189-224

———, 'Dessous economiques dans "*la Comédie humaine*": les crises politiques et la spéculation', *L'Année Balzacienne* (1981), pp. 267-83

Chevalier, Louis, '*La Comédie humaine*: Document d'histoire, *Revue Historique* (1964), pp. 27-48

Chollet, R., ' "Une Heure de ma vie" ou Lord R'hoone à la decouverte de Balzac', *L'Année Balzacienne* (1968), pp. 121-34

Citron, Pierre, *La Rabouilleuse* (Classiques Garnier, Paris, 1966)

Clark, Priscilla P., *The Battle of the Bourgeois. The Novel in France, 1789-1848* (Paris, 1973). Chapter V has as its subject 'Balzac and Stendhal in a Bourgeois World' (pp. 135-68)

Dimier, L. *Les Maîtres de la Contre-Révolution au XIXe siècle* (Paris, 1907). Includes a chapter on Balzac (pp. 115-35)

Dino, G., 'L'Aspect historique et social des types chez Balzac', *Europe* (Colloque Balzac) (January-February 1965), pp. 295-302

Donnard, J.-H., 'Qui est Nucingen?', *L'Année Balzacienne* (1960), pp. 135-48

———, *Les Réalités économiques et sociales dans l'oeuvre de Balzac* (Paris, 1961)

———, ' "Les Paysans" et "La Terre" ', *L'Année Balzacienne* (1975), pp. 125-42

Dubern, Eugene B., 'La Rente Française chez Balzac', *L'Année Balzacienne* (1963), pp. 251-68

Europe (Colloque Balzac) (January-February 1965)

Faillettaz, E., *Balzac et le monde des affaires* (Lausanne, 1932)

Ferry, G., 'Balzac candidat à la députation', *Revue politique et parlementaire* (10 December, 1901), pp. 566-88

Fischer, Jan O., 'Réalisme et "Conception du Monde" chez Balzac', *L'Année Balzacienne* (1974), pp. 265-80

Forest, Jean, *L'Aristocratie balzacienne* (Paris, 1972)

Fortassier, Rose, *Les Mondains de la Comédie humaine* (Paris, 1974)

Guyon, Bernard, *La Pensée politique et sociale de Balzac* (Paris, 1969)

———, *Un Inédit de Balzac, 'le Catéchism social', précédé de l'article 'Du Gouvernement Moderne'* (Paris, 1933)

———, 'La Province dans le roman', *Stendhal et Balzac II, Actes du VIIIe Congrès International Stendhalien*, Nantes, 27-29 May 1971 (Nantes, 1978), pp. 117-27

Haggis, D.R., 'Scott, Balzac and the Historical Novel as Social and Political

Analysis: "Waverley" and "Les Chouans"', *Modern Language Review* (January 1973), pp. 51-68

——, 'Fiction and Historical Change: "La Cousine Bette" and the lesson of Walter Scott', *Forum for Modern Language Studies* (October 1974), pp. 323-33

Larkin, Maurice, *Man and Society in Nineteenth Century Realism* (London, 1977). Chapters 4 and 5 are concerned respectively with the scientific basis of Balzac's determinism and with his attitude to the bourgeoisie, especially that of the July Monarchy

Leroy, Maxime, *Histoire des idées sociales en France*, 3 vols. Vol. 3 (Paris, 1954), has two interesting chapters: 'Le Romanesque social de Balzac' (pp. 170-87) and 'Le Césarisme social' (pp. 258-76)

Maistre, J. de, *Considérations sur la France*, 3rd edn (Paris, 1821)

Maurras, Charles, 'Balzac royaliste. Révolutionnaire comme Balzac', *La Gazette de France* (19 August 1900)

Perrod, P.-A., 'Balzac et les "Majorats"', *L'Année Balzacienne* (1968), pp. 211-40

Pradalié, G., *Balzac Historien* (Paris, 1955)

Prioult, A., 'Notes. Balzac et Lepître', *L'Année Balzacienne* (1965), pp. 317-22

Raphael, Sylvia, 'Balzac and Social History', *European Studies Review* (January 1971), pp. 23-33

Tolley, Bruce, 'Un ouvrage inconnu de Balzac: Les "Mémoires anecdotiques" de L.F.J. de Bausset', *L'Année Balzacienne* (1962b), pp. 35-49

——, 'Les Oeuvres Diverses de Balzac (1824-1831)', *L'Année Balzacienne* (1963), pp. 31-64

——, 'Balzac et les Saint-Simoniens', *L'Année Balzacienne* (1966), pp. 49-66

——, 'Balzac anecdotier', *L'Année Balzacienne* (1967), pp. 37-50

——, 'Balzac et la Doctrine Saint-Simonienne', *L'Année Balzacienne* (1973), pp. 159-67

Wurmser, André, *La Comédie Inhumaine*, 2nd edn (Paris, 1965)

Yaouanc, Moïse le, 'Balzac au Lycée Charlemagne et dans les pensions du Marais, 1815-1816', *L'Année Balzacienne* (1962), pp. 70-92

——, 'Précisions sur Ganser et Beuzelin. Balzac pensionnaire à Paris en 1813-1814?', *L'Année Balzacienne* (1964), pp. 25-38

IV Publications Concerning Specific Periods

(a) The Ancien Régime and the Revolution

(i) History.

Bretonne, Restif de la, *Les Nuits de Paris* (Paris, 1963)

Ford, Franklin, *Robe and Sword, The Regrouping of the French Aristocracy after Louis XIV* (Harvard, 1953)

Godechot, J., *La Contre-Révolution. Doctrine et action. 1789-1904* (Paris, 1961)

Goubert, Pierre, *L'Ancien Régime*, 2nd edn (Paris, 1969)

Greer, D., *The Incidence of the Emigration during the French Revolution* (Harvard, 1951)

Hampson, Norman, *A Social History of the French Revolution* (London, 1963)

Hugo, Victor, *Quatrevingt-treize*, Garnier-Flammarion edn (Paris, 1965)

Labrousse, C.-E., *La Crise de l'Economie Française à la fin de l'Ancien Régime et au début de la Révolution* (Paris, 1944)

Lefebvre, Georges, *Etudes sur la Révolution Française* (Paris, 1954): (1) 'Répartition de la propriété et de l'exploitation foncières à la fin de l'ancien régime' (pp. 201-16); (2) 'La Vente des biens nationaux' (pp. 223-45)

——, *La Révolution Française*, 2nd edn (Paris, 1957)

Leroy, Maxime, 'Les Spéculations Foncières de Saint-Simon et ses Querelles d'Affaires avec son Associé le Comte de Redern', *Revue d'Histoire économique et sociale* (1925), pp. 133-63

Lizerand, Georges, 'Observations sur l'impôt foncier sous l'ancien régime', *Revue d'Histoire économique et sociale* (1958), pp. 18-44

Marion, Marcel, *La Vente des biens nationaux pendant la Révolution* (Paris, 1908)

Richard, Guy, 'Un essai d'adaptation sociale à une nouvelle structure économique. La noblesse de France et les sociétés par actions à la fin du XVIIIe siècle', *Revue d'Histoire économique et sociale* (1962), pp. 484-523

Soboul, Albert, *Précis d'Histoire de la Révolution Française* (Paris, 1962)

Taine, H., *Les Origines de la France contemporaine*, vols. 1 and 2, *L'Ancien Régime*, 24th edn (Paris, 1902)

Tocqueville, A. de, *L'Ancien Régime et la Révolution* (Paris, 1887)

(ii) Balzac and the Revolution.

Barbéris, Pierre, 'Roman historique et roman d'amour. Lecture du *Dernier Chouan*', *Revue d'Histoire littéraire de la France* (March-June 1975), pp. 289-307

Butler, Ronnie, 'Balzac's *Jean Louis*: Some Links between a "Roman de Jeunesse" and the *Comédie humaine*', *Nottingham French Studies* (November 1977a), pp. 31-49

———, 'Les Acquéreurs de biens nationaux dans *la Comédie humaine*', *L'Année Balzacienne* (1977b), pp. 137-51

Dutacq, Jean, 'La Maison de famille', *Le Courrier Balzacien*, nos. 4 and 5 (May 1959), pp. 61-8

Hamilton, James F., 'The Novelist as Historian: A Contrast between Balzac's "Les Chouans" and Hugo's "Quatre-vingt-treize"', *The French Review* (April 1976), pp. 661-8

Regard, Maurice, *Les Chouans* (Classiques Garnier, Paris, 1957)

Wurmser, André, 'Le Trébuchet', *Littérature et Société* (Paris, 1973), pp. 135-46

(b) Consulate and Empire

(i) History

Las Cases, E., *Mémorial de Sainte-Hélène*, 2 vols. (Paris, 1961)

Lefebvre, Georges, *Napoléon*, 6th edn (Paris, 1969)

Lucas-Dubreton, J., *Le Culte de Napoléon* (Paris, 1960)

Madelin, L., *Histoire du Consulat et de l'Empire*, 16 vols. (Paris, 1946-54)

Tulard, Jean, *Le Mythe de Napoléon* (Paris, 1971)

———, 'Problèmes sociaux de la France impériale', *Revue d'Histoire moderne et contemporaine* (July-September 1970), pp. 639-63

(ii) Balzac in Relation to the Consulate and Empire.

Andréoli, Max, 'Sur le Début d'un roman de Balzac, "Une Ténébreuse Affaire"', *L'Année Balzacienne* (1975), pp. 89-123

Barbéris, Pierre, 'Napoléon. Structures et signification d'un mythe littéraire', *Revue d'Histoire littéraire de la France* (September-December 1970b), pp. 1031-58

Descotes, Maurice, *La Légende de Napoléon et les écrivains français du XIXe siècle* (Paris, 1967). Chapter III is devoted to Balzac (pp. 225-67)

Donnard, J.-H., 'A propos d'une supercherie littéraire. Le "Bonapartisme" de Balzac', *L'Année Balzacienne* (1963), pp. 123-42

Fleischmann, Hector, *Napoléon par Balzac* (Paris, 1913). This work consists of a series of extracts from the *Comédie humaine*, preceded by an introduction, 'Napoléon dans l'oeuvre de Balzac' (pp. 3-60)

Guise, René, *Une Ténébreuse Affaire*, Folio edn (Paris, 1973), Introduction (pp. 7-19)

Laubriet, Pierre, 'Autour d'*Une Ténébreuse Affaire*', *L'Année Balzacienne* (1968a), pp. 267-82

———— , 'La Légende et le Mythe Napoléoniens chez Balzac', *L'Année Balzacienne* (1968b), pp. 285-301

Michel, Arlette, 'Une Femme devant l'histoire: Laurence de Cinq-Cygne ou la fidélité', *L'Année Balzacienne* (1977), pp. 51-70

Saint-Paulien, *Napoléon Balzac et l'empire de la Comédie humaine* (Paris, 1979)

Savant, J., *Napoléon dans Balzac* (Paris, 1960)

Serval, Maurice, 'Autour d'un roman de Balzac. *Une Ténébreuse Affaire*,' *Revue d'Histoire littéraire de la France* (October-December 1922), pp. 452-83

(c) The Restoration

(i) History.

Artz, Frederick B., 'La Crise des assurances en 1830 et les Compagnies d'assurances', *Revue d'Histoire Moderne* (March-April 1929), pp. 96-105

Bertier de Sauvigny, G. de, *La Restauration* (Paris, 1955)

Dupin, Baron Charles, *Forces productives et commerciales de la France*, 2 vols. (Paris, 1827)

Gain, André, *La Restauration et les biens des émigrés*, 2 vols. (Nancy, 1928)

Kelly, G.A., 'Liberalism and Aristocracy during the French Restoration', *Journal of the History of Ideas* (1965), pp. 509-30

Richardson, N., *The French Prefectoral Corps 1814-1830* (Cambridge, 1966)

Soutadé-Rouger, Mme, 'Les Notables en France sous la Restauration (1815-1830)', *Revue d'Histoire économique et sociale* (1960), pp. 98-100

Vidalenc, Jean, *Les Demi-Solde* (Paris, 1955)

———— , *La Restauration*, ('Que Sais-je?', Paris, 1968)

Zeller, André, *Soldats Perdus. Des Armées de Napoléon aux garnisons de Louis XVIII* (Paris, 1977)

(ii) Balzac and the Restoration.

Barbéris, Pierre, *'Le Père Goriot' de Balzac* (Paris, 1972b)

Butler, Ronnie, 'Restoration Perspectives in Balzac's *La Vieille Fille*,' *Modern Languages* (September 1976), pp. 126-31

Castex, P.-G., *La Vieille Fille* (Classiques Garnier, Paris, 1957)

———— , *Le Cabinet des Antiques* (Classiques Garnier, Paris, 1959)

———— , *Le Père Goriot* (Classiques Garnier, Paris, 1963)

———— , 'L'Ascension de Monsieur Grandet', *Europe* (Colloque Balzac) (January-February 1965a), pp. 247-63

———— , *Eugénie Grandet* (Classiques Garnier, Paris, 1965b)

Chevalier, Louis, Preface to the Folio edn of *Les Paysans* (Paris 1975)

Donnard, J.-H., *Les Paysans* (Classiques Garnier, Paris, 1964)

Gaudon, Jean, 'Sur la Chronologie du *Père Goriot*', *L'Année Balzacienne* (1967), pp. 147-56

Jacolin, F., '"Les Paysans" et l'Etat social des campagnes de l'Yonne sous la Restauration', *L'Année Balzacienne* (1974), pp. 138-50

Laubriet, Pierre, *César Birotteau* (Classiques Garnier, Paris, 1964)

Lerner, Laurence, 'Literature and Social Change', *Journal of European Studies* (December 1977), including some interesting remarks on *Les Paysans* (pp. 231-52)

Macherey, Pierre, *Pour une théorie de la production littéraire* (Paris, 1966), including a chapter on *Les Paysans* (pp. 287-327)

Meininger, Anne-Marie, 'Qui est des Lupeaulx?', *L'Année Balzacienne* (1961), pp. 149-84

Reizov, Boris, 'Balzac et Paul-Louis Courier', *L'Année Balzacienne* (1970), pp. 241-57

Seylaz, Jean-Luc, 'Le Transport de l'or dans *Eugénie Grandet*', *L'Année Balzacienne* (1980), pp. 61-7

Yaouanc, Moïse le, *Le Lys dans la vallée* (Classiques Garnier, Paris, 1966)

(d) The July Monarchy

(i) History.

Caron, F., *Histoire de l'exploitation d'un grand réseau, la Compagnie du chemin de fer du Nord, 1846-1937* (Paris, 1973). Chapter 1 deals with the period 1845-52 (pp. 45-71)

Julien-Laferrière, F., *Les Députés Fonctionnaires sous la monarchie de Juillet* (Paris, 1970)

Kent, Sherman, *Electoral Procedure under Louis Philippe* (Yale, 1937)

Pinkney, D.H., *The French Revolution of 1830* (Princeton, 1972)

Price, R.D., 'Legitimist Opposition to the Revolution of 1830 in the French Provinces', *The Historical Journal* (December 1974), pp. 755-78

Tudesq, A.-J. 'L'Attraction Parisienne sur le recrutement parlementaire à la fin de la monarchie de Juillet', *Politique* (July-September 1958), pp. 271-86

———— , *Les Grands Notables en France. 1840-1849* (Paris, 1964)

Vigier, Philippe, *La Monarchie de Juillet*, 4th edn ('Que Sais-je?', Paris, 1972)

(ii) Balzac and the July Monarchy.

Barbéris, Pierre, 'Trois Moments de la politique balzacienne (1830, 1839, 1848)', *L'Année Balzacienne* (1965c), pp. 253-90

Bodin, Thierry, 'L'Accueil aux "Paysans". De l'anathème à la gloire', *L'Année Balzacienne* (1977), pp. 241-66

———— , 'Généologie de la Médiocratie dans "les Paysans"', *L'Année Balzacienne* (1978), pp. 91-101

Brua, Edmond, '*La Filandière*, Allégorie Politique', *L'Année Balzacienne* (1973), pp. 55-74

Fayolle, Roger, 'Notes sur la Pensée politique de Balzac dans "Le Médecin de campagne" et "Le Curé de village"', *Europe* (Colloque Balzac) (January-February 1965), pp. 303-23

Guyon, Bernard, 'Balzac héraut du capitalisme naissant', *Europe* (Colloque Balzac) (January-February 1965), pp. 126-41

———— , *L'Illustre Gaudissart* and *La Muse du département* (Classiques Garnier, Paris, 1970)

Kinder, Patricia, 'Balzac, "La Gazette de France" et "Les Paysans"', *L'Année Balzacienne* (1973), pp. 117-43

Malavié, Jean, 'Balzac sous le feu d'un légitimiste avignonnais, Armand de Pontmartin', *L'Année Balzacienne* (1980), pp. 209-37

Meininger, Anne-Marie, *Le Cousin Pons* (Classiques Garnier, Paris, 1974)

Picard, Raymond, *Les Petits Bourgeois* (Classiques Garnier, Paris, 1960)

Smethurst, Colin, 'Balzac and Stendhal, Electoral Scenes', *Balzac and the Nineteenth Century. Studies in French Literature presented to Herbert J. Hunt* (Leicester, 1972), pp. 111-21

Ubersfeld, Annie, 'La Crise de 1831-1833 dans la vie et l'oeuvre de Balzac', *Europe* (Colloque Balzac) (January-February 1965), pp. 55-68

Van Laere, F., 'Du *Député* au *Candidat*, ou trente ans après', *Littérature et Société* (Paris, 1973), pp. 119-33

(e) The 1848 Revolution

Gaston-Martin, *La Révolution de 1848* ('Que Sais-je?', Paris, 1959)

INDEX

absolutism, advocated by Balzac 247-8
'acquéreurs' (*see also* 'biens nationaux') 19-29; numbers of 19, 23,
24; size of gains 20; types of in
Comédie humaine 25; peasants
25-6; as moneylenders 26; resistance to émigrés 49, 62-4, 107;
during first Restoration and
Hundred Days 83
Albert Savarus, elections 187, 189-90,
194, 203; 'éligibilité' 175, 178
ancien régime, Balzac's admiration
for 259-62
aristocracy (*see also* Restoration
aristocracy) Balzac's admiration
for 47, 87; Napoleon's sympathy
towards 48-9, 64-5; struggle with
bourgeoisie 53, 66-7, 87, 219;
loyalty to Bourbons 78; relationship with bourgeoisie after July
Revolution 212-14; involvement
in economic expansion 216-20
Aristocratie Balzacienne, L' (Forest)
87
Autre Etude de Femme 54
Avant-Propos 253, 261

Baldensperger, F., on emigration 32
Bal de Sceaux, Le 66, 103
'ballottage' 188-9
banking, under Restoration 129, 142,
144-7; provincial 146
Barbéris, Pierre, on Balzac's hostility
to July Monarchy 258; on *La Peau
de Chagrin* 167-8; on *Lettres sur
Paris* 166; on Restoration
aristocracy 87-8
Bardèche, Maurice, on credit 145
Béatrix 60, 213, 234, 258
Bertier de Sauvigny, G. on éligibilité
179; on moneylenders 146
'biens nationaux' (*see also*
'acquéreurs) sale of 19; Balzac's
account of 19-29, 63; Church
property 20-3; émigré property
20-3; resale of 23-4, 26; peasant
acquisitions 25-6, 63
Bonald, L. de 260-1

bourgeoisie (*see also* Restoration
bourgeoisie; bourgeoisification)
acquires landed property 20, 24;
struggle with aristocracy 53, 66-7,
219; economic liberty under
Empire 71; seeks aristocratic
status 93; economic power under
Restoration 125-30; Balzac's
dislike of 238, 256-8; gains in
1830 249; struggle with working
class after 1848 249, 262
'bourgeoisie terrienne' 153, 158, 206
bourgeoisification of aristocracy
125-30
'bourgs-pourris' 193-5
'Bourse', shares quoted 142, 148,
160n39, 228; scope of activities
151, 229, 231; after 1848
Revolution 248
Bourse, La 99
Brittany 81, 144, 257
bureaucracy, growth of under
Restoration 143

'Cabinet des Antiques' 78, 91
Cabinet des Antiques, Le 22, 41, 48,
144
Cadoudal conspiracy 61, 73n29
capitalist economy, growth of
220-5, 237-8
Carraud, Zulma 65, 166
Castex P.-G., on Grandet 21, 232
Catéchisme Social 253, 255
Cavaignac, General 250
'cens d'éligibilité' *see* 'éligibilité'
César Birotteau 146, 151-2, 234
'Chambre des pairs' 115-16
Charivari, Le 204-5
Charles X 89, 94, 116, 260
Charter of 1814, Balzac's critique
83-4, 200, 242; and emergence of
revived aristocracy 92; electoral
provisions 200, 208n8
Charter of 1830 200
Chouans, Les, 'biens nationaux' 24-5,
37; changes in French society 10,
12; condemnation of émigrés 108-9;
provincial backwardness 257